Revealing Riches & Building Lives

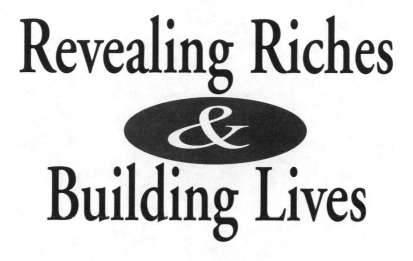

Revealing Riches & Building Lives

Youth Choir Ministry
In The
New Millennium

Randy Edwards

MorningStar
MUSIC PUBLISHERS
OF ST. LOUIS

MSM-90-27

Library of Congress Cataloging-in-Publication Data

Edwards, Randy, 1954-
    Revealing riches & building lives: youth choir ministry in the new millennium/by
    Randy Edwards.
    p. cm.
    Includes bibliographical references, filmography, and indexes.
    ISBN 0-944529-31-3 (alk. paper)
    1. Choirs (Music) 2. Church work with youth. I.Title: Revealing riches &
    building lives. II. Title.

    MT88 .E3 2000
    264'.2–dc21   00-025554

ISBN 0-944529-31-3

Published by MorningStar Music Publishers
St. Louis, Missouri
Printed in the United States of America

Acknowledgments

I f you are serious about a particular subject and if the content is generally worth writing in the first place, then putting together a book is bound to become a task of considerable proportions. Such was the case with this project. Actually, the most challenging part of the task has already been completed: the writing of 112 monthly issues (and counting) of *Youth Cue*, the travel, teaching, conducting and consulting, which has been done on behalf of the youth choir dream. The burden of concern for today's teenagers carried constantly within my heart has made the task heavier yet somehow lighter, more serious yet more joyful, more frightening yet all the more exciting.

I specifically want to thank my wife, Holly, for the support she has given me since the beginning of the *Youth Cue* project. I felt God's unmistakable call upon me for this ministry when our children were quite young: Preston (5), Ashley (3), and Kathryn Ann (newborn). Ashley was ill at the time, and we traveled many miles to discover the full nature of her ailment. Now, almost a decade later, everyone in our family enjoys good health, and our children are now entering adolescence and, yes, youth choir. Holly has sacrificed as much as anyone for the writing of this book, and I shall always treasure her constant love and unselfishness.

The family of faith at The First Baptist Church in Shreveport, Louisiana, has been an artesian well of encouragement and energy over eleven years of shared ministry. This is a rare congregation which provides its ministerial staff the space and support needed to maximize our gifts in the greater work of the Kingdom of God. The congregation is filled with smart, sensitive, compassionate friends who have encouraged the *Youth Cue* project to grow and flourish. As a result, the church in general and the Celebration Singers in particular have directly and indirectly benefitted from *Cue's* development.

Speaking of the Celebration Singers, these fine, young friends have been my inspiration over the past decade of music making and working together. Their fresh, bright faces have been a perpetual source of encouragement to me through the years, and the music they make has provided a huge part of my recent, personal soundtrack. Singers, you are my friends, and I love you!

It may seem strange to thank an adult choir for their input in youth choir ministry, but our Sanctuary Choir has provided amazing modeling for the Celebration Singers over the years. We have sung many worship services as a combined choir, and together we have performed major works with an orchestra. Aside from being first class musical role models, the members of the Sanctuary Choir have also provided a level of warm acceptance and encouragement for our kids that I have never before observed. Sanctuary Choir, you are the greatest, and the state of youth choirs here and abroad is healthier because of you and your extraordinary spirit.

Family members have also been present and encouraging on many levels. Marilyn Howland, my mother-in-law, keeps Youth Choirs, Inc. running very smoothly at our San Antonio office. Her skillful administrative work and faithful ministry to directors frees me to be productive and creative within the trenches of hands-on ministry. My parents, Truett and Joyce Edwards, are loyal prayer partners, festival groupies, and frequent sources of encouragement. Preston keeps YCI's feet to the fire in the arena of the latest technology. Ashley assists her daddy in numerous, thankless ways. Kathryn Ann, through her constant eagerness to help, provides an amazing level of energy and interest for the youth choir cause. My siblings, Judy Barber, Jean Hurry, and Mark Edwards, have always been there for me from my infancy. Their support and encouragement of the *Youth Cue* ministry is something I greatly treasure.

Thank you, Patricia Leath and Mary Gurski, for your skills in proofing, correcting, teaching, and informing. Both have earned degrees in English, and they also possess sensitive ministers' hearts. For their diligent work, I am eternally grateful. Mary Carter, my church secretary, has provided invaluable, above-and-beyond-the-call-of-duty support in my responsibilities as a full-time minister of music. Thank you, Mary, for being such an important member of the team.

Thank you, David Miller, for first hearing out my burden for kids and then for encouraging me to follow the dream. Thank you, Jerry Comfort, for being a dear friend and for actively and creatively sharing the vision with me for more than fifteen years. Thank you, George Mears and all the other members of the board of Youth Choirs, Inc. for your wisdom, professional expertise, direction, creativity, and love. Thank you for sharing the vision.

This book is dedicated to the hundreds of youth choir directors who love their teenagers and desire to serve them in a more profound way. You are my friends and colleagues. You are my teachers and my mentors. You have given grace and have worked willingly to see the youth choir dream become reality. It is a pleasure to be on your team.

Contents

PART EIGHT: INDEXES AND IDEAS

Jesus is calling us into a new community where leadership will be measured in terms of effective facilitation of others; where each of us will find the fulfillment of his own dreams as he encourages others to the fulfillment of theirs; where our task will not be to share our riches with others but to reveal their riches to them—and where the power of my self-esteem, my fullness of human being, will come to me as yours comes to you.

Robert Raines
To Kiss The Joy

Page 51
Word Books. Waco, TX 1973
ISBN 0-87680-324-9

PART ONE

1

The Calling
of a Kind Choral Builder

Why We Do What We Do

O ut of the corner of my eye, I noticed the Sanctuary door open wide and then quickly close again. Something seemed awry about the back and forth rhythm of the large, hardwood door, but I couldn't put my finger on the feelings I sensed. The tops of a couple of familiar heads on the other side of the thick, beveled windows were slowly bouncing in conversation—my wife, Holly, talking with my brother, Mark. Our youth choir continued to sing its final song of the concert, but I must admit I didn't hear much of the choral music I was conducting.

Something felt wrong. Very wrong.

It was a Friday evening in early June 1986. Our youth choir from San Antonio was on the second night of our annual choir tour. Our host church that evening was a sizeable congregation in Tupelo, Mississippi. We had driven all day in the rain to be there.

Holly was with us on that particular tour, something which seldom happened. She almost always stayed home to care for our children while I was away. On this particular trip, as providence would have it, she was traveling with us for the first few days, and then she would fly back to San Antonio from Florida. I thank God Holly was there.

Mark, who has now served more than twenty years as a minister of music in Nashville, was also providentially present. He had driven four hours to hear our group sing, since this was our nearest stop to middle Tennessee that year.

But something felt wrong.

As it turned out, something *was* wrong. Very wrong.

Toward the end of the concert, the host church office received one of those phone calls you hope you never have to answer. One of our front-row, high school sophomore basses had lost his father in a gyrocopter crash two hours

1

earlier; but, of course, the young boy was unaware of the tragedy. Scott Riggins sang his heart out all through the concert. Within a few short moments, his life would be forever changed.

Final anthem complete, I made my way to Holly in the hallway. Upon hearing the news, I couldn't help but weep. I spied Scott through that same beveled window in the Sanctuary door. He sat peacefully on the front row of the choir loft listening attentively as the host pastor made his closing comments. All was calm. All was bright. For now.

I turned to Holly and Mark and said with tears distorting my vision, "I can't do this. I just can't do this!" Holly, with all the love and determination of a Lamaze coach, took my face in both her hands and said, "Yes, you can. And yes, honey, you will. There's no one else to tell him but you."

Gathering my courage and silently praying as never before, I stoically staggered into the choir loft immediately following the spoken benediction. I took fifteen-year-old Scott by the hand and led him to a back hallway. Nearby, there were happy, muffled noises of kids talking and changing clothes in the adjoining rooms. When we reached an out-of-the-way place, I took Scott's face in my hands, much as Holly had modeled for me a few moments earlier.

Telling Scott the awful facts took only ten seconds. It seemed like ten hours. He reacted much as any normal fifteen-year-old boy would respond to such horrible news from home. I felt as though I had stabbed him in the heart. Like a remorseful attacker, I instantly began trying to fix the wound I had inflicted.

The next several hours were a nightmare, but one in which we felt the powerful hand of God in inexplicable ways. Since we received the death call so late in the day and since we were miles from the nearest commercial airport, we had to wait until early the next morning to fly Scott back to San Antonio. I put him in my room where we hugged, cried, prayed, reminisced about his dad and talked the night away. There was no sleep for the weary. At 4:30 a.m. we departed for Memphis in the church van, accompanied by two male counselors, Jerry Comfort and Kim Moore. Kim took the flight home with Scott. Jerry drove me back to meet the group in time for our 9:00 a.m. departure from Tupelo. It had been a wild twelve hours, something you would not wish on your worst enemy.

Although Scott had encountered a major tragedy in his life, he still wanted to rejoin the tour after his dad's funeral. Scott's mom thought this was a good idea. Unselfishly, she made arrangements for Scott to leave her again and meet the group in Florida the day following the burial. "This is where Scott wants to be," she said in a phone call. "His greatest support system is right there in the choir."

When the grieving fifteen-year-old caught up with us at a Daytona Beach hotel, he enthusiastically greeted everyone within hugging distance. After the dust settled, Scott told me he had something important to say to the group. We gathered everyone in the lobby to listen. Few of us will ever forget Scott's one-point, two-minute sermon. Few preachers have delivered anything as eloquent. It went something like this:

> From the moment I found out my dad was gone, I have been hearing music in my head. It has been going like a movie soundtrack nonstop ever since. The music was with me during that awful first night. It kept playing on the flight back home. It was with me at the funeral home and all through the burial service. The music played loudest as we drove away from the cemetery. It has surrounded me every night and has helped me go to sleep. It has been there every morning when that sick thud of realization hits to remind me this is not just another bad dream. It played again on both flights as I was coming back here to join you. What I am hearing over and over again, without end, is the song we sing near the end of our concert, "Cast Thy Burden Upon the Lord." I can't tell you how comforting this has been to me.

The anthem to which Scott referred was Claude Bass' setting of "Cast Thy Burden Upon the Lord," written in 1959 following the death of one of young Claude's close college friends. The text, taken from Psalm 55:22, reminds God's children to:

> *Cast thy burden upon the Lord, and He shall sustain thee;*
> *He never shall suffer the righteous to fall,*
> *He is at Thy right hand.*
> *Lord, Thy mercy is great, and high above the heavens;*
> *Let none be made ashamed who wait upon Thee.*
> *Cast thy burden upon the Lord, and He shall sustain thee.*

Why do we youth choir directors do what we do?
For one thing, we know deep in our hearts that what we do touches teens for time and eternity. We instinctively sense that much of life's crucial water hits the wheel during adolescence, and we know these events will have an ever-

lasting impact upon kids. The teenagers to whom we minister today will all too quickly become young adults, marriage partners, parents, and professionals.

Second, we also have learned that the Word of God, once planted inside teenagers' lives, will provide an eternal treasure-trove of strength for adolescence and well beyond the teenage years.

Third, common sense tells us that if there is to be a viable, vibrant church for tomorrow's adults, then there must be a community of faith in the present tense for today's teens.

Why do we do what we do?

There are a myriad of good reasons, and together we will explore them in every page of this book. It is my aim to help motivate all of us toward a dream. That dream is to touch today's teenagers deeply with the indescribable grace of Christ. Indescribable it is, for mere words are inadequate to express it. That's why we have to sing it.

Yes, touching new millennium teenagers and influencing their lives is best achieved through the medium of music. If you don't believe it, just ask MTV.

Why do we do what we do?

We do it because the job desperately needs to be done. When it is accomplished, even in small increments, it creates a huge wellspring of strength to all who are fortunate enough to experience it. The overflow of blessing also extends to directors and adult leaders who associate themselves with youth choirs, those precious and priceless mentors who invest themselves in the heavenly cause of kids.

Why do we do what we do?

Ask the thousands of teenagers for whom youth choir is having an enormous, positive impact upon their lives at this very moment.

Ask Scott Riggins and countless like him who are now well into adulthood and whose lives are forever enriched and fortified by the choral experiences of their youth.

Why do we do what we do?

God has called.

Our answer is, "Here am I, Lord, send me."

CHAPTER 1

Conflicting Entities:
The Nature of Music vs. the
Natural Course of Consumerism

Music was and is God's idea. Even in music's earliest recorded discoveries and innovations, God's people were encouraged, indeed commanded, to make joyful noises, to play instruments skillfully, and to sing. From the beginning, God designed us to express ourselves far beyond the verbal languages and dialects we would eventually learn to articulate. Words say only the sayable. Music is the universal language of the heart, spirit, and soul.

As we scan through the Old Testament, particularly the book of Psalms, there are several characteristics and uses of music which God's people were encouraged to embrace.

Music was participatory. In Old Testament worship, the Levites were commissioned to lead music creatively, but it was universally understood that every person would participate in the act of music making. There were to be no spectators in Old Testament worship, but, rather, each was to be an active, engaged and engaging participant.

Music was often very colorful, energetic, and loud. Music in worship pulled together all the resources of the people, all the available color, sound, energy, and talent. Music was inextricably connected to bringing one's best to God. Since most worship settings were held outdoors with worshippers numbering in the multiplied thousands, it was important that music rise to a decibel level adequate to engage the crowd.

Music was often used as a signal in battle or in large group projects. A battle cry was often a blast of the horn, the banging of drums, the crashing of cymbals, or all of the above. Music was a call to immediate action.

Music was enjoyed on many levels in many group settings. Worship, celebration and ceremony were all calls for the finest musical renderings the people could bring together into one place and time. Much of the identity of the people of God was mindfully molded by music. Although much of it was serious, sport, recreational and social gatherings were often musical events, as well.

Music provided therapy, comfort, meditation, and teaching. Young David became the first music therapist on record when he played the harp and sang in the courts of the depressed King Saul. Children were taught the songs of their ancestors along with their unique customs. As much as any other entity, the musical heritage forged their faith, commitment, and understanding of God.

Throughout the New Testament and forward into modern Christian history, music has continued to be embraced as a blessing and an enrichment to the human soul. The church's music through the ages has been a lifeblood, transporting spiritual nourishment and oxygen to the body of believers. This has never been more evident than in the twentieth century. Numerous universities and seminaries have established church music programs and have sent thousands of trained church musicians into local and international settings to advance church music on a global scale.

Commercial radio, network television, cable television, and other technologies have recently invaded and overrun the God-given gift of music. In 1981, the advent of MTV, the voice and face of a newly emerging youth culture, signaled the paradigm shift heard around the world. What we have witnessed since the early '80s is music transformed into a multidimensional commodity to be mass produced, bought, sold at the lowest price, consumed, and thrown away like a used paper cup.

Music is not the only victim of mass commercialization. Anything which can be used to make a quick buck is fair game for a society bent upon rampant consumerism. Produce it, package it, market it, move it, throw it away and repeat the process for power and profit—this has become a way of life for movers and shakers in big business. The use of people and their talents is not exempt from the mania.

Pop groups and appealing solo artists are listed in Exhibit A. Big-time promoters lock onto a potential up-and-coming pop sensation, and they immediately pour megabucks into marketing on their behalf. Music is only a portion of this picture. Sex appeal, product endorsements, concert promotion, CD sales, extensive product lines, and teen magazines work together to turn the group or individual into a veritable industry of their own.

The key to it all? Money, not music.

Check out what happens when the group's marketability is used up. They are thrown away like an old dishrag and left to fend for themselves. Remember

New Kids on the Block, The Spice Girls, Vanilla Ice, Hammer, Snoop Doggy Dogg, and Menudo? Talk about used merchandise, washed up, washed out, and hung out to dry!

As society's appetite becomes more ravenous for entertainment and thrills, the half-lives of sensation groups fall significantly. There is only a small window of opportunity in which to make the big bucks. The promoters and artists are keenly aware of this, which is why we see such incredible hype while the artist is hot. They must make it while they can, because this time next year, they are likely to be nobodies. Each group (and now each individual member of the group) as well as the promotion agencies are armed with an arsenal of legal teams to protect themselves when the inevitable comes down. This should be a strong indicator of what kind of business this really is. It's merciless, cut-throat marketing to the third power.

This is the society we have created for our teenagers, the only society they have known in their formative years. It is no wonder they feel little natural inclination to sing in something as seemingly uncool as a youth choir.

It is easy to come down hard on our culture of runaway consumerism, demonizing it in wholesale fashion. But before blasting away too hastily or harshly and declaring ourselves conscientious objectors, we need to face up to our own "techno" lifestyles.

For instance, I must admit that my family and I own a late model minivan as well as a neat, fun-to-drive SUV. Like thousands of other families, we have air-conditioning in our home, three television sets, cable, four CD players (six if you include the vehicles), and two home computers. Holly and I both carry digital cell phones everywhere we go. At this moment, the text and graphics of this book are being created and formatted on a state-of-the-art Macintosh computer with a twenty-inch monitor. At least, it was state of the art when I purchased it last month (ancient history)! Because of the speed of modern technology, the book I am writing today will be available to you in just a few short weeks, an unheard-of turnaround time even two years ago.

No, not all technology and commercialism are inherently evil, not by any means. We can readily cite the multifaceted benefits of everything from running water to internal combustion engines to MRI imaging to voice-recognition software. Some of us would not be alive today without the gift of advanced medical technology. And many of our lives will be spared or extended by it in the future.

However, when a gift as valuable and powerful as music is reduced to nothing but commercialism, then we have a considerable problem on our hands.

We are in serious danger of that potentiality becoming reality. In many ways, we are already there.

If you doubt the power of music in society, then take a closer look at MTV, now the largest network on earth. The worldwide youth culture is driven by MTV, its music videos, its programming, philosophies, and amazingly potent market savvy.

The purpose of this book is not to bash MTV, the youth entertainment industry, Hollywood, or music videos. Certainly, we need to be acutely aware and deeply concerned about the messages these forces incessantly send to our kids. Yes, the entertainment entities need to accept much more responsibility for what they produce and how it is presented and packaged to kids. As parents, we have an even greater responsibility. When the industry is so powerfully money-driven, there is something important we need to realize: if society doesn't buy it, the industry eventually won't produce it. It's really that simple!

As parents, we admit that some of what is happening in movies, music, and video is decent, some is marginal, and some is veritable pornography. There is quite a bit of fuzziness between those lines, as well. We get into trouble when we turn our backs on our teens and turn them over to the media without strong parental guidance.

As involved as we might become in a discussion of the media, my greater disappointment is with us, the church. Over the decades, we have failed to see the powerful possibilities of music lying underused and sometimes silent under our noses. We watch our children and teenagers lose hope and embrace destructive lifestyles as we wring our hands in mute despair. We fail to see the obvious: just as godless music can lead teenagers astray, God-centered music possesses the healing power to restore that which was lost.

Is it too late? Are youth choirs in the new millennium a lost cause?

You don't have to travel far or attend many gatherings of youth choir directors (or would-be leaders) to quickly conclude that the answer to that question must be, "Yes, I'm afraid it is a lost cause." If, for some reason, you enjoy listening to folks complain and whine, just crash a gathering of discouraged youth choir directors! Our quality of whining and sulking raises the water mark (or lowers it) to entirely new levels.

It's not hard to understand why. If you have ever tried to pull together a meaningful, challenging, and consistent youth choir program, then you have quickly been introduced to some of the most difficult challenges present in the world of ministry today.

Parents who did not receive the benefits of a positive youth choir experience during their own adolescence—and that is most—will likely allow their kids to choose to be involved in choir, but they will make little or no effort to actually encourage participation.

Even the few who did participate in youth choir as teens generally don't have a clue as to what it takes to implement a good program at this point in time. They remember glory days but are often flaky when it comes to helping their own kids make it to weekly rehearsals. They recall the warm fuzzies they felt when they sang in their beloved youth choirs in the 1970s and 1980s. What they feel is nostalgia, not necessarily to be confused with urgency. They had fun and provided a strong community for one another.

That was before MTV. That was before the advent of computer and video games and internet access in every home. That was before the ubiquitous digital television with hundreds of channels and the thirty-five-inch TV screens which are front and center in our family rooms. That was before youth baseball and soccer leagues rose to godlike status. That was when instant sensory gratification was not quite as instant as it is now. That was before church music for many was reduced to slick CD recordings and sexy Christian concert artists, six-figure Christmas pageants, the wholesale replacement of choirs with hip praise bands. That was before the scrapping of pipe organs paved the way for cheap, chirping synthesizers.

Ouch! The sentences above sound harsh! They are quite harsh when you and I possess a passion for reaching teenagers with the gospel through the miracle of musical participation. The above hits us very hard when we are ultimately responsible for the musical health of our teenagers. It is a tough commentary when worship and ministry for our kids are defined to a great extent by what we do or fail to do week in and week out.

Let's ask it again. Is youth choir a lost cause in the new millennium? If we believe it, there would be no point in writing or reading this book. What may not be obvious, however, is the swelling hope we have for the future of our youth choir ministries. What youth choirs can provide is not only the possibility of good choral music, as important as that is. The survival of the choral idiom is near and dear to many of our hearts, including mine, but that is only a small portion of the impact of youth choirs in the new millennium. Thriving choral music is only a by-product of what we do.

No. It is not a lost cause. It is not a pipe dream. It is not impossible nor is it irretrievable. Youth choir is not only alive in many pockets of our world, but in many places it is flourishing as never before. In fact, a youth choir in the new millennium will likely flourish or perish. There will be very little in between. Sheer maintenance is no longer an option.

Youth choirs will become extinct only when our commitment to them fades away. They will die only when our passion is extinguished, only when our fatigue overcomes us, only when we determine it is too much trouble or too much work. Youth choirs become history only when we cease praying for them and giving them front-burner emphasis: spiritual, organizational, musical, and even social.

In a world of throwaway pop groups, shallow relationships, capricious sports figures who themselves often live like spoiled teenagers, of disjointed and dysfunctional families, there is only one thing which is certain to stand the test of time. There is only one Person to whom we can look for true identity, transcendence, joy, and abundant life in this world and the next.

Youth choirs possess the power to renew and recharge, not only kids, but an entire church. To a large extent, the results are up to us, the directors. No amount of social pressure can remove a teenager's need to be loved, to belong to a positive peer group, to hunger and thirst for the Word of God, to be involved in a friendly family which is creative, giving, affirmative, and healthy.

Teenagers don't have to sell their souls to secular society. There is a much better way. Providing good musical alternatives is a big part of that picture, but it is only part. The real challenge for youth choir directors is to provide a total atmosphere, an actual counterculture, where teenagers are accepted, loved, nurtured, and encouraged in their young journeys of faith. The best place on the planet for that to happen, other than home, is in the youth choir setting.

When our homes fail, whom does that leave to get the job done?

Note: *Understanding Today's Youth Culture* by Walt Mueller (see bibliography) Chapters 4-6 is an outstanding digest of the current youth culture. This is a highly recommended resource for more in-depth reading on this subject.

CHAPTER 2

Conditioning for the Long Haul

The first pages of this book focus strongly upon the youth choir director and our understanding of the task before us. Directing a youth choir is a demanding enterprise. As discussed in the previous chapter, our teenagers quickly grow up in a world dominated by rampant consumerism, addictive entertainment, quick gratification fixes, technological overkill, and impoverished relationships. The vast majority of teenagers, even those who are regular church attendees, are basically clueless of the joys, benefits, growth, and fun that could await them within the embrace of a good youth choir experience.

Let's face it. Giving direction to such an organization is a very involved proposition and not one we should enter into lightly. It is a long process of education, outreach, motivation, and communication.

Unfortunately, visionless music ministers seem as plentiful as the clueless kids. So passionless about teenagers have many become that they have completely eliminated youth choirs from their music program offerings.

Educating, Motivating, and Envisioning

Before directors can provide education, motivation, and vision for our kids, we first must personally come to grips with these facets within our own lives.

We educate ourselves as directors by reading everything we can get our hands on regarding the youth culture. We go to current movies. We force ourselves to watch some MTV to seek to understand what kids are feeling and expressing. We get to know individual teenagers and what makes them tick. We also need to educate ourselves on what it takes to build a youth choir. Most importantly, we are disciples of Christ, ever searching for the hand of God at work in our world. Through prayer, silence, devotion, and commitment, God grants direction and determination for the task.

Going into it half-baked is ill-advised. Just as teenagers need a friend network within their youth choir, you and I need a colleague network of youth choir directors, support systems for times when we need to talk or share problems. This is what *Youth Cue* is all about, providing that level of professional support through the monthly newsletter, conferences, festivals, and our ever-present e-mail server list.

Motivating a group of teenagers is impossible if we ourselves have major motivation problems. Certainly, our work with teenagers will eventually recharge our batteries and actually provide incoming energy, but that is likely to be a long time in coming. You and I must be prepared to work off our own motivation batteries for many months before our kids generate anything to give back. In other words, we have to be ready to provide almost *all* the energy at the beginning. Fortunately, we are not alone. When God calls us to a task, He always provides what we need to get the job done. Oftentimes, another adult or two will join us in the task, and, together, we can help keep each others' batteries charged.

Scripture tells us that without a vision, the people will perish. We shall take up this Scripture and subject more fully in Chapter Five. For now, suffice it to say that the director's vision, her dream for what the youth choir can become, must be front, center, and in clear focus. True, the teenagers will eventually contribute much to the decision-making process, but, at first, the director must be assertive and paint clear mental images of the corporate direction. We must remember that we work with kids who are accustomed to virtual reality in three dimensions with millions of colors. With the nanosecond right click of the mouse, they can be in a totally different world. Our dreams must be strong, clear, and powerful enough to gain kids' attention and capture the most vivid of imaginations. Possessing a powerful vision is one thing; communicating it effectively is quite another. *(Chapter Eleven deals specifically with the elements of youth choir communication.)*

A Fact of Life

Even those of us who have made youth choir a ministry-long commitment will periodically lose energy for our work. For all of us, whether novice or veteran, discouragement is our most annoying nemesis. If there is one key to succeeding on the youth choir scene, it is this: outlast, outsmart, and outlive your discouragement. No director completely escapes it. Those who learn how to manage it and grow through it will develop divine dividends for their choirs and for themselves.

The Six-Year Phenomenon

Make no mistake about it. Growing a youth choir is a long-term and time-consuming project. There are no quick fixes in building lasting relationships with teenagers and teaching them how to sing. Those who have started programs and nurtured them for a decade or more will tell you the average gestation period is often five to six years.

What does this mean?

It almost always takes this much time to turn a major corner in youth choir development. To be sure, there will be many smaller victories, joys, and successes along the way during this time (along with the correlating frustrations), but six years is about the time it takes for the program to gear up totally and develop a life of its own.

Getting to Know You

There is practical reasoning for the six-year rule. For one thing, if you are directing a youth choir which includes grades seven through twelve—this is the most common age span for youth choirs, although most directors prefer having two separate groups for high school and middle school—six years is the length of time it takes for the group to become totally yours. To say it another way, the seniors by this time have known no other youth choir director, no other ministry style. There has been sufficient time for your ministry colors, personality and passion to run consistently through the program.

Secondly, your years spent in one place have given you the opportunity to perfect your own personal program skills and to hone in relationally with this specific group of kids. You have gotten to know the kids' parents, their local culture, and the *koinania* context from which they derive. This process takes time. Tenure alone does not guarantee success; however, some very important breakthroughs will not happen apart from it.

Making the Payments

Assuming most of us purchase or lease our automobiles using installment payments, let us pose an interesting and insightful question. When, over the term of the note, do we become the most weary of making those payments? May we suggest that it is right around the halfway mark? Here is the deal. We have been making payments long enough to become fully aware of the impact this vehicle has on our overall finances, and we know it's significant. By midterm, the SUV or sedan or sporty thing has been sufficiently dinged and scratched up, and the carpet inside is somewhat soiled. That fun new-car smell has long since dissipated. What's more, we still have another two years to go before we have the thing paid off! It's a drag making new car payments on a vehicle with fifty thousand miles. And oh, yes, don't forget that it needs new tires, brakes, and a battery, too.

Sometimes, making youth choir "payments" can feel this way, but please note one significant difference. Our vehicles begin to depreciate the second we drive them off the dealer's lot. On the contrary, the longer we keep our youth choirs, work with the kids, make those payments, and keep them growing and developing, the more value they have, both to us and to our kids. Youth choir is not a depreciating expense, far from it! Our youth choirs are an investment in lives which will post eternal gains from our contributions.

Midterm Tests

This is the way youth choir directors may feel come January. After getting excited about the August youth choir start-up, seeing all the possibilities and looking forward to a new season, we make our plans, talk a big talk in front of the parents and kids, and launch mightily into the youth choir year. We do a fair job of getting the program up and running. Then we hit the Christmas/Advent zoo zone. We survive December with all its demands and borderline insanity, and then we return to youth choir rehearsal during the first couple of weeks of the new year.

Thud.

It is a real test of our commitment, creativity, and communication skills to work our way out of such low-tide times.

Here is another August scenario. We are not excited at all about youth choir, but we are either obligated to it by job description or we feel obliged by conscience. Thus, we drag into the process half-prepared and half-baked, and the whole autumn is spent holding rehearsals and going through ministry motions.

We survive.

Come January, with its ubiquitous post-Advent fatigue, and behold, thou, I bring thee bad tidings of great concern. In other words, there is growing anxiety and serious stress brewing in the music minister's office.

Stirring Lemonade in January

If your car turns out to be a lemon at the midterm, that's a real bummer. However, if you find yourself with a youth choir lemon in January, then there is much hope to be found. It's time to get busy planning a popular summer thirst quencher, lemonade. One of the beauties I have observed over the years in the youth choir setting is this: for every downside (disadvantage, inherent problem, huge challenge) there is a corresponding upside (advantage, opportunity, need). The most effective youth choir leaders today are the women and men who see the pitcher of water half full rather than half empty. This is not to suggest that directors bury their heads in the sand and simply play the glad game. It is, however, to encourage all of us to search diligently for the hand of God at work within the community of our youth choir teenagers. When the reality of God's presence is recognized within a choir or within any Christian community, creativity and energy are not far behind.

Is youth choir ministry a long, challenging, and sometimes exhausting road? It certainly is. Anyone afraid of hard work should consider another area of ministry, for no program in your church will demand more energy from you than the youth choir.

There is no harder work. There is no greater joy.

Digging Deeper with Tenure

"Why does it take so long. . . so many years to build a decent youth choir? My problem is I am so discouraged waiting that I become bored and want to move on to some other church before anything really happens. I'm tired of waiting!"

Such were the words of a colleague who wants badly to develop a strong youth choir. Discouragement is certainly an occupational hazard for many of us, and overcoming it may be our greatest challenge.

This little conversation made me think about my own situation. The church I serve is not perfect (whose is?), but it is generally a healthy, sane, and happy place to work. The expectation level for excellence is high. The demands inherent in my ministry are not continually overwhelming, but they are consistently present and operative. It's a big job. It's not an impossible job.

At the writing of this book, I have been in the saddle here for almost twelve years, and it has been a good, growing experience for me, and I hope for our people, as well. As I think about it, there are some "buttons" of ministry that I am just now learning to push for the first time: opportunities and challenges that I was in no way prepared to face a decade ago or even two years ago.

The fact is that I am now uniquely prepared to accomplish some tasks which would have been impossible heretofore. Why so? Perhaps there are several reasons.

First, I hope I'm more seasoned, more mature, more insightful, more communicative, and more patient than in my earlier years. I hope I have grown as a minister, as a musician, as a person, as a friend.

Second, having celebrated some birthdays, anniversaries, graduations, successes, triumphs, and even disappointments with the good people of our church, I hope I have built a bank account of credibility with them. That does not mean that I can get away with murder, but perhaps it does indicate that I can be trusted. . .that I really love and care about the people I serve. . . that I don't have a hidden agenda to spring on them while they are not looking.

Yes, it often takes a while to learn the ropes and to know which buttons to push. In fact, as we stay in place for a good measure of time, we soon discover that there are new ropes, buttons, and approaches which emerge. These are called paradigm shifts; and, if we are alert to them, they can energize our lives and ministries for years to come.

An observation across ten years of studying and thousands of miles of travel is that anytime you see a youth choir dynasty in a church, high school, or community, one thing is certain. The common thread connecting these successful choirs is that somewhere in the choir's history, a dedicated director, one person with great passion for that choir, gave her/his lifeblood to that group for eight, ten, fifteen, twenty-five years. It not only takes talent and time to build a youth choir, it also takes tenure. No great program has ever been grown on a series of two-year and three-year directors. It simply takes longer than that. It takes more personal investment than that.

A new youth choir director can "successfully" begin to manipulate teenagers almost immediately upon arrival—no tenure required for that. And great will be the fallout if it is allowed to continue! However, if our goal is to provide conscientious and effective leadership to the people of God over a period of time, that's going to take some investment, energy, patience, wisdom, and self-discipline. In fact, it takes everything we have to give.

When working with teenagers, the best ministries among us are born and raised in an atmosphere of love, consistency, and commitment—all over the long haul.

CHAPTER 3

Creating a Soundtrack for Life

Hollywood producers are well-aquainted with the power of music. They spend millions each year hiring composers, conductors, musical producers, orchestras, and sound technicians to create and capture those just-right feelings for their movie soundtracks. A major motion picture without a soundtrack would be a sure failure, lifeless, dull, incredibly dry—a real loser.

Soundtracks Are Extremely Powerful

Sound and music are so important to a movie that, if you listen carefully, you will hear melodies and rhythms going on almost continually, even when most people in the theater are not even aware of them. The only times when the plot is not being underlaid with music are when the movie director decides to drop the soundtrack for a special effect. What is that special effect? A stark, silent, cold, alone feeling which emanates from the screen into the audience, all because music has been taken away.

Movies are not the only places where powerful, though sometimes undetected, soundtracks exist. Our own individual lives have, by now, developed their own special, unique soundtracks. The same can be said of every teenager in our youth choirs.

The Soundtrack Begins Before We Know It

My childhood and adolescence were spent in the sandy, rolling plains of South Texas. My earliest memories involve extended family gatherings where singing was a central activity. As a result, the *Coleman Songs for Men* and old gospel tunes and hymns became a huge part of my early soundtrack. On an almost daily basis, my mother played the piano or Hammond organ in our home and my dad sang semiclassical church songs: "Open the Gates of the

Temple," "The Holy City," and wedding songs, "I Love You Truly," "Because," and "The Lord's Prayer." My soundtrack had begun.

As a teenager, I memorized several Christian musicals and practiced conducting them in my living room during the summers. I also played in the high school band and sang in the motley school choir during that period, so those experiences became a part of my soundtrack as well. Pop music found new audiences during the '60s, and that style of secular music was recorded powerfully into my awareness. To this day, when I hear a particular pop song from that time in my life, I can close my eyes and almost be a teenager again. I see the sights, and I think I can almost smell the smells. Soundtracks are powerful, indeed.

But music is not all that remains as part of my soundtrack. I can still remember the timbre of my basketball coach's yelling, friends fighting at school, arguments between me and my siblings, angry things said during business meetings at church, and the voice of the principal when I was sent to his office for misbehaving. I may not be particularly conscious of my soundtrack, but it is certainly there. It regularly affects my thinking, and it colors my feelings about present issues.

Those of us who have grown up in healthy homes usually benefit from a positive soundtrack playing in our lives. The music we still hear and the voices we remember play on in our lives. They are components of encouragement for us during difficult times later in life.

However, adults who were raised in abusive homes or by alcoholic parents can "hear" their parents' fights for decades, sometimes for the rest of their lives. The soundtrack that was laid for these children and teenagers will be played and replayed over and over again.

Soundtracks Retain Their Strength

Soundtracks can be positive, negative, or a combination of both. In movies, we rarely notice the music, but the continual underlay of sound provides ambiance and sets the mood for the pervading pathos. The effect is usually outside our awareness. That is part of what makes it so powerful.

Not only do soundtracks *retain* their power, but they also can *grow* more powerful over the years. Psychologists' couches are often mashed by mid-lifers who are trying desperately to come to terms with the events, sights and sounds of their childhoods. On the positive side, scriptures and other sources of comfort often come back to adults who face particular stresses or crises in their lives.

Soundtracks Minister to Today's Teens

As youth choir directors, one of our greatest responsibilities is to lay down soundtracks in our teenagers' lives. Think about what has already been recorded in many of their memories by the time they come into our choirs: rock music, music videos, new age music, ugly sounds to accompany the violence they see on television, at the movies, in video games, and the sounds of rapid gunfire and explosions from watching the nightly news. Many come from dysfunctional families, and their soundtracks include the sad sounds of regular ridicule or constant verbal abuse.

Whether from healthy or unhealthy homes, there is a huge need among teenagers for someone to help them "record" positive, Godly sounds on their lives' soundtracks. We, as their youth choir directors, have the tools to help them transform their negative soundtracks into something which will sustain them. We have no greater task than to offer teenagers soundtracks which will bless rather than curse them through the remainder of their lives.

Scripture Set to Music Provides the Best Soundtrack

If we can get the Word of God into teenagers' minds and hearts, we give them the precious gift of life. Very few teenagers get into Scripture memory as such, but passages set to music and memorized will be just as effective as any kind of Scripture memory. *(Isaiah 55:11)* By teaching teenagers to sing songs with texts from the Bible, we prepare them for the pressures, temptations, and stresses they now face and will encounter in the future.

Part of the soundtracks that youth choir members replay as adults will be their memories of choir rehearsals and tours. What was the tone of voice and the attitude of the director? Was he always uptight, rigid, irritable or easy to provoke? Was he so loose that he never got the group to focus on what they were doing? Did she ever stop the grinding musical rehearsal to address a significant problem that the group faced? Was she ever able, with sensitivity and compassion, to lead the choir to worship God truly within the context of the rehearsal hour? Were tours fun adventures or mere exercises in more uptight activity? Has the choir ever seen their director cry?

Lay Down the Track . . . Carefully

All of these pictures will accompany the soundtracks we lay for our teenagers. What we do with kids may seem for today only, but our work with them is permanent. In fact, it is eternal.

As we help record the soundtracks for today's youth choir members, it helps us to remember with whom we are working. The teenagers in our youth choirs today are tomorrow's school teachers, bank officers, attorneys, home-makers, lawmakers, pastors, engineers, youth ministers, Sunday School teachers, deacons, and health care professionals. The way we teach these soon-to-be adults to deal with the challenges and stresses of leadership will have a profound effect upon the way they do business for the rest of their lives. The sights and sounds of the youth choir experience will be lived out in many places for time and eternity. Our task is that important.

What we have to give to youth is the sound of hope playing steadily and surely amidst the throwaway music which competes for their attention, time and money.

What we have to give cannot be bought and, once placed upon the sound-track of a teenager's life, it will not be sold.

CHAPTER 4

Casting Out Demons

Over the past decade of observing youth choirs and numerous directors, I am convinced that many leaders simply do not have a handle on their tasks. Struggling leaders often come at their youth choirs with old, outdated ideas about what a youth choir needs to be. We teach kids to sight sing, to form round vowels, to sit up straight, to quiet down at the right time and open up when it is appropriate. Directors often view themselves primarily as music educators who are hired guns to get a good-looking, great-sounding group together for worship services, tours, and mission trips.

All the elements of excellent musicianship are essential if we are to build a fine youth choir out of a group of previously unconnected kids. All the technical information we possess and utilize is our collection of tools for ministry.

However...

There are far more good musicians across the country directing youth choirs than there are great youth choirs. I wonder why. If the director is a fine musician, then why won't the choir naturally be a fine choir?

The excuse we give is that kids are uncommitted, untalented, untrained, undisciplined, unlovable, unsomething which keeps youth choir success from happening. We quickly excuse ourselves from the responsibility because everybody knows youth choirs are on the way out, right?

I am afraid we have missed the whole point.

The ninth chapter of the Gospel of Mark details the story of Jesus, Peter, James, and John descending from the Transfiguration experience. What a high that must have been! Peter had even suggested that they build three tabernacles in the higher, cooler elevations and forget the problems in the hot valley below.

What was happening down the mountainside? The other disciples were among the crowd working and ministering their heads off, healing the sick, touching the afflicted and laying hands on the broken. They were doing a good job and were probably finding a good deal of personal satisfaction as a result of their ministry well performed. They were probably quite good at what they did, and very likely there were people who lined up just to watch the disciples in action.

But one particular case embarrassed the disciples and caused them to feel frustrated. He was an afflicted young man, a teenager, whose malady the scripture describes in surprising detail. Mark 9:18 indicates that "an evil spirit" had taken up residence inside the kid and that it threw him to the ground, caused him to cast himself into the fire, made him grind his teeth and foam at the mouth. Sounds like some teenagers I have had in my choir! This kid was out of control.

The disciples tried their usual liturgy on this boy, and their efforts by the hour proved to be woefully futile. It was a perplexing situation. The disciples must have appeared as if they didn't know what they were doing. Perhaps some accused them of being frauds, or at least incompetent. Here, the trained and talented professionals gave it their best shot, but, alas, nothing happened but more severe seizures.

When Jesus arrived on the scene, he looked the boy in the eye, diagnosed his problem, and in a colorful, untraditional nonceremony, he showed compassion on him and healed him. It is a fascinating story and one which possesses powerful images for all youth choir leaders.

Later, after Jesus and the disciples managed to separate themselves from the crowds, the disciples must have huddled in around the Master. They asked, "How did you pull that off? Why could you cast out a demon in moments after a whole group of us had been working at it for several hours? We did what we had always done before! Why didn't it work?"

"I'll tell you what, guys," Jesus must have said with a twinkle in his eyes. "That kind of demon only comes out with prayer." Some translations report that Jesus said, ". . . prayer and fasting."

Yes, proper musical training is absolutely essential in youth choir ministry. The need to be highly professional is clearly indicated: open vowels, hard and crisp consonants, phrases, articulation, dynamics, and style. A large portion of this book pursues artistic excellence. All the choral components are essential to our ministry. But they are not our ministries. They are our tools. Our real ministry is about casting out demons.

With all this talk about demons, perhaps we should offer a definition of "a demon" as we use it in this chapter. For our purposes, a demon is anything which threatens the lives, well-being, joy, growth, and fulfillment of teenagers. Using this definition, one realizes that there are countless numbers of demons present on the youth scene today.

If you don't believe there are demons to be driven out, then you have not taken a good look at the current youth culture. In our society, there is so much for teenagers to stumble upon that there is barely enough space to walk. Walking straight is even more difficult. The by-products of the cancerous consumerism attack and threaten our teenagers' lives like tumors. Demons abound.

I am so excited about youth choir ministry because I believe it is, bar none, the very best tool available inside the church or out to drive demons from the lives of teenagers. No, we are not advocating exorcisms, snake-handling sessions, or bizarre healing services as we sometimes see on television. Casting out demons will happen much more practically, quietly, and gradually within the youth choir setting. The Scriptures the kids sing, the discipline they develop, the peer support they receive, the love they learn to give and share, the group dynamics, the teamwork, the relationships as they travel, the coming to terms with the hard issues of life—all, if embraced in prayer, will lead teenagers from darkness to light, from deception to truth, from demons to Christ.

Teenagers desperately need us to understand the world in which they live. We must realize that while we think about vowel formations, they are thinking about a friend who tried to kill himself last week. We think about the latest, hottest musical, while they try to come to terms with their parents' divorce. We think about recruiting ideas while they deal with guilt over the events of Saturday night.

It is going to take a lot of prayer.

PART TWO
2

The Design of a
New Youth Choir Home

A Rare Opportunity to Try It Again

T he thirteen-year period between 1967 and 1980 was a phenomenon in youth choir ministry. The overall youth movement was at an all-time high in the United States, partly because there were so many kids. Demographics were sky high, and the forecasters predicted we would never in our lifetimes see another youth population like this.

Enter the Youth Musical, Forever Altering the Course of Youth Choirs

Youth choir was coming out of the dark ages. The advent of the Christian folk musical brought kids out of the woodwork into youth choirs across North America. About all a director had to do was wave the latest musical release in front of a church full of teenagers and stand back. There would be an immediate stampede through the choir room doors. Everyone, it seemed, wanted to "do a musical."

After the folk musicals *Good News*, *Tell It Like It Is*, *Purpose*, and the all-time classic *Celebrate Life*, there followed a hotter style of presentation flowing from the publishers' presses. *Natural High*, *Life*, and *The Witness* were but three musicals of this era. As secular pop and rock music continued to push the boundaries, the Christian musical counterpart tried to keep up. Unfortunately, many of our musical composers became more interested in what "cooked" ("rocked" or "got down") than what spoke the truth. Predictably, what cooked sold. If it didn't cook, it didn't sell, and it was no mystery which direction the market-driven publishers were going to take. The shelf life for the average youth musical in the '70s and '80s was perhaps a year, about the same as a secular Top Forty hit.

The Beat Goes On

The youth musical has survived the past three decades, but the vast majority of youth choir directors who have built their programs on musicals alone have seen their numbers dwindle and their kids' concept of choral music go down the tubes.

In the '90s, a few composers made an admirable effort to reel in the youth musical and make it accountable for telling the real truth about current youth issues. I applaud their efforts and their ministries.

Musicals can meet certain specific needs in some youth choirs. Highly thematic, a musical can draw attention and focus on one particular issue in Christian discipleship. A musical can present a dramatization of a moral dilemma and a Christian response to it. This "picture" is often helpful to many teenagers and even to their parents.

The problem with most musicals is that they contain one or two strong, singable songs, but then there are the half dozen other substandard pieces which have to be learned and performed for the sake of the plot. Although hot and trendy and throwaway by nature, many are technically difficult, if not impossible, to sing well.

Many of the most popular musicals are actually collections of inferior choral arrangements derived from contemporary Christian artist solo hits. In other words, the songs were written to be performed and recorded in a studio as contemporary solos, not as serious choral music for worship. They were generally thrown together as an afterthought to sell. The biggest downside is that the kids and director spend an exorbitant amount of time and energy on something they will soon forget. Furthermore, music from musicals, for the sake of being catchy or cute, presents a very shallow theology, so forgetting may not be such a bad thing.

This is not the case with well-crafted choral music. Music written from the beginning to be choral music provides a much better training ground for teenagers. The harder the kids have to work at such selections, the longer the music will stay with them. This is why teens who are challenged to sing a classical piece or two will often, at the end of the year, declare it to be their favorite. Serious music is usually not particularly popular during the learning process. However, once conquered, choosing a classic as a favorite is not at all uncommon, even among the less experienced musicians in the choir.

Cotton Candy

Many of us cut our ministerial teeth as youth choir directors during the early days of the musical. Year after year, summer after summer, we bought our teenagers the latest, hottest things off the press, complete with all the packaged products to accompany the music: tracks, T-shirts, posters, recordings, multimedia, lighting and staging directions. Because of our young ages, lack of experience, shortsightedness, or perhaps all of the above, we as a guild failed to provide kids with much more than light music and surface spirituality. We didn't really teach them how to sing. We taught them show biz rather than worship. We taught them choreography but not choral discipline.

We Came Very Close to Losing It Completely

Alas, our attempts to play games and have fun with the kids didn't survive the test of time. By the mid-'80s, things were bleak in the youth choir arena. Demographics were down. Choir lofts sat dreary and nearly empty. Directors began to despair. Like the disciples in the valley below the Transfiguration, we were doing our normal thing which had always worked before. Suddenly, it seemed we were failures.

Market-driven publishers, having lost money on the plunging market of youth musicals, basically shut down the shop as far as any new youth music was concerned. The corporate cry seemed to be "Youth choirs are dead, they are a thing of the past! Sell, sell, sell. Cut your losses and run!"

By the sheer grace of God, some youth choirs and directors survived the decade. By the time we reached the early '90s and the advent of Youth Choirs, Inc., there was a renewed interest among many directors in rebuilding youth choirs. News was getting out that soon after the turn of the millennium there would be a youth population larger than even in the 1970s. The experts and forecasters had been wrong. The average family in the '90s would produce more than the earlier forecast of 1.736 children. With the economic growth of the nation, many families were having three, four, even five children.

The coming youth population will be like nothing we have seen before. There will be record numbers of teenagers in our towns and cities. Keep in mind, however, that unless we upgrade our programs, recommit ourselves to ministry with teenagers, and properly prepare ourselves to reach kids for Christ, most of the throng will never darken the doors of our churches.

A Second Chance

It's not every day that we get a second chance to correct something we botched the first time around. Teenagers seldom get the opportunity to go back and fix the relational, academic, or social blunders of their adolescence.

Youth choir directors have been given a rare second chance, and it begins immediately.

The kids are here.

The time is now.

CHAPTER 5

Dreaming the Dream, Seeing the Vision

Where there is no vision, the people will perish.
Proverbs 29:18

From our own personal experiences, we know the above passage to be true in any kind of organization—a church, a school, a youth choir, a city council, a classroom, a football team, a nation. Finding a clear vision is a major problem with traditional denominational structures today, and without that clear purpose, organized religion as we know it is floundering and will remain in serious trouble.

It is interesting to note that the passage quoted above is found within the context of instructions regarding raising children. The verse just before it says, "Correct your son, and he will give you comfort; he will also delight your soul." The NASB translates verse 18 thusly: "Where there is no vision, the people are unrestrained, but happy is he who keeps the law."

Where there is no youth choir vision, the kids are going to run wild. It is impossible to build a fine youth choir without vision. It can't be done, because the only thing which can continually motivate a group through the good times as well as the bad is a clear picture of the big goal.

How do you find a clear vision for your youth choir? Where does it come from? Where is it going? What does it do? What does it not do?

The dream has to begin, humanly speaking, in the mind and heart of the director. No football team ever exceeded the commitment, dedication, and vision of its coach. No company ever moved above the level of competence of its upper management. No church has soared higher than its Pastor.

If the dream does not first produce a fire in the bones of the director, it simply becomes some impotent idea of what might be, or perhaps what used to be. But when a director catches a glimpse of the possibilities within his youth choir, it will change his attitude forever. He will gladly take his rightful leadership in front of the group.

In Chapter Four, "Casting Out Demons," we looked at the passage taken from Mark 9 where Jesus healed the young man who had been possessed of a demon. When the disciples asked Jesus how he accomplished the miracle when they could not, his response was, "That kind of demon only comes out with prayer."

How many times have we, as youth choir directors, just assumed that we know what the dream for our youth choirs should be? We tend to mentally photocopy some old vision from 1978 or 1983 or 1998 and assume it will be on target for the needs of a new millennium.

It will not be.

Being still, praying, and continually seeking God's direction for today is prerequisite number one in effective youth choir work.

The Proverb makes good, logical sense. If a group doesn't know where it is going, the trip is going to be one of utter confusion, frustration, and lukewarm mediocrity.

It is no crime or sin to lose the vision temporarily or to be confused as to what it is. Through those times of uncertainty, God reminds us that we need to retreat into His presence. It is dangerous when we continue, for long periods of time, to go through the motions of ministry with little or no commitment to the importance and urgency of what we are doing. When we reflect upon God's love, grace, and beauty in our lives, the Spirit is able to recharge our batteries and infuse us with a new sense of purpose and passion.

Practically speaking, the beginning of a new calendar year or school year is a great time to get in touch with who we are and what we are about. Many directors find that the down time between school semesters and summer are lifesavers for them and their youth choir ministries.

As the dream shifts and develops over your tenure, that gradual transformation will have huge implications for the specific tasks which need to be begun, continued, and completed. Relationships must be continually cultivated. Communication is a never-ending process, always seeking better ways to impact the lives of teenagers. Administration must evolve and adjust according to the vision and in response to the personalities involved. The big events must reflect the overall design of the ministry, and they need to invest energy back into the ongoing program.

Sometimes our minds need a jump start in order to begin the dreaming exercise. The following questions offer a way of stimulating our vision mechanisms. As we think through our responses to these questions, perhaps we will become better aware of the possibilities and potentials of our ministries with teenagers. God bless us all as we dream and make the vital commitments needed to see these visions become, under God's guidance, realities.

Possible Questions to Stimulate Vision

1. Name one teenager who has great leadership potential, but who is still unaware of her/his gifts.

2. What three adjectives describe the way you want your youth choir to be viewed by the adults in your congregation?

3. Name one boy and one girl in your choir who are emotional orphans.

4. What is the smallest number you could have in your choir and still be considered "successful"?

5. Name a teenager who has never sung solos but with a little work and attention could do a good job.

6. Pretend it is 2021. What do you want your current senior class to take away with them when they leave your youth choir—some memory, feeling, song or text they will remember for years to come?

7. Which specific promises of God have been meaningful to you in your own Christian pilgrimage? How can you creatively communicate that truth to the teenagers you direct?

8. When your teenagers leave your choir, what range of music literature do you want them to have exposure to as a result of singing with you?

9. Name two healthy adults you know who could easily be motivated to work closely with you and your kids.

10. If you had the power to solve one perpetual problem in your youth choir, what would it be?

11. What personal qualities do you want tomorrow's adults to remember being modeled in your life?

12. Name someone in your choir who has talent in drama.

13. Name all the different musical instruments your teenagers can play.

14. Is there a place you would like to take your teenagers before they graduate from high school?

15. If funding were not an issue, what mission activities would you pursue with your youth choir?

16. Describe the way you want your choir to look when they make a public appearance outside the church.

17. What impact will your youth choir ministry have on your teenagers' future choice of a mate? Choice of profession? Choice of college?

18. Name two things you understand about teenagers today that you did not realize this time last year.

19. If you could push a magic button, how many pieces of music would your teenagers memorize this year?

20. What new ensembles could be readily formed using kids in your youth choir?

21. How might you enlist the help of other staff members to add a new dimension of relationship to the teenagers in your choir?

22. What do you want your teenagers to feel when they leave rehearsal this week? What do you want them to carry away from your time together?

The final three questions are about teenagers in your town or community who have never attended your youth choir and have never darkened the door of your church.

23. What could one of your current youth choir members say to an unchurched friend to get her attention about your youth choir? How would a girl in your choir describe the choir experience to another girl who knows nothing about it? Specifically, how would she likely word her description?

24. If your youth choir member is successful in getting the uninvolved girl to attend a regular weekly rehearsal, what would bring her back for a second or third visit? What would cause her to eventually join?

25. Answer questions 23 and 24, this time replacing the girls with boys. The new guy who has never been to choir is the captain of his high school basketball team.

Reality Check

Most of us wish things were different, but they are not. The new paradigms of current culture are upon us, and to ignore them is to miss out on ministry, not only now, but for generations to come.

Yes, teenagers will become involved in traditional, institutional church under the right conditions. But plugging their amazing energy and vital life styles into church calendars for the sake of preserving the program is a thoroughly dead paradigm. In fact, it's been dead for some time now. It's just that some have not bothered to bury it.

Neither kids nor their parents are particularly interested in sinking their precious time and personal resources into maintaining something which may have had meaning ten years ago. Trying to bolster the work of church programs for the sake of something so shallow as to build better attendance, is actually laughable to this generation. If teenagers and their parents are to become actively connected to a church, they will do so because specific and vital needs are being met in their own lives and in the lives of others. At church, they must get something they cannot get anywhere else. And that something they "get" includes the opportunity to give meaningfully to those around them—both those who are inside and outside the church.

Would we not agree that present opportunities abound and incessantly vie for teenagers' time, money, and involvement? For years , I was simply astounded at the sheer number of activities available to teenagers. Now, as a parent of adolescents, I am even more incredulous at the ways teenagers can fill their schedules. True, some of the activities may be relatively meaningless and eternally worthless. On the other hand, my children and many of yours have at their fingertips the kinds of programs, at school and within the community, which can change their lives and eternally enrich their minds, hearts, and talents. What is a youth choir director to do?

First, the program we administer must be on an organizational par with the finest opportunities the kids can get in our towns or cities. It has to have excitement, some pizazz, a lot of structure, and certain unique opportunities. And, yes, there must be significant financial resources behind it to keep it interesting and stimulating.

Second, we have to find a way to balance practice and performance. Teenagers love to sing what they learn, run that special play on the basketball court, perform the drama they produce, and play a gig with the garage band. They need regular exposure in their community if they are to remain energized and enthusiastic.

Teens also need to see that they actually make a difference in their world. Their influence may not be earthshaking, but it needs to be definite. For years, a teenager can carry the images of children smiling at them when they sing at a children's home. Youth choir members will never forget the tears of an inmate during a prison concert. Teenagers must see that they can make a difference, a difference that might seem insignificant to the average person on the street. When we give teenagers the opportunity to give, we open the doors of creative ministry.

The dream is beginning to appear.

The vision is coming into focus.

CHAPTER 6

Drafting for Things to Come: The Foundation

No contractor, regardless of his experience or expertise, would dare begin a major building project without a set of blueprints. Sometimes youth choir directors claim exemption from this need because we see ourselves as Spirit-led and thus providentially protected from potential problems on the construction site.

No master design? No blueprint? No specific plan of action?

Bad choice.

God gave Noah specific measurements for the ark and clear instructions about how to fill it. There was a detailed blueprint for Solomon's Temple. Gideon gave the gang no uncertain instructions for the use of their musical instruments as they surrounded the city that they were instructed to conquer. The birth of Jesus was prepared for on several fronts. Angels came and went, providing instructions and announcements for everyone involved.

Yes, God wants us to be led by the Spirit. No, God does not want us stuck in administrative ruts. Yes, human spontaneity was one of the trademarks of Jesus of Nazareth. No, the Son of God didn't go running off in his own direction any time he felt like it.

God is a Person of order. God is the Supplier of direction. God is the Inventor and Revealer of holy vision. As we follow God's lead, His plan is given to us, all in His time.

Following that lead and sensing divine timing is easier said than done. It is accomplished through prayer, diligence, and plenty of hard work.

A Concrete Blast from the Past

When I was a freshman in high school, my dad decided to build a three-car garage behind our South Texas farmhouse. Dad was and is a handyman of the first order. He can dream up, build, and fix just about anything. Over forty years ago, he built an above-ground swimming pool—above the ground to keep the diamondback rattlesnakes from taking a dip with us. To this day, the pool has not one crack in it, nor does it leak. The man knows how to build things that last.

The three-car garage project presented a challenge for which he was not totally ready. Spending several days preparing the forms for the foundation, he smoothed the dirt with care, placed steel in just the right places, and leveled out the tops of the forms. It was another one of his works of art. Now, we were ready for the cement. Or so we thought!

When the huge cement truck arrived from the city, the drum container was rotating slowly and the engine was whining, trying to keep the heavy material mixed up and churning. Dad thought that the truck driver would pour a section of concrete and that there would be sufficient, though hurried, time to smooth out the cement and level it before it permanently set up and dried.

Much to Dad's horror, the dude just backed up the truck near the middle of the forms, let down the trough, and in one motion, dumped the whole load of gray, wet muck into the big fat middle of what was supposed to be the foundation. Then, he hopped back into his cab and drove away, seemingly oblivious to the panic he had just created.

Dad, being the calculating type, immediately took inventory of the situation and almost panicked. Mom quickly called a couple of friends and neighbors, and luckily, an uncle showed up unexpectedly at the scene of the dump. The race was on! The cement was still wet and formative, but it was a race against the clock to clean up the mess and try to make something good out of it before it was too late.

This was about the time I arrived home from school. Changing clothes and removing my shoes, I bogged into the concrete. The first place I put my feet was on—or shall I say in—one of the few places my father had somehow managed to finish. I was there to "help." But as it turned out, the adults not only had to finish the job, but they had to redo the area I had innocently botched.

One thing could have made my dad's situation decidedly worse. What if, when the cement truck arrived, he was still measuring and cutting lumber, hammering two-by-fours, laying steel, and leveling the forms? Can you imagine how much worse the scenario would have been?

The thing that saved my dad was the fact that what he had set up and planned, he did so thoroughly and very well.

A Foundation for Youth Choir

What happened that day on our farm was a foretaste of what happens at some point to most youth choir directors. Through considerable education and experience, we prepare ourselves as thoroughly as possible to take on the challenges of building a youth choir. We do all the right stuff: prepare, plan, pray, and project great plans. We give considerable advance time and energy to make sure everything is ready to go.

Then, the kids arrive, pile on, or trickle in. Expecting a steady-yet-moderate stream of challenges in ministry to youth, we are absolutely blown away by the massive load of problems teenagers face and carry around as emotional baggage in their lives. No matter how complete our plans were, how finely tuned and well organized, we are still likely to feel overwhelmed. And yes, you don't need fifty or one hundred kids to feel overwhelmed. Sometimes, the dirty dozen can provide the same staggering effect.

If we stop long enough to assess the situation, we discover quickly that if we are going to have a significant impact upon these lives, we will have to act quickly and work fast. In short order, we must import some helping hands from the outside.

A Corporate Application

In order for a youth choir to begin healthy and continue to grow, there needs to be a clear sense of the goal. More and more choirs are adopting short, simple, yet focussed mission statements which provide a strong sense of vision and direction. A mission statement can and should be revised and updated from time to time as the need arises. Having the statement before youth choir officers and the whole choir will create a better sense of who we are and why we do what we do. A good youth choir mission statement could be as simple as the following:

The Chapel Choir is a Christian community which expresses its faith
in song through worship, mission projects,
outreach to other teenagers, and care for one another.

An Individual Application

When working with individual teenagers, we are presented with a window of opportunity. The window is open today, but soon it will close. The cement of adolescence will dry, forming a permanent foundation. Lives' foundations form and harden before our very eyes as we work with teenagers in music.

Certainly, it is still possible to make an impact upon people after they pass through the teenage years. But after adolescence, the basic foundation will already be set. The ministry process in working with adults is as complicated, time-consuming, and costly as correcting a concrete mess. It takes big, heavy equipment to deal effectively with hardened emotional cement. Counseling, psychotherapy, and even psychiatry are often needed to try to undo the damage and pain of lives scarred by warped foundations. Here, as much as anywhere, an ounce of prevention is worth several pounds of cure.

Shaping More Than Phrases

True, our task is to produce high-quality music using the developing gifts and abilities of teenagers. But our ministry to adolescents involves so much more than teaching kids to read notes, produce pure vowels, and spit out crisp consonants. Teenagers sit in front of us each week whose foundation materials are dumped onto our podiums by default. The cement of teenagers' lives often piles up in an undefined blob right in front of us. The clarion call is to those of us who are willing to perform an urgent service, a ministry of molding, of smoothing, of soothing, of balancing and shaping.

There is no way to perform this ministry other than to work hard and to be willing to get dirty. Most of us who minister with teenagers in the musical setting are not "professional cement workers." We are not trained psychologists nor even certified adolescent counselors. Although the skill of professionals is often indicated—and we must be sensitive to know when problems are out of our leagues—the greater need is for ordinary people who are willing to give of their time, energy, and resources to help build healthy foundations for teenagers' lives.

Meanwhile, Back at the Farm

Are you interested in knowing how Dad's garage turned out? It has now been thirty years, and the building is still standing strong against the weathering of time. About the only concrete remembrance of that spring day long ago is that the floor appears to have a slightly rough texture in a few places.

It reminds one of the aftermath of a moderate case of acne.

If we can bring adolescents into adulthood as strong, healthy, durable, and hopeful Christians, the small acne scars will seem quite insignificant.

Foundation for Youth Choir

Seven Practical Suggestions

1) Teach teenagers the Scriptures by singing straight biblical passages. (*spiritual and musical foundation*)

2) In youth choir, provide an environment for healthy adult-to-teenager mentoring. (*emotional foundation*)

3) Foster a sense of team spirit in the choir. (*social foundation*)

4) Through mission projects and other events, allow teenagers to give of themselves to those who cannot help themselves. (*spiritual, emotional, and social foundation*)

5) Develop student leadership by encouraging older teenagers to disciple younger youth. (*spiritual, emotional, and social foundation*)

6) Include regular times of leadership in your choir's worship schedule. (*spiritual and musical foundation*)

7) Allow teenagers to see you, the director, as a real person with real struggles. Let them see how a healthy, mature Christian handles the stresses of life. (*spiritual, emotional and social foundation*)

CHAPTER 7

Daring to Build Upon the Rock

W hen setting out to build a youth choir, it is important that the director, from the beginning, decide the nature of the program. This may
not be as easy as it sounds, since opinions on this subject vary greatly. To determine program direction, the director needs to take a look at 1) her
own gifts and commitments, 2) the level of experience or inexperience of the
teenagers involved, and 3) the expectations of the kids, parents, and congregation for this ministry. What follows can help guide our thinking about the
nature of youth choir under our own particular steeples.

God's Music Within a Very Secular Society

What kind of music is beautiful to God?
   In a world obsessed with what is hot, we tend to raise questions, develop
arguments, and choose sides based upon our own biases and personal tastes in
worship and music. It's a popular pastime for Christian teenagers and young
adults to develop elaborate lines of logic for why their favorite music style is
the most pleasing to God.
   "My kind of music pumps me spiritually."
   "Well, my favorite style challenges me to grow as a Christian. What could
be more important than that?"
   "But mine is better than yours because it leads more people to Christ. Isn't
life in the Lord all about leading others to Him?"
   "Mine is more spiritual than yours because my friends and I can just feel
the Spirit alive in it. God just speaks to me as I worship Him this way."
   "Mine is better because it has stood the test of time."
   "No, mine is better because it's the newest, the hottest, and the least ham-

pered by dead tradition. It just flows with the Spirit. And besides, it's every-body else's favorite, too. That many people can't be wrong!"

What's Hot and What's Not?

These are typical responses among teenagers, even those who grow as Christians. Unfortunately, most other teenagers grow into adulthood without thinking about worship music at all. They simply go with what they are fed and don't ask questions. They buy it at face value, a typical consumer reaction when presented with a packaged product. But by just following the crowd, even the church crowd, the deeper possibilities of worship and growth are often severely stunted.

Current Christian music is helpful in that it provides teenagers a viable alternative to destructive forces which are often vividly portrayed on MTV and on popular recordings. However, as good as it is for entertainment value and light listening, it is important to understand that the vast majority of Christian, contemporary, rock and rap is also market-driven. In other words, it is money-driven. Christian groups are more often than not managed and pro-moted by the same record companies and production moguls as those who keep MTV well supplied with the latest grunge. A study of major record labels will indicate that the big industry names promote musical products for a wide variety of tastes and markets: hip-hop, heavy metal, pop, blues, jazz, country and western, gospel, contemporary Christian. The latter is no more "set apart" for God's glory than any of the other categories designed to define a particu-lar market share. Again, it's a money thing.

Please don't misunderstand me. There is nothing inherently wrong with Christian musicians being successful or penetrating the secular market. However, the fact that their products are so heavily market-driven must cause us to evaluate them constantly and carefully with an eye for theological sound-ness and appropriateness in worship.

It is interesting to note that MTV is committed, not so much to music, as it is to building a global youth culture. This has become a reality before our very eyes over the past two decades. Even though the overall youth culture is the aim, the MTV people know that the best way to get the job done is through music. It is, after all, Music Television. Music is the most powerful tool for reaching kids in the new millennium. As we noted in an earlier chap-ter, secular society is more aware of the real power of music than are many Christian leaders. That is an indictment of us.

Who Owns the Music? Who Influences the Kids?

What kind of music is beautiful to God?

Again, music was God's idea, not ours. We neither invented nor discovered it, nor can we claim any of it as our own. Music flows from the human soul as naturally as blood flows through our veins and oxygen into our lungs. God created us that way. Obviously, some of us are much more musical than others, but I am convinced, after nearly three decades of working in music ministry, that there is God-given music inside all of us. The Old Testament is loaded with specific musical references. These colorful descriptions, commands, and instructions demonstrate without a doubt that music is important to God. He understands its power, and He desires for it to be used for His glory and for the education and edification of His children.

Underscore it again. The Old Testament instructions for music-making in worship involve everyone. Yes, there are sometimes worship prompters, Levites, trained musicians, and song leaders. But it is clear from reference after reference that God intends everyone to make a joyful noise unto Him. Worship has never been about sitting back and letting others do our work for us.

Worship or Spectatorism

We live in a society where almost everything has become a spectator sport: football, basketball, hockey, all-star wrestling, game shows, sitcoms, the Miss USA pageant, the Olympics, even tabloid news. To worship as a spectator is only natural for today's teenagers. They know nothing else. In addition to that phenomenon, the plethora of CDs and inexpensive CD players has made music yet another commodity to be mass-produced, packaged, advertised, bought, sold, used up, and thrown away. In order to "have music," all you have need is a disc and a Walkman, right?

Wrong.

Music, by its very nature, is participatory. *Listening* to music and *making* music involve two totally different dynamics. If humans were computers, we would each possess factory software which would allow us to listen to music. If we were to commit ourselves to making music, it would require a software upgrade, something which is not standard equipment for most new millennium kids. As music ministers, we must design, install, and instill that spiritual upgrade.

This is why music and worship function so wonderfully together. No spectators here, no groupies, no bystanders. Everyone is welcome. Everyone is challenged to join. Everyone is involved. Everyone's noise is joyful when offered unto the Lord.

Every spiritual awakening throughout history has had a musical component. During the great revivals of England where thousands of young people came to Christ under the leadership of John and Charles Wesley, there was a resurgence in singing, worship, and in praise to God. The musical medium was a popular new form, the hymn. The explosion of youth spiritual renewal in the 1960s was accompanied by the advent of the youth musical which brought life, participation, and new teenage involvement. Spiritual renewal is almost always accompanied by "a new song," a renaissance in active corporate worship and new forms, particularly among the young.

Praise and Worship Too Narrowly Defined

From what we read about the nature of God in Scripture, from what we experience in worship and Christian training, and from what we observe of God's presence in history, we know that God is a God of great diversity. "Alleluia" in inner-city Miami may sound very different from "Alleluia" in Vienna, South Texas, or South America. They are different because each is sung through the filter of diverse personal experience and culture.

Praise and worship must never be narrowly defined as a particular *style* or *sound* which incorporates a certain timbre or combination of keyboards, drums, or guitars. Yes, by all means, praise and worship can be expressed through these mediums! Go for it! But praise and worship can also be expressed beautifully in a new a cappella arrangement of "Come Unto Me" or through a classical Psalm setting which is accompanied by organ or chamber orchestra.

Teenagers are far more open to diversity than we think. Not only are they open to variety, but, once exposed to it, they will never want to return to a one-dimensional approach in their music and worship. To be certain, they will have to be taught the value of styles and variety, just as a six-year-old will have to be taught to broaden her diet to include more foods than Happy Meals, fries and chicken nuggets. They may complain and whine at first, but for their own good, we as parents provide a balanced diet which includes all the major food groups. It is essential for long-term health. Too often, we are not nearly as afraid of the teenagers' reaction to other forms of praise and worship as we are insecure about *our own abilities* to teach and lead them effectively. It is easier just to take the path of least resistance, to go with that which takes the least effort.

Easier? Yes.

Better? No.

Best? Not in a thousand years.

Characteristics of Renewed Youth Choir Ministries

For over a decade, I have led *Youth Cue*, an organization dedicated to rebuilding youth choirs in churches across America and beyond. Some say that the effort is futile, that youth choirs are dead, a foregone thing of the past. I might be tempted to believe these pronouncements if I had not seen the truth with my own eyes. In pockets throughout the United States, Mexico, Canada, Africa, Asia, and Europe there are youth choir directors who are committed to teaching their teenagers how to praise and worship and how to help others to do the same. The choirs which are doing the best work—many of which are eighty, ninety, one hundred, one hundred plus voices strong, and many sing every Sunday morning—sing a *very* wide array of music. They include in their programs everything from Michael W. Smith to Mozart, from spirituals to South African tunes, from a cappella singing to praise band, from DC Talk to Allen Pote, from Mendelssohn to original compositions composed by their own choir members. Not only are they on the cutting edge, but they are also developing a sense of history. They understand that they are not alone in time.

Kids love variety, and they will come to understand that God finds all styles beautiful when music, minds, and hearts are centered upon Him. Teenagers today are particularly responsive to Scripture texts, especially those which contain specific promises. Fortunately, a wide array of good anthems are being written today which set such texts to music.

As *Youth Cue* festivals continue to grow, often with as many as 600 teenage singers participating, the ever-present theme of these events is the power of the texts. Never has this been more poignantly demonstrated than when a youth choir from Jonesboro, Arkansas, sang for an internationally televised memorial service following the school shooting tragedy in 1998. The choir had recently returned from a Cue Festival involving 650 teenagers, and they sang one of the festival selections for the service. "You would not believe the power of that text (*excerpted from Isaiah 25*) in the midst of our community's tragedy," stated director Ric Hunt. "It was a time of true praise and worship."

Praise and Worship? Yes! Every Time We Meet!

Again, praise and worship must not be considered a particular style of music. Rather, it is an attitude toward God which finds expression in a wide variety of ways. Every one of us needs to dare to expand our boundaries a bit, to look for the hand of God in every aspect of worship. It is our responsibility, joy, and privilege to help our teenagers hear His voice in every possible way. God bless you in all your praise and worship of Him. He is, indeed, "worthy of worship and praise."

> *Worthy of worship, worthy of praise,*
> *Worthy of honor and glory;*
> *Worthy of all the glad songs we can sing,*
> *Worthy of all of the off'rings we bring.*
>
> *You are worthy, Father, Creator.*
> *You are worthy, Savior, Sustainer.*
> *You are worthy, worthy and wonderful;*
> *Worthy of worship and praise.*

Terry W. York.
Copyright, 1988. Van Ness Press, Inc. Used by permission.

Don't worry about giving your kids what is hot. Instead, dare to build upon the Rock, the One who is worthy of our very best.

CHAPTER 8

Debris, Rubbish and Other Natural Resources

Nehemiah was commissioned by God to rebuild the fallen wall of Jerusalem. Broken, burned, and in ruins, Scripture says the wall was "a reproach." Through a strong commitment to God and a considerable amount of dogged determination and enthusiasm, Nehemiah began his new task. At first, there was much energy and eagerness.

However, it didn't take long for problems to surface. Enemies taunted the laborers all along the work site. The masons and their families became discouraged as quickly as they had become excited. They began to whine and complain. There was so much broken rock and rubbish in the way that they barely had room to work on the new construction.

Sound familiar? Youth choir leaders are also Nehemiah-types. Called and chosen to rebuild a fallen dynasty called youth choirs, we too encounter challenges, difficulties, and motivational problems.

There are subtle and not-so-subtle enemies which continually work against us and try to woo and discourage our teenagers. All of the debris sits on top of the work site! There is so much psychological baggage and scar tissue in the lives of many teenagers that getting close to them with healthy relationships, music, and the Gospel sometimes seems impossible.

Building from Scratch or Remodeling

Which, would you say, is more difficult to do: build a house from scratch or completely renovate a structure that is already standing? When you pose this question to a group of youth choir directors, the overwhelming consensus is that building from scratch is much easier, much quicker, and much cleaner. This seems particularly true if you compare a totally new job to a major renovation.

When I was a kid, we remodeled our home. For three months or more, we stepped over boards, scaffolds, paint cans, and new appliances awaiting installation. It was an enormous mess. The problem was that we had to live in the house while the crew worked in it. If we could have just moved out for a few weeks, allowed the construction to be completed, and then moved back into our "new" home, it would have been much easier. That was not an option, so we continued on with our lives, homework, chores, food preparation, laundry, housework, yard work, baths and sleeping, all the while stepping over debris. It was a long three months.

Your Youth Choir: A Scratch Project, Major Renovation, or a Minor Tweak Job?

The Scratch Project. The advantage of beginning a youth choir from scratch is that you are not dealing with old baggage from other directors, old program traditions, and preconceived ideas. The downside is that there probably is not much of a concept of youth choir either. There is likely a general shortage of vision, and that is where the weight will fall heavily upon your shoulders at first. You will have to establish the mission, set the agenda, sell your idea, develop the goals, and evaluate the results based on no heritage or model in your church's history.

The Major Renovation. Depending on the recent history of the youth choir, this can range from very difficult to fairly simple. The upside is that you already have kids to work with, teenagers who know what a youth choir can be, and who are generally committed to attending rehearsals and performances. The disadvantage could be if the programming previously instilled in the kids and parents was poor. Accomplishing this renovation around the rubbish of bad youth choir concepts could be very complicated and time-consuming.

Here is a fairly common example. You want to develop a first-rate choral program for sixty kids that you inherited from your very popular predecessor. This last director, who has now been gone for almost a year, was a fun guy who had a very lighthearted approach. His philosophy was simply to go-with-what-is-hot.

Thus, the teenagers' hard-wired idea of youth choir is sitting around in a circle with chairs kicked back, drinking pop, chewing gum, and singing passively with a contemporary CD track for an hour while at least a third of the group is engaged in animated conversation about who knows what. The kids *love* this time together, and they don't want it taken away. As a director who wants to bring more into kids' lives, you can already feel the conflict rising and the tightness growing in your chest.

We could spend the rest of this book discussing how to deal with the specific example cited above. In fact, much of the latter chapters will deal directly, specifically, and practically with this and other difficult situations. No instant recipes will be offered, because there are none. However, insights will be provided for practically any youth choir situation. Each individual director must determine how to apply the principles in his/her particular situation.

The Minor Tweak Job. For some reason, very few of us seem to move to ministries where a good, strong program is already in place and where all we have to do is tweak the system. There are probably a couple of reasons for this. First, there are not yet that many excellent programs in existence. Secondly, those directors who do have superb youth choir ministries tend to be happy and stay where they are for the long haul. Good for them! And good for their kids! Remember the previous discussions on tenure?

How Would You Rather Have It?

After fairly lengthy discussions in our conferences about which is easiest (scratch, renovation, or tweaking), which is most difficult, which is most frustrating, and which is completed faster, we all had to stop and laugh.

Regardless of our opinions, the fact is we don't usually get much say in the situation. Whether it's a scratch project, a major renovation, or a minor tweaker, that will be determined by the shape of the program when we arrive. Most of us make our decisions to work on a particular staff based upon a wide scope of major factors: our family's well-being, salary, opportunity for advancement, geography, the kind of church it is, worship style, job expectation, professional opportunities in the community, overall church potential, chemistry with the pastor and staff, and an overall feel for the calling of God. The kind of youth choir a church has will certainly be one consideration in our final decision, but it is unlikely to be all we think about when we accept a new job.

Thus, the decision is usually made for us. The question then becomes, "How will I move forward to maximize this program? How can I take it from where it is to where it needs to be in the years to come? What changes must I make in my ministry to match the changes I am asking my new teenagers to make? How do I need to grow as a musician, as a leader, as a person, as a mentor, as a friend?"

After struggling, praying, growing, leading, and learning some valuable lessons, Nehemiah succeeded in getting the wall of Jerusalem rebuilt, and the refurb was better than the original. It is a wonderful story. As Nehemiah fulfilled his calling, so you and I can also be effective in leading teenagers to Christ through music.

Enjoy the project!

And, while you are at it, please pass me another brick, will you?

Youth Choir as a Mutual Fund

Over the past decade, mutual funds have taken the financial world by storm. Although not quite as popular today as they were in the early to mid-'90s, these rather complicated combinations of funds still possess interesting possibilities for those who invest in them. Offering much larger gains than ancient passbook savings accounts and newer but just as ineffective certificates of deposit, mutual funds have become accessible and popular for even small investors. For instance, ministers of music saving for their own kids' higher education often invest in mutual funds as part of a larger financial plan.

Here is how a mutual fund works. It involves the stock market, but it is not nearly as risky as buying only one stock. A mutual fund takes in huge amounts of money from a large pool of investors, usually into the hundreds of millions of dollars, and invests the money into a wide variety of interests. A mutual fund may have its money spread over stocks in more than one hundred companies.

With this spread of resources over a wide variety of industries and investments, the fund is not likely to suffer when a few investments slump (underperform). With experienced management, a wide and solid base of investment, and a little of what we might call luck, mutual funds can grow dramatically over time. There is risk in varying degrees, however, and it is also possible, though highly unlikely, that the investor will lose money. Mutual funds are usually the most beneficial over the long haul, during which the bumps and rebounds in the market are cushioned over time.

Mutual funds live up to the "mutual" definition in two ways. They are mutual in that all investors benefit (or lose) in direct proportion to what they invest. They are also mutual in that they are linked financially to numerous other businesses across the nation and/or world.

Youth Choir Economy

There is a certain "economic" structure which is similar in youth choir work. The currency is not stock options or cash. Rather, "investments" include energy, time, enthusiasm, and program interest.

There are many benefits to teenagers for their involvement in a good youth choir: spiritual, musical, emotional, social, educational, psychological, and leadership development. Youth choir directors must invest wisely in all these areas if a youth choir is going to see long-term growth and health.

If a youth choir is a mutual fund of teenage talent, potential, and possibility, then the director becomes the manager of that fund, always seeking to shore up the weak spots (under performers) and to invest in a few areas which could show dramatic gain (over performers). A good manager will even take some calculated risks for the sake of growth.

Some years our choir will not have as good a musical showing (musical gain) as it will in other seasons. This provides the astute director with an opportunity to keep investing musically, and also to look for other areas where the group can truly shine. It may not be the best year musically for the group, but the choir may have a wonderful, energetic, and inclusive spirit. This might be the year to invest major time and effort into the social or emotional growth of the group. Some years will be strong musically. These high choral times need to be celebrated and strong musical challenges need to be issued, but never to the abandonment of the choir's other needs. It takes a sharp investor (director) to "see it coming" and prepare the group for what lies ahead.

The youth choir is different from a mutual fund in that, no matter what happens in the world, we will never totally lose our investment. What we do in this arena is eternal. What we do out of love for teenagers is going to last, and it will never be lost or given in vain. One strong similarity exists between mutual funds and the youth choir—those who invest the most will receive the most in return. This is true for directors as well as for the teenagers.

A word to the wise: diversify.

YOUTH CHOIR MUTUAL FUND

Portfolio Manager: Youth Choir Director

Distributor: Your Church or School

Advisor: Holy Spirit

Subadvisors: Youth Choir Officers, Parents, Staff Members

Analysis: (by Randy Edwards, 4-1-2000) Current youth choir directors hope to build a strong ministry base from what used to be a relatively weak, one-dimensional program. Since its inception in the 1940s, youth choir ministry stock has performed fairly well at times, but now and in the future it can do much better. Managers lost a prime opportunity during the '60s and '70s when youth demographics were in their favor. They boasted great gains during that period, but they failed to build substance into their ministries. The same stock which skyrocketed in the '70s plummeted to record lows in the '80s and '90s. Youth choir managers are beginning to wise up and diversify their investments within the Youth Choir Mutual Fund. They are seeing that the musical product is but one way to measure youth choir effectiveness.

Portfolio

Security	% of Assets
Spiritual	10-25
Musical	10-25
Emotional	10-40
Social	10-50
Ensembles	10-15
Mission Endeavors	10-25
Tours, Musicals, Big Events	10-25
Weekly Responsibility	10-30
Officers Group	10-20
Adult Support Group	10-20

When Teenagers Come to Choir for the Wrong Reasons

When I began directing youth choirs a quarter of a century ago, I spent a lot of time preaching to my teenagers about priorities and their motivation for being in choir. Guilt lectures were not an uncommon feature at weekly rehearsals. As I look back, I am amazed that those teenagers hung with me, and today as thirty-something and forty-something professionals and parents, they still speak to me! At this point, I console myself and ease my embarrassment by remembering that I was literally a teenager myself when I preached hot and heavy about priorities. Incidentally, the longest of these sermons were on days when I had not prioritized my own time properly. I was not prepared for that rehearsal; so when things began to fall apart, all I could think to do was preach to them about their own shortcomings. Bad news.

A Pause for a Bit of Monday-Morning Quarterbacking

Let's discuss one of the major mistakes churches made with our youth choirs during the boom years. Rather than calling out and training a mature, energetic adult to minister to teenagers, we often enlisted and deputized one of the older kids and laid the mantle of responsibility upon him or her. Perhaps the huge, newly discovered "generation gap" played into those particular decisions. Perhaps adults were afraid of teenagers, and maybe teenagers of that era would not have responded to adult leadership as they do today. It seemed most youth choirs were directed by big brother/big sister types.

Whatever the case, it's no wonder we lacked substance in the '60s and '70s. Most of us in charge of youth choirs were ourselves adolescents, either actual or emotional or both. We just put ourselves in the front car of the roller coaster and held on for dear life.

It has long been my contention that as a director ages, she can actually become more effective in ministry with kids. This flies in the face of the well-worn adage which says, "I'm too old for this." I certainly understand the feeling, and I have said it myself on a number of occasions. However, once the fatigue fades and we look at the situation more objectively, it becomes obvious that the more a person matures, the more experience he gains to share with a group of kids.

Certainly, the aging process causes all of us to wonder how long we will be able to keep up the pace. Yes, everyone needs to step down before we fall down, never again to get up! However, many of those who give away their youth choirs do so too soon.

The boom years' big brother/big sister directors gave way in the '80s to more favorite uncle types. In the '90s, more directors were playing surrogate mother and father roles. Now, some of us are filling grandparent roles for teenagers, and this too is proving quite effective.

It is okay to be older, a lot older, than teenagers. The issue is not age, it's energy. It's not looks, it's love. It's not being a buddy to the "in" kid crowd, it's becoming a mentor to all.

Now, Back to Teenagers Coming to Choir "For the Wrong Reasons"

Reviewing a bit, we recall there are four major benefits for a teenager's participation in youth choir: spiritual, musical, emotional, and social. These benefits are also the four general motivations for a teenager's joining a choir in the first place.

In my early years of youth choir leadership, I insisted that everyone be present and participate "for the right reason." I was intolerant of the teenager who strolled into rehearsal just because it was the "in" thing to do. To me, that was an unacceptable motivation. The only appropriate reason for being there was to grow spiritually, to advance musically, and to minister to others. Period.

It began to dawn on me much later in my ministry that many, in fact most, of the teenagers I direct came into the choir "for the wrong reasons." They are there because, socially and emotionally, the choir meets a real need for them.

In all honesty, how many teenagers will turn out for choir for the first time primarily because it is a place of spiritual growth? A couple, maybe. How many will come because they seek an environment where they might advance themselves musically? A few more may sign up on that list. Now, let's see how many will give up their Sunday afternoons and come through the doors because they are told choir is fun and that they will get to see their friends.

Aha! There is the real draw for most teenagers! The vast majority of adolescents will come into the choir and stay as a way of meeting their own social and emotional needs.

Don't look now, but the same is true for adults.

Is this "the wrong reason" for joining a choir?

The answer is a sort of yes and no. Yes, any choir can become ingrown, self-serving, self-perpetuating, self-centered. All of us would likely agree that such a group is falling very short of its potential in ministry, service, and Christian growth.

It should not surprise us, scare us, or insult us that most teenagers are drawn into the youth choir for social reasons.

Notice the order of benefits listed: spiritual, musical, emotional, and social. Think of each level as a door that teenagers can enter. Why should we expect all teenagers to enter through the highest, noblest doors: the spiritual or musical levels? Most will not, and if we insist upon it, we will shoot our ministry in the foot from the beginning. Teens should be allowed to participate in choir at any "entry level" of motivation, at least for awhile.

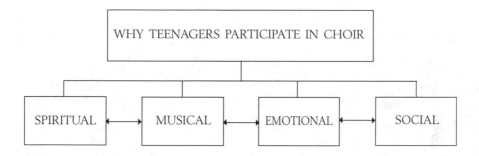

Perhaps the social aspect is the least noble, the least "spiritual" reason for being in a youth choir. But think of it in broader terms. If we were to provide teenagers *only* a dependable, safe, affirming environment to hang out safely with their friends, we would still be offering a valuable service to the kids, the parents, and the community. Most cities have a tremendous shortage of safe places for kids to come together, play together, socialize, and be themselves. Government grants are actually awarded to organizations who do only this. Yes, this in itself is a viable and legitimate ministry!

Obviously, as youth choir leaders, we want to do more, more, so much more than baby-sit teenagers in relative safety. We have such a wide world of marvelous tools at our fingertips that it is a travesty not to maximize them in the lives of teenagers.

The social aspect is essential for a thriving and vibrant youth choir ministry. We cannot separate any of the four elements from the others. Each depends to some degree upon the other three.

Yes, it is developmentally unthinkable that many young adolescents will, from the beginning, participate in choir only for the right reasons. It is up to us as leaders to help teenagers move from mere socialization to spiritual awareness. It is a director's task to build in a love for God and an appreciation of

Scripture and the great gift of music. It is a process. It takes time and patience. It takes more sensitivity and fewer sermons.

With God's help and guidance, our teenagers will end the year with higher motivation than when they first entered our lofts. Your prayers, preparation, hard work, endurance, and patience will bear wonderful fruit as you move all the levels of commitment in an upward, Godward direction.

CHAPTER 9

Don't Stop Thinking
About Tomorrow

One of the sad characteristics of new millennium kids is that many suffer from a severe, sometimes deadly loss of hope. Adults often wonder why so many teens involve themselves in "at-risk" behavior. "Why would a teenager these days start smoking? It is common knowledge that smoking is horrible for your health, terribly addictive, expensive and offensive. Surely they know smoking can shorten their lives and inflict them and their families with all kinds of medical problems!"

Yes, they *do* know. And they don't care.

"Well, that makes no sense! Why *don't* they care?"

Because they have lost hope. When you lose hope, you lose life. You envision your own life cut short by a nuclear holocaust, war, violence, disease, suicide, or by any number of other sad endings we see in the media—and in the hallways of our schools.

If we lose hope, we will do terrible things to ourselves because we are convinced, at least at that exact moment, that it doesn't matter. Pretty heavy stuff, wouldn't you say? And yet, millions of teenagers live this way every day of their lives.

Unfortunately, MTV tends to exacerbate the situation. Claiming to deal honestly with real adolescent issues, they actually do a superb job of asking all the right questions, exposing the inconsistencies and injustices and suffering within the adolescent society. They ask all the right questions, something the church as of late has been quite slow to do. We have become quite adept at ignoring the real issues of adolescence.

The problem with MTV is that it presents no decent solutions. It may reflect society, but it provides virtually nothing to redeem it.

On the other hand, the church thinks that we know all the right answers. But the answers we give tend to go with questions nobody is asking. Kids don't want our answers, because we are not listening to their questions, nor do we adequately respond to their loneliness.

Youth choir directors, through their ministries and their love for kids, can become distributors of hope for an entire generation. Hope is a rare gift, but one which Christians can possess in great abundance. Youth choirs can provide a vital link which brings hope to the hopeless.

It all has to do with our willingness to give major energy to our kids. It takes praying, planning, and preparation. Our intentions are good, but unfortunately our work skills and lack of self-discipline continue to hold us back. We want to be a lighthouse in a dark world, if only we could get around to it.

Procrastination? Who, Me?

Would it be too much of a generalization to suggest that, artists as a group, including youth choir directors, are chronic procrastinators? If, indeed, this description is too harsh and sweeping, then please accept my sincere apologies. If you are not, to some extent, a procrastinator, then it might be best to skip over this chapter and continue reading with the next section. I, however, am going to continue to write *and read* this chapter, because I am one who needs it.

Stated as simply as it can be put, we don't begin soon enough.

"Begin *what* soon enough?" we might ask.

"Generally, we don't begin *anything* soon enough," returns the reply.

As a group of youth choir directors, the vast majority of us stay approximately two steps ahead of the administrative steamroller. We produce when we have to produce; but, when there is no deadline bearing down upon us, we tend to flitter away the hours with substandard productivity. It's an artist thing.

The Futuristic View from Today

We must never, not even for one solitary work day, stop thinking about the future. Most directors pass that test without much problem, but we make an enormous mistake when we don't think *far enough* into the future. One way to get a grip on this is to do what might be referred to as working backwards. Fast-forward in your mind to the next big event, and make a list (yes, an actual written list) of all the things which will have to be decided, planned, executed, and organized in order for this event to come off without a hitch. Don't be afraid to write too much.

From that vantage point, work backwards, making a detailed list of all which must be done and when. Assign a specific date to each level of preparation, using deadlines which will give you a margin of a few days for the possibility of unforeseen difficulties or detours. At this point, we need to remind ourselves of something important. All of these things *will* get done. It's just a matter of when. We can discipline ourselves to take care of them in advance when we are calm, controlled and collected. The other option is to wait until the details absolutely must be done, the deadlines are screaming at us, and the pressure is relentless.

One of the reasons we don't plan this way is because it can be very tiring to look at such a *long* to-do list. And, to make matters seem even more grueling, this list needs to be made at what point? Immediately following the completion of our last big project, which has left us exhausted and mentally drained!

Unfortunately, many of us work in a defeating, or at least less than creative, cycle. Here is a common pattern: We procrastinate planning and accomplishing the components of a major event until the deadlines hang threateningly over our heads. Only squeaky wheels are oiled. Eventually, only the combination of an *absolute* deadline and the fear of failure provide enough fire under our flasks to get us to produce. Because we have not allocated the proper amount of time and energy for each task, we begin to work under stress in an increasingly frantic pattern. Everyone around us, including our secretaries (and yes, our families) begin to feel the pressure mount. Our support systems are on edge and are not happy campers. They may mask their disgust for our lack of organization, but don't let this fool you. Our co-workers will always give less when they are feeling overworked or abused.

If this pace continues or if the project is big enough, our panic will soon turn to frenzy. The order of the day is survival. Creativity, innovation, and the joy of the ministry are tossed out the window.

The bottom line is that we *will* make it. The deadline will come and go, and the event will pull together by the grace of God. It usually does, doesn't it?

But at what price?

The process has left us totally spent. Thus, immediately following a major event, when we need to plan for the future, we are mentally and emotionally useless for the next two or three weeks. While we "veg out", trying to recover, the program and expectations march on. Alas, the cycle begins all over again.

When we think in terms of the long haul, we discipline ourselves to plan productively and steadily through the down times as well as the more stressful hours.

One of the ways we can gauge our effectiveness and efficiency is to watch the work flow of our secretaries. So often, our support staff will work themselves into a lather during the crunch times, putting in overtime and working through their breaks and lunches. Then, when things shut down after a big event, there is little else to do but read a book or stand around visiting with church members or other staff. There is an art to working with a support staff, and the evenness or inconsistency of their work load indicates how efficiently *we* work. The challenge is to provide as even a work load as possible. Everyone is more productive that way, and a whole lot happier, too!

What keeps us from being more organized and futuristic in our planning? It is usually one simple thing: plain old lack of self-discipline.

A Ministerial Balancing Act

While a university student and a very young music minister, I served a church south of Houston. I will never forget the words of one wise elderly lady, Aunt Maude Rhoads, who said one day, "Son, life is a balancing act. Your success or failure as a Christian leader is going to depend a great deal upon your ability to nurture the real treasures, juggle the important things, and drop the stuff that doesn't amount to a hill of beans."

Such words don't mean much to a nineteen-year-old who knows everything there is to know about life and ministry. As the saying goes, "There's nothing smarter than a college sophomore!" However, the admonition about balancing makes more sense now that I am pushing forty-five.

A balancing act.

Remember the swimming pool mentioned in Chapter 6? This concrete circle was the center of summer activity among rural community kids. The end of school meant one important milestone for all of us tough guys: for six days a week, we would wear neither shoes nor shirts. By the time the school bell sounded in August, you wouldn't be able to tell the Edwardses from the Ludwigs from the Martinezes from the Garzas. Not only that, we could make sparks fly with our big toes! It was a guy thing.

One of the many games we invented was "stand on the inner tube." This was a gross misnomer from the word go, because nobody was going to do any standing. "Make a fool of yourself trying" would have been a more appropriate designation for our impossible water sport. Sure, standing on an inner tube in the middle of a pool sounds easy enough, doesn't it? Yeah, right! Across four decades of Hispanic and white kids, I have never seen anyone balance for more than three seconds at a time. Something else: the longer you stay up, the more fierce the flouncing and the more violent the fall. Guaranteed.

A balancing act.

There is a principle regarding inner tube standing which we all need to recognize. When you get one part of it submerged and under control, another part pops up. Every time. No exceptions. Take one side under the water and the other is on its way up. It is only a matter of time, either right now or two seconds later. So why does a pack of pubescent neophytes keep working on this impossible task? Maybe for sport. Maybe because "it's there."

A balancing act.

I wish I could tell you my life as a Christian and as a leader never feels that way. But truthfully, there is so much to balance. Frankly, it really doesn't matter how big or small the inner tube is. It's still a tough and potentially discouraging task. In the pool, we would struggle with it, working in shifts, until we finally said "forget it" and went on to something else. However, by the next morning, we were ready to take on the donut again. We were drawn to the challenge, even though we were often discouraged.

Work. Rest. Family participation. Time alone with God. Physical fitness. Spiritual readiness. Hard work. Play. Stress. Relaxation. Cleaning up the clutter. Letting it go for now. Staying professionally current with technology and trends. Staying committed to what we have already mastered. Remaining dedicated to that which will not change. Financial planning. Casting our cares upon the Lord. Providing for those we love. Laying up treasures in heaven. Being a good, true friend. Being a sensitive husband or wife, a kind, compassionate, and guiding father or mother. Making money. Using it wisely. Giving some of it away. Job efficiency. Having time for someone who drops by to chat.

A balancing act.

Most of us balance our checkbooks once a month, although you may know some folks who go months and months without doing so. Talk about producing stress! If you use Quicken or some other computer financial program, your job has been made much easier once you invest the time and resources to set it up. All checks, debits, ATM transactions, withdrawals, credits and deposits have to be regularly reconciled to keep your personal finances in proper order—if your checkbook is to balance (*there it is again*).

A balancing act. No joke.

However, if we wait until the end of the month to balance our emotional selves, we will find our lives in a terrible mess. God provides us with a highly sophisticated internal system which seeks to find balance every day of our lives, every hour of the day. All the psychological debits, the expenditure of what psychologists call "psychic energy," the affirmation we receive, the emotional hits we take in the course of a day—all these have to be balanced by the hour if we are to find sanity and meaning in our Christian pilgrimages.

Oftentimes, the task is more challenging than balancing a checkbook, and it is sometimes appropriate to seek outside professional help to discover that place of emotional health. Our own personal childhood and adolescent issues often emerge as we work closely with teenagers. This is one reason that youth choir work threatens so many of us. Such intense emotional work has a way of hooking the unresolved issues and insecurities of our own teenage years. If we don't face the skeletons in our own closets, we won't be of much real help to teenagers.

As followers of Christ, we possess priceless promises which sustain and build our lives.

Come unto me, all you who work hard and are weary and weighed down, and I will give you the rest you need. Take my yoke upon you and learn Who I am, for I am meek and lowly of heart. You will find rest for your souls, for my yoke is easy and my burden is light.

Matthew 11:28-30

God's yoke and burden are balanced, as well. The Great God of Reconciliation can do His work of balance in and through our lives, even though we live in the midst of a society which is woefully unbalanced.

All we need to do is ask. Remember, Jesus can not only stand on inner tubes, but he can also walk on water.

Who needs the inner tubes, anyway?

The Fight Against Compassion Fatigue

The reality of compassion fatigue has received a lot of press lately among those in helping professions. It is not an uncommon occurrence in the youth choir setting. We periodically hear a new and stunning manifestation of compassion fatigue: a well-known leader has burned out, a director has fallen prey to his own huge ego, a talented leader has hit the wall with her choir parents and feels she cannot take the kids one single step further. Compassion fatigue takes its toll on our lives and ministries in many ways.

The term itself, "compassion fatigue," is not as hot as it was in the mid-'90s. Like many other phrases adopted by society, it comes and goes. But just because the term is not used as much, don't be fooled into thinking the reality is gone. It is not. Whether you hear about it or not, chances are that you will feel it, and that feeling may press hard on you sooner rather than later.

For obvious reasons, summer events with teenagers often produce a bumper crop of compassion fatigue among youth choir leaders. During tours and camps, we connect with the kids, hear their stories, and seek ways to help. We become emotionally involved. We sometimes think about the problem kid to the detriment of relationships with kids who aren't so troubled. We see the pain, the hurt, the dysfunction, and, as ministers, we react and jump into the situation with both feet to try to fix it. These are the blessings and hazards of caring. This is the line which calls for an intense balancing act. This is the point of entry for compassion fatigue.

Perhaps there are three basic ways to deal with compassion fatigue among youth choir leaders. First, we can take on more and more and more, giving no thought to our own well-being and energy . . . thinking we can handle anything any time any place. We become oblivious to our own emotional health or lack of it, and we focus totally on what is going on at the point of the present crisis. This is a dangerous scenario for several obvious reasons.

A second reaction is to completely avoid the stress that comes from getting close to kids. We simply put up our personal barricades and determine never to be hurt, pulled down, or affected by what is going on around us. We stay at arm's length and never really engage. Unfortunately, many potentially effective musicians end up here with their kids in the youth choir setting. They never let down. They never become real people to their teenagers. They are always in a different reality.

Finally, there is a balance between the two positions that represent a place of health for everyone. Directors can, and indeed must, engage themselves emotionally in the lives of their teenagers. This is undoubtedly one of the greatest needs in our society today—adults who are willing to become emotionally connected to kids. But that is not to imply that the director jump headlong into every situation without first looking and taking inventory of the situation. A caring director can find a good balance between genuine compassion and distance. Our effectiveness as leaders depends on it.

Before you crash into your next big emphasis, let me encourage you to take some down time for yourself. Go hiking for a few days. Go to the country and drive a tractor for an afternoon. Get away for awhile to regain your focus, to fine tune your vision for ministry.

Keep in mind that compassion fatigue hits hardest when we are uncompassionate with ourselves. We can't care for others over the long haul if we abuse our own bodies and emotions. Compassion fatigue is an occupational hazard for caring directors, but it need not be an enemy which defeats us.

Steps for Minimizing Compassion Fatigue

1. Take care of yourself. Exercise regularly.

2. Talk regularly to a good, trusted friend. Unload your stress in small doses, before it becomes unmanageable inside you.

3. Keep your daily devotional life active.

4. Read *The Gift of Peace* by Joseph Cardinal Bernadin.

5. Write your feelings in the form of a journal and don't show it to anyone.

6. Use part or all of your professional development time and budget or even some of your vacation to spend time with a good professional counselor.

7. Enjoy a change of pace, however simple, before launching into the next intensive period of ministry.

8. For one solid day, do only what *you* want to do.

9. Take a couple of days away with the family. Lose the cell phone.

10. Even though you may not feel like it, do something active which will leave you physically exhausted and thus able to sleep soundly.

PART THREE

The Costs
of Construction

The Necessity of Personal Investment

I t usually goes something like this:

I came to this Youth Cue conference today to try to find more creativity and energy for my youth choir ministry. I used to just sort of survive youth choir from week to week. But now that I have an eighth grade daughter in my choir, I want the experience to be more, to mean more to her and her friends.

There are often slight variations on the theme, but many directors' stories sound surprisingly similar. Youth choir may be a lackluster thing to endure from week to week until a son or daughter is old enough to become involved. Then, all of a sudden, the purpose of youth choir seems a little clearer, the cause more noble, the stakes much higher.

That is okay. If having a child of your own in choir causes you to take your youth choir ministry seriously, that is good.

On the other hand, there are directors who have no teenagers of their own in choir, but their programs are vibrant, energetic, and growing. If you get them talking about their choir ministries, they will almost always tell you stories about individuals. They report the crises in these kids' lives and how the choir ministered to them in their time of need. They talk about kids who have unusual gifts and who need to be given constant direction and consistent affirmation.

Before long, you get the picture. These directors have teenagers in their choir for whom they feel a special attachment, a closer bond than a pass-you-in-the-hallway, see-you-at-rehearsal relationship. Successful directors don't build exclusive cliques around themselves. However, they do develop strong, healthy relationships with teens who have specific needs, a budding talent, a special problem, or a desire to give more to the choir.

Whether or not you have a child of your own in choir, one of the keys to effective directing is having a vested interest in your group. One young director reflected at a recent conference, "I often think about Emily and Amy and Rob and Ryan. Aside from being in the youth choir, they are special friends of mine. I want the whole youth choir experience to be as good as it can possibly be for them. I want them to take the feelings and friendship and love with them for the rest of their lives."

Do you and I want our youth choirs to be effective and successful in our ministries to teens? If this is going to happen, you and I, the directors, must have some personal, vested interest in our work. It needs to matter to us personally. When it does not matter, motivation and inspiration will be inconsistent and shallow. When it does matter in our hearts and minds, the sky is the limit in our creativity and sensitivity in the youth choir setting.

Nothing can substitute for personal investment.

When the Jacksons Outnumber the Carters

As a kid, I always wanted to be a musician. I never had much talent, or even discipline, for that matter, but I found a great deal of satisfaction picking out melodies on the spinet piano at home and banging out new rhythms on an old set of drums in the school band hall. It was a release from teenage tension and a whole new world of discovery for me. It was fun, and, looking back, I now realize that my investment in music kept me sane through adolescence and into early adulthood.

Mr. Carter was there from the time I started band in the fifth grade until I graduated from high school. A forty-something nice guy trained late in life as a band director, Fred Carter had been a geologist who became weary of digging. Instead, he began working to unearth and polish children's musical talent. About the only holdover from his former career was his chain smoking. Didn't all band directors smoke in the '70s?

This was the age of the Osmonds and the Jackson Five. They were some of my idols growing up in 1969. My changing vocal chords always felt comfortable crooning along with "The Twelfth of Never" and "Got to Be There." Donny and Michael and I are all about the same age, although I don't think either of them know my birthday. In fact, I believe neither Michael nor Donny know I exist, nor do I imagine they care.

Mr. Carter cared. And, in the eighth grade, when I first heard the old adage, "those who can, *do*, and those who can't, *teach*," I knew in my gut it didn't apply to Fred Carter. He could. He did. *And he taught.*

Taking a horrible Hooterville band in a tiny South Texas school, Mr. Carter went to work. We were his first job out of music school. Within three years, the Lytle—pronounced with a long "i," although more accurately described as "little"—High School Pirate Band won the state marching contest in Austin. It was a miracle, a musical version of the scene from the basketball movie *Hoosiers*. Ninety-six pubescent horn blowers, flute tooters, drum beaters, and tuba suckers danced around the astroturf like Super Bowl champions. We accomplished something incredible. Carter was our man!

Thirty years later, I believe he still is.

Entertained to death—My friends and I were lucky. We had a teacher who cared about us and showed us we could make music and march. Through sheer energy, hard work, and long hours, he convinced us that we could do something positive and extraordinary. It was no small miracle. Without that teacher, my friends and I would have been cursed for life just to pantomime the recorded sounds of the Osmonds and Jacksons coming through our radios. We would have been entertained all the way to our own artistic graves, never learning how to express the music inside us. We would have ended up like the vast majority of teenagers in our world today, entertained to death and bored stiff.

From the beginning of time, music has possessed the power to accompany miracles, to create, sustain and enrich lives. At its best, it can renew the spirit of a grieving community, unite a nation, soothe a deranged mind, discover the hidden treasures inside a teenager, and bless all those who come into earshot. The Fred Carters of the world realize this and have devoted their lives to discovering and developing the music within the gold mines of adolescents.

Only a couple of fellow band members became professional musicians, which is the way it probably should be. But all of us learned more about ourselves, how to work as a team, how to give, and how to become decent, productive human beings.

Isn't that what education is all about? Isn't that what God has in mind for the church and the world?

In the larger picture today, some music has ceased to bless and has now begun to curse. For money, it is prostituted by promoters in the marketplace. It is sometimes dark, deadly, dangerous, and cheap. It is being peddled, pimped, and pushed for the immediate sinister satisfaction it promises. For a growing number of teenagers, music is not a miracle at all. It is simply something else to buy at the cheapest price.

New kids in the dark—Parents have repeatedly sent the message loud and clear to their kids: we will spend money to entertain you, but we won't pay the price for you to learn. Play this video. Plug in this CD. Watch this game. Go to the movies. What? I'm not going to waste money on violin lessons!

Parents often play the theme song long before their children reach adolescence, "Do anything you want, but don't bother me." By the time a kid reaches puberty, he has often been shoved thoughtlessly aside into dark worlds of isolation and unquenched consumerism, a kingdom where earphones are crowns and where music videos reign supreme.

Out of control—We know the miracle of music has been sold out when all we hear about are the stars, the endorsements, the contracts, the bodyguards, production teams, record companies, lawsuits, and press conferences denying sexual abuse charges.

Not only has the entertainment orgy exterminated untold potential among our youth, but it also eats at the flesh of the stars themselves. Once today's icons exhaust all of their big-time marketing potential, they are tossed into the trash. Today's hunks are tomorrow's junk. "Rico suave," if you can remember the song from a few years ago, has become more like, "suave reeks . . . " or worse, if we were to choose today's vernacular!

As Michael Jackson's career almost came to an end in 1994, it was a near-perfect example of a carnival musical cruise turned cannibal. The very stage the promoters and public had set up for Michael exploded underneath his moonwalking feet. His strangeness was his trademark, his most marketable commodity. The more bizarre he became, the more money we heaped upon him. We kept on rewarding his unbridled bizarreness, tempting him to step deeper and deeper into the Land of Weird. All seemed well on the outside until he appeared to take one step too many down his mysterious road. He suddenly fell off the edge into unacceptable strangeness. Society's double standards can be confusing and confounding.

The whole truth about Michael Jackson's alleged moral wrongdoings may or may not ever be fully known. Everyone involved suffered greatly. And yes, the young boy in question also suffered, too. Think about it. Which would scar a fourteen year old boy more: sexual abuse by an adult male or scamming an innocent person out of $20 million. Either way, the boy has been used. The only ones not hurt by the ordeal will be the entertainment industry which has an uncanny way of capitalizing on the sins and/or misfortunes of everybody and everything. And you and I, our teenagers, their parents and their friends are the ones who buy it all up and encourage it to continue.

Upside down—Something is systemically wrong with a society which pays teachers starvation wages, while, at the same time, lavishing rock stars, professional athletes, and movie actors with annual salaries in the multiplied millions. We have gone to seed on entertainment, and the consequences of our mismanagement are unavoidable and already haunt us.

The Tribe of Carter—Despite the obvious concern we have for the youth of our world, we celebrate and see a great deal of hope knowing that the Tribe of Carter is not extinct. There are women and men in many places who are responding to the epidemic of neglect among our teenagers. You will find them teaching in public and private schools, coaching YMCA sports leagues, directing church youth choirs, counseling teenagers in synagogues and churches, and directing junior high debate teams. They help children and teenagers see the possibilities for the future, and they nurture the kind of expression and discipline which builds a strong, colorful fabric in our society. Each one of them is more valuable to the future of our world than a dozen rock stars. And, since this is a labor of love, they often accomplish their work at great sacrifice personally and financially.

May the Tribe of Carter increase.

Selling the souls of our kids to the god of entertainment is going to leave all of us singing the blues. If consumerism continues to grow unabated, nobody in the future will know how to sing . . . except, of course, the stars! So, I suppose we will all have to buy a new CD to sing our sad song for us. There is probably one in production right now!

Not cynicism, but reality with great hope—Reading back over the past couple of paragraphs, I must say it does appear rather dark, bleak, cynical and negative. Sorry about that!

We are not really singing a song of despair, not by any means. Rather, we hope to face our world honestly and build ministries based upon the realities around us and within us. Christianity has always been about going against the grain, about providing an eternal alternative to the superficiality of secular society.

Jesus said, "Be of good cheer, for I have overcome the world and all that is in it" *(John 16:33)*.

CHAPTER 10

Essential Ingredients for Healthy Relationships

T he explosive growth of the new church in Acts 2 is one of the most remarkable stories in all of history. In Acts 1, we find about one hundred and twenty scared, nervous disciples huddled together in an upper room, trying to figure out what to do next. By the time Chapter 2 rolls around, three thousand have joined the group. A few chapters later, the group numbers about five thousand. By the time we reach the middle of the book of Acts, there is serious talk about this group of Christians turning the world upside down, not so much by their sheer numbers, but by their involvement and influence within society.

What happened?

What blew down the four walls of the church and set the believers ablaze with the good news of the Resurrected Lord?

The obvious answer is Pentecost. The Holy Spirit came upon the frightened little group and gave them the power to move with effectiveness and courage. Although this is true, it really doesn't tell us much about what actually happened within the ranks of believers to transform their lives and to radically impact their society. Let's take a closer look at what this Pentecost was all about.

They Understood Each Other

It was a much-needed breakdown in the language barrier. People from one place spoke, and everyone, regardless of their nation or language or dialect, understood! They truly understood each other.

That is no small miracle, even among people who all speak English! We truly need to understand each other, not just our words, but also our deeper selves, those unspeakable feelings which need hearing.

They understood each other.

Do we?

Their Fellowship Was Based Upon Acceptance Rather Than Agreement

Holly and I have been married for nearly two decades. We have faced challenges typical in any marriage. We have also experienced a few pressures and stresses which are unique to who we are and the various roles we fill. We have had our share of illness, financial setbacks, joyful experiences, and disappointments. We share in raising and supporting our three children, and we make important and not-so-crucial decisions together as a couple—as a family.

I confess that there are times Holly and I don't agree on much of anything. We see things from different vantage points. We have our own personal goals which have to be incorporated into a family of five. Sometimes we disagree. But total agreement is not the basis of our relationship. What holds us together through the good times and bad is our unconditional acceptance of one another. Our unity, family, and fellowship are held together with acceptance rather than agreement.

The ministry of Youth Choirs, Inc,. spans a dozen denominational lines. It is very doubtful that all of us are in total agreement on every issue we face as youth choir directors. We hold different doctrinal views. We have various taste preferences. We celebrate and worship in different styles. Our backgrounds are different and unique. We may differ on the finer points, perhaps even on some of the basic points of the philosophy of church music. We even differ in our views of how to operate a good youth choir.

Despite these differences, we are able to love each other and work effectively together. Why? It is because of our overarching, overpowering, overwhelming and common love for Christ, our commitment to Christ's Lordship in our lives, and our concern and love for our teenagers. What unites us is much stronger than that which would divide us.

They Encouraged Each Other

Within the group of new believers, there was a scrawny little fellow moving around the group. His name was Barnabas, the son of encouragement. It is very unlikely that Barnabas ever preached a sermon, sang a solo, or took any major role of up-front leadership in the early church.

Instead, Barnabas seemed to move within the church encouraging people. Can you hear it now?

"You did a great job with that project!"

"I knew you could do it!"

"I'm very proud of you."

"Come on, it will work out, just hang in there!"

When we speak of encouragement, let's not confuse affirmation with flattery. The glad-handing, slap-you-on-the-back approach is not necessarily synonymous with encouragement. Flattery is designed as a setup to get something back from you. It is often loud, flashy, and boisterous. It is usually less than honest and reeks of showmanship.

Affirmation, on the other hand, creatively seeks to bless you at the point of your greatest need, taking into account your temperament and unique personality. Encouragement offers sincere assurance at the point of doubt and genuine acceptance at the point of insecurity.

Most of us have precious few people in our lives who truly know how to affirm and encourage us. It takes love, honesty, and genuine concern to encourage someone who needs it.

Thank God for those who know how to encourage you creatively and meaningfully. Ask God to make you a real encourager for someone else. Nowhere is this more important than in the youth choir setting.

They Possessed a Respect for One Another Which Bordered on Reverence

In a world where both respect and reverence are hard to come by, it is refreshing to realize that God's early church held one another in high regard.

How much respect do most teenagers receive, or consequently give, today? It seldom happens at school. A star football player or a well-known musician may feel some respect. That *may* be a certain kind of respect, but in this culture we easily mistake respect for *intimidation*.

What if you warm the bench on the B Team or don't make varsity band? What if you happen to be a boy who is very small for his age, or a tall, lanky girl wearing two or three corrective devices? Respect? I don't think so.

In far too many cases, it never happens at home. One way kids are shown respect is with the gift of our time. In fact, it's impossible to show respect to a teenager without spending time with him. The only place a teenager may find respect in her life is in a youth choir setting. Providing it is a heavy, heavenly responsibility!

A Series of Questions: What About Youth Choir?

What would happen if it became known to all that whenever a teenager walked into our rehearsal room, she would be met with real *understanding*. What would happen if every boy who came to choir received unconditional acceptance, green hair, earring, and all? What would be the impact on that lonely ninth-grade girl, if every time she set foot in our choir room, she felt sincere *affirmation* and genuine *encouragement*? And how would that little eighth grader react if he were treated with a *respect* that bordered on *reverence*, and those attitudes came from a senior soccer star?

Now this could change the world!

Youth Choir, Church, Any Christian Community

When understanding, acceptance, affirmation, and respect are distributed freely within the context of any Christian community, the body of Christ will grow as people are drawn into this amazing atmosphere of grace and love.

The four gifts we are called upon to provide for others are no strangers to us. As Christians who have given our lives to Christ, we possess these gifts inside ourselves. As Christ abides within us, He provides His children with a wellspring of understanding, acceptance, affirmation and respect.

In the Gospel of John (12:32), Jesus says, "If I be lifted up, I will draw all people unto me."

It happened two thousand years ago in the book of Acts because the Christian community became serious about giving away what they had received. It can happen again when we are intentional about embodying the grace of Christ through our youth choirs.

CHAPTER 11

Electricity in Communication

T he story is told of a man who went to see a psychologist with what he considered to be a big problem in his life. "Dr. Smellfungus," whined the poor, would-be counselee, "I just have the most difficult time getting people to understand me. I try and try to get my point across, but I can't seem to communicate with people what I am feeling."

After carefully listening to the man's story, Smellfungus replies, "Sorry, I don't get your point."

We have all felt like the man sitting on the counselor's couch. The complex processes of communication are so complicated and powerful that it is often difficult to figure out how to be properly understood by family members, staff colleagues, and our youth choir members.

Communication is a major key in getting our youth choirs "humming." Far too many directors have not taken a serious look at the communication process and the specific elements related to adolescents.

Researchers have committed entire lives to study the process, science and psychology of communication, and we will not be able to touch all of the bases in one chapter. We possess no vain hopes of being comprehensive, but perhaps we shall be provocative and helpful.

Principle #1

Good communication is always a two-way process; it involves receiving messages as well as sending them.

Though I speak with tongues of men and angels but do not hear what my youth choir members are trying to express back to me, it is going to get us nowhere as a group. Most of us have given time and energy to learn how to express our own feelings before a group of people—public speaking. We need to continue to improve those skills, but we *have* worked on them. Far fewer of us have done anything to improve our listening skills, to really hear what is being transmitted to us. When "communication" is reduced to hearing ourselves talk, then it is not communication at all; it has become something else. All telephones have an instrument for our ear as well as a transmitter for our voice. Without receiving and processing, we are not communicating. Blind and deaf talking is no more than the practice of broadcasting.

Principle #2
Every message has a meta-message.

In her book, *That's Not What I Meant: How Conversation Style Makes or Breaks Relationships,* Deborah Tannen explains to would-be excellent communicators that beneath every obvious message there is a deeper level of transmission. In fact, people may even say the opposite of what they really *mean.* Here again, just hearing the words will not get the job done. Inflection, expression, and the tension factors give a truer indication of what is really being said. For example, a teenager might say, "Everybody around here is unfriendly. Nobody ever talks to me," when, in fact everyone talks to him. What is the *meta-message,* the real message? "I am feeling lonely and I need some special attention."

Principle #3
Real communication is an intentional process. It rarely happens by accident.

Dysfunctional families and unresponsive youth choirs are the results of false assumptions about communication. Families often assume that they communicate well when they may not be understanding each other at all. Choirs who spend hours and hours together on Sunday afternoons may just assume that they are becoming a group when, in fact, they are just a bunch of teenagers sitting and singing facing the same direction in a rehearsal room.

Some significant serendipitous communication does happen in most youth choirs. When that occurs, it is most often a by-product of intentional interaction which has taken place at some point in the recent past.

Communication for Youth Choir Directors

Written Communication

We begin with written communication, because it is the most *under-used* form of building bridges with your teenagers. We have come to assume that teenagers will not read what we write to them, and this is a significant miscalculation. Teenagers will have to be trained to do many things which they need to do: open their mouths in order to make a good sound, produce quick, hard consonants, learn to be still when it is time to work, to be leaders in worship, on and on it goes. We will also have to teach our teenagers to read our written communication just as we teach them to read music. It will take conditioning, but in time the effort will be well worth it.

Some ideas we try to communicate cannot be adequately written into words, at least not completely. But some very important information can and must be disseminated effectively in written form.

Anything which can be put in writing, *put it in writing.* Keep written information, schedules, events, and requirements in front of the kids constantly. Surely, we will have to verbally emphasize certain instructions as time goes on, but the more the kids and their parents see in writing, the less you will need to say about it.

Rehearsal sheets with orders of rehearsals and announcements have become very popular with hundreds of directors across the country. Other leaders send a weekly mailing to their choir members, creatively updating them on upcoming events. A director can use the flip side of communication to write devotionals or letters from his heart to the choir.

At first, perhaps only a teen or two will read what you write. But with consistency over time, teenagers will learn the importance of reading their mail. They will eventually learn that there is important information in your mailing, and they won't want to miss any of it.

Incidently, what is the *meta-message* we send to teenagers when we consistently write or prepare a weekly rehearsal sheet? The message is clearly written on paper. The *meta-message* is, "You are important to me; I am prepared for our time together; I love you enough to give you my best effort and take the time to plan something special for you. I respect your time and want to make the most of it."

Spoken Communication

We list spoken communication second because it is the most *overused* form of communication with our youth choirs. It would be shocking for most of us to tape our rehearsals and clock ourselves on how much time we spend talking—giving minute details, repeating and repeating plans and instructions. We talk entirely too much, and one of the reasons we do this is because we have failed to communicate properly ahead of time with the written word. Having failed in our planning, we stand up and try to wing it on our feet in front of them. Our words become repetitious and monotonous. They often go unheeded because the kids know from experience that we are shooting from the hip.

Our voices must be used to communicate the most significant aspects of our time with the choir. But the overuse of speaking can cheapen the whole experience for the teenagers. They generally hate lectures, and the more the rehearsal can move along, the better they are likely to respond.

The spoken word is much like salt in our favorite soup recipe. Not enough leaves the soup (rehearsal) tasteless, flat, and boring. Dump the whole load into the pot and we render the whole recipe inedible. Generally, youth choir directors need to plan more, write more, and talk less.

Nonverbal Communication

If the written word is the most under-used and spoken communication is the most overused, then nonverbal communication is the most *under-recognized.* A sharp preacher or smart director will instantly be aware of how his audience (youth choir) perceives him. This is not to suggest self-consciousness, for youth choir directors cannot afford that luxury. However, experts in communication tell us eighty-five percent of all human communication takes place nonverbally, in the colorful realm beyond words.

Facial expressions. Body language. Tone and pitch and rhythm of speech. Tension. Ease. Stance. Posture. A sensitive director will sense when a group is growing restless, listless, or nervous. An experienced and in-touch leader can feel the barometric pressure in a room drop as she carefully observes responses, or the lack of them, within her group. When boys begin to put their elbows on their knees and start checking out of the rehearsal mentally, this is a more poignant statement than yelling, "We're bored out of our minds! Change the pace, please!" When we perceive body language, it often calls for a response (change or adjustment in pace) from us. Too many directors carry on as if body language doesn't exist. Many seldom watch their choirs; some rarely even look their singers in the eyes.

What about a director's own nonverbal skills? Again, thinking about preachers, how many of us have heard words that did not match the nonverbal communication expressed, thus producing a loud confusing double message? "God loves you!" the preacher screams at the top of his lungs with a tight-ly-clenched fist shaking stiffly in the air. We say one thing, but our face and eyes portray another. We communicate confusion.

Although teenagers may sometimes seem to be in other worlds, they are very perceptive. No matter what our words say, the way we communicate those words are just as important as the words themselves, often more so. Our eyes, faces and bodies have a way of telling the truth about the way we truly feel. Teenagers instinctively pick up on it. There is no place for a director to hide.

In its pure essence, what is the art of choral conducting? It is a nonverbal language which visually demonstrates musical line, phrasing, articulation, dynamics, mood, intensity, and even cueing. Good conducting is effective nonverbal imaging in perhaps its highest form. One way to involve teenagers more in the phenomenon of choral singing is to bring them to a point of responding to many types of nonverbal communication, including conducting. As they become more sensitive to subtle aspects of watching and responding, they will grow as musicians, as Christians, and as human beings. Not only has their musicianship blossomed, but so has their capacity to enjoy meaningful relationships throughout life.

Musical Communication

It only follows that if a director can communicate effectively with the written word, can motivate meaningfully and powerfully with the spoken language, and has a grip on the power of nonverbal communication, then the choir is naturally going to communicate musically. Musical communication is the most *underrated* element of the communication process for youth choirs. The musical communication of a choir will be the manifestation of all the above aspects coming together. Musical communication is a by-product of the other three.

Youth choir directors are notorious for accepting far less from their teenagers than they are capable of giving. We tend to excuse ourselves by saying, "Well, after all, they are just a bunch of kids!" All too often, the major musical limitation in a youth choir is the director's commitment, willingness, and ability to teach. The communication process must always begin with us.

Learning to Listen

In order to become effective youth choir directors, we must possess a good amount of get-up-and-go, develop a lot of initiative, refine a magnetic personality, manifest a large portion of flowing creative juices, and generally lead kids in ways that attract them into the group and help them feel special.

As you have already noticed, this is a big job! And it is a particularly huge task when you throw in one of the axioms we constantly drive home in *Youth Cue:* the teenagers' need for consistency. The pressure to be a consistent bundle of energy is, at times, absolutely overwhelming.

Yes, the responsibilities of directing teenagers call for all the extroverted characteristics we possess. For some of us, this comes easy by virtue of our basic personalities. Others have to work harder at it. For some of us who are painfully shy or secretly insecure, it is no less than a major hurdle which ominously looms between us and the potential in our ministries.

Whatever the case—whether we are loud and boisterous by nature, shy to a fault, or somewhere on the large playing field in between—we all can feel a certain pressure always to be up, excited, and energetic. This demand can actually lead to a frenetic way of life for many of us. When it does, we often fail at one of the fundamental points of our ministries—relationships. Simply stated, we fail to listen.

Is anyone out there *not* guilty of being a poor listener at times? Are you always perfectly in tune with the words, thoughts, and feelings of your family members, of your parishioners, of your youth choir members, and, most importantly, in your relationship with God? To be perfectly honest, there is no telling how many important messages I have not heard for one reason or another. How about you?

We need to understand something enormously important at this point. The pressure we feel as youth choir directors to build dynamic programs with ever-growing numbers is not conducive to effective listening.

Volumes of books have been written and millions of toner cartridges have been spent on this subject. Entire professions are based upon the art and science of listening. There is no way we can totally cover the territory, but perhaps we can outline some important items to think about.

In the following paragraphs, we take a look at some loose wires which short-circuit our attempts to listen. We also look at ways these "listening faults" can be corrected. Hopefully, what follows will cause all of us to think more and become sensitive to those around us and, especially, to God within us.

Common Faults in Listening

As a church music graduate student, a favorite and fascinating class was Vocal Pedagogy taught by Dr. James McKinney. As a part of that intriguing course, we were required to recognize, label, and prescribe cures for "vocal faults." Working off that concept, the following are recognizable and all-too-common "listening faults."

Fault 1: Too Busy to Care

When we are two feet ahead of the proverbial administrative steamroller, it is very difficult to be a good listener. As one has rather crudely said it, "It's difficult to clear the swamp when there is an alligator on your backside!" If we froth at the mouth with administrative minutia and last-minute detail work, we can forget being good listeners. It isn't going to happen.

Fault 2: Failure to Focus

Have you ever tried to speak to someone whose eyes darted around and who constantly looked over your shoulder? Not only is it frustrating, it is downright maddening. Too much of that kind of response (or lack of it) will send people away. Teenagers will simply give up trying to communicate with us.

Fault 3: Deadsville

Under the disguise of "being quiet to listen," some folks sit there and never say a word or show any facial interest. It is silence in overdrive, too much of a good thing.

Fault 4: "Uh-huh, uh-huh, uh-huh . . ."

"Deadsville" and "Uh-hu . . ." are neighboring villages in the countryside of communication. Deadsville just sits there. "Uh-huh" engages the voice over and over again, as if to agree, over and over and over again. "Uh-huh, uh-huh, uh-huh" to the point that you realize the person is not really listening at all, but is rather periodically kicking in his voice to fool you into thinking he's with you. He's not. He is not listening for your feelings. He is thinking his own self-centered thoughts and using you to confirm what he already "knows." It may look like listening. It may sound like listening. Alas, it is a cheap substitute which tries to rush you along.

Fault 5: The Chronic Interrupter

This person will really get on your nerves. If you are in a conversation with an interrupter, you may eventually become so frustrated that you will want to hit the person in the face for no apparent reason. But more than likely, you will learn simply to dread or totally avoid future contact. Interrupters are so absorbed with their own agendas that they scarcely, if ever, allow you to complete a sentence. They finish phrases for you. They tell you how you feel. They get what they need from you and leave you standing there with a handful of dangling participles which used to be your carefully thought-out position on an issue. After squeezing out what they need or want, they are on to someone else.

Fault 6: The Voice-Activated Eclipser

The eclipser is a chronic interrupter to the third power. What activates this person's loud and fast voice is the sound of another person's voice. It's all about power. There may be total silence in a room for three minutes and the person will remain silent like everyone else. But let another speak two syllables, and the eclipser will interrupt with lightning speed, using noticeably more volume and speed as a way of overpowering the other person.

As It Pertains to Youth Choir

All of us are sometimes guilty of sabotaging communication by engaging in some form of "fault." Our styles of communication evolve back to our childhoods when we may have had to fight to be heard or understood amidst noisy family structures. The dysfunction occurs when we bring those old patterns out of our childhood experiences and inflict them upon our families, our co-workers, and the teenagers with whom we work.

If we hope to be truly effective as ministers and mentors to teenagers, we must be extremely sensitive to *their* feelings and expressions. All too often, they feel misunderstood by parents by the time they come to us. They desperately need a place to express themselves appropriately, and we desperately need to listen to them as they do it.

The discipline we develop to "be still and know that God is God" *(Psalm 46:10)* will transfer to our relationships with others. Much of it is simply a matter of overcoming an addiction to the sound of our own voices. As we seek God and God's Word, God's agenda, and God's purpose, it is only natural that we will develop an interest in hearing other people's words, concerns, and feelings.

My good friend and mentor from years past, Dr. Frank Pollard, often reminds young ministers, "Everyone has a personal story. As ministers, we need to learn to allow people to tell us their stories, without interruption and without imposing our own agendas and images onto them."

This is very wise and timely counsel, particularly as we seek to minister to teenagers who, in today's society, are all too often *under-heard.*

More Barricades Which Hold Back Good Communication

The task of communication is constant among youth choir directors. Nothing is more important than developing the specific skills of friendship, and nothing is more universally overlooked. As obvious as the need for communication continues to be, directors by the dozens still dry up their ministries and kill their choirs by failing to communicate effectively with their kids. Those of us who recognize the value of this enterprise and consistently act upon it will find ourselves with energetic programs and viable ministries for teenagers and their families. Let us briefly discuss three general communication roadblocks.

Our Busyness—Groups of teenagers thrive on communication, and the most common cause of death among youth choirs is failure to communicate. If we think we are too busy to communicate adequately with our youth choirs, perhaps we should think again. What could be more important than meeting people's needs in the here and now? Teenagers are people, and they need as much help as any group of people we encounter. What on earth should take precedence over our equipping young lives to face the challenges of today and the uncertainty of the future? Too busy to communicate? Perhaps we are just too busy. . . period. A good review of our priorities as Christians and as leaders may be in order.

Our Shyness—Many of us are basically very shy. We may come across boisterous in a group, fun in a rehearsal, and a clown on a choir trip, but insecurity may lie just beneath the surface. For some of us, it was our basic insecurity which played some role in joining the ministry in the first place. For those of us who are shy, it takes work, prayer, practice, and self-discipline to continue communicating the way we should.

Our Drivenness—The capacity for intimacy is often thwarted by our need for speed. We put on a powerful front, seem to have everything together, and we let the fur fly as it will. For those of us who tend to be loud, overbearing, and rather narcissistic, the more subtle forms of communication must be carefully and cautiously developed. If we fail at this point, we run the risk of plowing under the feelings and sensitivities of the kids under our leadership. The torque of our intense leadership can often emotionally bruise or injure those we seek to serve.

Nothing is more important to a youth choir director than developing the art of communication. If one could profile a made-to-order youth choir director, she would embody the extraordinary combination of spiritual sensitivity, healthy relationships, excellent musicianship, and superb communication skills.

When we give time and energy to the development of these attributes, we are well on our way to becoming the world-class youth choir directors we need to be.

CHAPTER TWELVE

Effective Ministry Through Efficient Administration

How do you define effective administration? Rather than look it up in a dictionary or one of the popular best-sellers in business management, allow me to offer one simple statement:

Effective administration is a procedure which gets the job done.

Effective administration is not necessarily a procedure *designed* or *intended* to get the job done, rather it is that which *actually does accomplish* the task at hand. No matter how elaborate, how state-of-the-art, how well-executed, how clever, how simple or complex, if it doesn't get the job done, it is not good administration. Period.

In previous chapters, we have looked at some of the basic concepts and tools for building a youth choir in a church or school: vision, design work, conditioning for the long haul, dreaming the dream, building relationships, and developing communication skills.

Administration involves all of these areas and more. In fact, the above means little if we fail to engineer an administrative plan to handle the work load which our youth choirs will ultimately produce.

Obviously, volumes have been written and still could be said on the fine points of developing effective administrative skills. This chapter will paint with a wide brush some major considerations specifically for youth choir leaders and ministers.

For the unique tribe of youth choir directors, let us add the following components to the *effective administration* definition shown above.

Good youth choir administration is *realistic,* consistent with that which we are willing to give as directors. In other words, we must answer the question,

"Am I willing to take the needed time and make the necessary commitment to see my administrative plans work? If not, it's a faulty plan, and there is no point in continuing. We must return to the drawing board and be realistic in what we are willing to give. Plans will be made accordingly.

Effective youth choir administration is intensely *goal-oriented*. Teenagers respond to specific tasks, goals, challenges, and benefits which they can attain, celebrate, evaluate, and remember.

Successful youth choir administration is *flexible*. Here again, life is a balancing act. The program must possess strong structure and a definite mission. On the other hand, there must be a balancing component for the sake of overall health: flexibility. So, how do we balance these two seemingly opposite poles, high structure and flexibility? There is no recipe for this magic formula. It is discovered only through making the best educated decisions possible, working through trial and error, evaluation, and tenure. With steady work over time, the program tends to gravitate toward that mystical balance.

Productive youth choir administration *fosters and produces a noticeable advancement in the leadership qualities of the older youth*. In other words, the director has her program together to the point that she has time to spend helping, developing, and encouraging the leadership talents of the kids. It's one thing to do everything yourself. It's quite another to mentor teenagers to the point where *they* are a productive, creative force within your administration.

Comprehensive youth choir administration *develops a broader base of adults to support the director and teens*. The job is too big for just you and me. In the new millennium, we must enlist the talents and gifts of other adults around us.

Compassionate youth choir administration *employs loving and practical ways to reach out and embrace teenagers and their families in crisis*. This innovative ministry must be expressed in such a way that the individual teenager's problems will not put the ongoing ministry of the choir on hold. Such ministry may appear spontaneous, but we must prepare to deal with these eventualities in advance. Rest assured, crises surely will come.

Time Management for Youth Choir Directors

> *Therefore, be careful how you walk,*
> *not as unwise, but as wise,*
> *making the most of your time...*
> *Ephesians 5:15-16*

Good time management begins with a conscious decision, a new determination, a resolution for a better new year or a more successful choir season. Just wanting to do better will never get the job done. A commitment to the immediate action is essential. Notice we said "action" not "reaction."

For some of us, the stakes are now very high. Unless we think, evaluate, and act quickly, we could soon lose our jobs, our ministries, or perhaps even our families. Perhaps some reading this are so far behind that they aren't even aware of what is brewing. Take heart. There is hope.

For others, we are ready to move from crisis management to more control, more efficiency, and more balance. We have grown weary of a ministry where the daily mode of operation consists of oiling the squeakiest wheel. We no longer want to be reactors bouncing off the demands of others and the situation around us. We desire to become proactive people who help make creative things happen in a positive way. Our families and our ministries seem to be surviving well enough, but we want the daily experiences of life to mean more, to be richer and fuller for others as well as for ourselves.

There are also those who have been giving prime attention to managing our time for years. We discovered a long time ago that unless we developed plans and exercised strong self-discipline with our time and energy, we were on a course of sure frustration or even destruction. We have been consistently working to improve our efficiency and productivity. We get tired, but we periodically come up with new ideas and then pursue them with renewed energy. For those in this group, perhaps it is time for yet a new beginning.

Why discuss time management in a youth choir book? There is at least one good reason. Unless youth choir directors are superb organizers, there will be ten other things in our lives which will eat up all the energy we need to have reserved for our kids. Thus, our youth choirs suffer and a downward spiral eventually begins. A youth choir can be killed in a fraction of the time it takes to build one. Once a choir hits the skids, it takes double the energy to bring it back to where it was. If there was no energy to give the youth choir in the first place, where is the double energy going to come from? There aren't many full-time youth choir directors out there; although, there are a few. Most of us have pressing responsibilities in worship planning, with adult choirs and other groups. Many of us have families and even other jobs. Even the few of us who are full-time youth choir directors are also divided in our time and energy.

Because of our different temperaments and personalities, time management comes easier for some directors than for others. But regardless of who he is and his experience level, the wise director will constantly evaluate the matter of his own time and energy.

Here are a couple of suggestions to make us think about great personal time management:

1. *Plan some down time before you "start up" another major project or launch into a new season.* Yes, personal down time is important, but we also need maintenance time for our offices and programs. City buses, theme parks, ocean liners, automobile engines—all these need regular down time for service and maintenance if they are to run smoothly, cleanly and properly. One great way to begin a new year is to engage in a massive office cleaning . Throw old things away; make new files for items you need to keep; update old files. Psychologists tell us that even rearranging furniture in the room will remind us that something is new and updated. Make your area look clean, fresh and organized. If you do this regularly, it will tend to stay that way. If you wait until spring to clean, chances are that spring break, Easter, and choir tour will prevent it from happening. As you clean and work, think about new ways to organize your files and work load. We will deal with this issue in more detail later in this chapter.

2. *Each day, prepare a new to-do list.* Whether on your computer, on a legal pad or in your calendar, keep your daily list updated. Like coffee, it is best if made fresh every morning. The first thing you might write on your list is "Make to-do list," and you can feel good about checking off one thing immediately! This may seem silly, but it actually does get the creative juices flowing.

3. *Do not shuffle paper, mail, messages or correspondence on your desk.* If you pick up a piece of paper, deal with it immediately. Do not move it from one place to another.

4. *Leave your desk clear and clean at the end of each day.* It will help you feel better when you walk into your office the next morning.

And now, for our edification, education, and entertainment, too, please allow me to present several true scenarios which deal with the issues of administration, time management, and adequate planning.

Things That Make You Go "Ugh!"

How much time and mental energy do we spend cleaning up messes that we create for ourselves and our choirs? Not all consequences are as dramatic as those described below, but some we don't know about are probably worse. Oversights are often the cause of much pain and grief within our groups. Because we do not adequately think ahead, because we overlook something fundamentally important, because we fail to be thorough enough in our planning, we find ourselves and our kids in king-size jams.

Ugh #1: Stripped Gear

Christmas morning, 1992, 2:00 a.m. Holly and I had just completed a three-hour-tour of putting together Ashley and Kathryn's Barbie Dream House. Barbie House of Horrors would be a more appropriate designation, particularly for us poor schmucks who put it together at the last minute. The last touch of the evening (morning) was to spread multiple gifts under and around the tree. Holly is the absolute best at preparing these types of presentations. My final task was to place new batteries in our seven-year-old Preston's Game Gear, the hottest computer toy in 1992. After installing the four AA batteries, I tested the new toy to be sure it worked.

You guessed it. It did *not* work! The chip in its powerful little brain must have suffered a massive stroke because it was as dead as a hammer.

Preston told us for months that all he wanted was a Game Gear for Christmas. "I don't care about *any* other gifts but a Game Gear," he often liturgized. Sure, we bought him other presents, but this was the biggie. And now, his Game Gear was dead.

I felt like a heel. Actually, I *was* a heel for not testing the thing before the stores closed. We survived that Christmas morning, however, and our seven-year-old ended up in better shape than his mother and I.

The moral of the story? Test anything you can test. Many things we cannot change or control: weather, taxes, the alto who always complains. However, it is relatively easy to test what we can *before* show time. It takes just a minute and a little discipline. It could save us endless grief and headaches. Whether it's microphones, advent candles, or the processional, you need to test them. Make sure they work.

Ugh #2: Bad Date

It was the spring of 1977, the same year I graduated from college. I was working as a music director in a small church south of Houston. For six months we planned a choir trip to North Carolina. There were two youth camps scheduled in back-to-back weeks at a particular conference center in the Blue Ridge Mountains.

From the beginning, I had a difficult time deciding which dates would work best for our group. I went back and forth between the dates and toyed with arrangements for both, trying to figure out which would be more feasible.

I changed my mind so many times that I actually became confused and registered my group for the second week and publicized and planned for the *first*. Buses, hotels, counselors, preparation schedules, everything was geared to attend the first week. Alas, the crowded conference center was expecting us a week later. No way could they adjust to accommodate us.

Seven days before I thought we were supposed to leave, I discovered, to my horror, what I had done. It was by the grace of God that I discovered the mistake when I did, although I didn't feel very blessed at the time.

The situation was a fiasco of the first order. I had to change everything on a very short time frame: bus companies, financial arrangements and all the overnight stops between Texas and North Carolina. The afternoon I discovered my problem, I called every parent of every teenager, told them what I had done, and begged for forgiveness. Everyone seemed understanding enough. All the teenagers made the switch without a hitch; we lost no one. On the other hand, we lost *all* our counselors, every last one of them, and thus, I had to start over again with two weeks to go.

You can imagine this was the absolute worst trip I have ever been responsible for planning. By the time all the adjustments were made and the buses were spotted at 4:30 a.m. on departure day, I was so fragmented that I barely knew who I was or where I was going.

This was a classic case of using all of one's energy to undo a royal mess. There was absolutely nothing left for creativity or personal ministry. My energy had departed long before the group left. And our departure was certainly not the end of the ordeal. Actually, it was just the beginning. Several subplots developed during that week. Let me tell you about just one which shall forever live in infamy.

The Great Gatlinburg Goof

The program at the conference center was atrocious. After a couple of days of the worst preaching and music we had ever heard, my counselors (the substitutes), pulled me aside and expressed in no uncertain terms that this camp wasn't worth attending, no matter which week I had chosen. They would take the bull by the horns and provide a good week for our kids anyway, away from the camp program and on our own. We would continue to lodge and eat some meals at the conference center, but from that point on, we would provide our own program.

Part of Plan B involved taking a trip over to Gatlinburg, Tennessee. But instead of taking the three-hour route over the interstate, I made the executive decision that we would bus over the beautiful Blue Ridge Parkway.

Another mistake. Almost six hours later, we arrived in Gatlinburg, hungry, nauseated from countless hairpin turns on the bus, sick, tired, and cranky. Upon our arrival in beautiful Gatlinburg, half of us were drunk on Dramamine, heavy on the "drama." Before we broke for lunch, I swore by the gold in the temple that I would never again make a group of kids ride a bus over the Blue Ridge Parkway . . . I have never broken that vow.

After lunch, we visited a wax museum depicting the life of Christ. We saw a few more sights and then headed back to North Carolina, this time on the interstate.

I instituted a "great" new system for keeping track of all the kids while on the road. This roll-taking system was called "The Traveling Buddy System (TBS)." Everyone on the bus was assigned a mutual buddy. Everyone was responsible for his/her buddy to be certain that the other person was on the bus. If no one reported their buddy missing, then everyone must be there, right?

Not so fast, maestro!

We were two hours into our return trip from Gatlinburg to the conference center when a junior girl made her way to where I sat comatose at the front of the bus.

"Uh, Randy, my brother Brett is not on the bus," she sheepishly reported.

"That's impossible, Misty," I said with confidence. "If Brett weren't here, Michael would know."

"Michael's not here, either," she winced.

I'd rather not say what I said at that point. Indeed, we had left the two thirteen-year-olds at the museum. I made my way up to the bus driver and told him we had to go back.

"Sorry, friend," he said. "I'm already over my time limit for today. If I get pulled over by a state trooper right now, I'm already in serious trouble. I'm breaking the law just taking you straight to the conference center. There is no way I can go back."

The driver stopped the bus long enough for me to find a phone booth and put out an APB on our two lost boys. This was several years before anyone heard of a cell phone.

We arrived back at the conference center where one of our men counselors and I rented a car and headed back toward Gatlinburg. The entire way back up the mountains, I thought, "This is the kind of situation which makes national headlines every day: "Young Boys Abandoned, Abducted and Murdered in the

Hills of Southeastern Tennessee." Once back on the interstate, God had a long talk with me on the road to Gatlinburg. I prayed and told God that if He'd get me out of this mess, I would gladly do anything. I surrendered to be a foreign missionary four times that night.

It was midnight when we arrived. The quaint little mountain town, sleepy and lazy by day, had turned into tourist central by night. People were everywhere. All we knew to do was go to the police station and pray the boys would be there. Drum roll.

They were. I hugged the displaced and dazed duo, who were sleeping on the police chief's couches when we arrived. They didn't seem shaken, just weary of being in a police station for six hours. They had called their parents back home, and their dads had scolded them for missing the bus. The fathers instructed them to sit tight in the police station and wait for whatever would happen next.

All told, we had been separated from the boys for nine long hours. It was a miserable, dark, lonely, and chilling time. At 2:30 a.m., we finally returned to the conference center, turned in our rental car, walked the two young men to their rooms, and turned in for what was left of the night.

What is the moral to this epic adventure, the half of which has not yet been told? Plan carefully. Check your work often. Have someone follow behind you to double check you at strategic points, and do it all while there is still time to recover!

Ugh #3: Snuffed Symbolism

Several years ago, I attended a wedding ceremony which was to feature the new couple's unity candle. The ceremony was lovely and the music was unusually appropriate. Then came the moment for the lighting of the unity candle. The candle would *not* light, not for love nor money, or at least not for love. The couple stood there for several moments coaxing and nursing it, but to no avail. The candle produced great billows of black smoke; it looked and smelled as if someone were burning old tires in a landfill. It was as if the muted strings providing the background music suddenly turned into banjos. Everyone in the chapel smiled embarrassingly, and at the reception people joked about the candle being a bad omen.

Again, test it if you can.

The same thing happened during an Advent service I attended one December. Carried reverently down the center aisle of the cathedral, the Christ candle suddenly went out. The culprit? A faulty wick which would have been detected by the simplest of trial burns. Need we expound upon the symbolism of the Christ candle going out? It would be a dark world indeed!

Ugh #4: The Big Rotten Apple

In 1986, I spent a week in New York City studying conducting, attending shows, opera, ballet, and enjoying the Big Apple. One evening, our small group went to eat in the Little Italy district. Walking along the sidewalk, we noticed a church bus from Texas rolling slowly down the cramped street. Soon the bus stopped and fifty kids and adults emptied into several nearby eating establishments. We spotted the person we thought might be the director—I suppose we might all look alike—and we struck up a conversation with him.

Actually, the person with whom we were speaking wasn't the director but, rather, a counselor with the group. According to the young man, the director had brought his group to New York City sight unseen. This director had visited twelve years earlier, but to his amazement things "had changed!" He booked his entire group into a hotel, again sight unseen since twelve years ago. When he and his group arrived, they discovered it was a flophouse and left before they even checked in. So now the group was eating dinner, trying to figure out what to do next. Every other hotel they had checked was too full or too expensive or both.

What can we learn from this true story? Never *ever* take a group of teenagers to a place which is not familiar to you and comfortable for you. A pre-tour familiarization trip six months earlier would have completely prevented this situation. When traveling to a major city or a very distant location, this is doubly important.

To some degree, the "Ugh phenomenon" has happened to all of us. Before coming down too hard on any of these situations, let us look at the ways in which we fail to prepare for what is ahead of us and our choirs. The "minor details" of an event can quickly evolve into monster problems if we do not tend to them in a timely, efficient manner. Or, if we don't plan adequately and are still lucky enough to somehow avoid a major fiasco, then the meaning and joy of the experience, the positive effects, will never be maximized.

Who among us has arrived in the mastery of our time management? Which of us cannot improve our own productivity, effectiveness, and efficiency in our work with youth choirs? There is room for improvement in all our ministries. The challenge is to learn to balance efficiency and spontaneity. It can be accomplished.

Organization for Major Events and Weekly Routines

Our work loads are often divided into two broad categories:

1) Routine, weekly deadlines and ministries.

2) Big events which need considerable advance planning.

One youth choir director states: *I spend so much time putting out the daily brush fires in my program that I have a difficult time ever getting to the point of being creative. When I finally get the time to create, I'm too frustrated and weary. I guess I'm in a rut.*

Another: *Bottle-feeding temperamental people takes untold amounts of precious emotional and mental energy. Just when I think I'm getting somewhere, I have to stop and nurse another complainer back into the fold. And adults are as bad or worse than teenagers!*

And another: *When I get busy and preoccupied, I get careless. I wish I could move ahead rather than clean up the messes I create when I'm under pressure.*

A Weekly Schedule

Aside from your daily to-do list, consider setting up a schedule of tasks which you follow each week. Even by habit, most of us discover that we tend to work on worship planning at the same day and time each week. Why not schedule this and dozens of other tasks which must be completed each week? Allot yourself specific time frames to complete each job.

It is absolutely crucial to instruct your secretary or receptionist to hold your calls during certain times of the week. If you have no support staff, allow your calls to be taken by voice mail. If we remain a slave to the telephone, we set ourselves up for sure frustration.

As you place your tasks on a schedule, be sure to include personal ministries in the scheme of your work, i.e., a time set aside to write communications of encouragement, e-mail messages, and thank-you notes. Some designate this "people time" with a name, such as "Sunshine Ministry."

As time goes on, you will refine your schedule. The first attempts usually need significant revision after you live with them for a while. The advantage is that it provides a place to begin, and the scheduling of our time also allows us to have some standard evaluation for our use of time.

See the sample schedule below. There is certainly nothing sacred about any part of this suggestion. Each director's schedule will be somewhat different. Church calendars, designations for days off, various job descriptions, and the director's personality are but a few of the considerations in planning a weekly schedule. Be flexible, change it, update it, and modify it just for the sake of remaining fresh and keeping the feel of something new. In time, a written though flexible approach to scheduling could become your good friend. At least, it's certainly worth becoming acquainted.

Sample Schedule

Times with * should be designated for your secretary to hold all calls except emergencies or those from immediate family members. If you do not have a secretary or receptionist, allow your voice mail to answer your calls.

MONDAYS

8:15 - 8:30 *	Quiet time
8:30 - 8:45 *	Organize day, week / to-do list
8:45 - 10:00 *	Orders of worship
10:00 - 10:30	Sunshine time
10:30 - 11:15	Music staff meeting
11:15 - 12:00	Special projects
12:00 - 1:15	Lunch
1:15 - 2:00	Return phone calls / e-mail
2:00 - 3:30 *	Ministerial staff meeting
3:30 - 5:00 *	Teach voice classes

TUESDAYS

8:15 - 8:30 *	Quiet time / today's to-do list
8:30 - 10:30 *	Special projects
10:30 - 11:00 *	Return calls / e-mail
11:00 - 12:00	Rehearsal plans for all groups
12:00 - 1:15	Lunch
1:15 - 1:30	Return calls / e-mail
1:30 - 2:45	Choir communications *rehearsal notes, mail, web page*
2:45 - 3:45 *	Devotional article(s) for choir(s)
or 2:45 - 3:45 *	Ministerial staff meeting
3:45 - 5:00 *	Appointments / tour interviews

WEDNESDAYS

9:15 - 9:30 *	Quiet time / today's to-do list
9:30 - 10:30 *	Rehearsal preparation
10:30 - 12:00 *	Special projects
12:00 - 2:00	Long lunch
2:00 - 3:00 *	Rehearsal preparation
3:00 - 3:45	Return calls / e-mail
3:45 - 5:00 *	Meetings / appointments
5:00 - 5:30 *	Dinner at church
5:30 - 9:00 *	Rehearsals and / or meetings

THURSDAYS

9:00 - 9:15 *	Quiet time / today's to-do list
9:15 - 9:30 *	Finalize orders of worship for printer
9:30 - 12:00 *	Hospital rounds (away)
12:00 - 1:00	Lunch
1:00 - 1:15	Return calls / e-mail
1:15 - 2:00 *	Rehearsal preparation for Sunday
2:00 - 4:00 *	Special projects
4:00 - 5:00	Clean up for Sunday

FRIDAYS AND SATURDAYS OFF

Exceptions will certainly arise for weddings, funerals, retreats, and other church-related activities.

SUNDAYS ON AUTOMATIC PILOT

Begin the day with some quiet time for prayer and reflection.

Sharpening Our Tools

Back to South Texas. When I was growing up in the country, I was responsible for the yard and vegetable garden during the summers. Although it was tiring and often very hot, the work was very satisfying. I could eventually see and taste the results of my labor, and that was always encouraging and motivating. As ministers, we do not usually enjoy that advantage in our work. Ours is an ongoing task which has no definite beginning place, and there is also no time when we can say it is complete.

As a gardener, there was one lesson I was always slow to learn. While weeding the garden and flower beds, I would often allow my tools to become impacted with heavy, moist soil. Over an hour or so, my hoe, shovel or tiller would build up a thick layer of compacted sod on the blades. The result would always be the same. The tool became increasingly heavy and cumbersome. The sharp edge, the blade which penetrated and loosened the dirt, would become dull, fat, and imprecise. It was such a gradual thing that I seldom even noticed.

Someone else in my family would usually have to come up behind me, take a look at what I was doing, and then say, "Hey, why don't you stop a minute and clean your hoe?" I never wanted to do that because it seemed to be a waste of time. I have always hated to push the pause button for the sake of maintenance. I would rather press forward, move ahead and get the job done. It's my personality, as it is in many people.

Eventually, they would talk me into cleaning my tools. It meant stopping, finding a flat, sharp rock , sitting down and scraping the debris from the metal.

It took maybe one minute to get the job done.

As soon as I went back to work with my sharpened tools, I was always amazed at how much difference it made to work with clean, unburdened equipment.

Clean the tools in the music office. The application to music ministers is plain, but please consider several obvious observations.

1) As a guild, music ministers and teachers are generally some of the "stacking-est" people I have ever seen. Whatever comes into our office, we stack it in piles. True, we have more materials to deal with than most other teachers and ministers, but that should encourage us to be *more* organized rather than *less*. Our offices often look like disaster zones, and incredible amounts of energy are spent just trying to locate what we need. And bar the door if we are ever out of town when someone else needs to find something important.

2) I have also noticed several directors across the country who are model managers of their facilities. Their pencils are lined up in the desk drawer by length and eraser size. They can put their hands on what they need right now. The office area looks nice. It feels in control, open, light, and motivating. These directors tend to be much more productive and time efficient than some of us who can't get organized.

3) Whether, by our personalities, organization comes easy or seems impossible, we can all learn something here. Engines, toys, computers, refrigerators, air-conditioning units, pianos, lawn mowers, oboes, minivans, fireplaces—you name it. It must be clean in order to work at its best. The cleaner it is, the better it will operate for you. Our music ministry facilities are no exception.

Time Out: A Simple Suggestion for an Amazing Transformation

Most directors have times when ministry activity slows down significantly. During one of these slow periods, go to work as you always do, only this time wear jeans and tennies. Take two uninterrupted days, maybe three. Make it known to your colleagues that you are "not in" as far as ministry business is concerned. If you can, use only a back entrance and don't go up front where the action is. Let the calls go to voice mail as if you are out of town. It is "time out" for the program!

This concept is so crucial to my own ministry that I have been known to sacrifice a vacation day or two for the sake of having a time out. We normally do this two or three times a year. During these days, the only thing I do is clean and reorganize the music suite. Our music staff and I throw away junk seem-ingly by the ton. Old files, sample music, demo cassettes—in a year's time there is enough stuff coming into most music offices to fill an industrial-size dump-ster.

"But what if we will need those nine cardboard boxes?" is a common ques-tion among us "stackers." The fact is, we probably *will* need cardboard boxes at some point, but we can deal with that when the need arises. Even when some-thing is thrown away prematurely—this *seldom* happens—it is always easy enough and inexpensive enough to replace. We are still far ahead in terms of efficiency and time management when we keep things highly organized and clean. What is the use of keeping potentially useful materials or supplies if we can't find them when we need them?

So why don't we do a better job of keeping our facilities organized? One word—laziness. I would like to challenge every music teacher and minister to take periodic "time outs" to sharpen our tools. When the system is clean, pre-pared, and ready for action, it makes an enormous difference in the way we feel when we go to work. Nothing defeats us more than feeling that things are out of hand. Nothing is as productive as keeping all our tools in order, clean, and ready to use in creative, productive ministry.

Blow the whistle on disorganization! Time out!

CHAPTER 13

Excellence Established
by Bringing It All Together

by Neil Sherouse

"Neil is my favorite choir director," quipped 14-year-old Lee, easily within my hearing. There was a hint of humor in his voice as he anticipated my response. "Lee, I'm the *only* choir director you've ever known! You don't have anyone with whom to compare me!"

It was true. I came to First Baptist, Gainesville, Florida, when Lee and his twin brother, David, were about three months in the womb. I saw them in the hospital on the day they were born, watched them grow and became their choir director long before their voices changed. Though the reality did force me to count the years, it also reinforced the deep sense of satisfaction at having played a role in their lives since the day of their birth.

I cannot say I came to this staff position anticipating a stay of this length; but, having served here for over fifteen years, I am certainly willing to extol the benefits of a protracted ministry. There is probably no area of my ministry that has brought me more personal satisfaction than my work with our Youth Choir.

I cut my teeth in youth choir work during the late '60s and early '70s. In those days, little attention to organizational details was required. Nor, I should say, was there much of an attempt to provide a balanced repertoire for kids to sing. Most youth choir music was trendy and written in an idiom with a shelf life of about six months. The concept that we might wish to teach kids an anthem that could sustain their spirits for the rest of their lives was unheard of. We simply announced the commencement of the newest folk musical and stood back from the doorway to avoid the stampede of kids who had free time to participate in something that was geared toward their needs and wants.

From those heady days, I went on to an overseas missionary stint, a seminary degree and a five-year tenure in the pastorate. Then, in 1984, I reentered the field of church music and, in doing so, discovered a changed world. I discovered kids who wanted to sing but who were jaded by even the newest musical still warm from the publisher. I discovered a dearth of quality music being written for youth. I discovered that teenagers themselves had become very time poor, with scores of alternatives and activities demanding their precious hours. I inherited a youth choir that was, from all evidences, on life support if not already clinically dead. And, of greatest significance, I had joined a staff that was about to self-destruct and a congregation that was entering a five-year free-fall into controversy and despair.

I will spare you the details, but I will make the observation that churches who fall into a pattern of strife and disharmony are *seldom* selected by families with teenagers who are looking for a church to join.

During this period of staff resignations, terminations, lengthy interims and large-scale defections, I felt much like the young Dutch boy with his thumb in the dike except that, in my case, I was powerless to stop the hemorrhaging of our membership and *koinonia*. Though I often wondered why, I seldom doubted that God's intention was for me to remain here and be faithful to my call. In truth, my motives may have been no more noble than a reluctance to be the last rat to abandon a sinking ship, but I stayed. My choirs languished.

Finally, a period of stability ensued, and the flow of departing members slowed to a trickle. Then in the early '90s, with the arrival of a new pastor, the church began to heal and to grow. At the same time, the few older children who sang in our children's choirs entered middle school. It seemed to be the right time to attempt the rebirth of a youth choir. Also during this period, a letter from Randy Edwards came across my desk inviting me to subscribe to a newsletter for youth choir directors, called *Youth Cue*. It seemed the sort of resource I was seeking, so I sent in my subscription.

I devoured the first and subsequent issues of the newsletter. Within it, I found practical ideas to nurture my kids, useful tools to organize my ministry, and a wealth of first-rate literature to add to our repertoire. Through the honest stories of success and pain, I began to sense that a renaissance in youth choir work was under way. It was a wave I determined to ride.

Bolstered by articles in the first few issues of *Cue*, I began to plan our first choir tour for this faithful group of middle school singers, a loop through our home state. With seventeen young teenagers, we crisscrossed Florida during the first week of June 1991. Upon our return home, their enthusiasm reached a contagion that compelled them to reach other youth. Since that first tour, there have been seven others. We have outgrown church vans and now have outgrown a tour bus. Our travels have ranged far from our home state. They have taken us into New England, the Southeast, Mid Atlantic and Southwestern U.S., as well as the Caribbean. The gradual numerical growth that has followed each summer's tour has enabled us to begin a select high school ensemble that has toured England and will visit eastern Europe this coming summer.

Has *Youth Cue* been the sole catalyst for this growth? Or has it been as easy as it sounds? In a word, no. We are a downtown church, so growth has been slow. I forced on myself a discipline of nurturing and encouraging our kids that requires constant and consistent attention. *Youth Cue* and the circle of relationships it has provided have been invaluable resources for ideas, evaluation and inspiration. Through *Cue* I have learned ways to intentionalize the nurture I extend to our kids and ways to organize them to provide enthusiastic and positive peer leadership. I have also discovered ideas to enhance our tour and retreat experiences and, perhaps most important, I have gained an understanding that this calling to direct youth choirs includes very few easy formulae and hours of grinding labor. It is for me a humbling fact that any successes I enjoy in youth choir ministry are the result of the willingness of many of you to share ideas that have worked for you.

Through these years of service, I have learned that it is much more challenging to continue to grow and innovate, to retool and reevaluate, than it is to move elsewhere to repeat the same successes and failures. I have learned to gauge my own faithfulness, not in terms of the number of kids, but in terms of the number of years I will minister to these kids who sit before me this week. I have learned that kids need the assurance that some things in their lives are not likely to change too soon, that I am likely to be there to watch them learn to drive, graduate from high school, enter college and exchange their wedding vows.

Though I have weathered some difficult years here, the church has been gracious, affirming and patient to allow me to grow. Perhaps my deepest satisfaction comes from the fact that my own sixteen-year-old daughter has grown up here and sings alongside the finest friends a parent could hope for. Little else in life is of equal value to that.

Neil Sherouse is Associate Pastor/Minister of Music at First Baptist Church, Gainesville, Florida.

Bringing the Youth Choir Together

by Neil Sherouse

As a youth choir director veteran with the scars to prove it, I share the follow-ing with all who undertake this work of youth choir ministry, one concept for each year I have served:

1. *Communicate often* and personally with your kids through every means avail-able: personal cards and notes, group mailings, e-mail, phone calls, etc.
2. *Demonstrate an interest* in the other aspects of your kids' lives: sports, academics, hobbies, and try to attend their games, and concerts.
3. *Stay current on youth culture*, what they wear, watch, listen to, and who their heroes are. Lead them to evaluate the message, but do so without impugning the messenger.
4. *Be intentional* about developing and using peer leadership.
5. *Remind yourself* on a regular basis that the primary objective of our work is to move these kids toward spiritual and emotional maturity. The music is a means but by no means the end.
6. *Admit to your kids your failures*, oversights, and insecurities when the context is appropriate. They already recognize our inadequacies, and being honest with them about these will make it easier for our kids to be forthcoming with us about their own problems and faults.
7. *Don't fear the imposition of discipline.* Our medium, music, demands it, and our faith assumes a reasonable measure of it.
8. *Communicate often* your highest expectations for musical attainments, spiritual maturity and social responsibility. Point them always higher, as they will achieve no more than our lowest expectations.
9. *Be fair and evenhanded,* serving up grace with a big spoon.
10. *Provide them with a balanced repertoire:* a few classics, a few pieces that are con-temporary, and a good portion of solid anthems which will serve them throughout their life.
11. *Love them unconditionally* and communicate that love often.
12. *Be organized.* Kids will appreciate the fact that you do not waste their time.
13. *Share with your colleagues* in ministry the responsibilities of spiritual nurture. The big events—tours, retreats, etc.—should always have a spiritual focus and a unified theme.
14. *Don't be discouraged by slow growth*, and resist the temptation to move on when the church takes a downturn. It is at such times that the church and your kids will need you the most.
15. *Finally, let me encourage you to consider an open-ended tenure.* Weigh the benefits of growing up with your kids, sharing in their lives over the years and watch-ing as they move into adulthood as responsible believers.

PART FOUR

The Floor Plan for Ministry
with Kids

Forging Ahead with Newfound Focus

More than a quarter of a century ago, I tried my hand and heart at "real ministry" for the first time. At the seasoned age of eighteen, I set out to tackle a thirteen-week appointment at Medina Baptist Church, Medina, Texas. Situated in the heart of the Texas Hill Country, the tiny village of Medina was a beautiful little clump of houses, a couple of churches, and a school with two buses.

Meditations from Medina

Having begun college the previous January, I was between my first and second semester of my freshman year when this opportunity to serve came along. As music and youth minister for the next thirteen weeks, I went out to set the ministerial woods afire. I had a thing or two to learn. Now beginning a new millennium, there seems to be even more to learn than there was in 1973. There's nothing smarter than a college freshman, you know!

Actually, I learned quite a lot in the summer of '73. Living alone for the first time, I discovered the power and serenity of silence, although sometimes it overwhelmed me. I learned about myself, as well, because my long-distance girlfriend became more interested in someone else and never seemed to be able to work me into her schedule.

Much of what I learned in 1973 didn't really bear fruit until much later in my life. For instance, I have recently realized that when I hear Paul McCartney's "My Love," I am immediately transported back to Medina. The strains and phrases of the hit ballad work magic in my mind. All I have to do is be still while listening to it, and I feel eighteen years old again. I smell the smells, hear the sounds, feel the feelings. The soundtracks we lay down during teenage years are with us forever.

The dozen or so Walton-like teens in Medina taught me about community and relationships. Riding in open jeeps through the valleys and up the mountains was a new kind of fun for this way-too-serious ministerial wannabe. They taught me how to water ski on July 4 at the Garrisons' private lake. Ever since that Independence Day, I have known how much strength and balance it takes to stay buoyant on the waters of youth ministry. Most of our Bible studies consisted of sitting on the hoods of our cars leaning against the windshields parked in a huge opening in the middle of the mountains. There is no sky like a Hill Country sky, wide as the world! The stars are phenomenal. We held flashlights to read the Scripture verses. We then turned them off to save the batteries and watch for shooting stars as we talked about God, spiritual things, and ourselves. Not a bad setting for a rap session! Medina taught me how to be still, how to get to know teenagers intimately, and how to worship outdoors.

The church paid me a fair wage for my work and time with their teens. Actually, I should have paid them for the experience. It was the beginning of a lifelong lesson, and I shall be forever grateful!

Remembering How to Listen—Again!

Until we learn how to really concentrate on what our youth choir members are communicating to us, it will be very difficult to provide meaningful ministry for our teenagers. We discussed this at length in Chapter 11.

If we commit ourselves to hear, respond rather than react, and build relationships with teenagers, then we are off to a great start as we put together a program around this wonderful thing called music.

Listening, hearing, and perceiving properly are only part of the leadership challenge. Once we accurately hear, we then need to move, get active, and get creative. It's time to get with it!

Learning How to Boogie

In his 1992 book entitled *Liberation Management*, organizational guru Tom Peters dedicates the second section of his book to "Learning How to Hustle." We started to use that title but thought better of it, because the term "hustle" rustles up some rather raucous connotations. None of us want to be hustlers in any sense of the word. But, since we are musicians, it might be perfectly acceptable for us to learn to boogie.

Many musicians are wonderful dreamers and are creative beyond words. But we often come up short in the implementation process as we seek to move from point A to point B. Bringing our dream along from vision into reality can be one of our greatest challenges.

It takes more than a gifted athlete to be a successful distance runner. More than strength, agility, power, and even more than endurance are required. If a runner wants to win a marathon or even finish in a respectable position, she or he must develop not only the disciplines of running but of *pacing* as well.

Nothing is more important in youth choir work than going for the long haul. The benefits of excellence combined with *consistency* cannot be overestimated. Unfortunately, many of us do a good job with our youth choir in spurts. We have days, weeks, or months of high energy, and then, exhausted, we crash and burn physically, emotionally, mentally, and even spiritually.

The "I'm-thinking-about-maybe-looking-into-it" Syndrome

Many ministers think aloud, and, as we do, we talk about various program possibilities. In order to keep from committing ourselves, we use tentative language. We use "maybe," "thinking about," "considering," or "looking into." If we stack up enough tentative text before revealing a particular plan, we then separate ourselves from it and never really have to *do* anything. So, why don't we simply say, "I'm exploring this or that?" We subconsciously want an "out," to be released from the responsibility of seeing a project from inception to completion. After all, "I was only thinking about it."

The "Talk-it-to-death" Syndrome

Early in my ministry, I sat through innumerable staff meetings fostering detailed discussions about things which never happened. I began to realize at that point that many ministers' idea of ministry is talking. Most of the programs never materialized. Those which did launch usually fell to earth before reaching any real long-term effectiveness. There was no overall plan for ministry, instead, only a series of half-baked dreams.

The "Someone-else-is-ultimately-responsible-for-it" Syndrome

Artists in general and ministers in particular (alas, as ministers of music, we fit into *both* categories) are notorious for dreaming dreams and quickly handing them off to people who have no idea how to realize them. It is a rare person who can be both a dreamer and a technician. As youth choir directors working with fragmented teenagers and parents, this is exactly what we are called to accomplish.

Boogie or Die

It is time we clearly define the term "boogie": to *work hard, effectively, smart, and with passion to bring something to pass; to get with it and waste neither motion nor energy in the process.*

Most youth choir directors are willing to work diligently and spend the needed time it takes to build a program. However, over the past ten years, we have discovered that precious few really know how to work *effectively*. In the world of music ministry, there is *hard* work and there is *smart* work. The two are not necessarily synonymous.

Hordes of directors fail to work "smart." A huge number simply do not know how to organize their labors and manage their time in order to maximize their hours in the office and out. If we cannot get a handle on our own lives, how can we possibly expect to help teenagers find balance and sanity in theirs? Our ministries can quickly evolve into inanimate objects like giant leaky inner tubes, constantly receiving air (time and attention) but incessantly leaking through every seam. It is very possible for us to spend the greatest measure of our energy huffing and puffing and seeing little more than maintenance as a result.

Beginning to Boogie. . . A Reminder from Chapter Twelve

1) Take some down time simply for the task of getting reorganized. Hold your calls, spend the needed time to get a handle on your "systems." For maximum effect, discipline yourself to do this at least every six months. Arrange your office so you can put your hands on what you need immediately without wasting time.

2) Be realistic about what you can expect from volunteers. They can be wonderful assistants, but volunteers cannot take your place.

3) Pray for wisdom as you determine what is important and where your priorities will be. Some of us simply have impossible combinations of tasks, and these issues must be confronted.

4) Work to keep a steady pace.

CHAPTER 14

Finding the Freedom to Fail

From our earliest recollections, most of us have developed a real disdain for failure. It's only natural. Nobody likes to fail. In fact, in this success-driven culture, almost everything is seen as forgivable. Everything, that is, except for one: failure. You can be a criminal and still be a celebrity, a moral reprobate and still a star, a drug addict and still a hero, a narcissistic user of others and still a political icon.

Failure . . . The Unforgivable Sin? I Don't Think So!

Failure is often viewed as the one unforgivable violation in secular society. It is an interesting irony to note that in order to become a Christian one must admit failure. The admission that I have failed badly is the first step in becoming a follower of Christ.

A Disease Called Fear of Failure ("failphobia")

Most people carry fears of failure well into their adulthood, many to their graves. More times than not, the fear is so buried that we aren't even aware of its stifling presence. It sits heavily upon us without our even realizing it, and it ultimately affects life's most crucial decisions. Somehow, we lose sight of the fact that without the possibility of failure (trying) there can be no success (progress, growth). We learn to be successful only when we deal effectively with our failure. Those of us who can let go of our fear or pride or security long enough to try new things will discover that horizons are brilliantly broadened and new life is discovered. Because of our fear of failure, many of us fail to really live. We are dead though still breathing.

Artistic Advancement Arrested

This stifling effect also happens in smaller ways, such as with our development in the arts. The serious study of music, for example, causes us to quickly develop a sense of what is correct and what falls short of perfection. Normally, our teacher stops us when? When we make a mistake, when we have failed! We try and try to avoid getting stopped and corrected. Our greatest goal is to get it right.

Training Creativity Out of Kids

Ken Medema says that most musical training, though it has obvious benefits, often stifles creativity in many people. Says the improvisational genius who is also blind from birth, "What happens is that we, through strict and inflexible teaching systems, in effect train most of the creativity out of our children. They become scared to attempt something unique or different because they're afraid they'll get it wrong. Rather than making our own sounds and rhythms, we limit ourselves to playing someone else's creations."

If you know Ken Medema and have watched him work with an ensemble of teenage singers, you know that he does it all: classical, hymnody, show biz, and every kind of popular idiom. But he is also creating nonstop—building musical masterpieces on the spot and from scratch. When around him, you catch the infectious energy of his mind-boggling creative process.

To Ken Medema, imagination is the key. "Our creative sides die when our imaginations go to sleep. If we can free ourselves from the tyranny of failure-fear, we become much more colorful and productive as God's children."

Creative Leadership in Youth Choirs

There are a hundred ways that the fear of failure can thwart the spiritual and even physical growth of a youth choir. When the director carries around a foreboding fear of failure, the kids feel the insecurity. They will be affected by the stiffness and will hesitate to engage in the process.

On the other hand, when we are secure with ourselves—stable in our adulthood, confident in our leadership skills, comfortable around teenagers, secure in our faith, well-balanced in our priorities—we will possess enough self-esteem to break new ground and test new water. Sometimes the experiments may fail, but those trials are not signs of failure as long as we don't lay out a long trail of flops. If we learn from our attempts to improve, we will eventually hone in on systems, concepts and ideas which produce creative results. It all depends on our willingness to "fail," which is not really failure at all. Actually, the trial, error, learning, and improving over time brings our youth choirs into a powerful age of innovation and energy.

Enjoy the Flowers Blooming

As you and your choir develop this freedom to explore, you will discover another phenomenon. The individual teenagers in your group, particularly those who are naturally creative, will blossom with their own dreams and visions. When they see us, their mentors and adult friends, willing to stretch, grow, and "fail," the whole process becomes less threatening for these young lives. In an atmosphere of security, peace, joy, and acceptance, teenagers will thrive as they join you in the creative process.

A Strange Admonition

A young inventor was said to have sought advice from a very successful CEO. The inventor was discouraged because none of his ideas had yet caught on, and he wasn't making enough money to sustain himself. The wise CEO said, "Well, friend, what you need to do is double your rate of failure."

The CEO knew that as the young inventor tried more approaches, created more useful tools, built more helpful gadgets, that sooner or later one of the ideas would catch on and be successful.

I am certainly not suggesting the notion that we set out to fail. But when setbacks and disappointments occur, it is time to take notes, learn all we can, and redouble our efforts and energy.

It is a tough thing to do, but it is an effective way to create. Here's to all of your successful failures!

CHAPTER 15

Fielding and Maximizing the Talent: Recruiting

S peak to any successful collegiate coach, and he will tell you one of the major keys to a winning team is the art of recruiting; discovering young new talent, convincing them to invest themselves in your school and program, and helping them to rise to a position of leadership. This process is essential if a team is to continue to play competitively.

The same holds true of any youth choir. Directors who put all their energy into today's kids and neglect looking down the road are in for a future shock. It is a major mistake made by many youth choir leaders. Most do well just to minister to the kids present and accounted for today. Who is thinking about four, six, eight years from now? The wise youth choir director, that's who!

It's That Tenure Thing Again!

Again, this touches on the concept of tenure. Unfortunately, many directors, from the day they move into their offices, have no intention of staying with their current ministries for the long haul. Thus, the thought of recruiting for the future seems unnecessary. We tend to work for the fast fix today, the thing that will produce instant and easy results, causing our ministries to show quick growth. When that happens, we will be able to climb the ladder to a larger church and do our three-year thing again and thus "move up" yet another notch.

Certainly, there is a time to move. God leadeth and God calleth away. We know this, but it is also cause for great concern that there are not more significant tenures within music ministry today. Is it any wonder that our kids are suffering from a lack of consistency and continuity? Sometimes we even have the audacity to call *them* inconsistent and undependable for the long haul. "It's me, it's me, O Lord, standin' in the need of prayer."

The Personal Touch

Nothing can take the place of a friendly, winsome director who loves kids and enjoys connecting with them. Some of us who are basically shy have to work at the discipline of becoming more outgoing. Some teenagers test this discipline to the max, manifesting almost backward behavior in the presence of an adult leader.

A fine balance must be employed at this point. To be sure, we are the physical embodiment of the youth choir. After all, we are the adult who has committed a big chunk of his life to build the ministry. We are viewed by most of the kids as "the choir director," whether they participate in choir or not. We must always represent warmth.

At the same time, when we enter a room, we don't want the kids to see a treble clef coming at them! In other words, we really need to be viewed by the kids as more than a one-dimensional creature who does nothing but direct youth choir.

If every time we see a kid we have choir on the brain, we communicate a "one-dimensional" approach. Not only will we seem one-dimensional (boring), we will also be viewed as trying to cast *them* into a one-dimensional role. In other words, if we don't care anything about them except that they sing in our choir, the non-musicians are going to become terribly resistant to talking to us. The burden of proof is on us to demonstrate to them that *we care about them, whether they ever sing a note for us or not*, whether they ever show up for a rehearsal or not.

For this reason, it is so important for us to become involved in activities other than music. Coaching a basketball team, taking the kids to a movie, playing softball, or going camping with a group are great ways to break down this one-dimensional relationship barrier. A youth choir director needs to be accurately viewed by teenagers as a multidimensional person with many interests, experiences, and involvements.

Specific Suggestions for Recruiting Teenagers into the Youth Choir

1. Make a specific beginning and ending to each choir year, preferably with at least one month break in between. Year-round youth choirs in the new millennium will be few and far between. Each summer the teenagers need a break. Don't look now, but the director and accompanist need that break as well. When the new season begins, this is a perfect time for the group's major recruiting push.

2. Meet with the officers and choir *before* bringing in new recruits. The returning choir members need to have their acts together before they are ready to welcome new friends into the group. Be sure the officers and choir members complete all the registration processes for themselves before the new recruits arrive.

3. Incoming rookies (that is, the lowest grade moving up from the choir below) should undergo some kind of basic training before they are thrust into the larger group. Communicate with them what the youth choir is all about, what is expected of them, and what the wonderful benefits will be. Many directors use the choir officers to lead the basic training. This establishes the officers as the leadership core of the choir community.

4. When the new recruits (whether rookies or older youth coming for the first time) first walk into the choir room, the choir and the officers must be in an "anti-nerd mode." This means that we are going to have to work hard to help our visitors feel at home and at ease in this new, strange environment. They will naturally feel like nerds if we don't prepare ahead of time. Every detail of the rehearsal should be studied to discover how it can be made more user-friendly.

5. Many choirs begin their seasons with a retreat or another special activity designed to "draw the net" for teenagers in the church and community. Retreats and other concentrated times are good, exciting introductions into the choir's ministry, activity, and friendship community.

6. Getting a person to come to choir once is one thing. Holding on to that kid and assimilating her successfully into the program is quite another. During the first rehearsal, show a slide or Power Point presentation of last season's trips, ministries, and other highlights. Put the visuals with background music and make it both high-energy and thoughtful.

7. Immediately connect the visiting teenager with a social group. The officers can make sure that the new recruit connects with the group through e-mail, a phone call, and other contacts. If the kid has a specific need or encounters a loss, the other teenagers and director must immediately respond to provide friendship and support.

8. Quickly merge the teenager into the mainstream. This seems obvious, but it is amazing how many new teenagers slip through the cracks in their first few weeks of choir membership. Here is a checklist to be sure this does not occur.

   - Get her uniform ordered/robe assigned.
   - Be sure he is on the choir mailing list to receive all updates.
   - Prepare her own personalized music folder with her name on it.
   - Make sure he has an opportunity to audition for any ensembles.
   - Director must write a personal note of welcome.
   - Officers must systematically stay in touch.
   - Make other possible ministry connections: Sunday School, etc.
   - Be certain the new member is paired up with veteran member.

Recruiting Over the Years

Something magical happens when a youth choir meets the kids' needs. The recruiting *almost* takes care of itself. This is true because teenagers are, by nature, talkers. Many parents don't seem to realize this, but most adolescents do a lot of talking with their friends. A lot. This is one of the reasons they are often silent and even sulky at home. Many are actually tired of talking, spent of the emotional energy it takes to energetically communicate. By the time they get home to us at night they are exhausted.

Not only is chatter constant, it is usually selfish talk. They incessantly tell stories of what they did last weekend, where they went, how much fun they had, or what a drag it was.

The school hallways are more effective than CNN news for getting the word out about something. The reports brought by the hormone-driven communication are usually very colorfully described, but they also express feelings in black and white. Usually, an event was either awesome or it sucked. For teenagers, there is very little that lies in the gray areas, between awesome and awful, between love and hate, between cool and boring. It is one or the other. This is why a youth choir in the new millennium will either thrive or perish. There will be very few choirs in the mediocre category.

When a youth choir hits on all its cylinders or even most of them, it is going to meet major needs in teenagers' lives. When this happens, the kids *will* talk about it in some way. They will report the mission trips, the ministry projects, and the tours to friends. Again, their vignettes will be colorful and definite. As they talk, they are recruiting.

Notice at the beginning of this section that I said recruiting will *almost* take care of itself when the youth choir is functional and vibrant. Recruiting will never be maximized without the director's commitment. A wise director keeps his singers focusing outward, constantly searching their horizons for those who will benefit from the choir.

Finally, it is important to understand that it is usually the *social* aspect of youth choir which keeps teenagers connected. Even among the most serious musicians in the group, the word "friends" keeps coming up over and over again. In my youth choir's exit interviews, we have discovered that the music is important, the spiritual applications to life are treasured, the worship experiences are remembered, and the mission endeavors are inspiring. But the glue of the youth choir experience over the years is friendships, close relationships with peers, directors, accompanists, and other involved adults.

Yes, a new millennium is here, but the need for friendship among kids is unlikely to change anytime soon. When you recruit for your choir, offer kids more than a choral experience. Offer the opportunity to connect with a healthy, fun group of friends with whom they can share these exciting, turbulent, and challenging years called adolescence.

Mark Acker, longtime Director of Music at Brentwood United Methodist Church in Brentwood, Tennessee, provides insight into the recruiting practices of his effective youth choir ministry. "Provide teenagers with something they can't find anywhere else, and then do it better than anyone expects." Year after year, they keep coming back for what Mark provides, bringing their friends, neighbors and schoolmates. They have found something vital to their lives that they haven't found anywhere else.

CHAPTER 16

Focusing the Choir
to Give and Grow: Discipline

"When I was a kid, I would not have done that. It would have never crossed my mind to talk to a teacher or my parents that way!" When working with kids, particularly in the '90s, many choir leaders, ministers, and directors were shocked at the attitude of teenagers toward each other, adults, and society. In fact, so prevalent has the in-your-face behavior become that it is actually called "attitude."

Having "an attitude" is synonymous with an "I ain't gonna take nothin' offa nobody" lifestyle. It doesn't take a psychiatrist to perceive that this form of "attitude" is driven by nothing more than anger, fear, and hate.

Providing focus for a group begins with the focus of the director. How many times have we made such a statement in this book? "It all begins with the director." We may be weary of hearing it, but that does not reduce its truth or power.

Many directors who decry the attitudes of kids toward discipline are themselves lacking it in their own vocations. As a simplistic example, let's look into a youth choir rehearsal room. If a director stands before his choir having failed to discipline himself to adequately prepare for that rehearsal, the kids' lack of discipline will likely lead to anarchy. This is one of those "without a vision, the people perish" realities. The only thing which can tame the beast of corporate adolescence is a focus so strong, a vision so powerful, and a mission so clear that it will override the negative "attitude." So when we speak about lack of discipline in our society, we must begin with the discipline deficiency which rests inside us.

How much discipline does it take to keep a group of kids focused for a solid hour? Much! But, this discipline is not primarily the behavioral patterns of the kids in rehearsal. No, I'm referring to the commitment which took place on

Tuesday morning when you and I planned and prayed over this rehearsal! How disciplined were we on the front end when the plans were laid and the vision carved out? How can we criticize teenagers for doing what comes naturally when we fail to prepare and provide adequately for them?

Yes, a powerful vision and a strong image of ministry will overcome even the most disgusting of "attitudes." We will overcome, but no one said it would be easy . . . or instantaneous.

Remember when Jesus healed the young man in the ninth chapter of the Gospel of Mark. We discussed this scene at great length in Chapter 4 of this book, entitled "Casting Out Demons." After teaching that particular passage for years in our conferences, something incredibly comforting suddenly dawned on me. Even Jesus' work of healing took some time to accomplish. Reading back over the passage, what happened when Jesus cast out the demon from the boy? Was the young man instantly okay? Not quite. For a few horrible moments the demons took one more shot at the young man, this time with a vengeance. With a few final yelps and more seizure-like contortions, the young man writhed out of control and finally lay exhausted in the dust. For a moment, the crowd thought the young man was dead.

Even the direct touch of God often takes time to manifest its full effect. Isn't that comforting? It is with great joy that I announce to struggling directors who work hard, labor relentlessly, and still encounter discipline problems, that the boy at Jesus' feet threw a fit as well, even after Jesus healed him!

Here is something to think about as we work with kids in this culture. So many teenagers come to us from dysfunctional, unhappy, and chaotic families that some kids know nothing but strife from the time they wake up in the morning until they fall asleep at night. Logically speaking, how is such a kid likely to respond as he walks into an atmosphere of strong love, acceptance, affirmation, and understanding? Although it may feel good, it's an alien planet to him. He has little or no experience in that kind of environment. He doesn't know what to make of it. He doesn't know how to act. In some cases, the demons themselves may be dictating the kids' actions, recoiling from the spiritual presence of Christ in that room.

Too strange? Too far out? Spend a few years working closely with a group of teenagers, and you may not be so sure. Scripture clearly tells us that, as we minister in the name of Christ, we deal with powers of the air and principalities, things not readily seen or recognized. When Jesus provided pure love to save the life of this young man, the demons went nuts. But they eventually went away. Love drives out fear.

Let's backtrack a bit. Directors who thoroughly prepare for rehearsals must not be overly concerned with a few discipline problems along the way. It is going to happen.

On the other hand, the director who goes into a rehearsal half-baked can expect little else but frustration. There is no use trying to spiritualize it. When we arrive unprepared, we get what comes naturally, a bunch of loud, boisterous kids who can't be disciplined or focused. It all began on Tuesday morning when we couldn't discipline ourselves and properly focus on our own preparation. How many times have I been there? More than I care to remember!

Let's make one last reference to the story in Mark 9. After the demons departed from the young man, he was left on the ground as if dead. The crowd actually thought he was gone. A number of years ago, I was called upon to direct a youth choir following the forced termination of the former minister of music. The fellow was an outstanding musician and technician. He had built some strong relationships with the tiny group of leaders within the youth choir. They had invested themselves under this fine director's leadership, and they had all anticipated a bright future ahead. The situation which surrounded the minister's departure devastated the kids. As I entered the choir room for our first youth choir rehearsal together, I heard dead silence. Kids sat looking at the floor with their legs and arms crossed. Eye contact was almost nonexistent. The silence was not a sense of respect for the new director. The awkward absence of sound was a vivid reminder of death. No kids jabbering with each other. No energy. No wildness. No fun. No "we're so glad to be back together" feeling could be found. There was little hope and not a modicum of joy. It was as if we were dead.

From a personal perspective, let me offer this word of observation. I would much rather try to work with a group manifesting too much unbridled energy than to try to raise a choral corpse. I will take the wild, crazy energy any day to the hard, silent, jaded faces of anger and disenchantment. The good news, however, is that both can live abundantly. It depends on our willingness to point our kids to Christ through music, rehearsal times, ministry organization, and vision.

Specific Suggestions for Disciplined Rehearsals

1. Prepare your rehearsal thoroughly.

2. Pray daily for individual kids in your group.

3. Plan the rehearsal to move very quickly from start to finish.

4. Keep verbiage in rehearsal to a minimum. Too much talk by the director causes a loss of focus for the kids. Keep them singing.

5. Deal with any major discipline problems then and there, but keep personalities out of it, if possible. Be strong, but not brutal. Don't get into a yelling match with anyone. Keep voices down.

6. Be clear about what you expect and don't back down on the basics.

7. Be compassionate. Try to understand why a person reacts a certain way. At times, some teenagers are not completely in control of their own actions.

8. Continuous discipline problems need to be discussed with the individual kid and/or parents. Do not hold the entire choir hostage because of one teen's misbehavior.

9. Generally, if the rehearsal times are well-prepared, the discipline problems tend to take care of themselves.

10. Your choir officers can be an incredible resource for group discipline. We shall take that up in the next chapter.

CHAPTER 17

Fashioning Friendships to Work Together: Choir Officers

J esus' model of mentoring His disciples is a strong foretaste of how the Kingdom of God would deepen and expand through the millennia. Yes, Jesus ministered to the multitudes. He reached out to people who were not inside His immediate circle and offered them abundant, eternal life. He was touched by strangers in desperate search of comfort, healing, and restoration. Jesus' ministry to His world and culture reached far and wide.

It was within Jesus' batch of disciples that most of His teaching and intimate nurturing occurred. This motley group of twelve, combined with Mary, Martha, and Lazarus, formed the inner circle of the Savior. Their down-to-earth discussions about heavenly matters stand today as the epitome of group interaction and relationship.

Surely there would be a quicker, more time-efficient way to begin the church than to call a group of unconnected, diverse, blue-collar workers together and ask them to volunteer without salary or benefits. Certainly, the Master could have used the help of people with more influence, more education, money, and social standing to begin His work. The truth is, Jesus did allow people of wealth, visibility, and education to be involved, too. But He began with what must have looked like the dirty dozen. This was the group which comprised the majority of His three-year ministry.

Jesus poured His life, His time, and His teaching into this diverse group. He worked with them from morning until night. He taught them gently. He looked them straight in the eye and told them how it was. He sometimes hurt their feelings. He surprised them over and over again. He exasperated them at times. He loved them always.

As youth choir directors work with a group of officers, nothing is more poignant than studying the work of Jesus with His disciples. It is fascinating in every way, and we should take note of the energy at work among this often turbulent team.

We Have to Know Why We Are There *(so do the kids)*

When a teenager joins a youth choir, he does so because it meets some perceived need in his life. If it doesn't meet a real need, he is out of there. One of the basic differences between this and future generations is the motivation behind institutional involvement. Twenty-five years ago, kids could be motivated to pack pews, fill lofts, and attend for the sake of "filling their places" in church. Those days are very much gone; and, as long as we continue to push those ancient buttons of motivation, we will be continually frustrated. Guilt, although the lowest form of motivation, could be used with some short-term results in the mid-'70s. No more.

Kids need to see the specific purpose in what they are doing. They perceive their own time as being just as valuable as ours—and it is—and teens are not happy when their time is wasted. If *they* choose to waste their time, and they sometimes certainly will, it's okay. But if we keep them from doing what they want to do for no good reason, we are in trouble. What we do with our teenagers not only needs to have purpose in our minds, *but the kids must also see that purpose.*

Designating Offices, Electing Officers

When we decide to elect a group of leaders, there needs to be a purpose. So often we elect the traditional slate of officers: president, vice-president, secretary, treasurer, social chairman, section leaders, librarian, and so on. What does each of these officers *do*? What is the purpose of a youth choir secretary? A treasurer? What exactly do the section leaders do? What is the vice-president's function?

Offices need to be created and named to reflect specific jobs and duties that relate to particular needs within the choir. Determining those needs depends on the mission statement set forth by the director and the group.

When choosing which offices should be elected, be sure to call the office something which reminds the group of what the officer will do. Feel free to use unusual and nontraditional designations which meet your specific group's needs. The old "president" designation may be transformed into "coordinator," "liaison," or "chairperson." Section leaders may now be referred to as group leaders or section directors. Use whatever designation works to tell the choir what is taking place within the officers' group. Be creative.

How many officers should a youth choir have? That depends upon how many jobs need special, specific leadership. It may be six, sixteen, or in some instances, twenty-six.

Don't be afraid to adjust the number of officers you elect from year to year, based upon changing needs. Also, no officer designation (title) is set in stone. Feel free to change the titles when the need arises or when a more accurate designation seems to better fit the task.

The Rules of Election

Generally, only the older youth choir veterans should serve as youth choir officers. The president (or however your number one officer is designated) should almost always be a veteran senior. Serving as an officer needs to be an honor for those who have served well in non-officer capacities as a singer and leader within the group. When we elect officers at too young an age, we tend to burn them out, and the sense of honor quickly disappears.

Elections are best held by secret ballot and accomplished in a way to minimize taking precious rehearsal time for campaigning, voting, and runoffs. The simplest way which seems to work the best is a popular voting system on an 8.5 x 11 ballot. Allow the choir members to write in the names of those they would like to see as their officers with first, second, third, and fourth choices. The director, along with another adult or two, should count the ballots and determine the slate of officers. Since this is basically a popularity contest for the kids, the director needs to reserve the right to appoint anyone he feels is worthy of holding an office but was not elected. The teenagers don't need to know who got how many votes, who was appointed rather than elected, and all the details of the election. Integrity demands that the kids' choices be honored, but the director can provide balance to the officers slate if needed. Announce the election results the following week, or better yet, through the mail on Tuesday or Wednesday.

Officers–Elect System

Director David Pierce adapted a system of youth choir officer elections based upon several other organizations. David's choir elects officers each year, but the officers elected this year are for the following season. In other words, David's choir always has a group of officers and also a slate of officers-elect, already elected and right behind those serving this year. This is done for training, mentoring, and building choir continuity. It works beautifully; and, when put in place, every senior returns to fulfill the responsibility of the final year.

Under this system, the dropout rate for older youth is practically zero.

The two officer groups working at once has no significant downside. However, the start-up on this system is a little confusing, because you are electing two separate sets of officers that first year. When this happens, it is a good idea to list all those eligible for officers in each of the years and split up the actual elections over two rehearsals. This will eliminate as much confusion as possible. The good news is that this double-election only happens once, and then you are set for the future.

Possible Officer Configuration with Responsibilities

Limitless possibilities exist as your specific needs dictate.

PRESIDENT
- Chairman of the officers
- Official liaison between members and director
- Keeps his ear to the ground on all choir matters
- Calls meetings as needed for decisions, training, and fellowship
- Oversees the work of all other officers
- Tour assistant

SECTION LEADERS (four to eight members)
- Provide connection with four sections for music and ministry
- May or may not lead section rehearsals, based upon ability

SOCIAL COMMITTEE (three or four members)
- Plan food for after-choir parties
- Plan all social events

Alternative to the Fixed Officer System

PRESIDENT
- Same list of responsibilities as above

OFFICERS-AT-LARGE
Give them a name: The Entourage, The Movers and Shakers, The Steering Committee, The Coordinating Council, The Choir Vision Task Force, The Singing Servants, etc.

Within this at-large grouping, specific task forces can be assigned to accomplish specific, one-time tasks. One advantage of this system is that it is fluid, dynamic, and flexible. Members of the officer group have the opportunity to work together in various combinations on a variety of projects.

Make no mistake about it, the driving force of the officer group is normally still going to be the director. There are rare exceptions to this rule, but choir presidents are normally very busy, connected teenagers who have many irons in the fire at school, home, church, and even a part-time job. The youth choir director will have to gently and persistently lead the president and the officers along, knowing when to seek their input and when to back off and take another approach. The officers don't need to make all the decisions pertaining to the choir, nor should they be allowed to carry that expectation of total power. They have neither time, energy, nor expertise to pull off that task. You need their input in the area of wide, sweeping concepts and the implications for their fellowship with each other. They need to hear your heart, and, just as importantly, you need to hear theirs.

Back to Jesus

In the final chapter of the Gospel of John, Peter decides he is going to go fishing. There is a strong suggestion in this decision that Peter wanted to put space between himself and this strange call to follow the Lord. Jesus had been crucified, was resurrected and had appeared to the disciples two times, but Peter wanted to go back to his old life, the way it had been before this whole Jesus era. Peter felt out of control, and he just wanted to go back to where he was comfortable, to where he knew he could be successful, to the fishing boats on the lake. Successful he was not, because they didn't catch anything all night. Finally, spotting someone on the beach, the disciples began to wonder who it was. Suddenly, the person spoke, "Not catching much, are you fellows? Try throwing your nets on the other side of the boat." The fish hit the nets like a squirming ton of bricks.

Suddenly, the disciples knew it was Jesus, but they remained aloof. This was Jesus' third appearance to them, but none seemed eager to run up and greet Him. I wonder why. When they reached the shore, Jesus invited them to have breakfast. The disciples ventured to ask Jesus who He was, but the Scripture says they already knew it was the Lord.

What happens next is a picture I hope will remain with us for the rest of our lives. Here is Jesus, Emmanuel, the Savior and Lord, fixing a simple yet abundant breakfast for a group of guys who still had not totally bought into

His program. The disciples had grown weary of waiting around praying, so they decided to return to their comfort zone—fishing. Jesus was not angry. He did not preach to them or chide them for not being more committed, more serious, or more mature. He simply fixed breakfast and served it to them.

I have to admit there have been times I have felt betrayed by my youth choir officers. Either through immaturity, lack of experience, selfishness, or downright meanness, there have been isolated times when officers have said things which hurt my feelings, frustrated me, and caused me great pain. I have been known to snipe back, ever ready to defend my territory and stand my ground. May God help me in the future not to return the jabs, but rather to serve a hearty breakfast to the whole group.

The relationships we establish with our choir officers are intensive at times: intensively close, intensively loving, intensively fun, and sometime intensively frustrating. In many ways, we are like a family, hopefully a *functional* family, which deals lovingly with everything we face together.

The only time in my life I have led a foot-washing service was with a group of youth choir officers who gathered for a retreat in my home. It was an amazingly special experience, one that I cannot adequately put into words and have not attempted to duplicate in the fourteen years since it happened.

Christ calls us to be servants to one another and to communicate, solve problems, and minister within our group and beyond. If Jesus chose and trained a core group of friends to carry the light into the future, then so must we. It is slow and sometimes tedious, but it is the only way the gospel can change teenagers, reveal their riches, and build their lives.

CHAPTER 18

Freedom to Change

T hose of us who spend the greater parts of our professional lives in the institutional church know it well: many of the folks we are called to serve are bent in the direction of preservation. Holding firmly to the events, feelings, or accomplishments of yesteryear is the national pastime of the faithful. It is a temptation for all of us, even as career church musicians, perhaps *especially* for church musicians!

From Preservation to Permission

Success feels good. Most of us would rather revel in the reality of what *was* than to embark upon the pain of moving into what *is* or what needs to *be*. Lest you feel I am bashing the past, let me set the record straight. Memory is one of the priceless treasures we possess as the children of God. Without remembering who we are and where we have been, we are a pitiful tribe. Over and over again, Scripture reminds us to remember. Not only are we to recall and celebrate the acts of God in the past, but we are also to be faithful in passing down those stories to future generations.

Sometimes, memory alone sustains us through the toughest parts of our lives. One of the horrors of Alzheimer's Disease is that the memory is either gone or terribly skewed and inconsistent. Without memory, we are a boat without a rear rudder to steer our souls. Make no mistake about it. It is a terrible thing not to remember.

We need a balance between remembrance and refreshment. Even as we thank God for His provisions in the past, we need to feel permission to move forward. The future of our youth choirs depends upon it.

From Memorization to Motivation

Early in our ministries, most of us learned to avoid criticism creatively. Many of us have become master avoiders of confrontation, even positive conflict. For many of us, our early lessons in conflict-resolution were painful, one-sided (from the *other* side), harsh, and downright mean. We discovered that church people can be some of the cruelest people in the world. As we move into a new millennium, we are discovering that these fine people and their offspring are still out there, but now they are under more pressure than ever before. As ministers of music, and especially as youth choir directors, we often find ourselves standing in emotional harm's way.

What could be more emotional in church than one's personal taste in music? There is only one thing I can imagine: a person's children and grandchildren. Get the picture? As youth choir directors, we work in perhaps the two most emotionally charged arenas in organized religion today. As scary as that may be, it also accounts for the great opportunities at our fingertips.

After we get our noses bloodied a few times—if we decide to continue in the ministry—we tend to allow others to set the tempos and textures of our programs. Through fear and abdication, we also let other people select the style of our leadership, along with the forms of music we produce. But most damaging of all is that we slowly begin to bury our real feelings and deepest commitments. If we do this long enough, we may discover that our commitments are no longer alive. We slowly suffocated them under the weight of public opinion.

I think of case after case where men and women in the mid-lives of their careers are going through the memorized motions of ministry. They learn how to survive and to stay out of trouble. Their major motivation, admittedly or not, is self-preservation. The memorized choreography they dance has literally pounded the passion they possessed in earlier times. The passion becomes so bruised and the dream so distant that many, silently and secretly, give up.

Soon after the death of passion comes atrophy and the lack of motivation. After all, when there is no passion, what is there to motivate us? Yes, motivation derives directly from passion. We can attend all the seminars we want and learn all the latest techniques of ministry development, but until we have passion, it does not help us or our teenagers.

From Piddling to Passion

How do you find passion? What do I have to do to receive it, retrieve and to recharge it?

Discovery—Passion is a two-way street. In some regards, we discover passion when we uncover a vast need which is unmet. On the other hand, passion discovers us in a mysterious way which grips our very souls. It is not something we drum up; rather, it is a power which overtakes us. It is God. It is our calling to serve God. It is verdant vitality in our vocation.

Development—If you have been in youth choir ministry for a long time, you know that it is not an experience marked by constant growth, continually and steadily gliding upward to utopia. Yes, there are glorious moments when we see the glints of the glory of God. But generally, it is hard, time-consuming, and energy-demanding *work*. There are times when it doesn't seem worth it. There are times when it may not be worth it. However, it is through these peaks and valleys—and the vast distances in between—that we fine-tune, focus, and develop the passion within us. And yes, there will be times when only our passion, our calling, keeps us going.

From Discouragement to Joy—We have taken a short but aggressive hike around the issue of "permission to change." When our focus for ministry is preservation, maintenance, holding the position, or keeping up an image, then creative, passionate energy for ministry ultimately fades. It is terribly tempting and damnably easy to fall into comfortable patterns of ministry which does not challenge anyone (including myself) to change or grow. If we compromise enough times in enough places, we create a passionless program which piddles at ministry.

It is time for us to put aside the piddling in youth choir ministry. We must pray for passion, understanding, and where needed, change. God not only gives us permission, but He encourages us to take those scary first steps.

Let us look to God. May we pray without ceasing. We must dream big dreams. Let us commit to grow within and have the courage to allow those changes to flow to the teenagers we touch. It will be change for the good.

Permission granted.

Permission received.

CHAPTER 19

Floundering with the Funding

For the past eighteen chapters and for the next twenty-one chapters , we have discussed and will continue pursuing the weightier matters of youth choir ministry: understanding the task, dreaming the dreams, seeing the vision, administration, organization, and time-management. We have looked to the Bible as our guide and to God as our source of vision, hope and energy.

We know that "God owns the cattle on a thousand hills," and He, in fact, owns it all. "The earth is the Lord's and all it contains." We all know it costs a lot of money to function in today's world. No one in his right mind would marry and have children without a decent source of income for his family. Certainly, God takes care of His own, but He also expects us to work, to create, and to join Him in the effort to provide what we need to sustain our lives. We are laborers together with God.

A family cannot survive long without income. Likewise, a youth choir cannot meet the needs of teenagers without the financial support and significant underwriting of the congregation. Building a youth choir is a fairly expensive proposition. If the church leaders are more interested in saving money than they are in reaching teenagers, building a youth choir will be a tough uphill battle.

Practically speaking, it makes no sense to hire a youth choir director to work, pay salary and benefits, and then give him nothing to work with in terms of program dollars. If a youth choir is to be conceived, born, and raised to maturity, it will require a substantial amount of money in the coming years. Church leaders need to understand and deal with it.

Why does it cost money to effectively operate a good youth choir? Here are just a few of the considerations most lay persons never think about:

Postage	In order to keep kids informed, postage costs will be significant.
Computer	E-mail is becoming essential in connecting with kids.
Literature	New music, which enables us to stay current, costs big.
Mission Trips	The church needs to provide healthy support.
Tours	The church must see the value and get behind the effort.
Scholarships	Some teenagers will not be able to participate without the help of a scholarship.
Uniforms	Whether robes, formals, or matching shirts, the teenagers should not be expected to bear the entire cost.
Social events	The church provides social events as a way to enhance fellowship and say "thank you" for worship leadership.
Retreats	The choir will need underwriting to keep the costs from being prohibitive for teenagers, especially multiple teens from one family.
Programs	Funding is needed for special events with instruments, orchestras, and printed programs.
Festivals	Underwriting is needed to keep the cost feasible for kids.

When the church provides significant financial underwriting for the ministry of the teenagers, it sends a message to the kids. It says, "We think you are important. We believe your work is important. We want you to know we are behind you, praying for you, and pulling for you."

On the other hand, if a church finance committee must be begged or constantly coaxed to provide support, the opposite message is sent. "We don't mind you being around here, but we are not going to encourage you in any significant way. We will throw a little money at you, but don't expect much from us, because we certainly don't expect much from you. You are basically on your own. Good luck."

Generally speaking, the church budget should provide the needed resources—growing a music library, rehearsal space, robes—to equip a youth choir and keep them growing. The budget should also underwrite at least fifty-percent of the costs associated with ministries away from the church. Many churches are set up to provide all transportation and lodging costs for mission trips and choir tours. Meals, insurance and other expenses can be covered by charging the participants a per person fee. If the fee becomes too high, the kids will begin to bail out. This must never happen. Otherwise, the choir could be viewed as an exclusive travel club only for those who can afford it.

Many church budgets are not where they should be in youth choir support. As funding for the arts continues to be cut in the public schools, the church must rise to the occasion and provide more for the teenagers. Such underwriting must be viewed, not as a dead expense, but rather as an investment in the future, for that is precisely what it is.

Fund-raising is on the increase among youth choirs in North America. If the church is unable or unwilling to provide direct support, the second best solution is to allow the choir to hold fund-raising events. We have heard of several churches who strictly prohibit fund-raising, but they also provide practically nothing for youth choir ministry. This leaves only one option: the kids have to pay for everything out of their own pockets. Just a simple five-day tour costs each kid $500. There is no way this will work, even in today's crazy economy. It is doomed to fail before it ever begins. The real question which looms is, "Why hire a youth choir director or expect any kind of program if the church refuses to support it?" It's irrational.

With fund-raising on the increase, we have amassed a small collection of fund-raising ideas which work effectively for many youth choirs across the country. The possibilities are virtually limitless, depending only on the creativity of the director, kids, and parents, along with their willingness to work hard.

The funding of your youth choir projects may be difficult at first. However, when the financial movers and shakers in your congregation begin to see the results and hear the glowing reports, they will likely begin to support your program. It is a slow process, and there is certainly pressure to produce. As the church underwrites the teenagers' ministry, they inevitably want to see and hear good returns on their investment. With this reality before us, the youth choir director must put on the hat of public relations, making certain that key people are present when the choir shines the brightest. Such strategizing may seem unspiritual, but it is the law of the jungle when the youth choir is under the auspices of the institutional church.

Fifty Effective Ideas for Youth Choir Fund-Raising

Dinner Theater

Coupon Sales

Magazine Sales

Lawn Services

Auctions and Silent Auctions

Business Sponsors

Sub Sandwich Sales

Painting Days

Babysitting Services

Bus Washes

Breakfast/Brunch

Spoof Fashion Show

Barbecue Sales

Walk-a-thon

Golf Caddying

One-day Offering

Grocery Shopping

Recording Sales

Golf Tournament

Basketball Tournament

Feature Concert by Major Artist

Selling "Tour Stock"

Concession Stands

Selling Program Ads

Church Custodial Work

Talent Show/Dessert Dinner

Wrapping Paper Sales

Bake Sales

Aircraft Washing

Service Sales

Seed Sales

Pizza Sales

Landscape Work

Car Washes

Flower Sales

Fashion Show

Comedy Club

Window Washing

Marathon

Local Grants

Singing Telegrams

Firewood Sales

Book Sales

Tennis Tournament

Football Game

Benefit Concert by Choir & Friends

Choir Grandparents Club

Commercial Handbill Distribution

Valet Service

Childcare During Worship

PART FIVE

The Growth
of Christian Musicianship

Gaining Grace, Melting Weapons

The writing of this book has brought on a colorful and often bothersome realization. I have changed. It is not the change that is difficult to face. In fact, I am eternally grateful for my inner spiritual and emotional growth as a result of my close work with teenagers over the years. Even though I still have a long way to go, I can see progress. What pains me is the realization that from the beginning of my ministry, I carried emotional baggage around with me and regularly dumped it on the very kids I was trying to serve.

It is probably already clear that this chapter is going to be quite a confessional, and that is okay. Although there will be obvious differences between my story and yours, I wager that we are not totally dissimilar. If, by sharing some of the struggles and failures I faced as a young minister, I might help others avoid some of the same snares and common traps, then I thank God for the opportunity to tell it.

In the early years of my career, I was so insecure with my musicianship that I felt I had something to prove to everyone. Not only that, but I felt a general underlying sense of unworthiness that constantly badgered me and drove me to try to prove the same things to myself that I tried to display to others. Working with something which, in retrospect, seemed like a first cousin to paranoia, I saw danger behind every bush. I knew something would soon go awry, because, deep down, I did not deserve to be successful, fulfilled, or happy. Thus, I spent my life and ministry in a foreboding, angry, depressed and manic mode.

Developing a close circle of friends had always come fairly easy for me. Looking back, I can always remember intimate groups of eight to ten people that I would hang out with in each stage of my childhood, adolescence, college years, and graduate school. Most of these relationships are still strong and satisfying today.

I was not good at the more casual connections with people. Being friends was almost all or nothing for me. You and I either had to be intimate or we would not be friends at all. That is how I dated as well. Either you want to marry me, or I won't waste my time taking you out. My friendships had to have function. It couldn't be just for fun or for the sheer joy of it!

This translated into an awful scenario in the choir setting. I frustrated both youth and adult choir members, because I was totally distant and even brittle toward the masses, and entirely too intense with a precious few.

When I took my first full-time position out of seminary, I was still single. Arriving at a huge church at the ripe age of twenty-five, I followed on the heels of a music ministry legend. Lanny Allen is winsome, incredibly creative with kids, musically on the cutting edge, a caring minister of the first order, and a world-class human being. Linda, his wife, is the perfect partner in ministry. For more than a decade, Lanny and Linda ministered to the people with integrity and class, pouring out their souls with love through some of the best years of their lives.

Then I arrived, the green kid with the attitude. I was scared to death. Intimidated by everything that moved, I immediately began working ten hours a day, seven days a week just to figure out which programmatic buttons to push. I became weary to the bone, and the more stressed I became, the worse I handled my choirs and my relationships.

Although I was painfully insecure deep within, I came across just the opposite: aloof, arrogant, and cocky. It was all a front, protecting me from what I feared might hurt me.

The newly-gained musical skills I developed in graduate school came fairly easy for me. Conducting, teaching technique, and rehearsing were apparently my strengths, judging from my grades. Consequently, I torqued them up and drove them down my choirs' throats. With the massive insecurity I experienced professionally and ministerially, the musical skills I developed gradually became instruments of warfare. My skills became a veritable shield, protecting me from relationships which would expose my shortcomings and work against me. Tyrannical, quick-tempered, sniping, sarcastic, and joyless in rehearsals, I kept the flame under the pressure cooker and the technical torque high in an effort to mask what I felt and feared. When things became a little uncomfortable, I would sling out a string of terminology, intentionally intimidating the choir by speaking a language they neither fully understood nor could appreciate. I constructed a wall between us right before their very eyes. This technique kept an especially large gulf between me and the youth choir.

Pretty unhealthy stuff here, wouldn't you agree? And if it appears unhealthy from the outside, imagine how it felt on the inside.

I then learned that there is truth to the bumper sticker which says, "Just because you are paranoid doesn't mean they are *not* out to get you!" My actions and reactions began to become a self-fulfilling prophecy. A low-key petition began circulating among some vocal people in the music ministry who were seeking my resignation. Who could blame them for the way they felt? There was a scared young boy occupying the Music Office, trying to do a man's job.

At that point, my pastor and friend, Frank Pollard, saved my ministerial hide. He went to those who were petitioning and gently said to them in effect, "You have to give this young man some space and allow him to grow into his ministry. If you put too much pressure on him now, you could ruin him for the rest of his life." They mercifully put the petition to rest, and that was about the time I sought professional Christian counseling, an experience which totally changed my life.

I was so self-absorbed that I was not even aware of the petition until several years later. The counseling ministry was lovingly provided by Charlie Prewitt along with Clint and Pamela Dunagan. Not only did this incredible trio save my career and ministry, I also believe they saved my life.

It was also during this time that I met Holly Howland, a nineteen-year-old sophomore beauty at Baylor University. Holly grew up under Lanny Allen's ministry. She was a youth choir veteran and remained an avid enthusiast. Holly and I began dating, and this new relationship opened up a host of new awarenesses. Her whole mind-set regarding people was so healthy and joy-filled that it caught me off guard. She was bright, cheerful, trusting, but not at all naive or gullible. She possessed keen insights into people's feelings and shared sharp wisdom regarding all kinds of relationships. Holly was able to cut through my cynicism towards adults, my frustration and often anger with teenagers, and my gnawing insecurity deep inside myself. Summarily, I began to feel my musical weaponry melt into tools of helping, into instruments of care.

I am convinced that God provided everything I needed to see me through my troubled early days of ministry. The group of unhappy church members attempted to get my attention and provide me with a reality check. A kind and strong pastor went to bat for me even when I was ignorant of his support. Three Christian counselors worked me over spiritually and emotionally, leaving no stone unturned. Finally, there was and is sweet Holly, the love of my life.

Through all these factors and relationships, the Lord provided the spark which consumed my anger and ignited a passion for teenagers and adults alike. Who could ask for more?

Through the grace of God and the patience of His people, I was able to serve eight fulfilling years in that church. Holly and I were married and our first two children were dedicated there. Truly God is able to take a disaster of our own making and turn it into a blessing. Thanks be to God.

What weapons do you possess which could be melted into tools of love and ministry? What protective shields have you erected which might be transformed into opportunities of significant youth choir ministry? May God transform our protective armors into arsenals of hope, peace, joy and love.

> *And they will hammer their swords into plowshares,*
> *and their spears into pruning hooks.*
> Isaiah 2:4

Because of my early experience in ministry, the Isaiah passage will always contain powerful musical imagery for me. Perhaps it does for you, as well.

CHAPTER 20

Gaining the
Skills of Choral Singing

The Posture of a Good Rehearsal

We have heard it all our lives, and our kids have probably heard it, too: "practice makes perfect." Sounds good, seems right, should be so. But alas, it isn't. Practice does not make perfect. And why not, we ask? Because we can practice mistakes all day long, and the practice of those bad habits only makes our singing worse rather than better.

Practice does not make perfect. Only perfect practice makes perfect. Good practice makes good. Fair practice makes for a fair sound. The better the practice, the better the choir and vice versa.

How do you "posture" your youth choir for success? What can you do to motivate your kids to produce successful results in practice and in a performance?

Preparation

The director must know what she wants the choir to accomplish. When putting together your rehearsal plans, don't forget to include, not only what you want your kids to learn, but also what you want them to feel, to experience, to hear, to sense, and to "suspect."

The Rehearsal

Getting the singers to sit with correct posture may be a difficult task. Begin by explaining that they will not be expected to sit like soldiers from the beginning of the rehearsal to the end—only when they actually sing. When they are not singing (during prayer request time or when the director is talking), they may sit however they want, just so they do not disturb anyone else.

Using sports illustrations, describe how important it is for an athlete to be in the proper position to play his game. Talk about how ridiculous it would be for a lineman on a football team to stand upright at the line with hands in his pockets when the ball is snapped. How well would a baseball player hit the ball if he stood on top of home plate leaning on his bat? They will get the point.

Briefly describe good singing posture and then demand that your singers adopt it into their rehearsal habit. Good coaches never think twice about making similar demands on their players. Lovingly, yet firmly, hold the teenagers' feet to the fire on posture. No lecture alone will get the job done. Just like any sport, you will have to go back to the basics from time to time. Insist that posture be kept up among your singers, and in a few weeks, it will become second nature. When the choir is into its regimen, it is always interesting to watch a new teenager come into the rehearsal. His posture will stick out like a sore thumb compared to the veterans.

Transferring Posture to Performance

Nothing is more important in performance than a choir's posture. A good seated posture can immediately be transferred to performance posture just by standing up. Frame and chest held comfortably high and tall, feet pointed toward the audience, about eighteen inches apart and one slightly ahead of the other, and hands comfortably to the side.

Your youth choir is "heard" before their mouths ever open and even before the anthem's introduction begins. The audience makes a preliminary assessment of the group's quality just by the way they enter the room. Even choirs with musical problems can make a fine presentation just by the way they carry themselves before, during, and after the concert.

Want to know how your choir will look and sound next time you "perform?" Then take a look at the group during the rehearsals leading up to that performance and you will get a clear picture of what to expect. Our choir's performance and worship leadership bears an uncanny resemblance to the effectiveness of its rehearsals! We *will* perform *exactly* the way we practice.

With hard work and a little discipline, your choir can master its posture technique. They will know it when it happens, because they will never want to go back to the old sloppy ways of sitting and standing. When your group's singing posture becomes second nature, you have already reached a high degree of success. It doesn't take a musical genius to pull it off, but it does take some creative coaching skills. Go for it!

The Dynamics of Good Singing

How many youth choirs have you heard sing with good dynamics? Think about it. The last time you sat through a youth choir festival with eight or ten choirs performing, how many of those choirs sang anything other than very loudly or very softly or very blandly?

Frankly, getting some kids to sing at all is a great accomplishment. Directors of inexperienced choirs often spend a great deal of energy in the rehearsal just getting the teenagers to drop their inhibitions and sing out. In early rehearsals with starting-from-scratch choirs, I have been known to say to the young singers, "I don't care how you sound right now, just give me some sound. I can't improve nothing, I can't shape silence into a beautiful sound. I can't create something out of nothing. Give me something, anything to work with!" The result? After weeks and sometimes months of coaxing and praising, the teens slowly begin to sing unashamedly, and then we are on our way to building a good sound together.

"Louder, louder, more, more" is the theme song of many directors, and I must confess that I have been one of them. However, kids often improve upon their sound *quantity* as directors fail to improve significantly upon the sound *quality*. Actually, we are just so grateful to have *any* sound at all that we often settle for a second rate sound. After all, we don't want to discourage the kids. A youth choir that can actually be heard puts a group way ahead of the norm.

The kids are learning, advancing, developing, changing and growing musically. The question is, are we? As directors, we constantly strive to learn new ways to build sounds and colors and phrases and textures. If our advancement as directors begins to lag, then our kids will stagnate, as well. They will get stuck with their wide-open volume of sound.

Teaching teenagers to sing with dynamic variation can be a fun musical learning adventure. A session on dynamics can be almost game-like. However, a one-shot session on dynamic levels just won't cut it. You must remind the kids over and over again within the context of the songs they sing.

Do your teenagers know the difference between piano and mezzo forte? Sure, many of them understand that piano is soft and mezzo forte is medium loud. But, do they have a sense of where the two dynamics lie in relationship to each other? How much louder is mezzo forte than piano? Is there some sense of how the sounds feel different inside the mouth as well as sound different to the ear? How do you teach such things? We need to be creative.

To increase teenagers' speed in learning, develop a teaching tool which uses multiple senses: sight, sound, feel, and even touch. A simple blackboard is very useful as you teach dynamics. Write on the board a horizontal line of the dynamic progression: *(ppp) pp p mp mf f ff (fff)*.

Ask the teenagers to put their music down, freeing their hands of any distraction. Then, giving them no verbal instructions on how loud to sing, ask them to sing one short phrase that they know like the backs of their hands. After they sing it, ask various choir members to determine the dynamic level. There will be several opinions, but they will probably guess within a dynamic level or so of each other. After they express their opinion, tell them what you think. Your judgment will be the final say. Show them on the board where they sang the phrase. Ask them to sing it again, the very same way.

Now, point to *pp* on the blackboard and ask them to sing the phrase *pianissimo*. Then, move on up, having them increase their volume at each dynamic level. If your choir is like mine, they will come on too strong too early and will leave themselves "no place to go" for *f* and *ff*. This is another example of the impulsiveness of adolescence—launching in a direction without regard for pacing themselves or keeping reserves for the future.

Once you complete this exercise, move the dynamic level around within the phrase to create *crescendo* and *decrescendo*. Explain to the teenagers how to create an energized sound when they sing softly. *Pianissimo* requires just as much energy, support and sustaining as *fortissimo*. In fact, most conductors teach that as the sound becomes softer, it must take on more energy to keep it from dying.

In other words, as you move from right to left on the chart, replace decibels with energy. And when your singers go left to right, adding volume, be sure to remind them that the sound needs to become not only louder, but bigger, fatter, heavier, fuller, and more supported.

Hopefully, the images suggested above will inspire youth choir directors to get serious about singing with effective dynamics. As you can see, numerous opportunities exist to develop fun experiences using the various elements of dynamics.

I suggest that you keep the chart up or at the drop of a hat draw it again. When they see the chart go up, they will immediately know what you're doing: you are working on dynamics. Keep them aware of how they are doing with their dynamics. Once they get the idea and begin to feel the difference inside, your choir will begin to discipline themselves.

Choral music is an emotional art. Adolescence is a time of greatly charged emotions and feelings. When we successfully open up the world of dynamics to our young singers, a whole new horizon of expression and communication dawns for them. The teenagers can and will learn dynamics and appreciate their full power. The only question is whether you and I will take the time and energy to teach it to them.

Vocal Production in the Youth Choir Setting

"I've heard *college* choirs who don't sing as well as your kids do," said a prominent pastor in the South after a great youth choir from the Midwest performed a Sunday evening concert in his church. "Why is it that your teenagers sing so well, and other youth choirs we have had sound so puny?"

Good question. When you listen to youth choirs as much as we do, you find a vast difference in the way some groups sound as opposed to others. Why? What's the difference?

Varied Experience and Exposure

Several variables apply to this reality. To name a few: the teenagers' choral experience outside the church (school and community traditions or a lack thereof), the teenagers' varying backgrounds in church children's choir programs, the "modeling" the church adult choir provides every week, the church's openness (or closedness) to the use of good choral literature in worship services, and the director's understanding, skill and commitment (or lack of) in developing a beautiful choral sound.

A Step in the Right Direction

Books, theses and doctoral dissertations have been devoted to the science, art, and psychology of developing choral sound among teenagers. Obviously, in one chapter we will be able to hit only the high spots, to point out the tip of the iceberg of choral development. Perhaps these insights and general principles will move all of us a little further down the road of choral development with our kids. And, by the way, anything you can get your hands on to read on the subject will help, even if you don't agree with everything that is theorized.

Earlier Physical Maturity

Teenagers grow and mature earlier and faster than a generation ago. Improved baby vitamins, better ongoing health care as children, and an awareness of proper nutrition all contribute to the early physical maturation of teenagers. There may even be other factors we have not yet discovered.

This earlier physical development has obvious implications for the ways we train teenagers chorally. We can expect more of them vocally than we could a few years ago. We can push them a little harder without the fear that they will "strip their gears." Incidentally, I have noticed this fact with the choirs I have directed over the past twenty years. My group today is far more consistent, stronger, and has more physical stamina for rehearsals and concerts than my choirs a decade ago.

Knowing What You Want to Hear

A choral conductor must know what she wants to hear from her teenagers. If she is uncertain, the singers will, by default, determine the rehearsal's agenda and will set the pace vocally. This scenario invariably produces an insipid, anemic choral sound that is hopelessly cursed by a lack of precision and energy. How do you know what you want to hear? What is a good choral sound for your teenagers?

Open, Energized, "Unaffected" Sound

We alluded earlier that it is an accomplishment just to get some teenagers to sing at all. Achieving an efficient sound, free from breathiness and strain, can be a difficult and tedious task. Don't let anyone tell you it doesn't take patience; it does! Often, when teenagers do come out of their shells to sing, they will try to do so like their favorite pop or rock stars, crooning, sliding, and straining their way from one note to the next, pushing and tensing at the extremes of their ranges. It happens!

Voice training could be defined as practically solving vocal problems, finding the roots of all vocal faults in a student and helping him, through vocal therapy, to overcome them. Like all therapy, it is a process, is sometimes painful, and it takes time to complete. It also is best accomplished in regular, consistent intervals with relatively small steps. And, if therapy is to be successful, it needs to be supervised by someone who understands the physical and psychological components of the process.

So, how do you know what to do? How do you and I come to understand the components and principles of vocal production?

Listen, Listen, Listen

Listen #1: Listen to others. Serious composers often listen to music written by other composers. They obtain ideas, concepts and techniques by listening to what the masters and their own contemporaries produce. Serious choral directors will do the same; we listen to other youth choirs, to school groups, and to all-state festivals. Nothing is a better teacher than listening.

Incidentally, this is one of the major reasons that we, at Youth Choirs, Inc., produce recordings featuring youth choirs. This allows us to familiarize ourselves with what others produce chorally, and we can then develop ideas and insights simply by observing their work. The recording helps discover good repertoire.

Listen #2: Listen to your own internal concept of what sounds good. When you hear the stark difference between a fine youth choir and a not-so-great group, you begin to develop your own definition of good choral sound. Your group and my group need not sound exactly alike. Our individual voices, talent levels, numbers, and other factors determine the more subtle qualities of our sound. But no sound can be successful until it has energy, is in tune, is balanced, is together, and has musical line and integrity.

Listen #3: Listen to the reality of your group. Once a director forms an internal ideal sound inside his head, he then must work to move from Point A (where the group really is) to Point B (where he wants them to be).

Suggestions for Moving from Point A to Point B

This is where the task falls apart for so many of us. How do you break the news to your group that they need to improve their sound without killing their spirit? It's not so much that we don't hear the problems or that we don't know how to solve them technically. We must approach it in such a way to encourage the teenagers rather than turn them off. Here are some practical suggestions:

- Use vocal warm-ups at the beginning of each rehearsal.

- Use various forms of sectional rehearsals to solve in-depth problems within individual sections.

- Always compliment the choir before correcting them. The compliment must be sincere, and the correction must be very specific with clear instructions on how to solve the problem.

- Isolate trouble spots and "do therapy" on the specific passage. Be sure to include everyone in the choir as much as possible so that no one gets bored.

- Develop a mental catalogue of practical, nonmusical images which illustrate musical concepts. Sports images are especially effective with teenagers.

- Use humor. But beware; don't use humor that puts down the choir or intimidates anyone within the group.

- Be consistent in your insistence.

- Be kind in your demands.

- Be fun and fulfilling to sing for.

- Allow your teenagers to see how you are growing personally as a musician. Share some of your goose-bump moments with them.

The Fun Phenomenon of Consonants

A statement which, admittedly, has some notable exceptions: Church choirs in general and youth choirs in particular do not sing with good consonants. Here are a few characteristics of the relatively few choirs who DO sing with crisp consonants.

The choir's congregation or audience can understand practically every word of the text.

- Choral releases and attacks are clean and solid.

- The group's "ensemble" is superb.

- The choir generally sings with beautiful vowels.

- The group's rhythmic precision is extraordinary.

- Tuning is much better than average.

- The youth choir almost makes a game of seeing who can sing with the strongest initial and final consonants.

- The director, in a quest for musicality, must actually ask the choir for less consonant "explosion" from time to time.

The choir and director spend time "in the trenches" learning what it means to spit out consonants within the context of choral singing.

A Good Rule for Singing Consonants

Teenagers can be quickly taught that consonants must be sung 1) hard and 2) quickly. So often, we do just the opposite. Our consonants (and vowels, too, for that matter) are "chewed" softly at different times, and the tuning and choral unity are thrown out the window.

Motivating Kids to Produce Their Words with Energy and Vitality

If your kids already want to be their best, then selling them on singing consonants will be relatively easy. If they don't care how they sound, then motivation needs to begin with something deeper than just learning how to sing good consonants!

The biggest problem is getting the young singers to remember how important consonants are. They must be taught to exaggerate the consonant sound. In our speaking voices, particularly in the South, consonants are downplayed or at times almost eliminated in the spoken voice. It is a lot like getting kids to open their mouths—they really think they do it, when in fact, it does not happen at all. Teenagers think they are singing strong consonants, but alas, they are inaudible to the director, congregation or audience.

Teenagers love rhythm. When a director decides to move his youth choir toward choral excellence and excitement, he must use high energy (high torque) during the rehearsal. Things must go somewhere positive and fun. As a percussionist from my youth, I think of good consonants as the percussion section for choral music. A good strong final "t" reminds me of a rim shot on a snare drum. A "buzzed n" on the end of an "amen" feels solid and secure like a soft timpani roll. "Ch" sounds resemble cymbal crashes. None of the above works, however, unless they are produced absolutely together.

Games Directors Play

Make a game of it. Isolate consonant sounds and ask the choir make the sounds on cue. Remember, the rule is: 1) hard and 2) quickly. When you game-play, you need to get your act together and know exactly what you want, because teenagers will have fun with this. In fact, my problem in the past is that they enjoy it a little too much and the group loses its focus as a few wise guys exaggerate the consonants too much. After isolating single consonant sounds, get them to happen at exactly the same time, then throw in combinations of sounds and words, words such as KiTe, BiKe, LighT, GoD, inDeeD, etc.—the possibilities are endless.

I have noticed a strange phenomenon in working consonants with my choirs. In youth choirs, the guys first catch the spirit of consonants, and it becomes almost a macho thing. (Maybe it has something to do with adolescent boys' love of spitting.) In adult choirs, however, the women remember and get into their consonants. (Not many nice ladies I know are into spitting, but they do actually perform better consonants.) Getting adult tenors and basses to sing with good consonants is often like pulling teeth.

As in all areas of choral teaching, creativity is the name of the game. Know what you want to hear and motivate your teenagers. It will mean the difference between excellence and mediocrity.

Go For iT!

Get Together with Vowel Unification

First, a Disclaimer

Volumes have been written on the art and science of vowels in choral music. No small chapter will provide all the knowledge a director needs to train his choir to properly sing vowels. We have no delusions of being comprehensive; rather, we hope to be provocative. Read all you can from other sources and constantly study by listening to other great choirs and even home-made recordings of your own group. The director's open ears and innovation are the keys to greatness in any choral setting. If the teenagers commit themselves to work with you and you work as a team toward excellence, then half of your battle has already been won.

We hope that we give you a place to begin and continue your quest in choral excellence. If you discover one new idea, or if you remember something you already knew, then it was worth the writing as well as the reading.

What's Opera Got to Do with It?

A few years ago in my "spare time," I directed the Shreveport Opera Chorus, preparing them for several major productions each season. I want to share a couple of choral clues and cues I rediscovered while working with the opera chorus.

The production of *Aida* was performed in its original language, Italian. What an avenue for good singing! The vowels are pure and clean in Italian (eh, ih, ah, oh, oo). Impurities have no part of this lovely language. This is the primary reason many of us cut our vocal teeth in the studio singing Italian songs and arias.

A Lesson from the Cast of 275

Working with the chorus one evening (a huge group of volunteer singers from the deep South, mind you), vowel impurity was reeking havoc with our sound. We were woefully out of tune, and there was no focus at all in the vocal production. It didn't take long for "choral depression" to set in—the choir becomes so discouraged with its own sound that the singers emotionally give up. They just want to forget the rehearsal and call it an evening. You can just feel it. It can happen to any group, but directors can do things to help rescue them from their own feelings of inadequacy. The solution that evening was unifying our vowels.

The Pleasures and Pitfalls of Vanishing Sounds

Many English vowel sounds contain vanishing sounds—the major vowel and the vanishing vowel combined are called diphthongs. "My" (pronounced MAH...ee) has as its major vowel "ah" and its vanishing sound "ee." "Light" (pronounced LAH...eet) has the same major and vanishing vowels as "my." A key in choral singing is to keep the choir from moving to the vanishing sound too quickly. Pop singers and crooners do it all the time. Sinatra became famous for his "Ah...eeeee did it mah...eeeee weh...eeeeee." It may work in solo singing, but it never works within a choral setting. "Chewing" of the vowel causes disunity in the sound, tuning loss and focus problems—first fruits of bad technique.

Both the primary vowel and vanishing vowel are necessary in proper singing. The important thing, however, is to be sure that the primary vowel is, indeed, open and primary, and that the vanishing sound happens together (and very quickly) among the singers.

To Begin the Kids' Awareness, Banish Vanishing Vowels in an Exercise

Begin this process by using words which have no vanishing sounds at all. Since many of our youth choirs don't sing in Italian (yeah, right!) or Latin (some do occasionally sing in this language), there are other ways to practice key words so that young singers can test their vocal wings and choral unity.

Basic Training—Back into the Diction Trenches

In warm-up exercises, work these words using open chords (see Example #1). Allow the teenagers to hear and feel the open, round, tall vowels. If your group is not used to hearing these sounds, they will seem strange at first. If they never hear them modeled correctly by the adult choir or school choir, your challenge is even greater, but not impossible! If you affirm the kids' efforts and their energy, they soon begin to get the picture of what rich choral singing is all about. Keep using the warm-ups in creative ways at the beginning, in the middle, or at the end of your rehearsal. If you can plug what they learn about vowels into the actual anthems, it catches on even faster.

Keep up the good work of listening and improving as you go. Vowel purity and unification are common challenges for any choir, whether you sing in an auditioned graduate choir at Westminster Choir College or in the volunteer junior high ensemble at St. Mark's Episcopal Church.

Help teenagers to know what a good sound is and why. The teacher (director) is responsible for not only listening and teaching innovatively, but also for training teenagers to do the same. Sometimes it is very effective to allow the young singers to listen to other choir sections and describe what they hear.

The Opposite Game

When our children were young, they occasionally declared a day as "opposite day." If one said, "I hate ice cream," it really meant, "I love ice cream." If another said, "I want to go to the doctor for a shot today," it meant that she "wants to go anywhere *but* the doctor's office, and she certainly does NOT want a shot." It is a very confusing game for which haggard adults have little appreciation.

But the opposite game works to make vowel training fun in the youth choir setting. If you experience trouble getting the kids to produce the sound you are modeling, then model the opposite of what you want—even exaggerated a bit—and have them sing it back to you just as corny as they can. They will enjoy this technique. Then, using a continuum line on the blackboard, move your hand back and forth on the line. Ask them to go back and forth between good and bad sounds and everything in between. The best vowel for this exercise is "oo."

Be creative. Be a good listener. Be patient Be fun. Be consistent. Be a cheerleader. Be demanding. Stay with the program, and your kids will eventually produce beautiful vowels every time they open their mouths to sing.

Example #1

VOWEL SOUND	KEY WORDS
eh	led, red, fed (pure *eh* sound)
ih	kid, rid, bid
ah	cot, hot, got
oh	doe, go, low (pure *oh* sound, no *oo* vanishing vowel)
oo	who, cuckoo, boo (pure *oo*, not *eeeooo*)

Example #2

(Place on chalkboard and have choir sing bad sound to desired sound, back and forth.)

Bad Sound	Desired Sound
eeeeeeoo	oooooooo

Creating Beautiful Phrases

Harvard Dictionary of Music defines "phrasing and articulation" as:
"terms used to describe clear and meaningful rendition of music (chiefly of melodies), comparable to an intelligent reading of poetry. The main (though not the only) means of achieving this goal is the separation of the continuous melodic line into smaller units varying in length from a group of measures to single notes."

(Harvard Dictionary of Music, the Harvard University Press, Willi Apel, Editor, 1975, page 668.)

Clear and meaningful phrases are best taught by demonstration. Youth choir directors who take the time to demonstrate and cultivate the appreciation of beautiful phrases will find the teenagers turn on their feelings for the music they sing. They will eventually become comfortable making an emotional investment in the music, and when that happens, half of the phrasing battle is won. We must teach our kids what a beautiful phrase sounds like, how a boring line comes across, and how to make the difference with their own voices. As we teach, the contrast between beautiful and boring must be absolutely obvious. We can demonstrate the difference with our own voice, by the use of recordings, and by challenging the teenagers to "sing it both ways" to see which feels more exciting. As we train kids to sing phrases, keep the following in mind:

1) A slow, simple, sustained melody is a much better training ground for phrase interpretation than highly rhythmic, fast, accented pieces of music. Is it any wonder that choirs who sing strictly contemporary music with a beat usually do not have a clue about beautiful phrasing? They seldom, if ever, get the opportunity to put a phrase into use.

2) The use of dynamics within the phrase is a must. A sustained note that does not crescendo or decrescendo simply sounds weak—without energy. A good place to begin with dynamics is to try your best to adhere to the composer's suggestions. Too often, we never notice the dynamic level. Review the section on "The Dynamics of Good Singing."

3) Stagger-breathing must be included in phrase training. This can be transformed into very fun exercises that demand teamwork.

4) A beautiful phrase will always reflect the deeper pathos of the text.

5) Most teenagers will be clueless of phrase production until we teach it—and it never happens automatically. But, when a strong text is connected to a beautiful phrase, the kids will soak up the meaning like dry sponges.

6) Since phrasing is concerned primarily with melody, reinforce the choir's awareness of phrases by first practicing a simple melody. The more flowing, the better.

Music is art, comparable to an intelligent reading of poetry. Too often, we are afraid to admit to the artistic nature of music. We hesitate to lean into the deep emotions, the pathos of the art, because we fear that we will be seen as weak, strange, or over-emotional. Thus, our ministry becomes more science than sound, more program than ministry, more technique than joy, and more work than fun. Music must be more. Our youth choir ministry depends on it.

Phrases in the Youth Choir Setting

1. A line must be memorized before the group begins to make phrases with it. No printed music when you work on phrases!

2. Use a rubber band in each kid's hands to stretch as the phrase stretches.

3. Use hands to shape the phrase, and work with the kids until they sing the line EXACTLY the way you conduct it.

4. To practice stagger-breathing, have the choir hold final chords for many seconds, keeping the sound solid and balanced during the stagger-breathing.

5. Let the choir sing bad phrases on purpose to point out the contrast between great and bad musicianship.

Great Anthems for Phrase Training

Lord, I Stretch My Hands to You
Althouse, Providence #PP140

Know My Heart
Harlan, GlorySound #A-6836

Blest Are They
Haas, GIA #G-2958

At the Break of Day
Cox, Hinshaw #HMC-1311

Teaching Teens to Sing in Tune

Scenario 1: "God gave us two ears and one mouth!" says Joyce to her youth choir, emphasizing her point by leaning forward and looking intensely into the eyes of her young singers. Then she silently pointed to her two ears and then one mouth to drive home the point. "That means we're supposed to listen twice as much as we sing. However loudly you sing, you have to listen twice as much!" Joyce thinks they get her drift. They continue.

The definition of "tune" in the dictionary is an educational experience for musicians. According to Webster, *tune* 1: quality of sound, manner of utterance, phonetic modulation 2: a succession of pleasing musical tones 3: correct musical pitches (but also) 4: frame of mind, mood, agreement.

Joyce knows that good tuning in a choir cannot happen until the group is listening—to the accompaniment, to each other, to themselves—all at the same time.

Good tuning in any choir begins with awareness: awareness of pitch, of balance, of vowel formation, of how my voice fits (or does not fit) into the whole sound.

Aside from these technical listening skills which we must teach and our kids must learn, there is the entire meaning described in Webster's definition 4: frame of mind, mood, agreement.

It sounds simplistic, but it's true. A group will only sing in tune when they bond emotionally as well as musically. We fight a losing battle if we try to fix their tuning without nurturing their fellowship.

Scenario 2: Bart cringes as his six sopranos splatter a melodic line that hits a glancing blow on a high G. "Gosh, gals," he says with a look of good-natured bewilderment,"that sounded like a cat caught in a fan belt!" Everyone laughs, but they get his point. However, they still don't know how to fix the sound.

The more intense pressure to sing in tune, the less likely in-tune singing will occur—particularly true of volunteer choirs. Too much tension quickly brings the group to a point of diminishing returns in the intonation arena.

So, what is a director to do? Our kids have to be made aware of the need to listen. They must be constantly trained to sing with their ears open as well as their mouths. How do we instill the need for concentration without putting them under self-defeating stress?

One way is through humor. However, we need to be careful that we laugh *with* our choir and not *at* them. If you can get the group to laugh at you, you will be the winner. Kids love funny people.

But humor will only get your foot in the door. From there, we must creatively train for in-tune singing.

Scenario 3: "Let's do it again," groans Gary, his voice weary from working and failing. "Let's run it at measure 17 and try to sing it in tune this time." "Try" is the key word here. Gary's gang has "tried" to overcome this one knotty place in the anthem. No mat-

ter what they do, they can't sing it in tune. It is always flat. Or is it sharp? They've worked so long on it that nobody can tell any more! Gary has tried every trick in the book, and he is now about to decide that those eight measures were predestined from the foundation of the world to be sung out of tune.

Just "running over it again" isn't going to cut it. An eighteen-wheeler can back up and "run over it again," but the damage to the object lying on the street will only be worse instead of better on the second "runover." If we are going to rehearse a line again, the choir must know the specific purpose for doing it again. In as few words as possible, tell them what you heard, what is wrong, and demonstrate specifically how to fix it. Solutions may include vocalizing the passage in various keys, toning down the piano, singing it *a cappella*, and/or isolating parts or even small groups within your four sections. Breaking into section rehearsal for tuning can be effective, as well. Vowel modification, rhythmic accuracy, hearing the right pitches internally, and acquiring a good balance are all essential aspects of tuning.

At some point, it is important to back off. The director needs to be aware that on any given day, every choir will sing out of tune. Call attention to it, work on it, but do not constantly make a big deal out of it. After all this, we must look suspiciously and ask: 1) Is this a good piece of music? and 2) Is it appropriate at this point in our choir's development?

The Crucial Art and Skills of Balance

Working with a youth choir requires a balancing act on numerous levels. To a large degree, our success as directors will be determined by our ability to get a handle on these tiers and maintain equilibrium as we strive for balance in all areas. It can be a tough job, but this is what makes it such fun!

Balance Between Work and Play

Youth choir needs to be fun. In fact, it *must* be fun if the choir is ever to accomplish anything. But the youth choir experience also must be more than fun. We must always strike the mystical balance between work and play, between fun and concentration on the task at hand.

Balance Between Musicianship and a Strong Spiritual Emphasis

These need not be in conflict, but directors sometimes view them at cross-purposes. It all has to do with time. There is so little time in a rehearsal that it is tempting to spend every precious minute killing notes and memorizing music. Sometimes the spiritual emphasis within the music takes a back seat due to tough time constraints within a rehearsal.

Balance Between Styles of Music

The best youth choirs sing a wide range of musical styles. The musical diets of these fine choirs have been carefully planned and prepared by directors to resemble a loving mother's preparation of balanced meals for her family. There is a little of this and a little of that, giving the children's bodies the chance to flourish and their taste buds an opportunity to expand. Variety is not only the spice of life in youth choirs, it is also good health—musically, spiritually, emotionally, and socially.

Balance Between S, A, T, & B

Every veteran youth choir director knows the challenge of balancing an adolescent choral sound. Voices, temperaments, and abilities change so rapidly that achieving a choral balance is a never-ending process. It is very common for youth choirs to be very strong in one section and virtually nonexistent in another. Who hasn't lost a good group of seniors and wondered where the sound would come from next season?

Here are some specific suggestions to balance your choral sound with teenagers. First, move singers around within the sections. Stronger singers should generally be placed within a section, not out front or on an end. Experiment from time to time and discover how and where your singers sound their best. It is fascinating to watch John Yarrington work with a group of teenagers. He often moves guys and girls around like pawns on a chessboard until he achieves the desired balance. He does all this within the rhythm of a rehearsal so that his choir's concentration is not broken and time is never wasted.

Second, move the *sections* around in search of the best balance. Be flexible enough as a director to be effective in any configuration so that your choir sounds its best.

Third, rewrite some voice parts. Make the music work for your unique group. Allow a few of the altos to double the tenors in a difficult place. Develop a group of switch-hitters who can jump down and sing another part, as the balance requires. Some youth choirs have three or four switch-hitters in each section to provide support and reinforcement for other sections who may need help. Switch-hitting may take place for only four measures, perhaps even for just a short weak passage which is crucial to the overall sound.

Fourth, teach your singers to listen to the corporate sound. Recordings are a good way to provide a shock treatment, but keep the goal of good listening and sensitive singing before them.

Finally, it is impossible to provide any kind of real balance for teenagers without pointing them to Christ. When we do that, our sound improves and our ministry deepens.

Communication: A Two-Way Street

It has often been said that a group eventually reflects the personality of its leader! Scary, isn't it? I know this to be true in a number of organizations, particularly within the church.

With an angry pastor, the congregation eventually begins to take on anger to resolve conflict. If a minister of music is aloof and uptight, the adult choir will also become tense, terse, and cold. If the youth minister gossips, the kids will watch the real-life struggles of their friends just like a soap opera.

On the other hand, if a pastor is a caring leader and servant, the church will eventually become more caring and gentle. If the minister of music is warm, friendly, and open, the choir becomes a fun place. If the minister to youth is a trusted friend to the kids and their parents, then trust and compassion will bloom within the group.

There is no greater rub-off from leadership to lay people than in communication. If the leader (youth choir director) is an excellent communicator with his teenagers, the kids themselves will become articulate, sharp, aware, and skilled in communication. Entire semester classes in college and graduate school study the fascinating world of communication. Let's look at a quick overview. From it, perhaps we can all improve our skills and our kids' abilities in the arena of communication. For the purposes of this discussion of choral technique, we will look only at the way a choir communicates with its congregation or audience while leading in worship.

True communication is always a two-way street. The sender obviously sends the message, and the responder answers or sends back messages. Those responses are most often in the form of nonverbal communication. Communication specialists tell us that eighty-five percent of all communication (responding and sending) is done nonverbally, without saying a word! Think about that next time you stand in front of your kids. It's an awesome thought!

Good communication involves sensitizing your teenagers to the needs within your congregation. Teach them to carefully watch the congregation during the service to pick up "cues" from them. If the teenagers memorize their music (which is a primary step in a youth choir's ability to communicate through song), the kids can learn to be very attentive to the director while still staying aware of the nonverbal cues (mainly facial expressions) of the congregation. This takes a great deal of training and concentration for adolescents, but it is not beyond their capability.

Your conducting is a form of nonverbal communication. As you sensitize and train your kids in the finer points of responding to your conducting (facial expressions, size and articulation of beat patterns, etc.), you also teach them to be sensitive to the nonverbal communication of others. Since every rehearsal needs a little play and fun, creative directors can invent a myriad of game-like exercises as part of the rehearsal. Be creative. Be fun. Don't kill precious time, but try different ways to help teens become aware of what goes on around them. This will greatly enhance their ability to lead in worship.

Once you make teenagers aware of the power of nonverbal communication in worship, you must teach them how to use it appropriately. It is not enough to notice someone weeping in the congregation. The teenage singer needs to know what to do with that message. Teach the teenagers to pray right then for that person and ask God to use your choir to touch that hurt, whatever it is. Show the teenagers what a bored person looks like in worship and encourage the kids to sing well enough to hold that person's attention.

Youth choir directors spend the vast majority of rehearsal time improving the choir's sound, and rightly so. The sound always needs improvement. But don't be fooled into thinking that your choral sound is the only communication tool. The way the choir looks is just as important as its sound, and its appearance actually affects the quality of the choral performance. Pensacola director Bob Morrison is a master in this area. Not only does his choir sound great, but they also look wonderful! Whether in T-shirts or in tuxedos and formals, this group always makes a stunning appearance. The group has learned the value of communication in worship. They communicate excellence even before they open their mouths to make a sound. That attitude of awareness and attention causes their sound to be all the better when they do sing.

Want your choir to have the best choral experience possible? Want your kids to be real worship leaders? Want your choir members to give their best to every aspect of their choral presentation? Then creatively communicate it with them, and they will reflect it back!

Learning to Sing in Time, on Time, for Time

Among the large family of musicians, singers are notorious for being the poorest sight readers of all. We are viewed as having less than an average sense of rhythm. Simply put, instrumentalists often say, "Singers can't count." (I hope they don't mean to imply that we don't count within the ranks of musicians. Surely we count for something whether we are good music readers or not!)

The "singers can't count" joke hurts because there is truth to it. When compared to instrumentalists, we are, as a class, quite poor with rhythm. There are many possible reasons for this, but suffice it to say that we tend to learn more by rote than other musicians. Our rehearsal technique over time—or lack of good technique—leads us to depend more on feeling and memory than on actual counting. After all, it's fairly easy to "sing along" passively with anything: in the shower, within a congregation, along with a CD, or even in the ranks of an actual choral group.

But an instrumentalist is, from the beginning, perceived to have a much more exacting task. Let a handbell ringer miss his cue or a second oboe miss her entrance, and the "sin" will likely be exposed at once. When you are an instrumentalist, you have fewer places to hide.

Singing can either be active or passive. Of course, part of our task as youth choir directors is to make singing a thoroughly active, engaging experience for teenagers. We can accomplish this by teaching teens to read rhythms and to sing them correctly and together.

If we are to be anything to our kids, we must become their teachers. If we are teachers, then we must understand that our students will never advance further than the limits of our own ability as leaders. Certainly, a few individual kids will become better musicians, and some may even far surpass our own ability. But as a group, they will never be better than their director. We say this to remind ourselves that directors need to work hard to overcome deficiencies, including those in the rhythm arena. Before we try to teach anything, we must get a good grip on the material ourselves. We must be able to go one step beyond; we must teach these principles to a group of squirming teenagers.

Below are some specific suggestions to help our young singers make up for some lost territory in the rhythm department.

Make Them Read Rhythms

Within each rehearsal, incorporate clapping, speaking, stomping or all of the above, of notated rhythmic patterns. We do this in children's choirs all the time, but we tend to stop as the kids advance in years and singing experience. We always need to make sure our singers become better music readers. This may seem like a waste of time; but in the long haul, it will pay rich dividends.

Allow Them to Experience a Wide Range of Rhythms

Sing a wide range of music stylistically. Every youth choir should have some experience with everything from slow, sustained phrases to Baroque melismas to the patterns prevalent in contemporary Christian music. Why not give them experience with all of it? Why limit our kids' exposure and appreciation by giving them a steady diet of one kind of music? They can and will handle the variety if we know how to teach it to them. When we sing many styles of music, rhythmic accuracy becomes a way of life.

Isolate, Slow Down, Deal with It

Isolate trouble areas and slow down the tempo—even the pace of the rehearsal. If a choir cannot sing a passage slowly, then they can't sing it fast either. Directors often close their eyes and ears and repeatedly pass over the trouble spots, hoping they will go away with time. They never do. This "let's just run over it again" mentality exists for one of three reasons: 1) the director honestly doesn't know how to solve the problem, 2) the music is written so poorly for a choral group that it needs to be rewritten and the director doesn't want to take the time to do it, or 3) the director knows what to do but is too lazy to deal with it.

Challenge Their Best Concentration

Teenagers are generally very good at feeling rhythms. In fact, they can catch on to them so well (by rote) that in our haste to get through the rehearsal, we fail to teach them to read the rhythms. Learning a rhythmic pattern and actually reading it are two different tasks.

Teenagers can best be challenged when you approach them as a team. Games of football, basketball, soccer, and baseball are won or lost because of timing. If you challenge your youth choir to become a high-minded unit, they will want to be together. They will work together until their rhythms sparkle.

Teach. Teach. Teach.

Sight-Reading: How, What, Why, and When?

Teenagers are very quick learners. If properly motivated, youth choir members can absorb a large body of music and commit it to memory in a relatively short period of time. Most kids are so sharp that we can successfully "rote teach" them a concert or musical within the one-rehearsal-a-week time-frame. So, if teenagers can effectively rote-learn, why teach teenagers to read music? What is all the fuss about kids learning to sight-read?

It all depends upon our goal. Do we try to find a quick fix in youth choir, or do we commit ourselves to enrich teenagers' whole lives and prepare them for long, fruitful futures of ministry through singing? If we are in music ministry for the long haul, then there are several practical reasons to teach kids to sight-read music.

Why?

First, we subscribe to the philosophy that the more you know about art the more you will enjoy it. Learning to read music effectively only enhances the student's knowledge and appreciation of choral singing. Good readers make better choir members, regardless of their age.

Second, given the speed with which teenagers memorize, good music reading will allow a choir to broaden its repertoire and stretch its experience to include many styles and techniques. Good sight-reading inevitably stretches repertoire boundaries and expands your choir's musical horizons.

Third, with age, most people, including choir members, experience a slowing down in the remembering process. Memorizing is not as easy as it used to be. Thus, rote-teaching with adults is a *much* slower process than it is with kids. I have worked with adults who "have sung in choir all their lives," but are very poor sight-readers. Now, as adults they struggle to remember the music from week to week. The director spends all her energy fighting notes and other very basic musical fires, never approaching real choral artistry. All because nobody took the time to improve these choir members' reading skills when they were at the optimum learning age.

I have a theory that the sluggish, boring adult choir we hear in the average church is a grown-up youth choir that never learned to read music. Nationally acclaimed conductor Anton Armstrong says, "Basic musical literacy is a major concern of mine as I work with young singers. The very fundamental aspects of reading a score are being overlooked, and we are sending more and more people through our choirs who cannot read. We can do better than that."

How?

We need to clarify something at this point. Earlier we talked about "teaching sight-reading." Strictly speaking, sight-singing is not something which can be taught. It can be learned, but until the singer struggles with it and develops his own system that works for him, decent sight-reading skills will never develop. As teachers, we must point out principles, offer hints, make explanations, and encourage students. Although we cannot teach students to sight-read, we can do things to help them learn.

What?

Expose your teenagers to a wide gamut of music and to a good quantity of selections. Kids will never learn to sight-read as long as they sing the same old threadbare songs. When we teach first and second graders to read, we put as many books and stories in front of them as possible. They aren't just learning to read words, they become involved in new, exciting stories. Their curiosity and fascination with the plot keeps them moving forward, trying to figure out the words they don't know. The same is true when we supply our kids with enough good music to keep them intrigued. They will want to read when they sing enough good music.

When?

Emphasize something "technical" in each rehearsal. Do it in short installments over a long period of time. Call attention to dynamics, pitch, rhythm, and explain it to the group in detail. Take a minute or two, make a creative presentation or explanation, and move on. Over time, you will cover a great deal of territory. Like a savings account with a small weekly deposit, you will eventually begin to see it grow and accrue interest.

Overly-critical?

Encourage the kids to read aggressively, to force their eyes forward in the score, to make some big mistakes. Babe Ruth led the league in strikeouts at the same time he was the home-run king. This was not a coincidence. You must swing the bat—and often miss—before you ever hit the ball. Don't put down kids' mistakes. Applaud their efforts and say, "Great going; now this time let's make it better by . . . " Be careful about telling them they sound bad. Nothing stifles an adventurous spirit more than being chided for trying.

What Else Can I Do?

Some school choirs begin every rehearsal with a sight-reading exercise—a great idea. No correcting, no rehearsing, just hit it and be done with it. If you can't afford the time every week, then at least do it periodically. Hymns provide a good resource here.

Anything Else?

How do you teach your children's choirs to read music? We teach with body movement, charts, flashcards, and clapping rhythmic exercises written on the board, to name a few. Many of these techniques can be translated into games that youth will enjoy—again, in very short installments. I must add a word of caution here. Some of the most frustrated youth choir directors are children's choir directors who try, with methods much too juvenile, to teach fundamentals to teenagers. Be careful. Be creative. Be funny. Be quick. And be consistent. Keep some kind of sight-reading in front of your kids on a regular basis. In time and with your help, your singers will become better readers and thus a finer choral group. Like anything else in youth choir ministry, it takes time. The rewards are worth your efforts.

Teaching Communication Through Conducting

Thirteen-year-old Eric rolls his eyes as he turns away from his mom. He stands for several moments listening to his mother "yell" at him for the third time about making his bed. Actually, his mom barely raises her voice, but the intensity and the insistence in her tone feels like "yelling" to Eric. Now, having stood his ground for a few moments, he does the eye-roll routine, turns his head and walks away, gaining distance from his powerful parental unit.

This very simple situation is loaded with nonverbal cues and communication—the mother's intense eyes, tone of voice, and stalwart presence—the kid's rolling eyes, sagging shoulders, slow swaggering shuffle, and the blank look in the face. These are signals.

Yes, teenagers are very sensitive and *responsive* to the nonverbal aspects of communication. Communication specialists tell us that eighty-five percent of all communication is accomplished nonverbally. But even as conversant as they are in nonverbal language, teenagers need to be taught how to receive and send meaningful nonverbal communication on the *conscious* level.

At its heart, what is choral conducting? Is it simply a bodily means of keeping the music together? Yes, it is a physical expression of the desired music. And yes, it is an outward manifestation of what the conductor wants to hear. But it can represent so much more, particularly to the church musician who works with adolescents.

As a student of both music and communication, I view choral conducting as the highest art form of nonverbal communication. True, the theater also makes good use of nonverbals, but an actor can be fairly successful doing his thing alone, devoid of other's responses.

Not so with conducting. Unlike the stage (with the possible exception of comedy), the conductor's podium requires *constant* adjustment and *continuous,* uninterrupted communication. Without it, the glorious art of choral singing falls flat.

Wise youth choir directors successfully use nonverbal sensitivity innate in teenagers. As communicators of the Gospel and as ministers and friends to teenagers, we have an awesome responsibility to awaken kids to the glorious possibilities of nonverbal language. As choral conductors, we are uniquely positioned to provide this special teaching. We are limited in how and what we teach only by our own lack of understanding and ability to create.

Conducting Technique

In order for teenagers to respond optimally to conducting, the director's technique must be excellent.

Consistency: As directors, we need to show teenagers what we want. As we demonstrate certain passages of music, our conducting must show consistency and dependability. Sometimes, we need to say, "Look here, it's going to look this way in my hands every time!" Consistency infers that we are in control of our conducting and feel at ease with it.

Clarity: By "clear" conducting, I am referring to the quality of technique which allows teenagers to easily follow. Conducting courses, private lessons, and advanced seminars are highly recommended for all of us. It is easy to fall back into bad habits or awkward, unclear technique.

Cleanliness: This refers to conducting without "hitches" or movements that will throw the choral sound off-balance or out of sync. Many times, practicing in front of a mirror or making a video of our conducting uncovers a style cluttered with hitches. The problem with clutter in our conducting is that it inevitably displaces elements of expression which could otherwise occur.

Commitment to Memory: Youth choirs do their best communicating when they sing from memory. A conductor does his best communicating with his choir when he conducts from memory. Need we say more? If conducting is communication, and it certainly is, then a music stand and paper create physical barriers in the communication process between director and choir.

Teaching as You Conduct

It is not enough just to know how to conduct. *The teenagers you direct must also know what you are doing* and even why. When your relationship with your singers is at its best, you can teach them how to respond by including them in a "feedback" process. Let them tell you how you could improve your conducting communication. This is a challenge and is even threatening to some directors, but overcoming the fear could open up whole new doors of communication.

There's Power in Your Hands and Eyes

When we understand the art of conducting and the psychological implications for a group of singers, we see the importance of being the best we can be. When singers feel the security that you pass on to them with your hands and body, you begin to feel power in your conducting. When this happens, the next step—to create a powerful performance—becomes quite natural.

If we commit ourselves to grow as communicators and conductors, the results will be felt in the lives of our individual singers and in our choirs as a whole. Choirs follow their conductors, whether good or not so good.

Conduct yourself well. We are being watched far more than we realize.

Stylistic Considerations

Webster defines *style* as manner or mode of expression in language . . .

> . . . *a way of using words to express thoughts. . . specific or characteristic manner of expression, execution, construction or design . . . distinction, excellence, originality and character in any form of artistic or literary expression . . . the way in which anything is made or done.*

For the thinking youth choir director, style is more than finding and buying what's hot and dropping what's not. But, in a society consumed by consumerism, even youth choir directors fall into a tricky trap. We buy into certain narrow musical styles because we think the musical style itself can make us successful with kids. Strangely enough, style as we usually think of it has little to do with whether or not youth choirs are successful.

A Rather Negative Remark

After several years of traveling the country and hearing hundreds of youth choirs in various settings, I have made a stark conclusion: real style is a phenomenon most youth choirs simply don't possess. Alas, an average youth choir is a styleless, finesse-less conglomeration of crooning, scooping adolescent neophytes yearning to stay with the latest musical trend. In fact, even directors fall into the unhealthy habit of defining "style" as a particular *kind* of music incorporating specific *types* of accompaniment. "What style do your kids sing?" we ask, as if we are asking a friend what kind of car he just bought. It is fascinating to note that youth choirs who sing stylelessly usually have ministry programs which lack innovation in their total approach.

Real style involves much more than singing a particular kind of music. It encompasses putting into practice a comprehensive philosophy of ministry. When you see a youth choir with original, creative style, people immediately recognize it. Style in youth choir ministry involves the whole, big picture of programming, with numerous implications. Even lay persons with little or no training can tell there is something good going on, although they may not know how to describe it technically.

Innovators in Style

I offer the following examples to illustrate the above paragraph. There are plenty more positive role models in the *Youth Cue* community, but perhaps these will be good examples of ministry style.

Bob Morrison's choir has a meticulous appearance and sings an incredibly wide range of music, and they always sing well. Classy style!

Randy Kilpatrick's choir possesses great style in their creative presentation of drama, readings, choral music, and small groups. Randy's style is distinguished by the way he connects all the elements together into a unified worship experience. Powerful, thought-provoking style!

Joyce Blakesley's choir is characterized by high energy and what looks to be total involvement of every singer. They are unique in their very intentional emphasis upon teamwork, unity and community-building. Exciting style!

Mark Edwards' youth choir possesses an extremely clean choral style. Their sound will never be confused with an adult choir sound. It is young, energetic, light, bouncy, flowing, and unusually in tune. Nice vowels. Beautiful lines. His boys sing as consistently in tune as any I have heard. Smooth, no-sweat style!

Allen Harris' youth choir is known for its consistent musical strength and the excellent level of involvement of the vast majority of the teenagers in his church. Allen has an unusually close relationship with his kids, and he teaches private lessons to many of them—family, mentor, favorite-uncle style!

Public school director Kim Clark practices a style of leadership all her own. Her award-winning high school choirs sing such a wide variety of musical "styles" that it makes the listener's head spin. But what's more, they sing the music *in the style* in which it was composed. They sing Rutter, blues, Vivaldi, spirituals, and everything in between, all in the style which they were intended. Her leadership approach is both stern and friendly. She cares deeply for her kids, but she doesn't put up with any foolishness. Dynamite style!

Style in youth choir ministry is born out of innovative excellence. In the examples described above, each director has discovered her/his own strengths and has built ministries and programs based upon these God-given interests and gifts. Given hard work and time, the director will begin to see the choir reflecting her style of leadership.

Nothing will be more effective with your youth choir than original, innovative style. Nothing is less effective than a borrowed set of ideas, repertoire, and a program concept superimposed upon the group by someone who is not in touch with these particular kids.

Which will it be for you and your kids? Innovation is a time-consuming process, but the rewards are eternal. The shortcut approach is more popular, easier, faster, and it doesn't demand any soul-searching. The down side is that it will not stand the test of time.

Youth choir ministry in the 21st Century demands a breed of men and women, both young and along in years, who are willing to make sacrifices for the long haul. It is up to you and me. Your kids and mine need ministry styles only we can provide.

Reading the Whole Score

Take a look at the average choral score and you will discover time signatures, clef signs, tempo markings, articulation notations, notes, accidentals, dynamics, key signatures, crescendos, diminuendos, text and stylistic suggestions.

An Important Musical Lesson

When we conduct professional instrumentalists, they usually do well at holding our feet to the fire when reading the whole score. I wrote this article backstage during Act I of a Saturday night performance of *Madame Butterfly*. The sound monitors are dark just over my head and the video monitor keeps me in touch with the stage. What magnificent music! Over and over again, the musical accuracy of professional opera singers astounds me. The conductor and orchestra members must be sticklers for details as well.

It has to be that way with opera. Opera scores are often so involved and intricate that the musicians depend mightily upon reading their scores (their whole scores) just to keep it all together. Yes, the real music making, the artistry, comes as we move beyond the mere instructions on the page. But, it is only when we accomplish what the composer wanted technically that we can soar beyond and develop our own interpretative impulses. Opera begins with the absolutely correct singing and playing of the score (no small accomplishment, even for the most seasoned musician) and advances from there.

In church music, we too often work just the opposite process. We tend to start with interpretation and move toward accuracy that we teach only by rote. We fail to realize that precision can be read as well as rote-learned. The score gives us valuable information we often overlook, and of course, so do our kids. Certainly, the goals set out for an opera company differ from those of a youth choir, but there is some common turf.

Keep Our Eyes Open on the Big Picture

As we work with teenagers on sight-singing, we must keep them reading the whole score. This is not only good musicianship, but also good theology and sociology. Teenagers can be self-centered and one-dimensional in observing things around them. Reading the whole score reminds them that other important things are happening that they need to understand. Other people have notes, lines and instructions, too. From the beginning, they can be taught to be in touch with others. It not only makes for good sight-reading and quicker learning, but it also enhances group spirit and the power of teamwork.

Motivating a Youth Choir to Read the Whole Score

Teenagers are very competitive, and you can use this to your advantage. Ask questions such as, "Sopranos, what is going on in the accompaniment while you are singing that high F?" or "Basses, what is your dynamic level here?" or "Everyone who has the melody at letter B, raise your hands." On that last one, chances are nobody really knows who has the melody—some don't even know what the melody is—and even the ones with the melody don't realize that they have it. As always, hit it in short installments and be very specific when pointing it out. Soon, the teenagers begin to gain an awareness of parts of the music other than just their own.

Making Sure Conductors Are Reading the Whole Score

As in all things musical, the kids will never go any higher than their leader. In graduate conducting classes, our major professor, Dr. Robert Burton reminded us in a hundred ways to "read the whole score." It is only natural that inexperienced conductors will follow their own voice part with greater interest. If you are a soprano, the temptation will be to follow the soprano line, even when you are conducting. If we want our kids to see the whole picture, we must force our eyes to see more than just our own little world.

Forcing Our Eyes Forward, Down, and Around

All the great sight-readers force their eyes forward in the score. When a great sight-reader plays the keyboard to accompany your choir, she will turn the page two to three measures before the singers even think about it. If our kids are going to be decent sight-singers and good "whole score" readers, they must move their eyes away from the measure they are singing.

In youth choirs, most of us feel fortunate to get kids to focus somewhere near the page of music. Perhaps one reason youth choir members have a hard time focusing their attention is because we do not give them enough to think about. Could they be bored just singing their own little part? Perhaps they need to be coaxed into a deeper involvement in the music that would demand whole score reading. Here again, teenagers are more capable than we often require.

Teaching Community Through the Whole Score

God bless you as you seek to teach teenagers that they are a part of a picture much bigger than themselves, that they sing music that involves much more than one isolated part, that they are a part of a church that is beautifully connected in community. Together, we can make beautiful music.

Singing with the Spirit

Thinking back over my most formative years, two vivid memories had a profound affect on my youth choir philosophy. The scenarios form colorful images of extreme ditches on opposite sides of the road. I constantly work to keep from veering off into one or the other. Both are unhealthy at best and deadly at worst. I seek to hold my youth choirs in a healthy balance between these two opposite positions.

Act One: Heavy on the Smiles

The year was 1968, and I was fourteen years old. Out of San Antonio, a large, big-city youth choir came to sing the hottest new musical for the residents of our tiny South Texas village. It was mid-August, and the group sang in our un-air-conditioned school gym.

It was a hot musical in more ways than one. The choir's production team arrived hours before the performance to set up massive light towers, hook up several sound systems, and plug in numerous electric guitars with wow-wow devices. By 7:00, the temperature in the room had risen into the upper nineties. At showtime, the music was so loud and the choreography so jerky that the entire audience just sat there stunned as the G-forces plastered our faces to our cheekbones. Our hair must have stood straight back in horizontal locks behind our heads. By the end of the first number, the oily-faced kids on stage had already sweated through their polyester uniforms and had stomped down six inches of their bell-bottomed pants legs. Their hair was stuck to their heads and when they raised their arms we could see the wet sweat rings running from under their arm pits past their waists. Tons of movement. Plenty of decibels. More equipment than anyone knew how to operate. Heavy-duty smiles. But alas, not much music and very little beauty.

After what seemed like an endless performance where nothing was sung softer than fortissimo into microphone channels cranked up to "9+," everyone in our little town tried to be gracious. As the natives moved around the gym to thank the performers, we discovered the responses were as rehearsed off stage as they had been under the lights. No matter what any of us said to the choir members, they all had the same canned comeback. "It was just Jesus," they each said through manufactured, industrial-strength smiles.

"It was just Jesus."

"It was just Jesus."

"It was just Jesus."

Oh really?

We heard it ad nauseam until our young pastor, a kind, gentle man with a warm smile, took all he could of the parroted response.

On his way out the door, he said sincerely to a final subgroup, "Thanks for coming. We appreciate all your hard work and your time in bringing your musical to us. You did a good job."

"It was just Jesus."

"It was just Jesus."

With slow inflection resembling that of TV attorney Ben Matlock, my pastor said, "Uh, yeah . . . well . . . uh . . . I think there's a *little* more to it than that. I don't think it was *just* Jesus, because, you see, it wasn't perfect. What you did was good, but I think it was more than just Jesus."

My pastor was not down on youth choirs. He always loved teenagers and was gifted at working with us. His was a noble attempt to get the adolescents to stop and think about what they were saying . . . and singing. When reminded of the event, my pastor friend says, "I should have communicated with the director rather than the kids. The leader was obviously the one who had fed the kids the shallow line."

I don't know if the visiting teenagers caught my pastor's drift, but I did.

There is something more than just singing with the spirit. There are issues to address other than just getting everyone excited.

Act Two: Is That All There Is?

As a twenty-something graduate student, I was called upon to substitute-direct a seasoned youth choir while their director was away for the weekend. The choir's reputation of excellence sat heavily upon my shoulders as I strode into the gorgeous Sanctuary to direct the late afternoon rehearsal. There they were, fifty smug high schoolers wrapped warmly in their lovely traditional environment, rich colors of crimson, gold, and blue bouncing off their mature faces from a sunset cutting through rich stained glass.

Their legendary sound was strong, though somewhat overstated (that's part of what made them a legend). They sight-read better than most youth choirs perform. When I asked for more roundness in a vowel, they immediately produced it. When asked for a spinning pianissimo, they made not only their sound spin, but my head as well. "This is scary," I thought to myself. "They already know everything. What am I going to do for the next fifty minutes?" About that time, a hand went up in the soprano section. "Mr. Edwards, do you want this eight-measure crescendo at letter 'C' to begin on the 'and' of beat three or right on top of beat four?" Making a face like Jim Carrey, I said, "Oh, right on beat '4,' absolutely."

Yeah, right.

And Now for a Little Balance, Please

In all fairness, I admit that I juiced both stories to expose the need for balance. Neither choir was as off-balance as I portrayed them, yet each might be a stronger group if they took a broader look at their ministry through music.

The Apostle Paul, in his first letter to the Corinthians, said it this way, "What is the outcome, then? I shall pray with the spirit and I shall pray with the mind also; I shall sing with the spirit and I shall sing with the mind also." (I Corinthians 14:15, NASV)

Seems simple enough, doesn't it? Yet contemporary denominations still construct dividing lines over the proper balance between heart and head, emotions and reason, subjectivity and objectivity, feeling and substance. We will not seek to solve these differences here.

There is one simple principle we can all espouse which is often overlooked when we work with teenagers. We need to give adolescents the tools to sing their music, as Mark Moeller says, "from the inside out." When Scripture text set to music comes alive in the everyday lives of teenagers, they will naturally want to use both sides of their brains when they sing.

So, which comes first, the spirit or the understanding? Both. Some teenagers will be drawn into the feeling of the music and will be moved along by their emotions to gain more understanding of what it means. Others will be challenged by the texts and technical aspects of a song, and from there they will hide its beauties deep within their hearts (the center of feelings). Still others can process both at once. These teenagers represent some of our most fertile soil to develop a deep ministry with kids.

However our teenagers process the music we set before them, we must provide them with an environment of openness, acceptance, and joy. Together, as we explore the riches of music and ministry, we will find the teenagers begin to sing with the spirit that is growing deep within them. It certainly is something to celebrate!

PART SIX

The Heavenly Rehearsal

CHAPTER 21

Hearing the Holy History

W hen we were pregnant with our first child, Holly intentionally set aside time each day to be in the presence of majestic choral music. She had read recent research which indicated that babies *in utero* could hear and respond to music. A favorite recording (vinyl record) she often played was the flip side of John Rutter's *Gloria*. Amazingly beautiful and, at times ethereal, this seemed to be the perfect music to expose to an unborn child. Whether the baby could hear it or not, we certainly enjoyed having it waft from the living room into the kitchen and nearby den.

Within a few weeks, there was little doubt that the baby heard the music. The first anthem on the recording, "O Clap Your Hands," is brilliantly orchestrated and contains asymmetrical rhythms and a plethora of excitement and energy. The brass soars, the pizzicato strings dance, the voices are angelic and full of fire. Upon hearing the first and second phrases, the baby often kicked and knocked around as if dancing a jig. We joked that the baby understood the words and was clapping his hands.

We repeated the same process with all three of our children with similar results. We are convinced that sounds surrounding the mother and unborn child make it into the baby's ears and brain.

When the children were young, we often played the same choral music around the house. They were just crawlers and toddlers, but whenever they heard Rutter, they would appear with great glee in the living room dancing, clapping, stomping, jumping and running around in circles.

What science had discovered about music and babies was true, at least some of it. As Holly and I experimented with the concept ourselves, we discovered it had great merit. In a nutshell, we discovered that babies begin to process music and respond to it in the womb, months before they hear it in all its clarity, and years before they produce similar sounds and participate fully themselves. They begin to dance to the rhythm almost immediately, but the complete effect will take years.

Is it an accident that all our children are natural musicians, though none particularly serious about it at this stage? Each has an amazingly good ear, and each matched pitch at an early age. Genetics may have something to do with it, but we are convinced that the *in utero* music followed by a steady diet of it has played a bigger part.

The bottom line: we develop recognition, appreciation, and skills in one phase of our lives that we don't fully use or realize until we reach another chapter, a later layer of our development.

Jesus said it another way, "Lay not up for yourselves treasures on earth where moth and rust . . . , but lay up for yourselves." Jesus encouraged us to develop sensitivities and disciplines which, yes, will bless our lives today, but will provide enormous benefits for tomorrow.

This tells youth choir directors that what we do is more about planting seeds than about final harvests. The spiritual and musical seeds we plant in teenagers today will not bear their most beautiful fruit until the kids have grown up, become parents, grandparents, and eventually, angelic singers. We are about the *eternal*, which is why we should be of good cheer.

It is so easy to become discouraged and disenchanted with our youth choirs because we don't see the results we want *now*. Certainly, an effective youth choir tends to produce important effects in the present tense, results which impact teenagers' decisions, morals, and choices. But there is far more to it than that. Whatever happens in the present, we can be certain that the "treasure in heaven" will be eternally more significant than anything we see in the here and now. If the present is disappointing, then be encouraged by dreaming about eternity. You might discover, as many already have, that such heavenly dreams can translate into vision for the present.

Teenagers need to understand that they are not alone in time. For hundreds of years, indeed through the millennia, Christian believers felt the same musical pulses, developed the same textual themes, and poured out their hearts to God in praise, thanksgiving, horrible anguish, and ecstatic joy. Fellow believers sang in impossible situations when they didn't know what else to do. Our brothers and sisters from the Old Testament to the early church and through the Holocaust have all made music to God in times of joy, grief, crisis, and celebration. Ours is a rich and holy history. The treasures laid up are not of the earthly variety, but they are on "eternal deposit" and held for us in the next dimension: eternity with God.

As a child, did you ever draw pictures by connecting pre-numbered dots on the page? In a real sense, our prophetic task is to help kids connect the myriad of seemingly random dots in their lives. It is our task to help them find the big picture and to know how to express praise in light of it.

The advent and proliferation of the internet miracle is perhaps the most amazing technological development of our time. We have a super highway of information which can be accessed from practically anywhere anytime. Old, young, rich, poor, educated, uneducated, white collar, blue collar, ring around the collar—all can access the internet. However, one thing must occur before your computer can link up with the superhighway. You must locate a server and discover how to make proper connections. The server provides a "ramp" for entering the "superhighway," and without it, your computer can never leave the "parking lot."

Youth choir directors are "servers," providing teenage connections into the river of life offered freely by Christ. We make music accessible to kids, motivate them to get on the ramp, and teach them how to link up with the eternal, abundant life Jesus offers freely.

Yes, we and our kids are a part of a holy history.

The miraculous melody is moving forward. Can you hear it?

The holy harmony is happening.

The regal rhythm is gaining new strength.

Feel the beat?

CHAPTER 22

The Youth Choir Rehearsal: Honing In

As youth choir directors plan weekly rehearsals, we must give prime energy and attention to the task. If we discipline ourselves to begin these preparations early in the week, we discover that we not only cover all the needed bases better, but we tend to be more at ease when rehearsal time rolls around.

In Chapter Twenty, specific rehearsal suggestions cover the musical considerations involved in working with teenagers. There are other dimensions of rehearsal preparation, and we will tend to those within the next few pages. I will make specific suggestions for rehearsal preparation as well as one or two more rehearsal techniques not covered in Chapter Twenty.

You might remember from our discussion of communication that directors tend to talk entirely too much at rehearsals. We often complain that the teenagers constantly run their mouths, but if we are not careful, we can do the same. This is why it is so important to provide our teenagers with as much information in written form as possible.

Example 1 *(p. 415)* is a four-month youth choir schedule. Provide this for the teenagers at the first rehearsal of the season and then mail it to the parents early the following week. Not only do *you* need to know your schedule, but you must communicate it with your kids and their parents, as well. Yes, you will need to make adjustments and tweaks in the schedule from time to time, but this is a good place to begin. Example 2 *(p. 416)* is a rehearsal page which provides the order of rehearsal, announcements, an excerpt from the master calendar shown in Example 1, and other pertinent announcements. Example 3 *(p. 417)* is a sample of a weekly letter sent to youth choir members. The director must keep up with the kids and keep them informed through the mail and/or e-mail.

Why all this paperwork? Why all the text and cutting and pasting from one document to another? Teenagers need to see information five to seven times in order for it to sink in. With everything else going on, they need to see the same information in many forms. If we try to communicate this same information with only the spoken word, they may need to hear it a dozen times to get the details straight.

When you arrive at the rehearsal prepared, you can concentrate on connecting with the kids emotionally, spiritually, and musically. The pace of each rehearsal should be brisk, leaving little doubt as to whether this activity is important, organized, and productive. The teenagers will feel good about spending their time in this type of rehearsal.

Discovering a Neglected Treasure— Creative Section Rehearsals

Section rehearsals can transform teenagers' choral singing. Whether your choir is small or large, whether your singers are seasoned or beginners, section rehearsals can enhance your sound and confidence. Sectionals are seldom, if ever, used in most youth choirs, because of a lack of planning and imagination by the director. Like any other aspect of meaningful youth choir ministry, productive section rehearsals don't just happen, and their usefulness is not automatic. Planning successful sectionals requires innovation, forethought, and strategy.

Learning occurs best in stages, in units, in small bites. Music, once thought to be unapproachable for teenagers, is being regularly conquered by the principles of sequential learning. The key is isolation and focusing on a bite-size chunk of material. With persistence and time, the fragments of a piece can be strung together like a musical strand of pearls or a colorful choral quilt. Section rehearsals can help us accomplish this when nothing else can.

What is a section rehearsal? It can be anything you need it to be. There are as many possible configurations and designs for sectionals as there are musical needs in your choir. The possibilities are virtually limitless.

For instance, most of us think of section rehearsals only as it relates to teaching a section its notes, and certainly this can be a great benefit. Some directors attempt to put an anthem together in the large group rehearsal only after each section spends time on their individual notes in section rehearsals. This can be a good idea, particularly in the case of new music which is beyond their current capability.

A few other directors have expanded their sectional rehearsals to include in-depth vocal training. Rehearsals are used to build a concept of sound, training the bass section, for example, to sound like a real bass section.

Later in this chapter, we will seek to outline basic types of creative section rehearsals. But before we expand on these possibilities, every director should consider the following guidelines before launching into sectionals.

First, a section rehearsal must have a definite, clearly-stated purpose. If learning notes is the object, then there must be clear communication as to precisely what notes need to be learned. This seems obvious, but teenagers can become impatient if they feel they are just killing time. The leader must clearly communicate the goal of the sectional, and this goal must be reinforced several times during the rehearsal.

Second, most sectionals need to be relatively brief. Ten to fifteen minutes of good, hard work accomplishes much more than thirty minutes of slow-paced boredom.

Third, try to utilize people other than yourself to lead sectionals. If the director plans sectionals as a part of the regular rehearsal hour, he will obviously need to recruit leadership for the sectionals he does not direct. Personnel is sometimes a problem, especially in smaller churches, but take a good look around. You might be surprised at the talent available which could help you in this area. If the talent cannot be found in the church, look to other parts of the community. In rare situations, one of the teenagers in your choir might possess the musical skill, plus the respect of his peers, to successfully lead a sectional.

Several directors utilize four or more leaders who can come in at fairly short notice to help the director by leading sectionals. Some directors never conduct any sectionals themselves, subscribing to the philosophy that other leaders can bring freshness to the rehearsal. Other directors "make the rounds," taking a different section from week to week.

Finally, make certain you can physically get in and out of sectionals in a short amount of time. Long transit time will rob your rehearsal of precious time and will result in a loss of momentum. Teenagers who move to and from energized sectionals need to be trained to move very quickly. Be certain your locations are reserved, climatized, and ready when your teenagers descend upon the rehearsal sites.

Types of Section Rehearsals

There are no hard and fast rules for sectional configurations, but several general concepts have proven to be very effective with teenagers. Directors can mix and match them into unlimited combinations, specifically designed to target the choir's immediate and most pressing musical need. Certainly, many more possibilities exist, but perhaps these will provide a place to begin.

Four-Part Sectionals

Each section (SATB) meets in a different room with a different director to "pound out notes" or develop a concept of singing, or, hopefully, both.

Semi-Sectionals

Sopranos and altos together, basses and tenors together meet to learn notes or to grow accustomed to singing their parts against.

Master Class Sectionals

One section or combination of sections gathers under the direction of a qualified voice teacher to learn the basics of good singing and how to produce a good sound. A director must plan well in advance in order to secure the services of the clinicians. The director must also make certain that the choir can, at that particular time, afford to spend the allotted time away from their actual literature learning and memorization.

Home Sectionals

Specially scheduled meetings can be held on week nights in teenagers' or leaders' homes to provide a different atmosphere and a sense of fellowship and warmth.

Director Sectionals

The director takes a section aside to impart precisely what he wants from them musically. This is especially useful to inspire weak sections. Time alone with the director says, "You are very important to the choir and to me."

In-Gear Sectionals

This type of rehearsal requires extra space and an extra keyboard or more in the rehearsal room. When a particular section encounters difficulty with a passage, the director can physically pull them out of the choir, gather them around a separate keyboard, and highlight their part while the large rehearsal continues. This technique brings focus to a floundering rehearsal and provides energy and a change of scenery for tired singers.

Circle Sectionals

In a large rehearsal room or even a makeshift space in a large fellowship hall or gym, provide four keyboards and four "pianists" who can accurately play one part. Encircle the keyboards with your sections and rehearse with the director stationed in the center of it all "directing traffic." For best results, let the singers stand. This is a superb way to introduce Baroque music or anthems which contain extensive counterpoint. Circle sectionals provide needed isolation, but they also introduce the ensemble concept. It may be difficult to keep the sectional focused, but a strong, properly prepared director can accomplish it beautifully, with great results. Circle sectionals probably provide the most fun for teenagers.

Progressive Sectionals

This is a combination of section rehearsals designed over a period of time to move a choir closer to a musical goal as they move together physically. For example, a director might introduce new music in home sectionals. A week later, she might reinforce the work with short section rehearsals at the beginning of choir time. The next week, the progression continues as circle sectionals begin. As the singers become more familiar with the difficult music, they come together physically as well as musically. As the circle sectionals progress, move the four circles closer and closer together, inching them from isolation to ensemble. By the time you move your choir physically together, the music should sound pretty good, and you will be ready to memorize and polish. Your choir has progressed systematically from one-dimensional sectionals into a solid choral ensemble.

Two directors reported that this was precisely how they taught their choirs Vivaldi's *Gloria*. Several weeks were spent in each phase of the sectionals. The first "circles" were reportedly musical disasters, yet challenging and fun. In time, the concept produced amazing results for these hard-working directors and their singers.

The sky is the limit in creating and developing productive sectional rehearsals. The director who is serious about imparting musicianship and understanding to his singers can benefit greatly from exploring the possibilities. Sometimes, it is necessary to divide our teenagers in order to multiply our effectiveness as a choir. Happy singing!

CHAPTER 23

Humor with Honor

omedy is big business. What began with stand-up comedians such as Jack Benny, Bob Hope, and Red Skelton has evolved into a huge, full-blown industry. Comedy clubs have sprung up everywhere. The advent of The Comedy Channel on cable television signals that this is more than a few jokes here and there. Comedy is no laughing matter if you have a vested interest in it.

Unfortunately, the proliferation of show biz comedy is, like the growth of many other facets of our society, not entirely healthy. In fact, some of the trends are downright destructive. Now you can say almost *anything* about *anybody*, slamming them, sniping at them, smearing their name over the airways, as long as it is funny. The funnier your one-liner, the harder you can hit the object of your fun. If funny enough, you can say anything and get away with it. The comedy entertainment industry is all about pushing the envelope. Sound familiar?

The worst cases, and funniest, are the late-night talk show hosts. Their job is to make people laugh at whatever cost. They slam everything in sight, but they never take a stand on anything. Their contracts must stipulate that if they ever really *said* anything, they would lose their jobs. Their whole purpose in life seems to be poking holes into other people. How healthy can that be?

I don't want to slam the slammers or suggest that comedians suddenly become aggressive to endorse particular causes. All we ask is that there be a little sensitivity and a modicum of compassion in the laughing place. Is that too much to ask?

The dog-eat-dog world of comedy has an indirect effect on our teenagers and the society at large. Many people have given in to a cynical, callous collection of put-downs in their daily conversations. If you listen carefully, you can quickly detect the sarcasm flung around the room from every corner. Today's kids are infected with this disease, and many of us fall into its symptoms before we realize it.

For our purposes, we intentionally make a distinction between *comedy* and *humor*. Although their technical definitions may be similar, I hope we can see a difference. Comedy is aimed at being funny for the sake of being funny. It is used to get laughs and to gain the amused attention of the audience. Humor, on the other hand, is funny for the sake of some larger cause. Humor is shared more as a group phenomenon and is not so dependent upon one person being hilarious to watch. Humor involves everyone and is enjoyed by everyone. Comedy spotlights the comedian, many times at the expense of someone else. See the difference as it pertains to youth choir ministry? It is a small distinction, but one with merit.

Let's talk specifically about humor with kids. A humorless youth choir director is a boring and tedious leader, no matter how talented, focused, or committed. Sometimes, things happen when everyone just needs to laugh out loud. Those who can't are naturally handicapped in working with kids. Make no mistake about it. Humor is essential for effective youth ministry. Many young teenagers, when asked to describe their beloved directors, will say, "He's really funny." Kids love funny adults.

Humor must also be free of put-down and sarcasm. If made at someone else's expense, its colors have changed to comedy for the sake of bringing attention to the comedian.

This is not to say that all comedy is bad. It is possible to be comedic and hysterically funny without putting anyone down. Sometimes, the choir will need a good laugh and the director may tell a joke, a corny story, or recount an amusing memory from his own adolescence. Kids love to hear funny stories at the *director's* expense. You will sense when this is appropriate, both for them and for you.

The rule for youth choir directors must be: humor aplenty, but with honor. When we develop the skills to express healthy humor, we equip teenagers with another important venue of emotional therapy, the need to enjoy pure laughter. Humor is a laughing matter—for everyone!

CHAPTER 24

Hours and Hours on the Road: Choir Tours

Tour. To members of many youth choirs, this word is greatly revered. Once an effective tour pattern is established within a group, nothing will be able to take its place.

Most directors agree that there are some spiritual awakenings, social graces, emotional developments, and musical advancements which cannot happen anywhere else but on tour. It is that corporate experience of being together away from the grind of normal life which frees teenagers to be themselves. Away from the excessive pressures of their local cultures, they are challenged to focus upon the presence of God in their lives. Tour becomes a microcosm of the greater Christian journey: traveling, changing, learning, ministering, praising, and becoming a community. Many teenagers look forward to the annual experience of tour.

There are as many ways to "do tour" as there are directors and choirs who take them. In this chapter, we will take a look at the major considerations in planning and traveling on a tour. All aboard!

Types of Tours

Choir Tour /Mission Trip

This is the most popular form of tour, because it allows the greatest degree of participation among the teenagers. Generally, the teenagers work in mission projects during the daytime and sing in the evenings.

Whistle-Stop Choir Tour

This type of tour covers much geography as the choir travels during the day and performs concerts in the evenings.

Musical Mission Tours

This is a rapidly growing trend among youth choirs today. Unlike traditional tours with youth choirs singing in churches along the way, a musical mission tour practically avoids singing in churches. Instead, the choir turns its energy to places which seldom hear the blessing of choral music: retirement homes, prisons, children's homes, detention centers, shelters for the homeless, battered women's homes, and disaster shelters. The group performs as many as four concerts in one day. Their nights are usually free for group activities.

Mystery Tours

For the director with a sense of adventure, a mystery tour is great fun. Several directors in the *Youth Cue* network have mastered putting these tours together, although they usually do a mystery tour only every five to six years. On the mystery tour: 1) Nobody knows the tour details except the youth choir director and 2) The youth choir director must prepare incredibly well. Since there is no common knowledge of the trip's details, the director is solely responsible for the details. It is a huge task and usually only attempted by directors who have been in their locations for many years.

International Tours

Normally taken only by older youth choirs, the international trip generally lasts at least ten days and demands a preparation time of at least fifteen months. Directors who take international tours should be seasoned professionals in leading domestic group travel. The director should also commit himself to a familiarization trip to the site prior to taking the group overseas.

Weekend Tours

Normally either overnight or over two nights, the weekend tour is designed to provide the youth choir with a trip experience and concert setting within its hometown region.

Festival Tours

With the advent of *Youth Cue* festivals and others across the country, the festival tour has become very popular with youth choirs, particularly those smaller in size. The group may or may not sing to and from the festival. In some cases, groups from the same region join together on their routes to festivals and combine to provide concerts on the way to the even bigger event.

Tour Preparation

The Director's Preparation

As noted above, the international tour takes a minimum of fifteen months' preparation time to work out the details and to give teenagers enough time to raise money. A domestic tour generally demands nine to twelve months, and a weekend tour within the region can be arranged in three to four months. Festival tours require as much as a year of preparation, since a full slate of festival music must be learned and, in the case of *Youth Cue* festivals, committed to memory before arriving.

The Choir's Preparation

When the director embarks on her tour planning, it becomes evident as to what needs to happen to get the kids ready by the designated tour dates. The dates of a major trip need to be set at least a year in advance to avoid family vacations and other conflicts.

As the director takes a look at tour preparation, the following categories should be considered and addressed:
- Musical
- Spiritual
- Emotional (homesickness, building community, etc.)
- Social (becoming socially adept, courteous, and gracious)
- Physical (preparation for rules about eating right, sleeping)

The Parents' Preparation

As tour directors, we must not only get our own acts together. We also need to communicate these details to the parents and to the youth choir members. Common sense should guide the director to communicate clearly and in due time, well before deadlines and other key dates.

The Congregation's Preparation

The person in the pew needs to be kept apprised of the overarching work of the youth choir. Before major events, it is always advantageous to provide good communication to the members of the congregation, especially to leadership committees and councils. The wise director who communicates well with the congregation often discovers a wealth of prayer support and even financial underwriting for the youth choir project.

Funding the Tour

See Chapter Nineteen entitled, "Floundering with the Funding."

Logistics

Modes of Travel

Although there are no guarantees of safety with any form of transportation, youth choir directors should secure the services of reputable professionals and commercial companies to transport their groups. Those who use church vans or buses should do all they can to ensure safety in travel, leaving nothing to chance. Youth choirs travel on all forms of transportation: vans, buses, airplanes, trains, boats, and even subways. Transportation, above all, needs to be safe. This is very precious cargo.

Lodging

Most of us who sang in college choirs enjoyed staying in host homes while on tour. This was a wonderful tour experience; one night you would find yourself in a very modest dwelling and the next in a mansion. Many great tour memories have taken place in host homes.

Lately, many horrible memories have been made in host homes, as well. Recent e-mails report an alarming number of abuse cases in host home settings. Unfortunately, some of the offenders were the most respected leaders within the host church. In a world of sexual abuse and other uncertainties within the home environment, it is virtually impossible to adequately screen those who volunteer to host our kids in their homes. And, as you might already know, it is normally very difficult to find an adequate number of homes for a choir, particularly with a large group. This translates into a situation where the host director tends to take anyone who volunteers, whether there is any firsthand knowledge of the home situation or not.

As a viable alternative, many directors are going to their church finance committees and explaining the situation. They ask for increased tour funding so the teenagers can be lodged in college dorms, encampments, or even inexpensive but safe hotel properties, as opposed to host homes. This is a wise move.

A note of importance: teenagers, particularly younger guys and gals, need to be trained to be good guests in lodging facilities such as college dorms and hotel rooms. This will not come naturally, and directors should give considerable energy to social behavior training. Lay out strict and nonnegotiable rules in advance. Make sure the terms are accepted by the teenagers long before they arrive on the lodging property. However, once you clear that hurdle, the older teenagers will provide the discipline you need for the younger kids. It is all a matter of creative communication and consistent training.

Should you eliminate the host home concept of touring? Only you can decide that for your teenagers. But before you decide, consider two factors:

1) If you have thirty kids in your choir, it will take fifteen homes to adequately house them each night. If your tour is eight days long, you will need a total of 120 rooms for your tour. If you serve in one location for five years, that's a total of 600 homes for all your tours. That is a lot of homes, and it only takes one to destroy a trip, to injure a teenager for life, to potentially ruin your career. The implications are monstrous for both churches involved: emotionally, programmatically, professionally, and even legally. Is it worth the risk?

2) When you call a church to ask them if your choir can sing a concert in their church, the response tends to be more positive if you say in the same breath, " . . . and we don't need housing." You can almost feel the barriers coming down on the other end of the phone.

A growing number of directors say, "I will put my choir on the floor of a gym or in sleeping bags in an activities center before I risk putting them someplace where I cannot guarantee their safety with some degree of confidence." After twenty-seven years of touring and doing the host home arrangement for many years, I am one of them.

The Tour Booklet

A tour booklet can be the most difficult tool to put together, but it is also one of the most helpful. Simply stated, the tour booklet compiles every possible detail regarding tour. It answers a thousand questions of how, where, why, and when. It is difficult to put together because it forces us to think forward and to solve problems before they appear. Once you address the questions, put it into an organized form so those answers can easily be found. "Tour manual" may be a better term.

The booklet should contain the following elements:
- Requirements for participation
- Expectation for behavior and attitudes on the trip

- Consequences of misbehavior
- What to bring / What not to bring
- Spending money
- Tour procedures
- Tour itinerary . . . day by day, hour by hour

Many other items of interest can be added to the booklet, such as:
- Daily devotionals
- Notes from the church staff
- Games
- List of roommates
- List of choir members and counselors

The director should keep his tour booklet on file from year to year to avoid starting from scratch every year. Much of the information will remain the same and will just need to be reformatted for next year's booklet. Once you establish a booklet format, it is easier to produce the booklet. The first year is the most difficult, but it is a superb investment of your precious time. Advantages of producing a tour booklet are:

1) It answers on paper a thousand questions which you will not have to verbally address with individuals who ask for information. This advantage alone makes the effort worth it.

2) It forces the director to get his act together for tour well in advance. If your plans cannot be put on paper in the form of a booklet, chances are they are not really together at all.

3) Parents love the tour booklet, because it provides a sense of security regarding their teenager's choir involvement. It also provides a check list of items to begin gathering for their teenager's trip.

4) The kids enjoy receiving the booklet a month before departure. They are then able to look through the book and anticipate all the wonderful adventures which await them.

5) The booklet provides a marvelous publicity piece to recruit teenagers into your choir. When produced creatively with colors and pictures, the tour booklet serves as a recruiting brochure.

As you produce the brochure, always print enough for:
- Each choir member to take one on tour.
- Your choir parents to keep one at home.

-   Church staff and tour supporters.
-   Prospective members.

A Calendar of Tour Preparation

Below is a sample planning guide for tour preparation. The plan is designed to provide a full year of planning. As you study the sample, consider the following:

1) The preparation calendar assumes that the actual tour will take place in the month of June. If your tour takes place at another time, simply adjust the months backward or forward to meet your specific need.
2) The plan also assumes that your tour will be domestic. Tours abroad demand at least twenty-five percent more lead time and require parent meetings to be held earlier and more often.
3) This is by no means the final word in tour planning. It is simply an example of how a director might plot out his year to assure that all his bases are covered in a manageable, productive time frame.
4) Developing a customized monthly check list will save the director a great deal of time and stress in the long run. It provides a way of monitoring the planning process, and it affords the director the peace of mind she needs to minister effectively to teenagers throughout the year.
5) Be creative in adapting the schedule to your own situation.

August	- Set up your tour filing system.
	- Set tour dates (do your homework on this).
	- Visualize concept/tour sites.
	- Discuss feasibility with staff.
	- Develop tour budget.
September	- Obtain approval of concept by committees, choir officers.
	- Communicate general concepts to choir.
	- Double check tour dates on church calendar.
	- Set tour locations.
October	- Begin "broad stroke" itinerary.
	- Discover mission potential, make contacts.
	- Discover recreational opportunities in area.
	- Church adopts budget/tour budget approved.

November - Begin booking churches for concerts.
- Book "anchor events" or concerts.
- Book bus(es) and other transportation.
- Begin recruiting tour counselors.
- Select and order all tour music.

December - Push the "hold button" on tour projects until after major Advent events, but hit January running!

January - Thoroughly publicize first rehearsal back as a "biggee."
- First rehearsal back, spell out in writing tour locations, mission, cost, and attendance requirements and other requirements for participation. A detailed rehearsal schedule should be included to spell out time and place of every rehearsal before tour. Take just a few moments in rehearsal to discuss.
- Follow up first rehearsal with letter to parents and enclose in it the schedule of rehearsals, costs, and requirements. Communicate to parents, "We need your help."

February - Hold tour registration day.
- Collect tour deposit (1st payment).
- Clean up cluttered tour files.
- Select/order uniforms if applicable.
- Begin in earnest "The Tour Booklet."
- Confirm all counselors and assign duties.
- Sign up singers for tour interviews.

March - Conduct private interviews with all singers.
- Familiarize yourself with trip to tour site.
- Receive and distribute uniforms.
- Communicate your financial receiving/spending plan to church administrator.

April - Expand regular rehearsal times to provide needed extra time for musical and non-musical preparation.
- Hold a picture day in uniforms.

- Prepay all transportation, amusements, and lodging.
- Keep copies of all correspondence and checks.
- Collect payment # 2 from choir members.
- Send a tentative rooming list to all lodging facilities.
- Obtain all medical releases, permission slips returned from youth choir members' parents.
- Print publicity poster.
- Meet with counselors.
- Plan printed program, design, and take to printer.
- Finish TOUR BOOKLET, to printer.
- Implement tour roll-keeping system, explain to choir.

May
- Distribute TOUR BOOKLET to choir and parents.
- Send out publicity packets to all concert venues.
- Meet with youth choir, parents, director, and counselors.
- Finalize details of home concert and after-tour party.
- Begin scheduled extra rehearsals.
- Send final rooming list to all lodging properties.
- Compose and duplicate formal evaluation form to be completed the last day of tour.
- Call to confirm everything regarding itinerary.
- Collect final payment from choir members.
- Receive programs from the printer.

June
- Hold final meeting with counselors.
- Attend to last-minute details.
- Pack everything you need, beginning a week before tour.

July
- Take a vacation / no youth choir rehearsals.
- Dream and plan following year.
- Order fall music and Christmas music.

CHAPTER 25

Help for Today
and Bright Hope for Tomorrow

A good youth choir contains so many facets that they are difficult, if not impossible, to count. We help teenagers to stay away from at-risk behavior. Certainly the support, spiritual development, and social connections we provide will help teenagers to broaden their worlds and open their eyes and hearts to the need for Christian compassion. The music we teach will enrich their souls and heighten their artistic awareness.

While quite true, there is even more to the picture. For many kids, youth choir ministry will not fully bloom until the teenager departs for college. For some, the full effects may come even later in life, in a moment of stress, crisis, or grief. The spiritual seeds we plant are on deposit for the teenagers-turning-adults throughout time and eternity. They provide incredible help to face today's challenges, sustaining them powerfully through their futures.

The positive effects of youth choir ministry are not limited to the teenagers involved. When we provide leadership, mentoring, direction, counseling, and training to teenagers, something miraculous happens. *We* begin to grow, as well. Yes, directing a youth choir is hard, time-consuming work. But it can also become invigorating, energizing, and life-changing for the director and other involved adults.

We could spend the rest of this book citing examples of directors in their thirties, forties, fifties, and sixties who have found that their youth choir work has brought them a surprise side benefit. They are having fun! Directors who were drained emotionally by every encounter with their kids have discovered that they actually gain more energy than they give. Such is not the case every week without fail, but the overall effect is that of gaining energy for life and ministry. Ironic, isn't it?

Perhaps it isn't as ironic as we would think. In Romans 11:35, Paul challenges us to find a person who has given to God and who is still owed a debt by Him, who has remained unrewarded for his service. "For who has given to

God, and God still owes Him the debt?"

As we commit ourselves to revealing riches and building lives among adolescents, we discover a miracle. Some of the new riches are those revealed inside each of us as directors. Some of the lives being built are our own.

PART SEVEN

FAQ
Frequently Asked Questions

CHAPTER 26

What Is the Best Age Breakdown for a Youth Choir?

O ver the past decade, we have discovered that the vast majority of directors, if they could push a magic button, would choose to divide their
youth choirs into two groups: a high school choir and a middle school
choir. However, many of us find ourselves in church situations which do not
lend themselves to this type of division. Below, you will find ways youth choirs
divide or combine themselves.

Description	Percentage of Informal National Survey
Grades 7-12	45%
Grades 6-12	32%
Grades 6-8 / Grades 9-12	16%
Other types of divisions	7%

There are numerous factors which will help you determine the most effective breakdown for your particular youth choir. Some of the considerations
include the following:

1) How does your church's youth group function?
If your youth group functions best as a 7-12 grade group, it will probably
be an artificial, unnatural division to separate them for the purposes of choir.
On the other hand, if your middle schoolers operate in a totally different
dimension (no wisecracks, please!) from your high schoolers, then combining
the groups may be less effective. For best results, the minister of music and
minister of students should address this issue together.

2) How do your local schools divide the kids?

In some churches, this question is asked first, and the youth division duplicates the schools. Some churches, however, cut across the grain of the public schools and intentionally provide another dividing line which they feel is more helpful to the kids. In some cities, having sixth graders in middle school does not work well, and thus the sixth graders are treated as their own entities on the middle school campus, practically avoiding the seventh and eighth grade schedules, traffic flows, and pressures. Good cases can be built on all sides of the issue regarding elementary, middle, and high school divisions. The bottom line is that the church staff and laity must come to terms with what divisions are best within their own church parishes. Gather information from other places? Yes! Carbon copy your program just because other youth choirs do it that way? No!

3) How many teenagers are in your group?

How many more do you intend to reach? If you presently have six high schoolers and three middle schoolers interested in choir, it may be advantageous to keep them together. If the group consists of sixty high schoolers and thirty middle schoolers, then explore the idea of dividing the group into two choirs. If you have one hundred high schoolers and eighty middle schoolers, then a division would be a good thing.

4) Never say, "I'll never . . . "

This insight comes from personal experience. When I changed jobs in the late eighties and took on my present position, I left a flourishing high school choir of sixty singers. They were a focused and fun group who were motivated to attack musical hell with a water pistol! After directing a number of seven-through-twelve groups for many years, I made the premature statement, "I'll never direct another combined group! The only way to go is a straight middle school and high school breakdown of choirs!" I still agree this is the ideal division. However, I have now directed a seven-through-twelve group for the past twelve years, and it has been great fun. Considering our particular situation and our overall youth ministry, it is a good way to go. With sixty to seventy singers, we feel strong, powerful and significant.

Good arguments can be made for various divisions in youth choir ministry. Discuss it with staff, parents, and the teenagers, pray diligently, be willing to change, adapt if you need to, and be intentional about how your groups are divided . . . or combined!

CHAPTER 27

How Can I Select
Good Repertoire for My Choir?

L ater in the book, we provide an entire section of four hundred annotated anthems. The list is a good place to begin to select your repertoire. The list appears in order of difficulty and the information gives a modicum of information regarding the character of each anthem.

Unfortunately, there is no easy way to find appropriate music for your teenagers. For most of us, selecting literature is one of our most time-consuming, seemingly thankless tasks. Choir directors play a maternal role, much like a caring parent preparing a balanced, healthy and tasty meal for the family. Although it might be easier to microwave fast food or bring in burgers and pizza from down the street, it is not a healthy habit if continued for prolonged amounts of time. All families can benefit from home-cooked meals where everyone gathers around to eat, engage in dialogue, and enjoy one another. A youth choir rehearsal needs to be a home-cooked meal, although you don't need to create everything from scratch.

Obviously, it's not necessary to personally write all the music our kids sing, but we do need to gather all the healthy ingredients (good anthems) and prepare the menu with love, care and competence. As in family meals, variety is the spice of life. A healthy array of styles, colors, textures, and flavors is hallmark of a good youth choir folder.

A growing trend in youth choir music today is this: Teenagers immediately warm to and resonate with scriptural texts set to well-crafted music, texts which contain hope and a promise. For this all too often hopeless generation of kids, the Word of God will transcend time, space, and style. Helping teenagers "record" personal soundtracks of Scripture will eternally bless their souls and enrich every aspect of their futures.

There are no shortcuts to finding a balanced repertoire for your group. Only you, the director, can make that determination based upon everything you know about the adolescents under your direction. A key here is the whole dimension of *appropriateness*. John Rutter's "O Clap Your Hands" is amazingly beautiful and exciting choral music, but it is not advisable to sing it with your middle school choir. Just because a choir boasts a steady diet of "only good literature" doesn't mean it is necessarily appropriate for that particular group's development. Good music sung poorly is not really good music at all.

Likewise, the four hundred anthems listed in this book work well in a youth choir setting. However, you must make the determination as to how and when to introduce these pieces and when to let them go. Some may never be appropriate for your group, but many could prove quite usable at one time or another. You must decide how. You must determine when. You must ascertain where. It is all based on the director's knowledge: knowledge of the choral idiom, familiarity with her particular kids, concern for the congregational culture, and an understanding of decent theology.

The steady diet of fast-food musicals and collections may soothe certain spiritual hunger pains, but too much can cause cancer in the colon of church music. Let the kids sing and enjoy the musical burger and fries—it is all a part of being a kid—but provide them with spiritual vegetables and musical fibre as well. It is essential for good health, spiritual as well as musical.

Any music publisher in the world will be more than happy to send you packets of new releases for your perusal. Most charge a nominal fee for this service, but it is worth the investment. Generally, the broader the base of the *publishers* you use, the better the variety of the musical packet. Be sure you have enough music. We speak of *enough* in two ways:

1) Be certain to have *enough* anthems in your packet. You will all become bored with the same five or six tunes. A good youth choir folder should contain at least a dozen and as many as twenty good anthems. You don't need to sing every note of every piece in each rehearsal, but over the weeks, the kids need to rehearse a wide selection of anthems.

2) Be sure to have *enough* music—an adequate number of copies of each anthem—for each teenager to have his own copy in his own folder. Don't allow yourself the temptation of photocopying. It is against the law with very rare exceptions. It takes advance planning to make certain, not only that you have a good repertoire of music, but that you also have enough copies for each choir member.

Many directors periodically block out an entire day or more simply to review new music. Several colleagues take their portable keyboards and head to a lake house, bags of music in tow. After a day and sometimes an overnighter, the director emerges from the personal retreat with repertoire selected for the next year. A concentrated approach to select music seems to work best for most directors.

Colleagues, the *Youth Cue* network, music conferences, reading sessions (although many reading sessions are one-dimensional and musically monolithic), recordings of other choirs, and this book are all good resources to select appropriate and challenging literature. Remember, the literature they sing is, to a large extent, the spiritual nourishment we provide.

In the second paragraph of this chapter, I said it was "unfortunate" that there is no quick, easy way to select good repertoire for your choir. Actually, it is a blessing that we have to invest ourselves in this task. The exercise of selecting music is not just a challenging, time-consuming chore. It is also a blessing, a privilege, and an honor. As we make the selections that will feed the souls of today's kids, we shape the future and fulfillment of tomorrow's adults, teachers, parents, and mentors. Nothing in our ministry is more important than that.

CHAPTER 28

What Should I Do with My Cambiata Voices?

ambiata, or changing voice, is the "C word" for many youth choir directors. It is amazing how much insecurity, anxiety and downright fear this natural phenomenon strikes into the hearts of even the finest choral directors. Few people claim any real hard-and-fast knowledge of this pubescent "disease" called the changing voice.

We won't solve or even mention all the issues in this chapter. For those who want to know more, the Bibliography lists an excellent reading on the subject. I encourage you to seek it out.

Listed below are some general suggestions for approaching real-life youth choir situations as they pertain to the changing voice. We welcome continued discussion and insights concerning this and other youth choir issues on our web site: www.youthcue.org

1) Read all you can get your hands on regarding the changing voice.

The more you know, the better equipped you are to handle the common and unique situations which develop with our younger boys.

2) Don't take it too seriously.

This seems to fly in the face of the suggestion above, but there need be no conflict at all. Using our acquired base of knowledge on the subject, take it seriously but stop short of obsessing about it. Some directors are so uptight about doing it just right, that they emit tension and cause many guys to recoil.

3) Watch out for a very subtle snare.

If the cambiata situation becomes too much of a concern, we may be close to a dangerous trap. Is it possible that we become more concerned with the cambiata *voice* than with the cambiata *kid*? The voice is only a part of what changes inside this pubescent neophyte. To him—unless he is a serious musician having grown up in a serious boy choir—the voice change is but a symbol of the mighty hormonal earthquake taking place within every fiber of his being. In other words, the boy needs help with more than just his voice. In order to be an effective youth choir director, we must concern ourselves with the whole person, the whole kid, the whole boy.

When we *do* encounter a rare young man in our choir who has benefitted from an intensive boy choir experience, take some extra personal time with him. Find out his concerns, let him express his opinions openly to you, and then help him find the place where he will function the most comfortably. In many cases, this young teenager already has a good idea of where he wants to sing. As long as his choice keeps him engaged and fulfilled, his decision should be affirmed.

4) The emotional/hormonal earthquake referred to above is, for most young guys, an 8.5 on the Richter Scale.

Boys need to be constantly assured that these changes are quite normal. It is natural and quite common that, during this period of time, the singing voice will react in strange, unexpected ways. The shifting sands of their vocal mechanism are a big deal for some boys, but usually nothing compared to the other pressures they face on a daily basis. Nonetheless, if handled improperly by the director, the cambiata scenario can unwind a young musician or want-to-be choir member. Take care, conscientious director, lest you become so scientific and uptight that you take all the fun out of the kid's early youth choir experience.

Encourage boys to take their changing voices in stride. They learn *how* from their director. They need to be led to understand that:
- Voice change is a natural part of growing up, and it should be celebrated rather than dreaded.
- It won't always be this hard to sing. "One day soon, you will be able to sing more than four or five notes!"
- There is more to singing in youth choir than just the sound you personally produce.
- Although the male voice usually experiences its big earthquake sometime between ages thirteen and sixteen, it may happen earlier or later. Even though the big shake-up comes and goes relatively quickly, there

are milder aftershocks in the voice, particularly in baritones and basses. The subtle shift often continues well into adulthood, sometimes as late as into the mid-thirties. Young guys love it when their director's own voice breaks in a rehearsal. The wise conductor will make the most of this fun experience and thus set at ease the cambiatas and recent cambiata graduates.

5) *Let the entire choir in on the basic information regarding the cambiata stage.*

Remind the older guys to mentor those younger, providing war stories of when their voices did strange things. Remind the girls that some of the guys with the squeakiest voices today will eventually have the lowest, fullest, and richest voices. As in all things pertaining to the Christian faith, it is important to impart hope and anticipation for the bright future ahead. "He who began a good work in you will be faithful to complete it" contains beautiful musical implications as well as a profound spiritual promise. The wise director reinforces it at every turn and with every squeak. Do everything possible to build up the boys' confidence and self-esteem, both musical and non-musical.

6) *Remember the girls.*

Although girls' voices don't take a huge plunge, many do become heavier and thicker. This change can be almost as unsettling for some girls as it is for the guys in the group.

7) *Logistical suggestions for placement of the cambiata voice.*
-   Allow "switch-hitting" among the vocal parts. Some guys can sing tenor part of the time, but when the line drops too low, they may need to switch and sing alto for a few phrases. Cambiata voices are not the only ones who might switch hit. Altos are sometimes called upon to sing tenor notes for a few measures to provide support in a section where the tenors are exposed in an upper register passage. Altos may be called upon to double the sopranos during unison melodies designated for the soprano section. Many choirs have regular switch hitters within the guys' sections, baritone types who sing tenor at times and bass at others. When switch-hitting is a way of life in youth choir, everyone learns teamwork, has more fun, and the parts are always covered. An alert director will capitalize on this principle with his cambiata kids.
-   Physically place the cambiata boys in the tenor section bordering on the altos. This makes the switch hitting easier to accomplish.

- Pull the tenors, especially the young ones, out of ranks from time to time for five-minute periods. Have them encircle a keyboard which isolates and reinforces their part within the context of the rehearsal. Isolate them with care and not too frequently. *(See more on section rehearsals in Chapter 22.)*
- As time, opportunity and appropriateness permit, spend individual or small-group time with the cambiatas. The purpose of this special time is partly musical but also to build relationships, trust, and confidence.

8) Keep the kid connected.

If you can get a little music out of a young boy, that's great. However, the most important task during the voice change is to keep the kid engaged, having fun, participating and building relationships within his peer group. We can also provide musical training for this age group which is not necessarily vocal. Not much is going to happen strictly vocally during this time, but much more can occur within broader musical experiences and training. Once the boy emerges from the cambiata earthquake, he will be better positioned to make a real vocal contribution to the group because of his broader musical, social, and spiritual training.

The theme song of the cambiata kid should be, "This too shall pass." Who knows? This may be the most important song they learn under our batons.

CHAPTER 29

Where Should I Place the Sections within My Choir?

This could be the shortest chapter in the book. Put rather succinctly, we must place our sections within our choirs where they will create the best choral sound. Visit twenty college choral rehearsals, and you will likely find eight or ten variations of placement. These configurations are normally developed from years of fine tuning and often experimentation. The most common placement of sections within a youth choir are illustrated below:

S=Soprano   A=Alto   T=Tenor   B=Bass   C=Cambiata

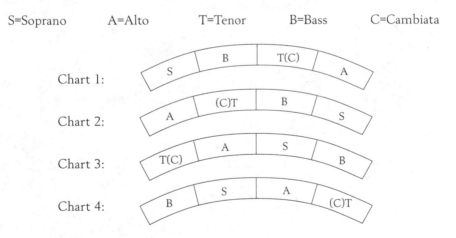

Although choral configurations thirty years ago often utilized a girls-in-front and guys-in-back arrangement, we seldom see this today. It makes little sense, except to provide better sight lines for the back rows.

The placement of individual voices within sections is as crucial as placement of the section. Keep stronger voices away from the front rows. Kids who lead their sections vocally should be placed in the back portion of the section.

Whether they are placed on the sides of the section or within them depends on the quality of the particular voice.

Likewise, uncertain singers should be buried within the section, surrounded as much as possible by strong musicians. Placing three strong vocalists together is usually as ill-advised as placing three uncertain singers in a row.

When it comes to placement of sections and individual voices, nothing can take the place of knowing the teenager, knowing his voice, and being sensitive to the psychological considerations in choral singing. We must know what we want to hear and know how to get there.

Experiment. Nothing in this realm is set in stone. Seating charts can be adjusted. As the teenagers grow musically, socially, and spiritually, let them learn to worship in dynamic settings. Go with the flow, have fun, and don't be afraid to try something new.

CHAPTER 30

What Is the Functional Difference Between a Youth Choir and a Youth Ensemble?

Ensembles are important components within the larger youth choir in many churches and schools. Various types of ensemble groups exist: handbell choirs, small vocal groups, praise teams, instrumental groups, orchestras, drama groups, and liturgical dance troupes. One choir in the *Youth Cue* network even sports a very proficient percussion ensemble.

The most advisable use of a youth ensemble is to make it an outgrowth of the youth choir. Teenagers perform best in ensembles when they are inextricably connected to the larger choral/social group. In other words, regular participation in the youth choir should be mandatory to become and remain a member of a select ensemble. With this foundation firmly established, the two entities—choir and ensembles—become valuable contributors to one another's effectiveness.

Differences Between Youth Choir and the Ensembles

1. Youth choir is normally open to any teenager who wants to participate. There are generally no exterior requirements to participate, no audition. However, there are usually attendance requirements (and should be) to participate in major events such as productions, tours, and other choir trips. Ensemble members are most often selected by audition and are required to meet more stringent attendance requirements. Some even sign covenant agreements.

2. Youth choir claims outreach as its major focus within the youth ministry. Ensembles are designed to build commitment and develop talent. Both are taught the principles of leading in worship by practical education and experience.

3. Youth choir is the backbone of the youth music ministry. Ensembles are subservient to the choir and, for best results, must remain as such.

4. Youth choir draws and connects kids, both musically trained and untrained, with one another in a large community of faith and spiritual growth. Ensembles draw a great deal from the talent and strong artistic motivation of those already involved in choir.

5. Choirs work from a high level of organization. Ensembles, being smaller and usually filled with older, more motivated teenagers, can afford to be lighter on their feet.

6. Good youth choirs and effective ensembles both reveal riches and build teenagers' lives.

CHAPTER 31

When Is the Best Time to Rehearse a Youth Choir?

T his, too, could be a rather short chapter, because the answer seems simple. The obvious solution is to meet at a time when the most teenagers can and will consistently participate. That seems easy enough, doesn't it? And bottom line, this is workable.

However, experience proves that it is seldom this cut-and-dried. Most of us, regardless of our church or school size, juggle a much larger load of responsibilities and schedule of demands. So do the kids. And so do their parents. Youth choir is just one of the things we do, which is all the more reason that we find the best possible time for rehearsal!

School

If you are seeking to build a youth choir from scratch in a school, you must sell the concept to your superiors and colleagues. At first, academic credit may or may not be offered to students for this elective or extracurricular, and you will need to be very creative as to how and when to meet. If, from the beginning, you are fortunate enough to be able to build the choir into the school curriculum and schedule, then count your blessings, rejoice and be glad.

If, on the other hand, your choir begins as a stepchild, you must build a case for its need and viability. This is a stressful endeavor, but many directors belly up to it each year with great effectiveness. Once the choir shows itself to be successful, engaging, and energized (in other words, it feeds energy and good PR back into the school), you then have negotiating power and will be taken more seriously. If you are successful enough and if you find yourself in an open minded environment, you might be able to write your own ticket. However, it is never good to demand such a privilege.

As the school youth choir grows, broadens, and develops, the director must stay alert and aware of the scheduling realities around her. Given your past success, you have obviously discovered a time which works for your kids. Be aware of the deeper reasons why this time works, but don't develop a territorial attitude. There is a thin line between freely going with the administrative flow, while, at the same time, protecting the continuity of your program. Time, experience, and a good deal of prayer will help us to find that mystical balance.

Church

The vast majority of youth choirs in North American churches rehearse regularly in the late hours of Sunday afternoons. Whether the kids attend an evening worship service afterward seems to be irrelevant. The Sunday afternoons have it, although no one is exempt from competing with soccer games, football, baseball, and a plethora of community and school activities. This is a fact of life in the new millennium: there is no way to find a youth choir time which is conflict-free.

According to our informal surveys, approximately fifteen percent meet on Wednesday evenings or another night of the week. Most choirs also augment their rehearsal times with periodic retreats and choir lock-ins. A few choirs meet twice per week, on Wednesdays and Sundays. In these cases, the Wednesday night rehearsals are brief, usually about thirty minutes, and are designed as much to touch base with the kids socially as to reinforce notes and rhythms.

Teenagers can be some of the most traditional people in town. Since so much in life spins and changes around today's youth, kids search for stability anywhere they can find it. If you find a schedule which works for your teenagers and they have a good youth choir experience as a result, the kids themselves will hesitate to make any major adjustment in it. If it is a good thing, they want it left alone. Part of the consistency we can offer teenagers is a secure place where they will be met with love, support, and great music.

On the other hand, if your time slot is simply ineffective to gather the most kids together, it is worth some study, discussion, and reworking. The smart director will do his homework thoroughly, and take into account the solicited ideas and suggestions from fellow staff members, parents, and the kids themselves.

The bottom line: there is no perfect time. Some rehearsal times are better than others, and some are outright disasters. If the teenagers and parents know your heart—that you are willing to rehearse the choir at 11:30 p.m. on Tuesday nights if that is what it takes to build this ministry—it is very likely, that working together, you will develop a good schedule for the vast majority of your group.

Observe the life patterns of your kids and families.

Study the possibilities.

Dream a little.

Do a reality check . . . often.

Plan diligently.

Discuss openly.

Launch with confidence and a willingness to adjust.

Stay focused and follow through with the dream.

Reevaluate periodically with commitment and an open mind.

CHAPTER 32

How Can I Plan Productive, Energetic Rehearsals?

Nothing is more important to this process than the selection of good repertoire (Chapter 27). If the rehearsal is a banquet, then the repertoire is the food we serve. The party will be only as good as the food provided. And when the food is really good, the party will be awesome!

Once you select and package the music into folders for the kids to pick up with one swipe of the hand, the rehearsal commences. In fact, the rehearsal begins the moment the first teenager arrives, perhaps ten minutes before the official start time. Although no musical training has to begin that early, the atmosphere, mood, and ambiance of the experience are already set. The "food" is prepared and waiting. The room is "decorated" and ready to go. The "fire in the fireplace" is lit and roaring. The host (director) is at ease and waiting to welcome the guests and to engage them in conversation.

Once a youth choir rehearsal begins, it needs to fly like an eagle. Part of the homework of the director should include the production of a rehearsal page which provides the order of rehearsal (anthems in order), announcements, and a choir calendar. Very little time lapses between one piece of music and the next. The accompanist is key at this point. He must be ready to give introductions a nanosecond after the last selection ends.

The wise, seasoned director will learn to keep the pace moving at a quick clip, working as many as eight to ten pieces in every rehearsal. On some pieces, you may choose only to isolate an eight measure phrase rather than sing through the whole piece every time. If you work ten anthems in one rehearsal, you may only complete half of them. The others will be rehearsed in isolated passages.

The success of any rehearsal depends on the commitment of the director to communicate with his kids. Please refer to the principles outlined in

Chapter 11 for more information.

Since youth choirs do their best work from memory, memorize *something* at every rehearsal. Again, your memory work du jour may be a sixteen-measure phrase or a page or two of a current anthem. Directors make a big mistake when we make our choirs wait until the last few rehearsals before a performance to begin memorizing. When kids memorize in small increments, beginning with their first rehearsal, they become much stronger musically over the long haul. We repeat— memorize something at every rehearsal. Not only does it provide stability in the future, it also provides the kids with a sense of success and satisfaction every time they get together.

The director's energy level is key in any youth choir rehearsal. The best directors are high-energy, fun, funny, and cheerful. A youth choir director simply cannot afford the luxury of self-consciousness. Nor can we allow ourselves the indulgence of explosive anger, biting retaliation (no matter how subtle), or vented frustration. These will eventually kill the finest community spirit.

Always include prayer time for your kids. Allow them to share concerns and also unspoken requests with a simple raised hand. Teenagers themselves can be called upon to pray, but choir members should regularly receive the ministry of prayer from the director and accompanist. "We have too much music to rehearse to spend time praying," is a common response of many busy directors. Although the stress of getting it all done is certainly understandable for anyone who has a serious choir program, it is nonetheless necessary for kids to be given the opportunity to pray in community. Nothing can replace it. Nothing will bind a group together more than sharing concerns and sharing a prayer ministry together. When it comes to prayer time in rehearsal, we must learn a word from Nike: just do it. In time, you will be very glad you did. Guaranteed.

Creating an Energetic, Productive Rehearsal Environment

1. Thoroughly plan your menu (repertoire). Be sure to have enough selections in the folder to capture your teenagers' imagination. Be sure to include enough copies of the music (without photocopying) for every teenager to have his own copy.

2. Provide a rehearsal sheet for your youth choir rehearsal to include the following:
   - Order of anthems rehearsed
   - Detailed schedule of coming activities and ministry events

- Announcements
- Special instructions
- Any other information you wish

3. Have your rehearsal space set up well in advance so that when the teenagers arrive, you are there for them and ready to engage them in friendly conversation.

4. Begin the rehearsal with a special time designed to focus mentally as well as warm up their voices.

5. Rehearsals must move very quickly from one entree to another—no wasted time. The director must not waste time with idle chatter or repetition.

6. It's okay to momentarily slow the rehearsal pace, but do so intentionally and communicate with the choir what you are doing and why. When the rehearsal kicks in again, it's *a tempo*.

7. Always include a prayer request/prayer time within the rehearsal. There are hundreds of creative ways to do this, and directors should be encouraged to give this area of ministry a great deal of energy and innovation.

CHAPTER 33

How Often Should a Youth Choir Sing for Worship?

I t is possible for a youth choir to sing too much, to be handed too much service responsibility. A heavy schedule of worship leadership or other outside concerts/performances may stress you and your kids. As a result of being overloaded, you will tend to do none of the above to your group's full potential. That scenario becomes frustrating and unfulfilling in a hurry, this lethal combination of being overloaded with responsibility and being unable to feel good about the leadership you provide.

However, the opposite scenario is most often the case in the majority of churches. In most situations, the youth choir does not get to sing enough. As a result, their rehearsals and other preparations lose focus and a sense of mission and urgency. In such cases, it is easy to fall into the routine of mundane rehearsals, always having more time than needed to get ready for the very limited responsibilities which await somewhere down the road. An ironic phenomenon begins to take place. When choirs have *too much* time to prepare, they often come across as unprepared, anemic, and energy-less when they finally do hit the loft.

Somewhere between the breakneck pace of singing too much and the lazy lounging, looking for something to do, lies a mystical balance known as a strong challenge with sanity. Only you, your fellow staff members, and your kids can find the acceptable and optimum range of "performance" for your youth choir.

Much of the answer to the question above lies in how much rehearsal time you have each week. If a youth choir sings every Sunday morning, the group should rehearse at least ninety minutes, either in one rehearsal installment or two.

Most youth choirs that rehearse an hour a week should be able to accomplish the task of singing an anthem from memory once a month. A faster, more advanced group can handle singing twice a month with the same amount of rehearsal time, an hour per week.

Space and schedules permitting, youth and adult choirs are often combined for Sunday morning worship services. There is a wide array of available literature which is appropriate for both age groups and can be used in combined configurations.

Youth choirs are also known for special presentations, Christmas concerts, musicals, Easter dramas, festivals, and other high-energy events. Teenagers are encouraged through these events, because they see that they are a part of an enterprise which is much larger than themselves. They are a part of a large community of believers and worship leaders. Major production events usually happen once or twice a year in most youth choirs.

Mission projects in and around the choir's community provide meaningful outlets for ministry through music. Creative youth choir directors will have their kids sing for everything from homeless shelters to detention centers to homes for battered women to nursing care facilities. Link up with community agencies and other ministries, and the sky is the limit in providing periodic opportunities for kids to share their faith through song. Local mission projects can be planned and completed on a fairly short fuse. Two or three of these a year is the norm.

Major tours lasting seven to fourteen days are common for the majority of youth choirs. Caring directors have discovered over the years that there are some positive results in kids' lives that take place only on a trip away from home. Community-building, discipleship training, change of scenery, and connection with new friends play big roles in providing this fertile environment for spiritual growth.

CHAPTER 34

How Should I Handle an Unsupportive Colleague?

Several other questions must be asked in this situation.

1) Who is this colleague? Pastor, minister to students, minister of education, your accompanist?

2) Is your program already established, or are you building from scratch?

3) Who has the most tenure, you or the person in question?

4) What is the chain of command? Who answers to whom?

5) Are the church members, including the kids, consciously aware of the conflict of interest, or is it still subtle, under the surface?

6) How serious a conflict is it? In other words, there is quite a bit of difference between someone who is indifferent to your program and inconsiderate of your schedule, and the one who actively works against you.

We will address this issue in general terms. Using your responses to Questions 1 through 6 in combination with what follows, perhaps this will provide a place to begin dealing with this very uncomfortable situation.

First and foremost, pray about it without ceasing. And yes, pray for the person you perceive as unsupportive. It is difficult to be angry with someone if you pray for them.

A few observations I hope will help:

1) If the unsupportive person is the pastor and if this person has been in the field longer than you, it is probably time to brush up your resume. If the pastor can't understand your heart and feel your pulse on this issue, then major roadblocks lie ahead.

2) If the unsupportive person is the pastor and he has just come on the field, you have to wonder if he will survive in that place very long. If he is as inconsiderate of others as he is of you, it's likely to be a stormy voyage.

3) If the unsupportive person is the minister of students and he has been there longer than you, this situation probably came up in your interview process. What was your thinking about it at that time? How did you plan to handle it once you arrived?

4) If the unsupportive person is the minister of students who has just come on the scene, and if you have already built a good youth choir program, don't panic. Chances are this person will be history within the next twenty-four months.

5) If the unsupportive person is your accompanist, seek the careful counsel of a colleague of kindred spirit, preferably on your staff. If the pastor is in your court on this issue, this will go a long way in finding a solution. Remember, the youth choir will never go further than its director or its accompanist.

6) If the chemistry between you and fellow staff members continues to deteriorate over time and seems to be going nowhere, you will probably do well to pray that the Lord move you to another place of service, one which would encourage and celebrate your particular gifts. That still doesn't mean you will necessarily go anywhere soon, but it does mean that you are open to a good opportunity. One possibility is that the Lord will move the other person.

7) The win-win situation occurs if everyone can adjust, give a little, become more flexible, and carefully communicate their passions and heartbeats. In this way, you reach a mutual understanding which maximizes the talents, gifts, and ministries of everyone. When this happens, we all win, especially the kids.

CHAPTER 35

How Can I Instill Interest and Vision within My Kids

P ose this to Lou Holst, and he is likely to say something such as, "The vision and passion has to begin in you, the coach (director)." Having fielded this question scores of times in our seminars, I have noticed that most who ask it are *themselves* looking for vision in their ministries. The "redirect" questions I ask often reveal that the questioner has been drafted to start a youth choir but has little personal interest in it. Or, perhaps, the person once had passion for the youth choir ministry but has somehow lost it over the years of cultural change.

Humanly speaking, the director is the key to the whole youth choir equation. Without her passionate spark and sparkle for the choir, very little will ultimately happen. We often try to lay it off on the kids, when actually, the problem lies deep within us. How, then, does a director gain the needed passion to pull off a good youth choir ministry?

From cover to cover, this book is designed to reveal, ignite, and creatively develop whatever passion exists within the youth choir director. Sometimes we have to dig deep to find it. There also is a sense in which *passion finds us.* We refer to this as our calling, something which tracks us down, captures us and fills us with a deep desire to engage in a particular labor of love. This *something* which calls us is actually Some*one*, God Himself.

If after reading this book, hearing the stories, and seeing others' visions for ministry, there is still no real drive or inner fire in your bones to carry out this work, your involvement with youth choir ministry will remain unfulfilling to you *and* to those you direct.

Strictly speaking, some activities in life cannot be *taught:* for instance, preaching, conducting, composition, communication, and ministry. Certainly, we offer classes aimed at *improving* our skills in these areas. We must all refine our skills to be the best we can be. Every one of us needs to learn from the masters, the brilliant professors who have given their lives to the study of our particular disciplines. Without education, we shall always be frustrated in the pursuit of maximum ministry. No one can teach another person to preach a powerful sermon, compose a beautiful anthem, or communicate effectively and creatively.

No, these spiritual skills cannot be taught, but they certainly can be *learned*. What's the difference? When a person is truly passionate about a concept, a subject, a ministry, he will want to learn about it from everyone he encounters, including the bag boy at the grocery store. So eager are we to learn that everyone becomes our teacher. We draw insights from everything that moves. A Chinese proverb promises: *"When the pupil is ready, the teacher appears."*

Vision cannot be *taught,* but it can be *caught.* And it will be caught when 1) Someone models it passionately, and 2) A few people are eager to catch it. This must be the case in the youth choir setting. The fires of passion in youth choir must be built, kindled, stoked, maintained, and steadily fed by the direc-tor. In time, the kids themselves, perhaps just a few at first, begin to "warm up in its glowing." Through the leader's modeling, then through the emerging choir leadership, through the ranks from oldest to youngest, the interest grows and the passion builds.

The key phrase is: *in time*. It does not occur in two weeks, two months or even two years. This kind of energy for ministry often takes several years to generate. Yes, God can provide passionate power and rain divine energy upon us at anytime He sees fit. However, the group must be ready to receive it.

Actually, there is much more insight, vision, passion, and energy within our groups than we are ready to receive. As previously mentioned, part of the dis-appointment expressed in the church is that we have, in many ways, abdicat-ed the power of music which can bless teenagers. We have given it away to MTV and other secular entities. Why? Not because God has not given the vision, but because we have not yet been willing to dig deep enough within ourselves to discover it. We remain fearful of the risk. O, we of little faith!

It takes work. It takes constant prayer. It calls for personal vulnerability. It calls for an element of risk. It demands more than many directors are yet will-ing to give, which is why, in many places, there is still a dearth of youth choir vision.

CHAPTER 36

How Can I Help the Boys to Move Beyond the "Choir Is for Wusses" Syndrome?

Many similarities exist between sports and choral training. At a minimum, directors can easily use sports analogies within the rehearsal context to illustrate musical principles. Directors who seek a more creative and "in-your-face" approach actually take a basketball, football, or baseball into rehearsal and demonstrate how certain principles apply to both disciplines (music and sports). Choir and athletics have the following concepts in common: consistency, stance, body technique, movement, concentration. One director takes a baseball bat into rehearsal at the beginning of every season (not for disciplinary measures!) and demonstrates how the stance of a batter relates to the stance of a singer. Certainly, there are differences, but the focus, discipline, alertness, and consistency are essential to both. Any use of athletic stories or references helps the athletes, both boys and girls, to feel more at home. Don't look now, but many of the non-athletes also enjoy the sports stories, as well.

In addition, anything a director can do athletically outside the rehearsal room will be helpful. Play golf with some of your older guys, coach a girls' basketball team, or a community soccer team.

When building a youth choir from scratch, it is quite common to begin with a large group of girls of all ages and a group of younger guys. Don't let this discourage you. As the younger guys grow up and mature, they will dispel the old adage that "singing is for sissies." Be sure to hang on to those guys as they grow and develop. They will provide a strong draw for the younger boys who look up to them as role models. In fact, when there are big guys in your choir, the pendulum swings the other way. The smaller boys can become actually intimidated by the older set, and you will have to work hard to be sure the older guys connect with and mentor the younger.

When there are a dozen or so tall, good looking guys in your choir—many of whom are first class athletes—the syndrome will disappear. It is unlikely this is going to happen overnight. Chances are, you will have to grow those young men through your program. This means that, today, you may have to work with a group of little guys. Remember, they will grow up quickly, and they will be your leaders before you know it. Invest in them! Don't stop thinking about the future.

An aside: The final nail in the coffin of the "choir is for wusses" syndrome is having your youth choir sing the National Anthem for a major league baseball game. As your group sings its heart out, they stand on the first base line of a huge stadium a few scant feet from the likes of Sammy Sosa, Alex Rodriquez, and Chipper Jones. Plaster those photos all over your choir room and in the youth building and you will never hear the "wuss word" again.

CHAPTER 37

What Should I Do About Cliques in My Choir?

Y ou don't have to hang around youth choir directors very long for the subject to arise.

"What do you do about the cliques within your youth choir?"

"How do you handle it when two or three little exclusive groups develop within your ranks and threaten to ruin the fellowship of the larger choir?"

"How can I break up and get rid of these ever-present cliques that sabotage our growth and kill our group spirit?"

There are no easy, quick-fix answers to these questions. Oh, sure, the director can choose to blindly bog into the situation, confront the offenders (clique members) and tell them that their actions and attitudes are out of line. However, you should not take this approach unless you are ready to lose everything you have worked for in the youth choir. Harsh confrontation will almost always produce diminishing returns. Such a move may further alienate the cliquish teenagers from the rest of the group and put even more distance between them and their director. Ignoring the dilemma will not make it go away.

As we struggle through this ubiquitous reality of youth choir ministry, let's construct some hooks on which to hang our thoughts. First, let's take a look at what cliques really are. Why are they there? What purpose do they serve? What damage do they incur to those involved and to those on the outside looking in. Second, we will take a look at various kinds of cliques. To lump all cliques together into one negative category is premature. Is there such thing as a healthy clique? Finally, we will share some suggestions to evaluate cliques and to find redemptive ways to deal with them.

What Is a Clique?

A clique is a relatively small group of teenagers who seem to develop an informal, club-like mentality. Those on the inside of the circle are privy to many inside jokes, private information, the latest gossip, social and romance news. Their proverbial doors of membership are closed to the group as a whole, with the exception of rare times when a person is drawn in and "blessed" enough to become a member. This opening usually occurs when a sharp new kid joins the group, and the cool clique snatches him before he can assimilate himself as a part of the whole choir.

Clique members are often perceived as going everywhere together and doing everything as a group. This may not actually be the case, but this is how it is perceived by the other kids. Already, we have touched upon an important component of cliques—perception. Clique members need to be perceived as "cool" or "in" or "hot," even if they do not feel that way—*especially* if they do not feel that way! In fact, this is one of the reasons cliques exist in the first place, to give teenagers who feel "out of it" the opportunity to be a part of something bigger and better than themselves. But the rest of the teenagers—the ones who are on the outside—seldom see this reality. They tend to resent the cliquesters and view them as having "made it" socially and emotionally. It is a strong perception, but more often than not, it is the *wrong* perception.

A notable variation of the clique theme is those who huddle around the banner of being different. When you get enough kids on the "outside," they can form their own clique where their central identity is that of a reject. Exhibit A: the "trench coat mafia" at Columbine High School.

Before blasting teenagers for becoming involved in clique cults, let's see where they came from. They are so prevalent in youth culture that common sense suggests that they meet some kind of need or perceived need.

Teenagers tend to band together and hang together in small groups because, however healthy or unhealthy it is, the group meets some of the adolescent's intimacy needs. A certain closeness manifests within the group, and teenagers who are starved for friendship go to great lengths to find it. Once you are "in," acceptance within the clique seems unconditional. This reality is at the root of the increase in gang activity in the United States over the past three decades. An inner city gang is a super-clique, much more developed and requiring a higher degree of loyalty to the cause. Cliques play the same roles within the larger society in which they exist (cliques in the youth group and gang in the inner city). Both can have disastrous effects on the whole, but properly motivated and directed, they can work for the positive.

More times than not, both gangs and cliques function as families, though not necessarily *healthy* families. Cliques usually consist of authority figures, father-types or at least big brothers and big sisters. They attract teens whose home situations are less than happy and where role models are fuzzy or nonexistent. Teenagers who grow up with healthy familial modeling will not feel a great need to find it on the outside, within a gang or in an unhealthy clique.

What is a clique? The bottom line is that it is a futile attempt made by teenagers to reconstruct their failing or already fallen families. Teenagers desperate for healthy relationships and appropriate intimacy appear on our church door steps looking for it. Should we be surprised?

This knowledge tends to cool us down from being so upset with teenagers who form these convenient little networks. On some level they are hurting badly. They need each other and are drawn into relationship with others who are also hurting.

For the perceptive youth choir director, this clue should provide a major hint for the building of a successful youth choir ministry. If a director abolishes and banishes all the cliques in his choir, he would effectively kill the spirit of the entire group. However, understanding the problem doesn't make the practice of cliques universally okay. Cliques still cause major damage to group spirit and choir unity. What is a director to do?

As I understand the disease, cancer is a growth in the body that runs amuck, that gets out of control, that does not focus in the right direction to sustain life. If this is true, then cliques can produce cancer-like effects upon any choir. The damage produced is a respecter of none. What are some of the effects of malignant cliques?

Choir unity suffers. Some kids are perceived as more important than others. Jealously abounds. Fault finding inevitably erupts. Inconsistencies are exposed with great delight. Real leadership is hard to come by. Directors become discouraged and even angry. Lack of teamwork persists. Attendance eases downward. Positive growth is all but shut down because new kids coming in for the first time feel negative energy, mysterious tension, and bad vibes. They won't be back. Generally, the health of the larger group decreases due to a lack of focus, purpose, and clearly articulated vision. Certain kinds of cliques, like more aggressive forms of cancer, will eventually kill.

A surgeon will often opt to watch a patient for a while and run a battery of tests before taking her under the knife for radical surgery. The physician knows that, even if surgery is indicated, he needs to have as much information as possible before cutting with the scalpel.

Sometimes youth choir "patients" suffer more as a result of the director's archaic "cure" than from the clique disease itself. In trying to "take care of this problem once and for all," directors have damaged teens' self-esteem and spiritual growth. Sadly, I confess that I, too, have been guilty of this type of malpractice, particularly in my early years of ministry.

Before trying to combat an infection in a patient, a good physician will determine what kind of bug it is so he will know how to treat it effectively. Certain antibiotics work miraculously on some infections, but they will not touch others. Similarly, a youth choir director needs to know as much as possible about what he is facing. What are the various strains of youth choir cliques, and what are the best indicated treatments for them?

Cliques That Quell

This group is oblivious to its own existence and disruptive nature. They never really set out to become an exclusive group, but they are so clueless of everyone else's feelings that they never even thought of themselves as being a clique. "Who, us?" Their little cult continually brings the spiritual and musical level of the group down a notch or two. Like a low-grade fever, it never really makes you sick. The larger group just lacks excitement, energy, and enthusiasm—everyone wonders why.

Cliques That Contend

This is normally an older group of youth who generally have the good of the choir at heart. They are probably the best leaders, and they give the most vocal input when a new director arrives on the scene. It is the unspoken task of this group to keep the choir together and the director in line. Vocally, they can be more powerful than anyone on the church's finance committee, and they expect results. They want to see things happen, even though the new director is not yet fully trusted. This group functions in overdrive if the previous director left the group at an inopportune time or under less-than-ideal circumstances.

Cliques That Conceal

When on a youth choir tour, this clique makes directors paranoid, angry, and old in a hurry. These teenagers seem bent upon protecting their activities with a code of silence. You can never figure out where you really stand with these illusive guys and gals, and in their presence, you get the distinct impression that you are not trusted. They seldom look you in the eye, and when they do, they just might be lying to your face. Deception, like many other sins, seems easier to pull off in groups, and there is less guilt if you get caught.

Cliques That Coerce

Peer pressure is an old term which we learned to throw around in the late sixties. Even though the phrase has become passé, the fact remains: teenagers feel incredible pressure, both spoken and unspoken, from their own peer group—pressure to belong, to be viewed as okay, to be successful in some sphere, to be viewed as an attractive person of quality and worth. Cliques comprised of strong personality types place intense pressure on those who find themselves on the outside. The leaders within the clique constantly pressure their weaker counterparts to conform, even when there is little hope that the new conformists will ever be granted passage into the clique. This clique has mastered the art of teasing and seducing, never providing real acceptance or satisfaction. This variety is exceedingly petty in its view of life on the outside. Coercion may seem too strong a term, but one must never forget the extreme, excessive power of the peer group in most adolescents' lives. It is not unusual for a teenager to feel totally powerless over the pressure of a peer group.

Cliques That Kill

A clique which realizes its own existence, power, and negative influence on the group, but does not care, has the potential to kill the most successful of youth choirs. Thankfully, cliques that kill are relatively few, but they do exist. One characteristic of killer cliques is that they randomly demonstrate the characteristics of all the other groups cited above. They are complex groupings which quell, contend, conceal, and coerce, many times simultaneously. A clique can kill when:

1) It is mishandled by the director, either through avoidance or improper invasion;

2) When the director's best leadership skills are employed, but the attitudes of those involved are so deplorable that they galvanize in the face of the director's loving care. In this case, it is time to get the parents, choir officers, and perhaps even the church leadership involved. No director should have to handle such a situation alone. But ninety-nine percent of the time, the damage is done to a group because of the first reason: the director mis-

handles the situation and exacerbates the problem. Please, fellow directors, be very careful with cliques. Like the surgeon, mishandling the situation could cause it to spontaneously metastasize into other parts of the body.

Handling Dangerous Cliques

Most teenagers are basically reactors. A few are initiators some of the time, but most live their lives in reaction to events and attitudes. The reason they seek shelter in a clique in the first place is because they are reacting to some kind of dysfunction in their social lives or homes. It is also important to note that cliques are born out of adolescence. To be sure, many adults are cliquish as well, but they react out of their own unresolved adolescence as they take on or continue this immature behavior.

As directors, we must be exceedingly patient with immaturity among teenagers, for it is certainly in great supply in our choirs. At the same time, our ministry to kids involves helping teenagers to move successfully *through* adolescence, to help them grow spiritually and emotionally as well as musically. The key word here is *patience*.

Occasionally, dealing with a negative situation with swiftness and directness is the only effective way to handle it. But most of the time, the wise director will find that improper or disruptive behavior can be better eliminated *indirectly*. In other words, work to provide your choir with such a positive and powerful focus that the immaturity will dissipate in the light of what is truly significant. Remember, street gangs are born out of boredom and lack of purpose. Cliques thrive in the same environment. When Mark Twain wrote, "The idle mind is the devil's workshop," he must have known something about cliques.

As directors, we have the awesome responsibility to keep ministry challenges constantly before our kids. In us, they must see openness to everyone and favoritism toward none. We must model acceptance on every level of our organization. In time, the choir's heart will begin to beat with the director's, provided the director's heart is beating for ministry. Many directors still have not caught a vision for what a youth choir *can become*. We need a fresh image of how revolutionary our work can be in the lives of the teenagers we direct. If we lose sight of that, our youth choir is susceptible to all kinds of unhealthy maladies.

The combination of music and ministry is powerful indeed. We are sitting on a keg of dynamite, for music is perhaps the greatest tool of ministry for teenagers in any millennium. Where do we turn for that renewed image of ministry which we all so desperately need?

Let's look at our ultimate Model in ministry, Jesus Christ. To someone who did not understand Jesus and what He was up to, one might think the carpenter from Nazareth gathered up a gang of renegades. He went to twelve select guys and asked them to follow Him. Then, upon several occasions, He took three of the twelve, Peter, James, and John with Him to special spots of inspiration and ministry. Was Jesus demonstrating the workings of an exclusive clique?

Bad News or Gospel?

We have come to think of cliques as exclusive and *exclusively negative*. Jesus did have a clique around Him, if we choose to refer to it as such, but it was *inclusive* and positive. With very few exceptions, the only ones left out were people who eliminated themselves. With Jesus, it was and still is "whosoever will may come."

Bacteria also have the same reputation as cliques. Most of us think of bacteria as nasty stuff which are always bad, but some good bacteria are, in fact, necessary for a healthy life. The same is true of cholesterol. There is good cholesterol and there is the dangerous stuff which clogs arteries and kills. So it is with cliques—there are good ones and bad ones. Jesus gave us a beautiful picture of a positive clique. Let's learn from the Master.

"Imaging" Your Group

If you can imagine a literal circle of kids, then you can picture the model of most youth choir cliques. It looks something like this: a few guys and girls standing tightly huddled in a circle, arms locked and facing each other, oblivious to others on the outside. Their "membership" is closed. The group is tight, claustrophobic, no air. The leader of the clique stands squarely in the center, dominating the group and demanding its undivided attention.

About Face

Now, imagine a second picture, the one Jesus gives us. It is still a circle, but the members' arms are unlocked, which allows healthy breathing room between each member, and most importantly, the entire group faces the *outside* of the circle, *facing away* from the center of the group.

The leader, still in the center, leans over the shoulder and whispers into the ear of one of the group members. One hand rests on the member's shoulder, and the other hand points in compassion to a person at a distance who needs nurture, attention, and care.

Seeing in All Directions

With unlocked arms, the group uses their hands to reach out to others. The ring leader whispers into the group members' ears, pointing out other teenagers who need a special touch or a word of affirmation. The amazing grace about this group is that, working together, they can see the landscape in all directions. They may need to huddle up from time to time for directions, worship, encouragement, and teaching, but the huddle time represents only a fraction of the time they spend ministering on the outside. The group focuses on others, ministering, reaching out, helping out, praying, and encouraging. Typical cliques are all about "us." Christian cliques are primarily about "them"—open, inviting, and accepting.

Feed My Sheep

"Do you love me?" Jesus asked His disciples. "Then feed my lambs. Take care of my little sheep." "Go ye into all the world and make disciples . . . " Jesus built his group around ministry and serving others. Even the disciples were not free of their own problems and attitudes they had to confront, but as a group, they worked through these challenges and eventually turned the world right side up for Christ.

Cliques? Yes, they can be bad news, but they can also be transformed to model good news. It all depends on the direction we face, and our willingness to be taught a better way. As directors, we have so much to do and so much to seek in prayer. If we use Christ as an example and open up to the Holy Spirit, we can accept the challenge to transform self-seeking cliques into God-seeking corps of ministry. As in so many other areas of youth choir ministry, great responsibility rests upon directors to gently, firmly, and lovingly guide our kids. As we do so, we will build not only our youth choirs, but the very church itself.

Practical Prescriptions to Help Choirs Move Beyond Unhealthy Cliques

1. Try to be extra-friendly and show genuine interest in every member of the choir, not just the winsome, easy-to-talk-to kids. This takes a great deal of emotional and physical energy.

2. Develop a system to jot personal notes to every choir member over time. Some directors discipline themselves to write a certain number of personal notes each week. Include everyone, and use the miracle of e-mail.

3. Using adult leadership, divide the choir into "family groups" of six to seven in each group. As director, you make the group assignments. Break up the tight cliques. Let the groups meet periodically as part of rehearsal to share and pray. The adult "family" leaders can easily be tipped off as to which groups need extra attention.

4. Ask another staff member or qualified outsider to come to your rehearsal or retreat and lead the choir in small-group building. Again, you choose the groups, and be sure to disperse clique members throughout the groups.

5. Bring in a successful coach who is known for building great teams. Have him or her talk to the choir about what it means to work together as a united team.

6. Assign older youth "little brothers and little sisters" among your choir rookies. Make the older kids responsible, in some way, for the well-being of the younger kids.

7. While on tour or any trip, require the choir members to stay with a variety of roommates. For instance, on certain nights, give the counselors or a rooming coordinator sole responsibility of placing kids together. This will need to be announced early and should be seen as a requirement for going on the trip, even before the group departs. This arrangement should not be a surprise to the group once they get on the road.

8. Talk to your group about inclusiveness, but do not dwell upon the fact that cliques exist. Certainly, you can acknowledge cliques, but if you harp on it, you will create a negative focus.

9. Most importantly, pray that God will give every person in your group, including directors, an openness toward everyone who ventures into the group. A friendly, inclusive group is a gift from God to teenagers who so desperately crave to be a part of this experience.

CHAPTER 38

How Can I Help My Choir Become More Chorally Oriented?

This question closely relates to the situation presented in Chapter 8 which we will address further in Chapter 39. I encourage you to read this chapter in tandem with the next.

Read the following scenario. A group of kids is interested in singing nothing but music that "cooks," stuff which reminds them of the commercial fare they hear on radios and on their favorite CDs. The lighter it is and the more trite the text, the more they seem to like it. How is it possible to move this group beyond this stage so they can be exposed to music which will actually bless their lives and give them "strength for today and bright hope for tomorrow"?

Remember that the word "change" is a curse word for many people. If the current status quo seems to meet a particular need, there may be very little interest to change the musical diet. In fact, there may be outright resistance. Here are some principles which I hope will help.

1. Use the word "expand" or "grow" rather than "change."

2. Always begin the growth process where they are. Push the envelope gradually, slowly but surely stretching their awareness and thus their appreciation of other music.

3. You must see, acknowledge, and affirm anything you can regarding the value of their music of choice. They need to see that we aren't just choral sticks-in-the-mud. Try to talk their language. If we subject ourselves to them at this point, they will teach us well, and having *been* the teacher for a while, they will be more open to *receive* instruction from you.

4. Begin introducing new styles very slowly. As you start to work with the kids musically, introduce new styles in short installments. We said, "begin slowly," but that is not to be confused with a slow-paced rehearsal. To the contrary, the stranger a piece is to the group, the quicker it needs to be addressed and then put aside for next week. In this sense, we actually should say, "Introduce new music quickly and then get off of it before they have time to grumble about it." Even if the group becomes down-right hostile to a style of music at first, they will still put up with it for sixty to ninety seconds. When you put it away, you are not giving up on it, rather working at it in short installments. As the kids become more successful with the piece, they will begin to warm up to it. Remember, we generally don't enjoy what we can't sing. On the other hand, if we can sing it, we usually develop some level of appreciation for it.

5. Remember, in order for kids to like a piece of music, they have to feel successful with it. When introducing new styles, it is wise to do so with simple, easy-to-sing, simple-to-be-successful selections from that particular style.

6. Don't be intimidated by the complainers. Most are just blowing off general frustration which may or may not have much to do with the music you select. Keep moving forward, stay positive, remain cheerful.

7. Refrain from preaching to the kids regarding their musical taste or lack of it. At this stage of development, they possess neither the self-understanding nor the theological insights to possess anything other than a subjective opinion on music. Give them time. Let them learn by doing. Be steady, consistent, and always loving. They will come around.

8. *Youth Cue* Festivals can be a good way to motivate teenagers into a broader base of choral literature. If a choir wants to go to a festival and participate in the fun and excitement, they must learn and memorize the festival repertoire. Period. The first year may be difficult, and only a small group may choose to participate. However, we have been amazed at the repeat traffic with the advent of the *Youth Cue* Festivals, and many individual choirs grow larger every succeeding year that they participate. In some cases, choirs have doubled, tripled, even quadrupled their individual numbers as they participate in festivals, festivals where choirs perform superb literature. When this happens, your literature battle has been permanently won.

CHAPTER 39

Let's Talk About That Situation Described in Chapter Eight!

Before reading this chapter, please refresh your memory on the scenario described in Chapter 8. You will also want to review Chapter 38. Here are the facts as we know them:

1) The former youth choir director was Good-Time Charlie with a winsome personality and charisma aplenty. His personality headlights were always on high beam. He was a lot of fun, but he also managed to minister to the kids on some level during their times of need.

2) The teenagers still grieve his departure.

3) The kids want to sing together, but mainly they want to be together as much as possible. They seem fixated upon their past experiences together, always remembering and talking about what happened during those golden summers filled with tours, trips, and mission endeavors. (By the way, this ceaseless reminiscing is also a favorite pastime in most nursing homes!) The time frame for rehearsal is the perfect meeting time for them. They love their "rehearsals."

4) It is a shallow musical experience to say the least. There is no discipline of any kind, and the hour has degenerated into a virtual rap session with Jesus-is-my-boyfriend type music playing in the background. For the most part, it is a sing-along.

5) About half the kids actually sing. The others talk.

6) The kids and some of their parents have made it clear that this time meets a real need for fellowship. Basically, the message is, "Don't mess with it!"

The situation described above is going to take a lot of prayer and the wisdom of Solomon to fix, and yet it is not at all impossible. Before reading on and hearing my suggestions, why not pause a moment and determine how you would approach it. There are certainly more ways than one to deal with the issue, and several approaches could prove quite effective. What do you think?

Practical Pointers

1. Set a meeting time to talk with the teenagers about their perceived choir experience. Include parents or other interested adults if appropriate. Allow approximately an hour. The director should consider talking very little. Listen attentively, try to understand the underlying meanings, and take notes of what is said. Be friendly, not probing. Keep it light. Ask lots of questions.

2. Hold a second similar meeting in which you paraphrase back to them everything you heard them say in the earlier meeting. Ask them to speak specifically about any point which needs clarification. Then ask if they would be willing to expand their time to include some other elements of musical experience as long as their other needs are met. If this is met with general approval, and it probably will be, then proceed to the next paragraph. If the folks are still hard-wired about "doing business as usual" without any changes, then skip to practical Pointer No. 6.

3. In "rehearsal," focus their attention toward their stated needs. Take prayer requests, hold a sharing time, exchange Scripture passages and brief testimonials, and pray together. Even let them sit informally and visit for a while. As a token of goodwill, provide the drinks and maybe even cookies or brownies. Kick it up a notch from what they used to do, even on their terms.

4. For a short time-period, perhaps placed in a different slot each week, introduce choral music to the group. For ten minutes, work at it like a house afire. Be intense, but always kind, winsome, and occasionally comical. Work hard, and provide them with music which will grant them some immediate success and provide good feelings. Do not go beyond the ten minutes time (or whatever amount of time you determine). Even if you are in the middle of a phrase, stop everything, shut it down, and go to the

next activity on the agenda. In time, the group will probably see the need and desire more singing time. Let them drive this development and grant it to them only after they have consistently expressed a desire for it. Up the time to fifteen minutes, then twenty, and eventually you will hold a real rehearsal again.

5. Meanwhile, work on another front—an indirect approach. Find the sharpest teenage choral organization in your area or region. It could be a church youth choir, a school choir, or perhaps even a college group. Bring them in for a full concert on a Sunday evening and let them "blow away" your kids, pulling out all the stops and providing an incredible choral experience. Then, do it again with another group in about six months, and then again if need be.

If you skipped from Pointer No. 2:

6. If the group is still unwilling to budge, offer the opportunity to sing in an ensemble (worship team, choir, however you wish to initiate it) at a different rehearsal time. Begin slowly with a poor time slot. As you grow and develop, the numbers and the demand for a prime rehearsal time will begin to take precedence. Now, go back to Pointers 3 through 5 and begin to implement these plans.

Some youth groups are so hard-wired into what they have "always" done and are now doing that they won't even consider the possibility of change. We thought only old people were set in their ways! However, the vast majority of teenagers will respond positively to 1) a director's genuine interest in the teenagers; 2) meeting their needs and expanding their focus, and 3) the modeling of a sharp group or two which expands their vision and ignites their passion.

Nothing is foolproof, and there are few "sure things" in youth choir work. However, until we give it our best prayerful effort with no results over a fair period of time, there is no good reason to give up on the youth choir dream.

Remember, it takes time, sometimes lots of time. Sometimes, the best thing that can happen to a youth choir is graduation. It happens without fail every May. Three months later, here come the bright eyes and fresh faces of a whole new crop. Little kids? Yes! Babies? Seems like it! Demoniacs? Some appear to be! The future? No doubt about it!

CHAPTER 40

What About Using Adults in Rehearsals?

In the 1990s, youth choir directors began to use adults in their rehearsals with kids, a trend that continues into the new millennium. Adults can serve effectively in this setting, and we will enumerate three basic possibilities. Variations and combinations abound. When it is natural and easy, adults can help our teenagers accomplish many tasks. However, one task should always be left for the teenagers to accomplish alone—singing in worship and in concert. A group of youth choir singers will seldom maximize their own vocal potential as long as they can depend on adult voices at their sides. Always allow the kids the privilege of performing alone—win, lose, or draw.

Although no one is perfect, and certainly everyone has his own share of life's difficulties, don't place unstable adults into the already tricky mix of adolescent hormones. An adult with obvious emotional problems, a hairpin trigger on his temper, or deep unresolved anger, should be kept at a distance. However, there are many wonderful adults who can perform an invaluable service for your kids if invited given the proper entree.

Adults as a Choir Booster Organization

A growing number of directors enlist a large number of adults, primarily parents, to accomplish many housekeeping tasks. While sixty to eighty parents may be choir boosters, they don't all need to be present every time the choir meets. In fact, the rotation may call for the parent to be present only once per semester. It all depends upon the amount of work and the size of the group. Tasks include: roll-taking, preparing snack suppers, selecting and distributing uniforms, coordinating transportation, helping with prayer ministry, organizing choir folders, providing retreat and tour counseling, and helping with social committees and outreach. Other tasks can certainly be

included in this group's responsibilities, but the work must be highly organized and structured. The more people involved and the more tasks which
need to be completed, the more organization they will require.

Adults as Care Group Leaders

Many choirs divide their teenagers into family groups or care groups. The
aim of the care group is to provide individual support for every member of the
choir and to help new teenagers assimilate into the larger group. The care team
leaders may or may not be parents. There are advantages and disadvantages to
parents serving in this capacity, but most of us will, by necessity, involve at
least some parents to head up such groups.

Adults as Section Leaders

Several successful directors regularly involve young adults to rehearse with
their youth choirs. Four to eight young adult singers (one or two in each section) help the section learn and feel their parts sung correctly. When the director calls for section rehearsals, the same adults take the lead to help the kids
feel secure about their parts. When the notes begin to take shape, the adult
section leaders quietly disappear or move off to perform another task. The
young adult singers do not remain in the section long enough for the teenagers
to overly depend on them, but only until they get a better handle on their
notes. This plan of adult section leaders serves an obvious musical purpose,
but it also provides great mentoring possibilities on other levels. When the
choir departs on tour, voilà, you have your tour counselors already in place!

CHAPTER 41

How Should I Handle the Teen Who Does Not Match Pitch?

I n graduate school, we always called them *uncertain singers.* However, most of us found out that it's not the uncertain singer who usually damages the choir's sound. It's that *very certain singer* who sings with gusto who unnerves us. The only problem with this enthusiastic and confident young man is that he is nowhere near the pitch! Confident? Yes, indeed! Enthusiastic? No doubt about it! Singing the right pitch? Not even close!

If you have directed youth choirs for a while, you know firsthand about this phenomenon. An unnamed colleague in another city refers to this phenome-non as *singing-impaired.* Another says *musically challenged.* Still another, *chorally under-gifted.* It is amazing how many grown people, particularly males, are inca-pable of matching a pitch with their voice. Incapable *thus far,* that is. With a lit-tle help, time, attention, and musical therapy, the problem can be improved if not totally solved. Very few folks receive this kind of training, mainly because it is viewed by many in the musical community as a highly contagious disease. Stay away from it, avoid it, pretend it isn't there.

I subscribe to the thinking which says virtually anyone can be taught to match pitch. Undoubtedly, there are some dear folks who have genuine hand-icaps which prevent them from accomplishing this task. However, the vast majority simply have not learned to listen and move their voice's pitch around until it matches the desired note. It's a matter of exposure, training, concen-tration, and practice. Eventually, like riding a bicycle, it becomes second nature, and the singer can then concentrate on the more advanced points of matching pitch, such as fine tuning and unification of vowels.

Two decades ago, I directed a large adult choir in San Antonio, Texas. One evening, a fine older gentleman who could not match pitch joined our choir. Unlike some adult choirs, we did not require auditions for membership. It was a "whosoever will" church choir, and usually, the sheer numbers could hide most individual problems which arose. Our singing-impaired friend was a gem of a human being, and you couldn't help but be attracted to his demeanor and spirit. He always wore spiffy little suits with bow ties. With his impeccable demeanor and sharp appearance, he looked like an English butler. It was a pleasure to have him aboard . . . in every way except musically.

After a couple of rehearsals of noticing "that horrible drone," as one alto put it, one of my dear friends came to me immediately after the rehearsal. A retired voice coach and violin teacher, Rosemary Smith said, "Hey, maestro, would you like for me to take care of that problem for you?"

"I sure would, Rosemary, if you can."

"Oh, I think I can if you are uncomfortable doing it yourself."

"What are you going to do, Rosemary? Please don't be mean to him."

"I'm not a mean person, and I'm certainly not going to be mean to him!" Rosemary said with a bright, toothy smile, peering peacefully at me through her large, fancy spectacles.

"Okay, go for it then. I am interested to see how it turns out."

I never really heard any more about it. Our friend continued to attend rehearsal. Over the next few weeks, "that horrible drone" went away and only surfaced for a nanosecond on very rare occasions.

I took Rosemary aside and asked in disbelief, "How did you pull that one off?" (Now, mind you, I already had a great deal of respect for this fine lady, a wonderful musician and a master teacher. Among her gifts was that of intercessory prayer, particularly as it related to real estate. Don't ask me how, and don't ask me why, but every time Rosemary prayed for someone's house to sell, it sold, even in a severely depressed market. We had already been the recipient of that prayer blessing several years earlier when we needed a larger house for our growing family.)

Rosemary's reply was swift, to the point, and gentle. "Oh, I just told Mr. Music that he was singing a little too strongly and that sometimes he wasn't matching the right pitch. You are going to do just fine, Mr. Music, but I'm going to put two of our best men singers on each side of you and right behind you. You need to listen more and sing softer. You sing exactly what they sing, and back off if you sense that you are not matching the pitch. Singing in choir is a team effort, and I know you are going to do just great. Remember, listen loudly and sing softly, not the other way around. After a while, it will become a lot easier for you."

Mr. Music (not his real name) was delighted and honored to get the attention of such an outstanding leader in the choir. He sang in our choir for a number of years, loving every minute of it. He was often the first to show up for rehearsals and many times one of the last to leave. I can count on one hand the number of times I heard "that horrible drone" after Rosemary talked with Mr. Music. Now you talk about a spiritual gift!

If this technique can work with a man in his sixties, it can certainly work with a kid in her teens. Spending individual time with this teenager also proves very helpful in such situations.

We make a big mistake when we treat the wayward singer as if he has a case of terminal halitosis or chronic B.O. Why do we avoid the issue like the bubonic plague? Certainly, it has something to do with our own sense of insecurity. The Rosemary Smiths of the world — direct, to the point, kind, genuine, gentle, and warm—provide us with worthy models to emulate.

Jesus always saw a person's need as a way to reach her with good news. The woman at the well needed water, and Jesus used the need to introduce a blessing. When we see or hear a glaring problem, it is the perfect invitation to build a relationship and to reveal new riches to a needy teenager. The right pitch is not the only thing for which most kids are hunting!

In closing this chapter, I remind all of us that Jerome Hines, the world-famous 20th century bass baritone, was rejected from boy choir as a child because his teacher diagnosed him as "tone deaf."

I rest my case.

CHAPTER 42

What Should I Know About Ministering to Teens in Crisis?

Ironically, I am writing this chapter just three days following the awful shooting spree at Wedgewood Baptist Church in Fort Worth, Texas. As I construct these lines, the people of Ft. Worth prepare for a community memorial service to be held tomorrow. This chapter is dedicated to the fine folks of Wedgwood and to all who have experienced recent grief, tragedy and senseless loss. The words across my monitor are blurry, viewed through the mist of mounting tears.

Tragedy is too mild a term for anyone who has lost a child, a sibling, or a close friend. Devastation, grief to the third power, sadness to the point of despair, and a living hell: these may come close to describe what really happens when we hit the cold concrete of cruel crisis. It all seems to be made worse, if that's possible, when the cause of grief is so evil, so senseless, so insane that it defies adequate description.

Whatever the situation, whatever the circumstances, whatever the loss, teenagers need help to deal with their pain and fear. Entire volumes have been written on this subject, but for the sake of space we shall limit our insights to just a few paragraphs. It is our hope and prayer that these suggestions will help if and when you are called upon to minister to teenagers in crisis.

Timing is crucial.

As ministers to teenagers, if we intend to help our teenagers, we need to be on the scene as soon as humanly possible. To wait on someone else to act, to delay until the kid calls on us, to hesitate because we are personally uncomfortable in the situation, is to ultimately neglect the teenagers in their greatest time of need. It is not always necessary to stay by the teenagers' sides around the clock (although this is sometimes necessary for real ministry), but if at all possible, we need to assert ourselves and connect as soon as the crisis hits. Timing is extremely important.

Don't worry too much about what to say.

In the shock of crisis moments, teenagers will remember very little of what people say to them. It is not necessary to be a spiritual giant or to come up with theologically profound statements. You don't need to be a professional therapist in order to be a good friend. The key is to be present.

Most of the time, it's best to remain quiet and supportive.

We get into trouble when we try to explain things we don't understand. There are no good answers for most of the tragedies which befall us. God does not promise us answers. He does, however, promise us His presence. As God's servants, we cannot improve upon the provisions of God. We can be God's hands, feet, and ears. Again, just be there.

Gently encourage the teenager to talk about what she is feeling.

The greatest service we can provide in a time of crisis is to be a good, compassionate listener. Allow times of silence, and don't feel uncomfortable by the lack of constant chatter. Silence doesn't mean you are not doing a good job. It only means that the situation is overwhelming.

Refrain from revealing the lessons which should be learned from this situation.

It is neither the time nor the place for preaching. As the teenager looks back upon this event, she will put it into perspective with the rest of her life. God will teach her what He wants her to know—all in due time.

When the Entire Choir Experiences Grief and Loss

A choir member is killed in an automobile accident. The father of one of our girls suddenly dies of a heart attack. A choir member's brother is sentenced to twenty-five years in prison. The youth choir director is diagnosed with terminal cancer.

These situations involve the choir as a whole, and steps should be taken to help the group deal with their corporate grief as well as their individual loss.

Set up a meeting for debriefing.

Following the drug overdose of a choir member, the youth pastor spontaneously opened the church's Activities Center for anyone who wanted to come by and talk. Over fifty showed up at one time, and the youth pastor led the group in a wonderful informal time which allowed the healing to begin. They talked about their deceased friend, read scripture, prayed, and sang a song or two. It was a very healthy and healing time. There was laughter, a lot of crying, and even more hugging.

The facilitator of the group session can begin the sharing process by recounting to the group his favorite memory of the one who has died. When looking back on the person's life, recognize the reality of death and then help the group to celebrate the joy of life . . . eternal life.

If the youth pastor or youth choir director is too close to the situation and does not feel comfortable leading the group sessions, there are professionals who can be called upon to provide this ministry. Another staff member or a Christian therapist would be excellent resources for this type of session.

Hold follow-ups to help the group process their grief.

Within the next several months, the youth pastor described above held several more informal gatherings for his teenagers to process their loss. Through the informal group therapy sessions, the teenagers learned to deal with their own feelings and to face the future with a knowledge that Christ will be there for them in their greatest times of need.

Sometimes, encouraging the teenagers to put their feelings in writing is therapeutic. Others may wish to write a song or draw a sketch. Teenagers react to grief in different ways, and they express themselves and employ various coping mechanisms. Whatever we do, the most important thing is to model Christ's presence for our kids by *being there with them* in the midst of their pain. This is what Christian community is all about.

PART EIGHT

Indexes and Ideas

CHAPTER 43

Knowing Where to Go for Help

The final section of this book deals with resources, places we can go to address our ongoing needs, issues, concerns, and questions. Since youth choir is a very dynamic ministry, and since the youth culture is always in transition, it is very important to stay up to speed with our kids and the ministry they need.

Some things never change: God's Word, a kid's need to be loved, the beauty of well-crafted music, the reality of our constant need of God and His care. All these are universal issues which will remain at the core of our ministries.

Some things never stop changing. Yes, change is here to stay in the arenas of popular music, worship styles, entertainment trends, tastes in clothing, and how societies view religion. One thing we know for sure. Whatever society develops, markets, and sells will change, because change keeps our crazy world economy ticking. The fashion industry is a prime example. If styles stagnate, the whole industry would go broke, because the pendulum swings, variations and revivals of the old keep the fabrics flowing.

Youth choir directors need to know what will not change and what will change. So often, we become clouded on that basic issue, and the ensuing confusion erodes our ministry potential.

Resource Number One in this chapter on "where to go" is the inspired Word of God, the Bible. From cover to cover across the millennia, it is loaded with stories of Christians on a sacred journey. These communities wandered, worshiped, sinned, repented, prayed, and sang. They experienced the miracles as well as the judgment of God, and they were careful to accurately pass down their stories of amazing grace to one generation after another. We are encouraged by their strengths and warned by their weaknesses.

We have filled this book with concepts, ideas, suggestions, and exhortations regarding the ministry of youth choirs. Obviously, I think all these facets are important, or we would not have put them into print. But nothing can substitute for intercessory prayer on behalf of your youth choir ministry. Our personal connection and relationship with God cannot be overemphasized as we seek to meet the massive adolescent needs before us. Yes, learn all you can about the nuts and bolts of youth choir work. By all means, study this book and anything else which proves helpful. But allow this passion to grow from hearts turned and tuned to God.

God often works His encouragement through the presence of other special people in our lives. I can't begin to fully relate the number of close friends who have been Godsends in my life to guide me, nurture me, teach me, and challenge me. People like my Uncles Glen and Travis, my teenage pastor and his wife, Roy and Kay Savage. Folks like Wilma Lowe, Rhealene Stewart, Letha Crouch, Tom and Gwynne Brake, David and Jeaninne Boyles, Eleanor Lester, Clint and Pam Dunagan, Charlie Prewitt. When you begin to count all those who have touched you in the Savior's name, you realize that they have indeed been His helping hands in your life.

When God places passion inside us, He gives us the provisions needed to get the job done. I hope you find more of these provisions in the following sections.

CHAPTER 44

The DOs and DON'Ts of Tour Counseling

Aside from your prayers and commitment to your choir's tour experience, the single most important factor in your tour's success or failure is this—your counselors. The counselors can make your tour or break it. See more about this in the touring chapter.

Below is a general list of warm-ups for your tour counselors. As you meet with them before the trip to prepare them, they might benefit by focusing their minds on the task at hand.

All the best to you, your counselors, and your kids as you travel together. Some wonderful experiences can take place in this venue that simply cannot happen in any other way. Godspeed to all!

Counselor Considerations for Tour

DO . . .

1. Ask someone's name if you don't know it.
2. Be inclusive.
3. Ask teenagers to help you with tour projects.
4. Move around the bus and visit with as many kids as possible.
5. Take care of yourself.
6. Be soft-spoken.
7. Affirm anything positive you see.
8. Help us monitor bus movies.
9. Be on the lookout for the lonely kid.
10. Ask questions about school.
11. Take a genuine interest in each teenager.
12. Take catnaps on the bus when you get a chance.

13. Without being overbearing, help maintain the tour rules.
14. Understand that teenagers are often loud.
15. Discourage name-calling or making fun of people . . . anyone.
16. Encourage kids to mix and mingle with each other.
17. Encourage teenagers to mix with people to whom we minister.
18. Encourage kids.
19. Encourage each other.
20. Encourage the bus drivers.
21. Try to find the fun where possible.
22. Eat right.
23. Make suggestions to individual singers as to how they can improve their personal concert appearance.
24. Encourage choir members to take care of their uniforms.
25. Encourage singers to give energy to personal hygiene.
26. Get away by yourself or in small groups of counselors every now and then. Let your hair down.
27. Put your hair back up.
28. Help teenagers relearn and perfect their music while on the bus.
29. Play games with the kids on the bus.
30. Help us keep the buses clean.
31. Get some exercise.
32. Go to sleep with confidence at the end of the day.
33. Pray for the youth choir and individual kids every day.
34. Be friendly and outgoing.
35. Have a great time.

DON'T . . .

1. Be a know-it-all.
2. Be exclusive.
3. Hesitate to ask kids to help you with tour projects.
4. Stay in one place on the bus all the time.
5. Eat too much.
6. Try to talk over a group of kids. It doesn't work.
7. Make fun of anyone.
8. Let kids watch anything they want on bus TV.
9. Neglect the lonely kid or the one who is homesick.
10. Hesitate to ask questions about school.

11. Only talk about surface issues.
12. Think you have to be on guard twenty-four hours a day.
13. Personally violate the tour rules.
14. Get upset when the buses get a little loud after a performance.
15. Engage in name-calling or fun-poking behavior.
16. Allow kids to stand around in small cliques.
17. Miss an opportunity to help a teenager reach out.
18. Avoid confronting unpleasant situations.
19. Prowl the halls at night.
20. Talk to teenagers about other teenagers (there may be exceptions to this, but really think about it first).
21. Try to sleep in a situation where you are uncomfortable. We will find you a roll-away or make other arrangements.
22. Hesitate to insist (within reason) that teenagers go to sleep.
23. Assume that everyone understands Christian lingo.
24. Forget to help teenagers keep up with their uniforms.
25. Be afraid to jump in and recruit kids to help you with a job.
26. Overreact to typical teenage misunderstandings. Be steady.
27. Be uptight.
28. Feel like you're the police force.
29. Yell at the kids.
30. Hesitate to creatively, lovingly deal with obvious problems.
31. Hesitate to bring anything which concerns you to the director.
32. Drink too many carbonated drinks.
33. Hesitate to make friends with the bus drivers.
34. Spend all your time with the teenagers. Get away somehow, sometime, somewhere.
35. Be surprised if you have as much fun as the kids do.

CHAPTER 45

One Hundred Effective Ideas . . . They Work!

Written Communication. . . Not Only That We Do This for Kids,
But We Also Teach Them to Do the Same in the Future.

1. Send a card to each teenager on her/his birthday. What you send needs to be personal—addressed in your handwriting with a handwritten message from you inside.

2. Have personal stationery prepared, preferably a small note card with an envelope. Keep these handy so you can quickly jot appropriate and timely notes of encouragement, congratulations, condolence, and affirmation to your kids and their parents.

3. Set up and keep current a youth choir web page on the internet. Very likely, there will be a teenager or two in your choir who can take this project and run with it. Remember, keep it current, which means it will need to be updated at least once a week.

4. Initiate and respond to e-mail messages to and from your teenagers and their parents. It's a good way to stay in touch. However, you might refrain from automatically placing kids and parents on your forwarding list. It is often irritating to continually receive messages, forwarded stories, jokes, and graphics which were not requested.

5. Set up an e-mail server list, billboard, or chat room for your youth choir members and/or parents. The same can be done with your choir officers and/or parent support groups.

6. Increase your postage budget to stay in close touch with your teenagers on a weekly basis.

7. Prepare and mail out a weekly update page for your choir members and potential members. Teenagers benefit from receiving something important from you every week.

8. Develop a logo for your group. This can be permanent, or you may decide to change it from year to year. Someone in your group or among your parents may be able to creatively design your logo, or you may do it yourself. A professional design artist can usually do the job for a minimal fee. The logo should appear on everything you send out and everything connected with choir publicity.

9. Order choir stationery, or at least envelopes bearing the choir's current logo—the more colorful, the better.

10. Prices for color laser printers have dropped greatly over the past several years. Budget now for a color printer next year so all your communication to teenagers can be bright, colorful, engaging, and interesting. If you still can't afford your own color printer, explore the possibility of sharing the printer with another office or two in your church.

11. Use what would normally be empty or filler space in your order of worship to spotlight a recent youth choir project. Remember, a picture is worth a thousand words.

12. Consider purchasing a digital camera. These technological wonders are becoming quite popular among youth choir directors. The advantage of the digital cameras is that JPEG files (photos) can be downloaded directly onto your computer's hard drive. This capability provides a world of opportunity for preparing web pages, choir directories, press releases, e-mail attachments, and much, much more.

13. Prepare a choir directory with pictures. This can be accomplished within the first couple of weeks of a new season. On the first day of choir, take candids or action shots of each individual. (If this is done with a digital camera, putting together a pictorial directory is a snap.) If you use choir

registration forms during the first couple of weeks, you can pull together all the needed data for your directory. Do not delay completing the directory and distribute it to every member of the choir. This will help to bring the kids together as a group. Update regularly as new teenagers join.

14. Prepare a bulletin board to display recent group photos of mission projects, rehearsals, and other youth ministry events. Teenagers love to see themselves in photos, especially if placed together with captions. Be sure to include symbols of the event on the bulletin board also: the logo, T shirts, a recently released choir CD, and a publicity poster.

15. Systematically make sure that every teenager in your choir receives a personal note from you. This will take determination and discipline, but nothing is more powerful than a personal written word from the director, particularly if it comes at a crucial time.

16. If you send your kids a weekly choir communique, write them an occasional devotional article that has nothing to do with the choir schedule or upcoming events. Instead, focus upon how you see the Spirit moving in their midst, about a spiritual application of an appropriate movie you just saw or a book you recently read. Show them how choir is a part of a larger landscape of the Christian pilgrimage.

17. Anytime you embark upon a major event, especially a trip, prepare a brochure or booklet containing all the pertinent information. Provide this publicity piece far enough in advance to help the teenagers and their parents plan and prepare for the event. More about the tour booklet is discussed in Chapter 24 dealing with choir tours.

18. Keep a journal of your experiences and impressions regarding your youth choir ministry, particularly while on tour. You will find your entries very interesting when you look back over them one, two, or five years later. A journal is encouraging in many ways.

19. Sometime each May, send your graduating seniors a classy personal letter on official church letterhead. This gift should be of framing quality, elegant and free of imperfections. This communique could be a lengthy letter which eloquently enumerates the qualities you have come to appre-

ciate in this teenager. Be as affirming as possible, and stay away from anything negative or preachy. Challenge yourself to make this a collector's item for the kids you are sending forth.

20. Keep a blackboard handy in each rehearsal and use it creatively. This innovative use of the board need not be complicated. Scribble out key words, key phrases in teaching concepts, and images which will remind the teenagers of what they are learning. Sometimes, the worse you draw, the better it is, because the teenagers will get such a bang out of your attempts to be artistic.

21. While midway through tour, distribute to the kids surprise letters from home. This is a ministry in itself, and it takes careful preparation ahead of time. Inform the parents of what you are doing. Instruct them carefully to:
    - Not tell their kids about the letters they are writing, the element of surprise is key,
    - Deliver them to your office sealed in an envelope with the teenager's name on the outside,
    - Deliver letters to your office by a deadline of at least two weeks before tour (this will allow you to "get on" parents who lag behind in writing their letters.) Come down heavy if you must: "Everyone else is getting a letter from home on tour, and I don't want your child to feel the pain of being left out."
    - Make letters COMPLETELY uplifting and PURELY positive, no "I hope you learned your lesson when ...," yes, say it in words: "I love you."
    - Tell your teenager how proud you are of him.

    Be sure to bring plenty of Klennex for this exercise, you will need it. To add an extra-special touch, provide the teenagers with paper, envelopes, and stamps to respond back to their parents. However, this response will need to happen quickly. They need to be mailed as soon as possible, because you don't want the kids to arrive home before the letters do. When you do arrive home, you will be amazed at the spirit of the reunion following the exchange of loving letters.

22. Rather than taking roll in rehearsal, have your teenagers sign in when they arrive. Include a column for them to enter the time they arrived. Place a digital clock next to the sign in sheet so they will be totally aware of when

they arrive. They will also need to sign out if they are leaving early. Attendance records are taken from the sign-in lists. The advantages to this system are numerous. 1) The system makes each person responsible for herself. 2) Each person will see what time he came in and what time he left. 3) Signing in teaches the teenager that he must account for himself while in choir. When the group leaves on tour, a similar system will be employed for taking roll before the buses roll each day. 4) This is an honor system in which we trust you to be honest. As one director has said it, "If you are going to lie about your church attendance, I'm not sure you will enjoy being here anyway."

23. In response to special needs (bereavement, congratulations, farewells, or the extended absence of a choir member) have the group prepare a gigantic greeting card, signed by everyone. With today's computer technology and Kinko's in every city, these creative projects are a lot of fun for the choir and prove to be quite meaningful to the recipients. If possible, include a big color photo of the group. As space allows, the group can write messages. For grief situations, be certain to sensitize the teenagers and give them guidance.

24. Encourage your teenagers to write devotional pieces for the choir. These writings can be included on the flip side of rehearsal notes, in the weekly choir mail out, displayed on the bulletin board, or used in other creative ways. Directors are often surprised to discover how much writing talent exists within the group. When a person enjoys writing, the need to communicate in this form will not likely be satisfied in any other way. Encourage your writers to write, and be sure you give them input as to appropriateness and sensitivity.

25. On the last night of tour, provide one white king-size pillowcase for each graduating senior. Have on hand colorful Sharpie markers and encourage each younger singer to sign the pillowcases, writing personal messages and scripture references. (For best results, stretch out the pillowcase on a hard floor or table, and place cardboard or plastic inside to keep the markers from bleeding through to the other side.) With the beginning of college, the new freshmen will discover this touch to be a meaningful remembrance of home. And yes, the guys like them as much as the girls.

Verbal Communication . . .   Modeling a Creative, Compassionate,
and Colorful Style

26. Occasionally tell your choir members a funny or embarrassing story about yourself as a teenager.

27. Make a point of personally greeting every teenager when you see them. Don't wait for them to initiate it.

28. As Andrew Carnegie wrote in *How to Win Friends and Influence People*, speak in terms of the other person's needs. We must step outside our comfort zones to communicate about the areas of interest for the *teenager*. Get the athlete talking about his sport, the actress talking about her play, the debater talking about the upcoming tournament.

29. Spend enough time with teenagers to understand their vernacular. It's not necessary to *use* their language, but it is always helpful to know it.

30. We can put teenage vernacular to good use in our own conversations, as long as it is appropriate and non-offensive.

31. Take a moment of time and energy to seek out an individual teenager to strike up a conversation. This will take discipline, because the times when teenagers generally stand around will come immediately before or after times when there are program demands upon us as directors. There need be no agenda other than being friendly and getting the teen to talk.

32. There are rare but real times in the life of the choir when a particular issue will need to be talked through. Sometimes, it is both timely and appropriate to give an entire rehearsal to discussion and group harmony. These times should not be totally spontaneous, but rather there should be some thought given to the content and ambiance of the meeting. The key words here are: be honest, open, loving, caring, and compassionate. Sometimes what is needed more than anything is for the director to become transparent and somewhat vulnerable to the group.

33. Seniors who have paid their dues in choir and have invested themselves over several years should enjoy a special privilege. Allow veteran seniors

the honor and privilege of addressing the choir anywhere, any time, for any reason. It may happen in the middle of the most intense rehearsal, on a tour bus, in the hallway before a performance, or after a prayer time. I have never known a senior to abuse this power. On the contrary, most disciplinary problems and motivational issues within the choir will be voluntarily addressed by seniors who carry much weight with their younger peers. When a senior disciplines the choir, it usually works.

34. Allow and encourage older youth choir members and officers to present five-minute devotions based on anthem texts at rehearsals. This is a wonderful feature if done just before or after the group prayer time.

35. Always take time for the teenagers to voice prayer requests. There are many effective systems to accomplish this. If possible, take the choir into the Sanctuary or a Chapel for the prayer time. Consider keeping the lights dimmed and use candle light. When a group becomes accustomed to the prayer time, they will not want to miss it for any reason. The requests which come out of these moments are sometimes amazing. Although some spoken concerns may be somewhat shallow or juvenile, some teenagers will open up in an amazing way.

36. Require your teenagers to make individual appointments with you for a Singer/Director Interview or Interface. These meetings should be done in your office or another appropriate and safe location. The interview process may be held as a beginning-of-the-new-season routine or a requirement for participating in choir tour. Most directors do not use the interview time for voice checks or auditions, (although there's no rule which says this shouldn't be done) but rather as a time of getting to know the teenager. Be sure to take notes for next year's reference. You may be surprised to see how the interviews become deeper as the teenager matures.

37. Give a parent an unexpected call when you see their child handle a situation well. Parents oftentimes wonder how their boy or girl is adjusting and connecting socially—how they act when they (the parents) are not around. It is always good to provide parents with positive feedback for the good things we observe in their teenagers. This also establishes a connection of goodwill with the parents. The phone call can be very brief—stay upbeat, friendly, and positive.

38. Recruit at least one teenager to lead in some aspect of worship each week. This can be accomplished with public prayers and scripture readings as well as solos and instrumental selections. The visibility and experience in worship leadership will provide teenagers with a sense of healthy importance and involvement in the larger ministry of the church.

39. Periodically, bring the pastor, youth minister, or other respected adult into the youth choir rehearsal to listen for a few moments and then to share a devotional thought with the kids.

40. Do you have an unusual or extra-important message you want your kids to hear from you? Consider putting the message on cassette tape, perhaps combined with other features. The cassette format can be used quite creatively, and it is also easy to weave humor and entertainment in, around, and through the message. Once completed and duplicated, mail the cassette with instructions to "listen to this hot cassette today!"

Non-verbal Communication . . . Modeling a Strong, Sensitive, and Warm Acceptance

41. Touch your teenagers—physically. In a world of sexual harassment, abuse, and litigation, do we have to be careful when we touch kids? By all means! In fact, we must be careful in *everything* we do with teenagers! However, if we lose the ability to provide a timely touch and the willingness to reach out a healthy hand of friendship, we give up entirely too much. We must be careful *where* we touch kids (where on the anatomy and where in our church facilities). The hows, whens and whys of touching are also important. We must be cautious and very sensitive. However, don't let this scare you from being a close friend—a person who hugs and is huggable. Always be appropriate, warm, and friendly. Be above reproach. Touch as Christ touched two thousand years ago. We are His hands in a new millennium.

42. As a part of rehearsal, work with teenagers to respond to specific conducting cues. Tell them what you are about to do before you begin, and then, for the next period of time, use no words except to tell them where to begin singing. All other instructions (cues) will be given non-verbally, with conducting gestures. One session you may work strictly on dynamics,

another on line and phrasing, and yet another session can be given to tempos. As you train the kids to respond, take them on a ride through the full range of expression for that particular session. Through exaggerating the cues and effects, you will sensitize your young singers to respond to your non-verbal communication.

43. Ask those who need specific prayer support to come to a central place in the midst of the group. No specific requests are verbalized, only the opportunity for those needing prayer to come together. As your group begins its prayer time, have the other choir members gather around, placing their hands upon the shoulders of those requesting prayer support. The prayers offered by the kids can be spoken or silent. Near the end, the director can lead in prayer pulling the group together as a united family.

44. Seek out Christian organizations which provide wilderness team-building or training in Colorado, Tennessee, Arkansas, California, Arizona, New Mexico or another location. Spend a day or two in the wilderness, building teams through group activities. Typical activities include white-water rafting, wilderness games, hiking, backpacking, horseback riding, and rock climbing. If you connect with the right group, they will provide a great experience for your choir, and at the same time will teach them how to work together and become community. Executives of major corporations and sales teams go through these adventures, and your group can benefit from them, too.

45. Sign language has a way of bringing sensitivity to a youth choir on a number of different levels. As a choir learns to sign one or two of their songs, the teens not only learn to express the music more effectively, they also develop sensitivity, respect, and appreciation for physically-challenged individuals in our society.

46. Your choir departs from a retirement village, prison, or children's home following a late-afternoon concert. The sky is clear and the sun is setting on the left-hand side of the bus. Everyone is buzzing with excitement following a productive day of singing and ministry. Get on the bus sound system and ask everyone to take their seats and be quiet for a few moments. "Look out to the left and look at the incredible orange sunset over the mountains. Sometimes we just pass by these miracles, never noticing their beauty and

color. Take a minute and be absolutely quiet. Give this time to God, thank Him for all the blessings of life and particularly for His presence among us today as we sang and ministered. I'll let you know when our quiet time is over." If your bus has a good stereo system, you might end the quiet time by playing an appropriate CD.

47. A groups' silence can be extremely powerful, but the teenagers will need to be prepared to make it happen and appreciate it. Before arriving at a memorial site, tell the story of what happened at this place. Try to help them feel the feelings, see the sights, smell the smells. As your group disembarks from their transportation, most will naturally go silently out of respect and awe. Those who do not will quickly be reigned in by the older teens in the group. Some of the most amazing youth choir experiences have been celebrated in total silence at places such as the Vietnam Wall and Holocaust Museum in Washington, The Oklahoma City Bombing Memorial, and on the street in front of Columbine High School in Colorado. Prepare and encourage your teenagers to feel the powerful impact of these important places.

48. For some of us, looking other people in the eye is a natural thing to do. For others, particularly those of us who are victims of low self-esteem, it is a real challenge. The good news is that we can learn to be better communicators simply by looking teenagers in the eye. Sometimes they are unable to reciprocate, but through time, patience, and our example, we will help them learn this communication skill.. People who do not look you in the eye when they speak seem insincere, shy, incompetent, unstable, or unconcerned. It's a simple skill to learn. Teach it through modeling.

49. It was said of Princess Diana and a number of other powerful people that when they were talking or listening to you, it was as if you were the only person in the world. Great communicators give great attention and energy to those they engage. What a gift this is to anyone, to be the center of someone's attention, if even for a few moments. It's a gift which is easier to describe than it is to give.

50. As a feature in rehearsal for ten minutes, play the "turn off the words game." Using a creative array of players (choir members) and situations, role play situations using no words, only facial expressions and body lan-

guage. Discuss as thoroughly as you can. Another way to achieve this effect is to play a video of a singing choir and turn off the sound. Discuss what the kids "hear" without really hearing. What develops from this discussion of non-verbal communication could be the beginning of better understanding within your group. This exercise may help with conducting, leadership dynamics, prayer ministry, and choir recruiting.

51. During your prayer request time at rehearsal, ask for those who would like to share with the group an unspoken prayer request, by raising a hand. You might be amazed to discover how many teenagers will share a prayer request in this way when they are not comfortable talking publicly about it.

Musical Communication . . . Where It All Comes Together

52. Sing from memory. Teenagers can and will memorize like lightning, much faster than their directors! When your choir sings for worship or in any other "performance" setting, have them sing from memory, with very few exceptions to this rule. The choir's sound will nearly double when you pull the scores out from under their musical noses.

53. Sing from memory, Part 2. In every rehearsal, be sure the teenagers memorize *something*, even if it is just eight bars of unison singing. From the beginning of their work on an anthem, encourage them to "think memory," quickly transferring as much as possible onto their "mental hard drives". With sustained encouragement, your singers' memories will actually increase and become more accurate. It's hard to believe, but it's true.

54. Sing from memory, Part 3. Actually, this idea should be called "Conduct from memory." When the conductor commits himself/herself to conduct a piece from memory while the teenagers are singing from memory, magic happens. The conductors and the kids' eyes meet often. The whole singing machine is immersed in a mode of trust and teamwork. Perhaps you are not comfortable conducting from memory on every piece. There will be, however, at least one selection in your repertoire you can conduct from memory. When you do, you may never want to go back to performing with a score. It's like sky diving. It gets in your blood.

55. Distraction drill. Simulate distractions, even small disasters. If you are like most directors, you may find it difficult to keep your singers focused during concerts. The loss of focus and energy manifests itself in dozens of ways in the midst of a worship service or concert setting. Preparation is the key. Make it very clear to the kids that *something* unexpected is sure to happen while you are singing. Someone will faint, someone will fall out of the balcony, a baby will shake the rafters with his crying, the director will knock over his music stand, the accompanist will lose her place. These are facts of life, and I can remember few concerts when *something* did not surprise me and/or the choir. Practice it. Simulate distractions. Tell the kids on a certain rehearsal day that there are several distractions planned, and they are going to rehearse handling those distractions without losing focus. Not only are these wonderful teachable moments, but they can be a lot of fun, as well.

56. Talk about how the choral experience relates to larger life. If you try idea #55 above, then why not take a moment for a fireside chat after the distraction drill. Life is loaded with distractions and detrimental detours. To a large success, teenagers' success or failure in life will be determined by the way they handle these situations. Will they lose focus for life or will they learn, recover, and move on?

57. Did you know the congregation (or audience) "hears" our choirs before they ever sing a note? Here's how and why. When we enter the choir loft to sing, people's antennas are already up, gathering information. They observe the group, and within the first few seconds of *seeing* the group, they form an opinion. Roger Ailes, in his book, *You Are the Message*, refers to this as "the seven second test." Within the first seven seconds of being in someone's presence, you already form an opinion. That opinion can change, but it will be more difficult to accomplish after the first seven seconds. Rehearse choir loft entrances, processionals, and other ways your youth choir gets into place. As director, provide funny demonstrations where you yourself model good appearances and sloppy ones. This, too can not only be educational, but also comical. Hold their feet to the fire. If the youth choir is going to communicate musically, it will have to first make a good appearance.

58. Does it make any difference what kids wear when they sing? Will their apparel have any effect on their sound? Will it affect their musical communication? There is no physical reason why this should be the case, but mentally and emotionally, the choir's corporate appearance is essential. Generally, the better the kids look as a group and the better they *feel* about the way they look, the better they seem to sing. This observation not only comes from the pew, but from the loft itself. We are not sure why, but psychology plays a significant role in this reality.

59. Sing from the inside out. Nothing brings musical communication to life more than a group singing their songs out of a sense of their own personal experience. The more reality music brings to the life of teenagers, the more they experience its power in their everyday lives, the better they will communicate musically. The connection between life and music is largely the director's responsibility: selecting good music, teaching it effectively, and connecting its meaning to adolescent reality.

60. Allow and encourage seniors or older singers to present "anthem devotions" based upon texts of your music. The devotions can be presented in the form of scripture study, personal testimony, group discussions, or all of the above. Again, when teenagers connect their music to life, the power to communicate musically begins to come naturally.

61. After a good concert, nothing is more powerful than scattering the choir into the pews to greet the congregation. This ministry is after-the-fact musical communication, but it is no less powerful. The sight of friendly teenagers breaking ranks to speak to children, parents, and the elderly is a beautiful way to wrap up the choir's gift of music.

At or Near the Beginning of the Season

62. Each season, invite every teenager in your church to participate in youth choir. Even the seniors who have never sung before should be invited. Several dynamics will be at work here. 1) You demonstrate that the choir is not an elitist organization. 2) Occasionally, a senior will join your choir for the first time. Once the year is over, that same senior is often in tears, wishing he had become a part of the group sooner. 3) Some teenagers need

to be invited several times before take the plunge. Give each teenager every chance possible to be a part of the youth choir.

63. Provide special recruiting activities for all incoming rookies. These can be in the form of parties, a night at the pizza restaurant, or going to a movie or baseball game together. Be sure many of the choir leaders attend, and above all, make it fun!

64. At the first rehearsal of the season, play a video excerpt from last year's tour or big performance. Try to give your visitors and potential members a taste of the youth choir in its very best, most exciting times.

65. Give a door prize every time the choir meets, or at least periodically as a surprise: a great new book for teenagers, a current Christian CD, concert tickets, or other less expensive and creative incentives. Make certain that different people receive the weekly gift.

66. At your first rehearsal, and then again through the mail the following week, distribute your choir schedule. The written schedule needs to include as much detail as possible between the beginning of school and Christmas break.

67. When the dust settles a bit from the beginning of the year, encourage the older choir members to throw a party for the younger teenagers. This could be a surprise event, perhaps at the end of rehearsal, as a way of saying, "Hey, you guys have done a good job of fitting in, and we are glad to have you." The seniors need to take the lead on this, and the choir president should make the we're-glad-you're-here speech at the party.

68. As best you can, make certain that the new kids in choir find friendships and healthy relationships within the ranks of veteran singers. The key is everyone knowing everyone else's names, and the pictorial directory (see Idea #13) is an excellent tool to accomplish this.

69. Sometime near Thanksgiving (preferably before), lead your teenagers to perform a local mission project of love. The project need not be complicated, and it may or may not involve singing. It may just involve a half day or perhaps more. Provide a viable ministry opportunity for your choir and

then encourage them to come out and get their hands dirty for the good of someone else.

70. Most of us have special kids in our groups who do more and work harder than most of their peers. Thanksgiving provides a great opportunity to write that extra-special member a personal note thanking him/her for her contribution to the choir. Your note might begin by saying, "Thanksgiving is a time of year when we all count our blessings. One of the blessings I am counting this year is my friendship with you! ...."

71. In worship, allow a group of four to six teenagers give mini-testimonies as to why they are grateful. Prepare the group, and you may want to actually rehearse the group before the service.

At Christmas

72. Allow your youth choir to present their own program sometime during Advent. This could be in the form of a weeknight concert or as part of the church's weekly worship schedule. However you choose to set it up, be sure the event clearly belongs to the kids. With a few years of successful Advent events, this may become one of your church's more meaningful holiday traditions.

73. Take your Christmas concert "on the road" to a care facility for the mentally disabled, a children's home, a prison, a geriatric center, or a hospital. Work at least three months in advance to set up such an event.

74. Give the youth choir a Christmas break which coincides with their school holidays and/or their Christmas concert (see Idea #72). The break not only allows the kids a couple of weeks of down time following a busy fall, it also tends to energize the choir after the first of the year. Don't look now, but you may need the break, as well.

75. As a Christmas party, take the youth choir carolling, perhaps as a combined party with your church's adult choir. You may want to go carolling in your community, or perhaps in a local mall or other public place.

76. Combine your youth and adult choirs for the morning of Advent IV (the Sunday before Christmas). Combining choirs on Easter also increases the potential for powerful choral music.

At Tour Time

77. Carry a state-of-the-art cell phone at all times. Be sure the parents and your the teenagers and counselors on your trip have your number. They will be able to reach you immediately in case of an emergency. Keep the phone on 7/24, and don't forget to take the charger.

78. When traveling in more than one vehicle (for instance, two buses or one bus and one van), carry walkie-talkies to communicate between the vehicles. This may seem unnecessary, but you will use them numerous times on the trip. Inexpensive-yet-dependable walkie-talkies units are now available in many stores and on the internet. Again, don't forget the chargers.

79. While on tour, write short daily devotions for your teenagers and counselors. The best devotions are those which spotlight an area or site you will visit sometime during the day. Tie the adventure of the day to the spiritual journey teenagers experience in life.

80. If you have a professional bus driver, remember to tip him/her at the end of the trip. A good tip range is 50 cents to one dollar per kid per day. This will need to be figured into your tour budget.

81. Train your tour photographer to be alert for good photo opportunities, particularly at well-known places. Any time pictures are taken, make sure there are kids in the photos.

82. Before departing on tour, we normally tell our kids how much spending money to bring. From your counselor group, assign a tour accountant. Instruct the teenagers that the accountant will take up half of their spending money at the beginning of the trip. The funds will be held "in escrow" until the midway point, at which time the accountant will redistribute the funds. The best way is to have individual envelopes with each teenager's

name on them. The accountant is responsible for the cash (usually thousands of dollars) until it is redistributed to the teenagers.

83. On your departure day, ask the teenagers to bring a six-pack of their favorite soft drinks. The church can provide ice boxes, ice, and paper goods so kids and counselors can enjoy a refreshment on board without stopping. When the six-pack is loaded onto the bus, it becomes public property; each person can select whatever they want to drink whenever they want it. The same can be done for other snacks if you wish.

84. Sometime during the tour, take the graduating seniors to a nice lunch and pick up the tab. A mall or another such location would work well. As the younger kids eat at a food court or at a fast-food place, the seniors and director can eat at a nicer upscale restaurant and enjoy a special time together. Allow at least an hour and a half for this event.

85. If your bus has a VCR player, watch one of the following movies each year as a tour tradition: Hoosiers, October Sky, The Sand Lot, Mr. Holland's Opus, Sister Act, or The Prince of Egypt.

86. Set up a tour web page, separate from your regular choir web page (Idea #3). In order to be effective, the web page should be updated daily. Someone other than the director (a computer savvy kid or counselor or both) should update the page. If you don't feel you are ready to do the web page, you can always send daily e-mail messages to all of your parents, complete with photos from your digital camera (Idea #12). The advantage of the web page is that it has more interesting possibilities to display your information. A second advantage is that the parents can pull up the web page at their convenience.

87. For no particular reason, pick up your counselors' tab for a nice lunch or dinner.

88. Learn the meanings of: 1) tour booklet, 2) fam trip, 3) points system, 4) tour prayer ministry, 5) awards banquet, 6) the roll board, 7) "Sunshine Mail System," and 8) tour task forces (Chapter 24).

89. Two weeks before the tour, meet with your counselors for a pre-tour meeting.

90. One week before the tour, hold a mandatory tour participant/parent dinner meeting to discuss the content of the tour booklet and other important tour information.

Keep Yourself Fresh and on the Cutting Edge of Youth Ministry (Youth Cue can help.)

91. Read *Youth Cue* every month. Go online with the free *Youth Cue* e-mail list server and interact with your fellow youth choir directors all over the world. (www.youthcue.org)

92. Periodically, check out the Center for Parent/Youth Understanding web site (www.cpyu.org) to access an incredible array of links for our education and inspiration. Although not geared to choral music, this site contains a treasure chest of insights into kids. Pick out a site or an article and study it. You will be enlightened by what you read.

93. Periodically, make yourself watch MTV. Try as best you can to learn from what you see and hear.

94. Watch anything you can on television dealing with youth. News shows such as Primetime, Dateline, Nightline, 20/20 and Good Morning America often spotlight youth issues. Local news also provides features regarding local youth issues. Take mental notes, become a student of these issues, and make needed applications within your own youth choir.

95. Read everything you can—new books and magazine features dealing with the current youth culture.

96. Develop strong friendships with parents of your teenagers. Through these relationships, you will learn a great deal about the kids you serve and will find yourself surrounded by a new level of support.

97. Become friends with effective coaches, dance instructors, school teachers, and others who successfully work with teenagers. The give and take of these friendships will encourage everyone.

98. Attend the National *Youth Cue* Roundtable, held annually in different locations across the United States.

99. Listen to recordings of good youth choirs. More and more youth choirs periodically record CDs and cassettes. The *Youth Cue* network can help you locate the choirs who have produced recent recordings.

100. Bring your choirs to a *Youth Cue* Festival. Held in various locations around North America, these major events involve from two hundred to six hundred teenagers. The Festivals are fabulous musical/spiritual experiences for the teenagers, and they also provide a veritable clinic of observation for directors. Some directors participate in Festivals without their choirs as observers. For the best possible experience, bring your teenagers. Together, we all accomplish and learn more.

CHAPTER 46

Web Sites

I would like to extend a special thank you to Walt Mueller and The Center for Parent/Youth Understanding in Elizabethtown, Pennsylvania. In my opinion, this organization bar non has a better handle on current youth culture from a Christian perspective than any other group. I highly recommend them for resources, education, workshops, and other enrichment events. The Center for Parent/Youth Understanding is a nonprofit organization which hosts a marvelous web page. Virtually all of the following web site information was provided by CPYU from their links page. Thank you, Walt, for this marvelous list, for your courage, your love of the Lord and your heart for teenagers.

Web site: www.cpyu.org
Email: cpyu@aol.com
P. O. Box 414
Elizabethtown, PA 17022
(717) 361-8429
Fax: (717) 361-0031

THE CENTER FOR PARENT-YOUTH UNDERSTANDING
Web site Listing
NUMBER OF SITES: 81

Online Ministries and Organizations

Barna Research Online

http://www.barna.org

The Barna Organization has been providing cutting edge research on cultural trends, generations, and issues affecting the church for years. Now you can tap into a wealth of helpful Barna information and analysis through this web site. You will find ministry resources, information on seminars, in-depth analysis, and a section on data and trends.

Breakpoint

http://www.breakpoint.org

Chuck Colson's daily guide to developing a Christian Worldview in post-Christian culture hits the net with Colson's insightful commentary on news and trends. Visitors can search the archives for scripts from past commentaries or listen to the day's broadcast.

CampusLife

http://www.christianity.net/campuslife

This web site is the online version of Campus Life, a relevant cutting-edge Christian magazine for teens. It features articles from the current issue, complete past issues, message boards, and an offer for a free hard copy of the publication. Lots of links to other sites (advice, humor, reviews, resources, trends, and stats) make this valuable for teens, youth workers, and parents.

Celebration Singers, Shreveport, LA

http://www.celebration-singers.org

Produced and maintained by a group of teenagers in Shreveport, Louisiana, this site is the home page of First Baptist Church in Shreveport's Celebration Singers. Up and running all year, the web page highlights the ministry of the Singers and posts weekly information and updates.

Center for Student Missions
http://gospelcom.net/csm
Nothing cements the faith of a student like a mission experience. This site explains the mission and ministry of CSM and outlines opportunities they offer groups for building faith through short-term inner-city missions.

ChristianCollege.org
http://gospelcom.net/cccu/christiancollege
Designed for prospective students and their parents, this online site of the Coalition for Christian Colleges and Universities allows users to plug in personal preferences and then conduct searches of 93 Christian colleges with a combined 300 undergraduate majors and 90 graduate programs.

Cross Search Online Directory
http://www.crosssearch.com
A helpful search engine this site helps you find your way to the best Christian resources on the Web.

Cult Awareness and Information Centre
http://student.uq.edu.au/~py101663/zentry1.htm
With a growing interest in spirituality sweeping through today's youth culture, many young people are turning to alternative religions and cults for fulfillment. This site is a good starting point for information on particular cults, their appeal, and their influence.

Gospel Communications Network
http://www.gospelcom.net
This ministry of Gospel Communications International serves as a helpful directory to online Christian resources. Included are links to dozens of member ministries and organizations, a searchable Bible, devotional materials, and chat rooms.

Group Publishing
http://www.grouppublishing.com
A leader in providing resources for ministry to children, youth and adults, this helpful site is loaded with information on books, magazines, curriculum, and training events. While you are here, check out "Ministry.Net" and its searchable library of articles from Group's arsenal of periodicals.

Internet For Christians Virtual Appendix

http://www.gospelcom.net/ifc/virtual.html

Christian media guru Quentin Schultze, creator of "The Internet For Christians" online newsletter, continually updates this guide to essential resources on and about the Net. Beginners will find this user-friendly site especially helpful.

Mars Hill Forum

http://www.gospelcom.net/ivpress/feature/apologeticsnow.html

This site features answers to pressing questions about the place of Christian faith in a post-Christian world. Authors Jim Sire and Doug Groothius will help you start discussions with anyone who has tough questions about Christian belief and practice. The hosts don't shy away from questions like "What is truth?"

National Center for Fathering

http://www.fathers.com

A great site for Dads! Fathers can find practical fathering tips, research on fathering, information on the fathering movement, humor, and an online version of *Today's Father* magazine.

Reaching Generation X for Jesus

http://home.pix.za/gc/gc12/genx

Created and maintained by Graeme Codrington, this growing site contains resources, links, helpful tips, research papers, and other interesting items related to Gen Xers ministry.

Reaching Generation Y for Jesus

http://home.pix.za/gc/gc12/geny

Youth ministers looking to connect with millennial kids will find information on today's teens, ministry tips and strategies, as well as many helpful links to other GenerationY sites.

Regenerator

http://www.regenerator.com

The site for *Regenerator Quarterly* magazine contains thought-provoking material addressing the distinctive experiences, concerns, and perspectives of today's emerging generation of orthodox Christians.

Sanctuary
http://www.webpulse.com/sanctuary
A unique Christian ministry that serves as "an alternative church for the disenfranchised music underground." A prime example of Christians actively seeking to provide answers and hope to kids heavily involved in goth, industrial, punk and other fringe musical genres.

Screen It!
http://www.screenit.com
This web site provides music, movie and video reviews specifically for parents needing insight into today's latest media offerings. Breaks down songs, movies, and television shows by content, theme, etc. This site also includes lists of possible parent/teen discussion topics.

Search Institute
http://www.search-institute.org
This helpful site provides practical research, tools and resources from an organization that has studied teen values, attitudes, behaviors and needs since the 1950s.

Sports Spectrum
http://www.gospelcom.net/rbc/ss/
The web site of this Christian sports magazine is a great place for fans of all ages. Look for stats, athlete testimonies, feature articles, article archives, and links to other sports sites.

TrueTunes
http://www.truetunes.com
A cutting-edge site both visually and in terms of its information related to the alternative Christian music scene. This online version of *Truetunes* magazine is great for kids who love music but have been turned off by the mainstream Christian music scene.

Understanding Your Teenager
http://www.uyt.com
Founded by youth ministry guru Wayne Rice, the Understanding Your Teenager organization conducts lively and informative parenting seminars

across North America. The UYT site features information on these seminars, a helpful online bookstore, and parenting tips.

Urban Youth Workers Resource Directory

http://www.iugm.org/yth-res.html

A joint venture of Kingdomworks and Urban Youth Ministries, the site includes a list of books, videos, magazines, journals, training conferences, and organizations. Urban youth workers will also find links relevant to the topic of urban youth ministry.

What Would Jesus Do? The Official Web Site

http://www.wwjd.com

The WWJD phenomenon that started with a bracelet has moved onto the web with a site designed for teens and youth workers. While the site is heavy on marketing WWJD products, it also features tips for witnessing, personal testimonies, and opportunities for real-time conversation through the WWJD chat area.

YouthCue

http://www.youthcue.org

Web site for youth choir leaders who care. Coordinates with the monthly edition of *Youth Cue*. Operated by Youth Choirs, Inc., the web site provides youth choir directors assistance on a number of levels.

Youth Ministry Bibliography

http://www.btc.co.za/model/bibliog.htm

This site provides an extensive online categorized bibliography with books on youth ministry philosophy, leadership, evangelism, discipleship, missions, counseling, education, worship, development, and youth culture. Many of the books are listed in hypertext which allows you to click and go directly to the amazon.com online bookstore for information, reviews, and ordering.

YouthPastor.Com

http://www.youthpastor.com

A new online ministry for youth pastors by youth pastors, this site is loaded with ministry resources, links, games, ministry listings, etc. Lots of good stuff on a site that's growing!

Youth Specialties

http://www.gospelcom.net/ys/

A must visit site for anyone working with teenagers. Constantly updated, the site offers information about Youth Specialties, their conferences, and youth ministry resources. In addition, you will find a list of youth ministry job openings, discussion areas, and a helpful growing list of links to other youth-related sites on the Web.

Online General
Organizations and Publications

Addicted To Noise

http://www.addict.com

A weekly online music magazine with news, reviews, and other information on the popular music scene.

All-Music Guide

http://www.allmusic.com

A gold-mine of information on popular music. Start with a search of artists, albums, songs, styles, or labels. In addition there are music maps, lists of helpful popular music statistics, essays, articles, artist bios, and more.

alt.culture

http://cgi.pathfinder.com/cgi-bin/altculture/home.cgi

An online encyclopedia of 90's youth culture that serves as both a "culture guide and online compass." The over 900 entries are loaded with hypertext links. A helpful search engine makes navigating this site easy. A must visit site for youth culture watchers!

blaze.com

http://www.blaze.com

Billed as Hip-Hop's home on the web, this new site is filled with information on the fastest growing segment of the popular music industry. The online home of *Blaze* magazine, visitors are told they will be informed of every development in the hip-hop world, with updates added several times a day.

CDnow

http://www.cdnow.com

This site is billed as "The Internet's Number One Music Store." It provides a wealth of information on artists, albums, and charts. Visitors will also find a list of helpful links and a site search engine.

Chillinonline

http://www.chillinonline.com

Looking to understand today's urban youth culture? Chillinonline offers "interactive urban relaxation" in the form of commentary and information on urban culture—everything from music, to issues, events, etc.

Cinemachine

http://www.cinemachine.com

This movie review search engine allows you to search by movie name and to scan reviews on upcoming and recent releases. A search quickly yields a short plot synopsis and links to just about every other online review.

The Den

http://www.theden.com

Welcome to the Daily Entertainment Network—a site where you will find daily news on music, movies, television, and the sci-fi world. Also a good site for keeping abreast of new developments in the electronic gaming industry.

Entertainment Asylum

http://www.asylum.com

Another extensive entertainment site packed full of pop culture information on movies, music, television, etc.

Entertainment Weekly Online

http://www.ew.com

Billed as "the most exciting new web site in entertainment" and "America's digital doorway to popular culture," the online version of *Entertainment Weekly* magazine offers up-to-date information on all aspects of popular media culture including television, music, movies, video, cyber space, and books.

Girl Tech

http://www.girltech.com

Created by a feminist software designer, this site is packed full of information and guidance for girls. Billed as a site that's "creating a world for the adventurous spirit," Girl Tech supports a feminist agenda and "girl power". Attractive and fun, it's easy to understand the site's appeal to young girls. The site includes areas for parents and teachers as well.

A Girl's World Online Clubhouse

http://agirlsworld.com

Peek into the world of today's young adolescent girls by visiting this "space on the Internet that's totally girl-powered." It's an interactive online magazine for girls, offering advice and guidance on everything of interest to the female middle-school set.

iMusic

http://www.imusic.com

This popular music site is a valuable window into the world of today's music. You will find artist info, music news, reviews, charts, bulletin boards and chat rooms. A great place to go if you want more information on who your kids are listening to.

The International Lyrics Server

http://www.lyrics.ch

Looking for lyrics to that song you just can't seem to figure out? Look no further! This site contains lyrics to over 100,000 songs!

Internet Movie Database

http://www.imdb.com

Everything you ever want to know about over 140,000 different movies. Includes plot summaries, ratings, reviews, links, and a search engine to guide you through overwhelming amounts of movie information.

JamTV

http://www.jamtv.com

Another valuable source of information on today's popular music, this site includes breaking news, links to live web casts, photos, videos, an artist search, and chat room.

Movie Review Query Engine
http://www.mrqe.com
Looking for information on that new movie the kids want to see? This site makes it easy with links to over 70,000 movie reviews on the Internet.

Movieweb
http://www.movieweb.com
The place to find previews of upcoming releases and information on past films. A link is provided to each movie's home page where you can download pictures, posters, production notes, quicktime videos of the movie trailers, cast info, and a plot synopsis.

MTV Online
http://www.MTV.com
The trail-blazing twenty-four hour music channel continues to blaze trails with this cutting-edge web site. Do you want to know more about today's pop culture? This is the place to find music charts, MTV news, and information on a variety of social issues.

Music Boulevard
http://www.musicblvd.com
Billed as "The World's #1 Online Music Store!", this site is loaded with music searches, charts, genre guides, and information on all of today's popular artists and their albums. Another valuable source of music information.

The Obscure Store and Reading Room
http://www.obscurestore.com
Looking for a good primary source of information on today's emerging generations? Here's a place to read the news and check out what young people are writing themselves. A difficult site to describe, but a valuable place to visit if you are searching to understand the heartbeat of this generation.

The Online Slang Dictionary
http://www.umr.edu/~wrader/slang.html
Wondering what your kids are talking about when they throw around words like "agro", "chim", or "dap", or any of several hundred other slang terms? This online dictionary of slang will help you sort it all out—over 750 terms and growing!

Platform/Transglobal Urban Lifestyles

http://www.platform.net

A site dedicated to "street-wise" cutting-edge youth culture. Visitors can purchase street wear and urban gear as well as access articles on hip-hop, DJ culture, music, skateboarding, and snowboarding.

rockontv

http://www.rockontv.com/

Billed as "the ultimate guide to music on television", this online guide keeps track of television shows that may be of interest to popular music fans. Frequently updated weekly listings track every music-related show and appearance on major networks and cable stations. A great connection to music on the tube.

Rolling Stone Online

http://www.rollingstone.com

The online version of the bimonthly paper edition of *Rolling Stone* magazine.

The Source

http://www.thesource.com

The online site of *The Source* magazine, one of the fastest-growing sources of information on the urban hip-hop youth culture. Check out the latest news, read commentary, view a full-length video on-demand, check out your favorite artist, or post a message.

SPANK! Youth Culture Online

http://www.spankmag.com

An online magazine about youth culture written and managed by members of today's youth culture. Focuses on youth issues, interests and happenings. It's a monthly, but there are daily updates on the site. This site offers a valuable peek into the hearts and minds of today's teens.

Spin Magazine

http://www.spin.com

This online version of the popular music culture magazine contains a wealth of sights, sounds, video clips, news, discussion groups, etc. Always on the cutting edge, *Spin* is worth a visit if you want to know what is going on in the popular music and entertainment industry.

Swoon

http://www.swoon.com

A popular site offering teens and young adults information on "dating, mating, and relating." This is not the place to send your kids for an education on relationships, but it is a great place to gain firsthand insight into some of the edgiest sexual and relational trends in today's youth culture. It is heavily advertised in many teen and young adult magazines.

Teenwire

http://www.teenwire.com

Another online place for kids to find guidance on sexuality, relationships, and other issues facing teens today. On our most recent visit we found a section called "Your Johnson and You: The Lowdown on Male Anatomy." This is another good site for parents and youth workers as it offers a peek into what kids are learning about sexuality from mainstream culture. Planned Parenthood operates the site.

The Totally Unofficial Rap Dictionary

http://www.sci.kun.nl/thalia/rapdict/main.html

Have you heard your kids using hip-hop street slang that you just can't understand? Here is an alphabetized dictionary to rap that will let you in on what they mean by "phat" and hundreds of other terms. The site also includes translations of rap star names and places.

The Ultimate Band List

http://www.ubl.com

This is the ultimate source for an overwhelming wealth of information on bands, radio stations, record labels, music news and more.

Ultimate Movies

http://www.ultimatemovies.com

Log on and scan the alphabetical list for the film of your choice. Click on the title and you will instantly connect to the official site of the flick you have chosen. A great place to go for some quick information on today's most current movie releases.

UltimateTV
http://www.ultimatetv.com
This site contains over 10,000 links for over 1,300 television shows including over 1,300 www pages. This is the "television index of the net." You will find press releases, rosters, chat areas, and plot information.

VIBE online
http://www.vibe.com
The online site of *Vibe*—a magazine devoted to today's urban hip-hop culture.

Vidnet: Videos On Demand
http://www.vidnetusa.com
Entertainment Boulevard has put together this helpful music and media site. After downloading the VivoActive Player, visitors can view music videos from today's most popular groups and artists. You will even find videos that have never made it to MTV. You can also conduct an artist search or scan the site's extensive pop music genre list.

WILMA: The Internet Guide to Live Music
http://www.wilma.com
More than a guide to who is playing where, WILMA has a searchable database of over 18,000 touring artists. In addition, you will find artist information, bios, interviews, a musical genre guide, charts, and audio/video clips.

Online Statistical and
Informational Sites

ADOL
http://education.indiana.edu/cas/adol/adol.html
The Adolescence Directory On-line is an electronic guide to information on adolescent issues maintained by the Center for Adolescent Studies at Indiana University.

American Demographics Magazine
http://www.demographics.com/Publications/AD/index.htm
A searchable archive of the definitive magazine on consumer and marketing trends with a wealth of information on the values, attitudes, and behaviors of children and teens.

Billboard Online
http://www.billboard-online.com
The online version of the weekly music mag featuring Billboard's charts, daily music news, music industry product information, and other music resources. Site visitors can access every Billboard album review from 1980 until present.

Centers for Disease Control and Prevention
http://www.cdc.gov
If you are looking for statistics and information on adolescent health issues, (sexually transmitted diseases, teen violence, suicide, etc) this CDC site is thorough and up-to-date. The site features a search engine and an extensive list of links to other related sites.

Directory Of Media Literacy Organizations
http://interact.uoregon.edu/MediaLit/FA/MLDirectory
This site contains alphabetical listing and links to dozens of media literacy groups and organizations worldwide. If you are concerned about what children and teens watch, log onto this site maintained by the Media Literacy Project at the University of Oregon.

Drug-Free Resource Net
http://www.drugfreeamerica.org
Created and maintained by the Partnership for a Drug-Free America, this site offers a complete and accurate compilation of information about substance abuse. Included are a comprehensive database on drugs and help for parents.

Electric Library
http://www.elibrary.com/id/101/105
A "personal online research center," the Electric Library provides multiple search features for quick and effective research. The site currently includes almost 8 million newspaper articles, 775,000 magazine articles, 400,000 book chapters, 1,110 maps, 85,000 TV and radio transcripts, and 58,000 photos and images.

Facts for Families
http://www.aacap.org/web/aacap/factsFam
Created by the American Academy of Child and Adolescent Psychiatry, this

site is loaded with 56 up-to-date and concise fact sheets on issues that affect children, teens, and families in today's world.

Great Transitions
http://www.carnegie.org/reports/great_transitions/gr_intro.html
This online report represents the culmination of the Carnegie Council on Adolescent Development's ten years of research on the adolescent experience in contemporary culture. The site contains a synthesis of "the best available knowledge and wisdom about adolescence in America."

The Monitoring of the Future Home Page
http://www.isr.umich.edu/src/mtf/index.html
This site is packed with current teen substance abuse data from the annual Monitoring the Future Survey conducted by the Institute for Social Research at the University of Michigan.

National Fatherhood Initiative
http://www.fatherhood.org/
The mission of the non-profit NFI is "to improve the well-being of children by increasing the number of children growing up with loving, committed and responsible fathers." The organization's site includes advice for Dads, a catalog of fathering resources, tips from other fathers, and a list of links to other related organizations.

National Institute on Drug Abuse
http://www.nida.nih.gov
This site provides information on drugs, drug use, and current research on illicit drugs. It includes a long list of links to other related substance abuse sites.

Parents Television Council
http://www.parentstv.org
A project of the Media Research Center, the PTC's mission is "to bring America's demand for values-driven television programming to the entertainment industry." The site includes up-to-date suggestions for family-friendly viewing, suggestions on how to influence television programming, a family guide to prime time television, and lots of research and analysis.

Search-It-All

http://www.search-it-all.com
Billed as "the ultimate reference tool", this easy to use site boasts a categorized collection of the best searches on the Web. It is a great place to start your next search for up-to-date information on today's youth culture.

Teen Health and the Media

http://weber.u.washington.edu/~ecttp/default.html
Today's music and media serve as powerful molders and shapers of young people's values, attitudes, and behaviors. This site offers extensive insight into how media influences body image, teen sexuality, violent/suicidal behavior, and substance abuse.

YouthInfo

http://youth.os.dhhs.gov
Maintained by the US Department of Health and Human Services, this site includes profiles of America's youth, reports, stats, publications, and speeches on youth topics. In addition, there is a list of resources for parents and links to related sites.

Used by permission of The Center for Parent/Youth Understanding.
Walt Mueller, Founder and President

PERSONAL WEB SITE LIST

CHAPTER 47

A Youth Choir Director's Reading List

G aining understanding and insights from others is an enormous part of becoming a qualified youth choir director in a new millennium. In this chapter, we list one-hundred books which provide unique and timely insight for our work with teenagers. The books are listed alphabetically by author. Each listing also includes information as to the category of youth choir ministry the book covers. Enjoy!

Adams, Jere
LEADING YOUTH CHOIRS

Convention Press
Nashville, 1988

ISBN (Library of Congress)

❑ Ministry
❑ Understanding Ourselves
■ Understanding Teenagers

❑ Communication
❑ Choral Technique/Teaching
❑ Leadership

Alies, Roger
YOU ARE THE MESSAGE
Getting What You Want by Being Who You Are

Doubleday
New York, 1988

ISBN (Library of Congress)   0-385-26542-5

❑ Ministry
❑ Understanding Ourselves
❑ Understanding Teenagers

■ Communication
❑ Choral Technique/Teaching
■ Leadership

Albom, Mitch   Doubleday Dell
TUESDAYS WITH MORRIE   New York, 1997
An Old Man, a Young Man, and Life's Greatest Lesson

ISBN (Library of Congress)   0-385-48451-8

❑ Ministry   ❑ Communication
■ Understanding Ourselves   ❑ Choral Technique/Teaching
❑ Understanding Teenagers   ❑ Leadership

Allen, Jimmy   Moorings
BURDEN OF A SECRET   Nashville, 1995
A Story of Truth and Mercy in the Face of AIDS

ISBN (Library of Congress)   0-345-40091-7

■ Ministry   ❑ Communication
❑ Understanding Ourselves   ❑ Choral Technique/Teaching
❑ Understanding Teenagers   ❑ Leadership

Anderson, Frances & Leeder, Joseph   Prentiss Hall
GUIDING JUNIOR-HIGH SCHOOL PUPILS   New York, 1954
IN MUSICAL EXPERIENCES

ISBN (Library of Congress)

❑ Ministry   ❑ Communication
❑ Understanding Ourselves   ■ Choral Technique/Teaching
❑ Understanding Teenagers   ❑ Leadership

Andrews, Moya & Summers, Anne   College-Hill Publications
VOICE THERAPY FOR ADOLESCENTS   Boston, 1988

ISBN (Library of Congress)   0-316-04233-1

❑ Ministry   ❑ Communication
❑ Understanding Ourselves   ■ Choral Technique/Teaching
❑ Understanding Teenagers   ❑ Leadership

Bair, Alisa   Good Books
A TABLE FOR TWO   Intercourse, PA, 1998
A Mother and Her Young Daughter Face Death Together

ISBN (Library of Congress) 1-56148-218-8

■ Ministry   ■ Communication
■ Understanding Ourselves   ❏ Choral Technique/Teaching
■ Understanding Teenagers   ❏ Leadership

Bernadin, Joseph Cardinal   Loyola Press
THE GIFT OF PEACE   Chicago, 1997
Personal Reflections by Joseph Cardinal Bernadin

ISBN (Library of Congress) 0-8294-0955-6

■ Ministry   ❏ Communication
❏ Understanding Ourselves   ❏ Choral Technique/Teaching
❏ Understanding Teenagers   ❏ Leadership

Beuchner, Frederick   Harper
LISTENING TO YOUR LIFE   San Francisco, 1992
Daily Meditations

ISBN (Library of Congress) 0-06-069864-0

❏ Ministry   ❏ Communication
■ Understanding Ourselves   ❏ Choral Technique/Teaching
❏ Understanding Teenagers   ❏ Leadership

Blanchard, Kenneth and Johnson, Spencer   Berkley Books
THE ONE-MINUTE MANAGER   New York, 1982

ISBN (Library of Congress) 0-425-06265-1

■ Ministry   ■ Communication
❏ Understanding Ourselves   ❏ Choral Technique/Teaching
❏ Understanding Teenagers   ❏ Leadership

Brandt, Leslie F.   Concordia
PSALMS NOW   St. Louis, 1973

ISBN (Library of Congress)   0-570-03230-X

■ Ministry   ❑ Communication
❑ Understanding Ourselves   ❑ Choral Technique/Teaching
❑ Understanding Teenagers   ❑ Leadership

Burroughs, Bob   Broadman
AN ABC PRIMER FOR CHURCH MUSICIANS   Nashville, 1990

ISBN (Library of Congress) 0-8054-3307-4

■ Ministry   ❑ Communication
❑ Understanding Ourselves   ❑ Choral Technique/Teaching
❑ Understanding Teenagers   ❑ Leadership

Burroughs, Bob   Tempo Music
CHURCH MUSIC IN THE REAL WORLD   Leawood, KS, 1996
A Church Musician's Handbook for the Rest of Us

ISBN (Library of Congress)   1-889411-00-0

■ Ministry   ❑ Communication
❑ Understanding Ourselves   ❑ Choral Technique/Teaching
❑ Understanding Teenagers   ❑ Leadership

Burroughs, Esther   Thomas Nelson
SPLASH THE LIVING WATER   Nashville, 1999
Turning Daily Interruptions into Life-giving Encounters

ISBN (Library of Congress)   0-7852-6958-4

■ Ministry   ■ Communication
■ Understanding Ourselves   ❑ Choral Technique/Teaching
■ Understanding Teenagers   ■ Leadership

Burroughs, Esther   New Hope
A GARDEN PATH TO MENTORING   Birmingham, AL
Planting Your Life in Another and Releasing the Fragrance   1997

ISBN (Library of Congress) 1-56309-197-6

- ■ Ministry
- ❏ Understanding Ourselves
- ❏ Understanding Teenagers

- ❏ Communication
- ❏ Choral Technique/Teaching
- ❏ Leadership

Busch, Brian R.   Schirmer Books
THE COMPLETE CHORAL CONDUCTOR   New York, 1983

ISBN (Library of Congress) 0-02-870540-5

- ❏ Ministry
- ❏ Understanding Ourselves
- ❏ Understanding Teenagers

- ❏ Communication
- ■ Choral Technique/Teaching
- ❏ Leadership

Campbell, Don
THE MOZART EFFECT   Avon
Tapping into the Power of Music to Heal the Body   New York, 1994

ISBN (Library of Congress) 0-380-97418-5

- ❏ Ministry
- ❏ Understanding Ourselves
- ❏ Understanding Teenagers

- ❏ Communication
- ■ Choral Technique/Teaching
- ❏ Leadership

Carter, Jimmy   Times Books
LIVING FAITH   New York, 1996

ISBN (Library of Congress) 0-8129-2736-2

- ■ Ministry
- ❏ Understanding Ourselves
- ❏ Understanding Teenagers

- ❏ Communication
- ❏ Choral Technique/Teaching
- ❏ Leadership

Chapman, Gary   Northfield Publishing
THE FIVE LOVE LANGUAGES   Chicago, 1995
How to Express Heartfelt Commitment to Your Mate

ISBN (Library of Congress)   1-881273-15-6

- ❏ Ministry
- ■ Understanding Ourselves
- ❏ Understanding Teenagers

- ❏ Communication
- ❏ Choral Technique/Teaching
- ❏ Leadership

Chapman, Gary and Campbell, M.D., Ross   Northfield Publishing
THE FIVE LOVE LANGUAGES OF CHILDREN   Chicago, 1997

ISBN (Library of Congress) 1-881273-65-2

- ■ Ministry
- ❏ Understanding Ourselves
- ■ Understanding Teenagers

- ■ Communication
- ❏ Choral Technique/Teaching
- ❏ Leadership

Cooksey, John M.   Concordia
WORKING WITH THE ADOLESCENT VOICE   St. Louis, 1992

ISBN (Library of Congress) 0-570-01344-5

- ❏ Ministry
- ❏ Understanding Ourselves
- ❏ Understanding Teenagers

- ❏ Communication
- ■ Choral Technique/Teaching
- ❏ Leadership

Dakers, Lionel   Marshall, Morgan,
CHURCH MUSIC AT THE CROSSROADS   and London, 1970

ISBN (Library of Congress) 551-05246-5

- ■ Ministry
- ❏ Understanding Ourselves
- ❏ Understanding Teenagers

- ❏ Communication
- ■ Choral Technique/Teaching
- ❏ Leadership

Dawn, Marva J.   Eerdmans Publishing
TRULY THE COMMUNITY   Grand Rapids, 1997
Romans 12 and How to be the Church

ISBN (Library of Congress)   0-8028-4466-9

■ Ministry   ❑ Communication
❑ Understanding Ourselves   ❑ Choral Technique/Teaching
❑ Understanding Teenagers   ❑ Leadership

Dawn, Marva J.   Eerdmans Publishing
REACHING OUT   Grand Rapids, 1995
WITHOUT DUMBING DOWN
A Theology of Worship for the Turn-of-the-Century Culture

ISBN (Library of Congress)   0-8028-4102-3

■ Ministry   ❑ Communication
❑ Understanding Ourselves   ❑ Choral Technique/Teaching
❑ Understanding Teenagers   ❑ Leadership

de Long, Alfred   Vantage Press
TO SING OR NOT TO SING   New York, 1987

ISBN (Library of Congress)   0-533-07091-0

❑ Ministry   ❑ Communication
❑ Understanding Ourselves   ■ Choral Technique/Teaching
❑ Understanding Teenagers   ❑ Leadership

Ehmann, Wilhelm   Augsburg
CHORAL DIRECTING   Minneapolis, 1968

ISBN (Library of Congress)   67-29816

❑ Ministry   ❑ Communication
❑ Understanding Ourselves   ■ Choral Technique/Teaching
❑ Understanding Teenagers   ❑ Leadership

Eshelin, Gerald
LIES MY MUSIC TEACHER TOLD ME

Stage 3 Publishing
Woodlands Hills, CA
1994

ISBN (Library of Congress)   1-886209-11-1

❏ Ministry
❏ Understanding Ourselves
❏ Understanding Teenagers

❏ Communication
■ Choral Technique/Teaching
❏ Leadership

Foster, Richard J.
CELEBRATION OF DISCIPLINE
The Path to Spiritual Growth

Harper and Row
San Francisco, 1988

ISBN (Library of Congress) 0-06-062839-1

■ Ministry
■ Understanding Ourselves
■ Understanding Teenagers

❏ Communication
❏ Choral Technique/Teaching
❏ Leadership

Friedman, Edwin H.
GENERATION TO GENERATION
Family Process in Church and Synagogue

Guilford Press
New York, 1985

ISBN (Library of Congress) 0-89862-059-7

■ Ministry
■ Understanding Ourselves
■ Understanding Teenagers

❏ Communication
❏ Choral Technique/Teaching
❏ Leadership

Fuchs, Peter Paul
THE PSYCHOLOGY OF CONDUCTING

MCA Music
Saddle River, NY, 1969

ISBN (Library of Congress) 74-93278

❏ Ministry
❏ Understanding Ourselves
❏ Understanding Teenagers

■ Communication
■ Choral Technique/Teaching
❏ Leadership

Fulghum, Robert   Ivy Books
ALL I REALLY NEED TO KNOW I LEARNED   New York, 1988
IN KINDERGARTEN
Uncommon Thoughts on Uncommon Things

ISBN (Library of Congress) 0-8041-0526-X

■ Ministry   ❑ Communication
■ Understanding Ourselves   ❑ Choral Technique/Teaching
■ Understanding Teenagers   ❑ Leadership

Garretson, Robert   Prentiss Hall
CONDUCTING CHORAL MUSIC   Upper Saddle River, 1998

ISBN (Library of Congress) 0-13-775735-2

❑ Ministry   ❑ Communication
❑ Understanding Ourselves   ■ Choral Technique/Teaching
❑ Understanding Teenagers   ❑ Leadership

Glasser, M.D., William   Harper Perennial
CHOICE THEORY   New York, 1998
A New Psychology of Personal Freedom

ISBN (Library of Congress) 0-06-093014-4

❑ Ministry   ❑ Communication
■ Understanding Ourselves   ❑ Choral Technique/Teaching
■ Understanding Teenagers   ❑ Leadership

Goleman, Daniel   Bantam
WORKING WITH EMOTIONAL INTELLIGENCE   New York, 1998

ISBN (Library of Congress) 0-533-10462-4

❑ Ministry   ❑ Communication
❑ Understanding Ourselves   ❑ Choral Technique/Teaching
■ Understanding Teenagers   ❑ Leadership

Goleman, Daniel   Bantam
EMOTIONAL INTELLIGENCE   New York, 1995
What It Can Matter More Than IQ

ISBN (Library of Congress) 0-533-37506-7

❑ Ministry   ❑ Communication
❑ Understanding Ourselves   ❑ Choral Technique/Teaching
■ Understanding Teenagers   ❑ Leadership

Gordon, Arthur   Revell Company
A TOUCH OF WONDER   Old Tappan, NJ, 1974
A Book to Help People Stay in Love with Life

ISBN (Library of Congress) 8007-5122-8

❑ Ministry   ❑ Communication
■ Understanding Ourselves   ❑ Choral Technique/Teaching
❑ Understanding Teenagers   ❑ Leadership

Griffin, Em   Intervarsity Press
GETTING TOGETHER   Downers Grove, IL
A Guide for Good Groups   1982

ISBN (Library of Congress) 0-87784-390-2

■ Ministry   ■ Communication
❑ Understanding Ourselves   ❑ Choral Technique/Teaching
■ Understanding Teenagers   ■ Leadership

Gurian, Michael   Putnam
A FINE YOUNG MAN   New York, 1998
What Parents, Mentors and Educators Can Do

ISBN (Library of Congress) 0-87477-919-7

❑ Ministry   ❑ Communication
❑ Understanding Ourselves   ❑ Choral Technique/Teaching
■ Understanding Teenagers   ❑ Leadership

Hallowell, M.D., Edward M.   Pantheon Books
CONNECT   New York, 1999
Twelve Vital Ties that Open Your Heart, Lengthen Your Life . . .

ISBN (Library of Congress) 0-375-40357-4

- ■ Ministry   ■ Communication
- ■ Understanding Ourselves   ❑ Choral Technique/Teaching
- ■ Understanding Teenagers   ❑ Leadership

Hamner, Russell   Scarecrow Press
SINGING—AN EXTENSION OF SPEECH   Metuchen, NJ, 1978

ISBN (Library of Congress) 0-8108-1182-0

- ❑ Ministry   ❑ Communication
- ❑ Understanding Ourselves   ■ Choral Technique/Teaching
- ❑ Understanding Teenagers   ❑ Leadership

Henrichsen, Walter A.   Victor Books
DISCIPLES ARE MADE, NOT BORN   Wheaton, IL, 1979
Making Disciples Out of Christians

ISBN (Library of Congress)   0-88207-706-6

- ■ Ministry   ❑ Communication
- ❑ Understanding Ourselves   ❑ Choral Technique/Teaching
- ■ Understanding Teenagers   ■ Leadership

Hersch, Patricia   Ballantine
A TRIBE APART   New York, 1998
A Journey into the Heart of American Adolescence

ISBN (Library of Congress)   0-449-90767-8

- ❑ Ministry   ❑ Communication
- ❑ Understanding Ourselves   ❑ Choral Technique/Teaching
- ■ Understanding Teenagers   ❑ Leadership

Hoffer, Charles R.   Wadworth
TEACHING MUSIC IN SECONDARY SCHOOLS   Belmont, CA, 1973

ISBN (Library of Congress) 0-534-00230-7

❑ Ministry   ❑ Communication
❑ Understanding Ourselves   ■ Choral Technique/Teaching
❑ Understanding Teenagers   ❑ Leadership

Holtz, Lou   Harper Business
WINNING EVERY DAY   New York, 1998
The Game Plan for Success

ISBN (Library of Congress)   0-88-730904-6

❑ Ministry   ■ Communication
❑ Understanding Ourselves   ❑ Choral Technique/Teaching
❑ Understanding Teenagers   ■ Leadership

Huckabee, Mike   Broadman and Holman
KIDS WHO KILL   Nashville, 1998
Confronting Our Culture of Violence

ISBN (Library of Congress)   0-8054-1794-X

❑ Ministry   ❑ Communication
❑ Understanding Ourselves   ❑ Choral Technique/Teaching
■ Understanding Teenagers   ❑ Leadership

Hunt, Jeanne   The Pastoral Press
CHOIR PRAYERS   Washing,ton, DC, 1986

ISBN (Library of Congress) 0-912405-22-8

■ Ministry   ❑ Communication
❑ Understanding Ourselves   ❑ Choral Technique/Teaching
❑ Understanding Teenagers   ❑ Leadership

Hunt, Jeanne   The Pastoral Press
MORE CHOIR PRAYERS   Washing,ton, DC, 1990

ISBN (Library of Congress) 0-912405-67-8

■ Ministry   ■ Communication
■ Understanding Ourselves   ■ Choral Technique/Teaching
■ Understanding Teenagers   ■ Leadership

Hybels, Bill   Intervarsity Press
TOO BUSY NOT TO PRAY   Downer's Grove, IL, 1988
Slowing Down to be With God

ISBN (Library of Congress)   0-8308-1256-3

❏ Ministry   ❏ Communication
■ Understanding Ourselves   ❏ Choral Technique/Teaching
❏ Understanding Teenagers   ❏ Leadership

Jansen, Dan   Villard Books
FULL CIRCLE   New York, 1994
An Olympic Champion Shares His Break Through Story

ISBN (Library of Congress)   0-679-43801-7

❏ Ministry   ❏ Communication
❏ Understanding Ourselves   ❏ Choral Technique/Teaching
❏ Understanding Teenagers   ■ Leadership

Johnson, Laurene   Thomas Nelson
DIVORCED KIDS   Nashville, 1990
What You Need to Know to Help Kids Survive Divorce

ISBN (Library of Congress)   0-8407-3174-4

■ Ministry   ❏ Communication
❏ Understanding Ourselves   ❏ Choral Technique/Teaching
■ Understanding Teenagers   ❏ Leadership

Keirsey, David and Bates, Marilyn   Prometheus Nemesis
PLEASE UNDERSTAND ME   Del Mar, CA, 1984
Character and Temperament Types

ISBN (Library of Congress)   0-9606954-0-0

- ■ Ministry   ❑ Communication
- ■ Understanding Ourselves   ❑ Choral Technique/Teaching
- ■ Understanding Teenagers   ❑ Leadership

Kimmel, Tim   Multnomah
LEGACY OF LOVE   Portland, 1989
A Plan for Parenting on Purpose

ISBN (Library of Congress)   0-88070-312-1

- ■ Ministry   ■ Communication
- ■ Understanding Ourselves   ❑ Choral Technique/Teaching
- ■ Understanding Teenagers   ❑ Leadership

Kouzes, James M. and Posner, Barry Z.   Jossey-Bass Publishers
CREDIBILITY   San Francisco, 1993
How Leaders Gain and Lose it, Why People Demand It

ISBN (Library of Congress)   1-55542-550-X

- ❑ Ministry   ❑ Communication
- ❑ Understanding Ourselves   ❑ Choral Technique/Teaching
- ❑ Understanding Teenagers   ■ Leadership

Lasker, Henry   Allyon and Bacon
TEACHING CREATIVE MUSIC   Boston, 1971
IN SECONDARY SCHOOLS

ISBN (Library of Congress)   79-124939

- ❑ Ministry   ❑ Communication
- ❑ Understanding Ourselves   ■ Choral Technique/Teaching
- ❑ Understanding Teenagers   ❑ Leadership

Lewis, C.S.
THE SCREWTAPE LETTERS

Touchstone Books
New York, 1961

ISBN (Library of Congress)   0-684-83117-1

- ■ Ministry
- ■ Understanding Ourselves
- ■ Understanding Teenagers

- ❑ Communication
- ❑ Choral Technique/Teaching
- ❑ Leadership

Lewis, Gordon
CHORAL DIRECTOR'S REHEARSAL
AND PERFORMANCE GUIDE

Parker Publishing
West Nyack, NY, 1989

ISBN (Library of Congress)   0-13-133398-4

- ❑ Ministry
- ❑ Understanding Ourselves
- ❑ Understanding Teenagers

- ❑ Communication
- ■ Choral Technique/Teaching
- ❑ Leadership

Link, John V. and Ware, Gerald
KEYS TO A SUCCESSFUL
YOUTH CHOIR MINISTRY

Church Street Press
Nashville, 1997

ISBN (Library of Congress)   0-7673-3456-6 DP

- ■ Ministry
- ❑ Understanding Ourselves
- ❑ Understanding Teenagers

- ❑ Communication
- ❑ Choral Technique/Teaching
- ❑ Leadership

Lucado, Max
SIX HOURS ONE FRIDAY
Anchoring to the Power of the Cross

Multnomah
Portland, OR, 1989

ISBN (Library of Congress)   0-88070-314-8

- ■ Ministry
- ❑ Understanding Ourselves
- ❑ Understanding Teenagers

- ❑ Communication
- ❑ Choral Technique/Teaching
- ❑ Leadership

Lucado, Max   Word
HE STILL MOVES STONES   Dallas, 1993
Everyone Needs a Miracle

ISBN (Library of Congress) 0-8499-0864-7

- ■ Ministry   ❑ Communication
- ❑ Understanding Ourselves   ❑ Choral Technique/Teaching
- ❑ Understanding Teenagers   ❑ Leadership

Lucado, Max   Multnomah
AND THE ANGELS WERE SILENT   Portland, OR, 1992
The Final Week of Jesus

ISBN (Library of Congress) 0-88070-487-X

- ❑ Ministry   ❑ Communication
- ■ Understanding Ourselves   ❑ Choral Technique/Teaching
- ❑ Understanding Teenagers   ❑ Leadership

Lucado, Max   Word
IN THE EYE OF THE STORM   New York, 1991
A Day in the Life of Jesus

ISBN (Library of Congress) 0-8499-0890-6

- ■ Ministry   ❑ Communication
- ■ Understanding Ourselves   ❑ Choral Technique/Teaching
- ❑ Understanding Teenagers   ❑ Leadership

MacDonald, Gail   Tyndale
HIGH CALL, HIGH PRIVILEGE   Wheaton, IL, 1981

ISBN (Library of Congress) 0-8432-1424-5

- ■ Ministry   ❑ Communication
- ■ Understanding Ourselves   ❑ Choral Technique/Teaching
- ❑ Understanding Teenagers   ■ Leadership

Madden, Myron C.   Broadman Press
BLESSING: GIVING THE GIFT OF POWER   Nashville, 1998
Finding an Identity That Makes Power Safe

ISBN (Library of Congress) 0-8054-5056-4

■ Ministry   ■ Communication
■ Understanding Ourselves   ❏ Choral Technique/Teaching
■ Understanding Teenagers   ■ Leadership

Mark, Michael   Prentiss Hall
CONTEMPORARY MUSIC EDUCATION   New York, 1996

ISBN (Library of Congress) 0-02-87915-8

❏ Ministry   ❏ Communication
❏ Understanding Ourselves   ■ Choral Technique/Teaching
❏ Understanding Teenagers   ❏ Leadership

Marshall, Catherine   McGraw-Hill
THE PRAYERS OF PETER MARSHALL   New York, 1954

ISBN (Library of Congress) 07-040598-0

■ Ministry   ■ Communication
❏ Understanding Ourselves   ❏ Choral Technique/Teaching
❏ Understanding Teenagers   ■ Leadership

McKenzie, Duncan   Rutgers Univ. Press
TRAINING THE BOY'S CHANGING VOICE   New Brunswick, NJ

ISBN (Library of Congress) 56-7611   1956

❏ Ministry   ❏ Communication
❏ Understanding Ourselves   ■ Choral Technique/Teaching
❏ Understanding Teenagers   ❏ Leadership

Mellalieu, W. Norman   Oxford Univ. Press
THE BOY'S CHANGING VOICE   London, 1934

ISBN (Library of Congress)

❑ Ministry   ❑ Communication
❑ Understanding Ourselves   ■ Choral Technique/Teaching
❑ Understanding Teenagers   ❑ Leadership

Michael, Fowler   Hinshaw
SING!   Chapel Hill, NC, 1988

ISBN (Library of Congress) 0-937276-08-1

❑ Ministry   ❑ Communication
❑ Understanding Ourselves   ■ Choral Technique/Teaching
❑ Understanding Teenagers   ❑ Leadership

Miller, J. Keith   Harper
A HUNGER FOR HEALING   San Francisco, 1991
The Twelve Steps as a Classic Model for Christian . . .

ISBN (Library of Congress) 0-06-065767-2

■ Ministry   ❑ Communication
■ Understanding Ourselves   ❑ Choral Technique/Teaching
■ Understanding Teenagers   ❑ Leadership

Moses, Harry   Parker Publishers
DEVELOPING AND ADMINISTERING   West Nyack, NY
A COMPREHENSIVE HIGH SCHOOL   1970
MUSIC PROGRAM

ISBN (Library of Congress) 13-204156-1

❑ Ministry   ❑ Communication
❑ Understanding Ourselves   ■ Choral Technique/Teaching
❑ Understanding Teenagers   ❑ Leadership

Mueller, Walt   Tyndale
UNDERSTANDING TODAY'S YOUTH CULTURE   Wheaton, IL, 1999

ISBN (Library of Congress) 0-8423-7739-5

❏ Ministry   ❏ Communication
❏ Understanding Ourselves   ■ Choral Technique/Teaching
❏ Understanding Teenagers   ❏ Leadership

Nouwen, Henri J. M.   Image Books Doubleday
THE WOUNDED HEALER   New York, 1972
In Our Own Woundedness, We Can Become a Source of Life

ISBN (Library of Congress) 0-385-14803-8

■ Ministry   ❏ Communication
■ Understanding Ourselves   ❏ Choral Technique/Teaching
■ Understanding Teenagers   ❏ Leadership

Nouwen, Henri J.M.   Doubleday
CREATIVE MINISTRY   New York, 1991

ISBN (Library of Congress) 0-385-12616-6

■ Ministry   ❏ Communication
❏ Understanding Ourselves   ❏ Choral Technique/Teaching
❏ Understanding Teenagers   ❏ Leadership

Oates, Wayne E.   Westminster Press
BEHIND THE MASKS   Louisville, KY, 1987
Personality Disorders in Religious Behavior

ISBN (Library of Congress) 0-664-24028-3

■ Ministry   ❏ Communication
❏ Understanding Ourselves   ❏ Choral Technique/Teaching
❏ Understanding Teenagers   ❏ Leadership

Parker, William and St. Johns, Elaine   Prentice Hall
PRAYER CAN CHANGE YOUR LIFE   Englewood Cliffs, NJ
ISBN (Library of Congress) 0-13-694786-7   1957

■ Ministry   ❏ Communication
❏ Understanding Ourselves   ❏ Choral Technique/Teaching
❏ Understanding Teenagers   ❏ Leadership

Peck, M.D., M. Scott   Tyndale
GOLF AND THE SPIRIT   Wheaton, IL, 1999
Lessons for the Journey

ISBN (Library of Congress) 0-51770883-3

■ Ministry   ■ Communication
■ Understanding Ourselves   ❏ Choral Technique/Teaching
■ Understanding Teenagers   ■ Leadership

Peck, M.D., M. Scott   Touchstone
THE ROAD LESS TRAVELED   New York, 1978
A New Psychology of Love, Traditional Values and Spiritual . . .

ISBN (Library of Congress) 0-671-24086-2

❏ Ministry   ❏ Communication
❏ Understanding Ourselves   ❏ Choral Technique/Teaching
❏ Understanding Teenagers   ■ Leadership

Peck, M.D., M. Scott   Touchstone
THE DIFFERENT DRUM   New York, 1987
A Spiritual Journey Toward Self-Acceptance, True . . .

ISBN (Library of Congress) 0-684-84858-9

❏ Ministry   ❏ Communication
■ Understanding Ourselves   ❏ Choral Technique/Teaching
❏ Understanding Teenagers   ❏ Leadership

Peters, Tom   Vintage Books
THE PURSUIT OF WOW!   New York, 1994
Every Person's Guide to Topsy-Turvy Times

ISBN (Library of Congress) 0-679-75555-1

❏ Ministry   ❏ Communication
❏ Understanding Ourselves   ❏ Choral Technique/Teaching
❏ Understanding Teenagers   ■ Leadership

Pipher, Ph.D., Mary   Ballantine Books
REVIVING OPHELIA   New York, 1995
Saving the Selves of Adolescent Girls

ISBN (Library of Congress) 0-345-39282-5

❏ Ministry   ❏ Communication
❏ Understanding Ourselves   ❏ Choral Technique/Teaching
❏ Understanding Teenagers   ■ Leadership

Pipher, Ph.D., Mary   Ballantine Books
THE SHELTER OF EACH OTHER   New York, 1996
Rebuilding Our Families

ISBN (Library of Congress) 0-345-40603-6

❏ Ministry   ❏ Communication
❏ Understanding Ourselves   ❏ Choral Technique/Teaching
■ Understanding Teenagers   ❏ Leadership

Pollack, M.D., William   Random House
REAL BOYS   New York, 1998
Rescuing Our Sons From the Myths of Boyhood

ISBN (Library of Congress) 0-375-50131-2

❏ Ministry   ❏ Communication
❏ Understanding Ourselves   ❏ Choral Technique/Teaching
■ Understanding Teenagers   ❏ Leadership

Ponton, M.D., Lynne E.   Basic Books
THE ROMANCE OF RISK   New York, 1997
Why Teenagers Do the Things They Do

ISBN (Library of Congress) 0-465-07075-2

❑ Ministry   ❑ Communication
❑ Understanding Ourselves   ❑ Choral Technique/Teaching
■ Understanding Teenagers   ❑ Leadership

Reid, Clyde   Harper and Row
CELEBRATE THE TEMPORARY   New York, 1972

ISBN (Library of Congress) 0-06–0668-17-2

■ Ministry   ❑ Communication
■ Understanding Ourselves   ❑ Choral Technique/Teaching
■ Understanding Teenagers   ❑ Leadership

Riley, Pat   G.P. Putnam's Sons
THE WINNER WITHIN   New York, 1993
A Life Plan for Team Players

ISBN (Library of Congress) 0-399-13839-0

❑ Ministry   ❑ Communication
❑ Understanding Ourselves   ❑ Choral Technique/Teaching
❑ Understanding Teenagers   ■ Leadership

Schalk, Carl   MorningStar
FIRST PERSON SINGULAR   St. Louis, 1998
Reflections on Worship, Liturgy, and Children

ISBN (Library of Congress) 0-944529-29-1

■ Ministry   ❑ Communication
❑ Understanding Ourselves   ❑ Choral Technique/Teaching
■ Understanding Teenagers   ❑ Leadership

Schuller, Charles   Harper and Row
MUSIC EDUCATION FOR TEENAGERS   New York, 1966

ISBN (Library of Congress) 66-10115

❏ Ministry   ❏ Communication
❏ Understanding Ourselves   ■ Choral Technique/Teaching
❏ Understanding Teenagers   ❏ Leadership

Seamands, David A.   Victor Books
HEALING FOR DAMAGED EMOTIONS   Wheaton, IL 1986

ISBN (Library of Congress) 0-88207-228-5

■ Ministry   ❏ Communication
■ Understanding Ourselves   ❏ Choral Technique/Teaching
■ Understanding Teenagers   ❏ Leadership

Sharp, Tim W.   Leawood Press
PRECISION CONDUCTING   Leawood, KS, 1996
The Seven Disciplines of the Masterful Conductor

ISBN (Library of Congress) 1-889411-01-9

❏ Ministry   ❏ Communication
❏ Understanding Ourselves   ■ Choral Technique/Teaching
❏ Understanding Teenagers   ❏ Leadership

Shaw, Harold   Wheaton Press
HOW TO GROW A YOUNG MUSIC LOVER   Wheaton, IL, 1994
Helping Your Child Discover and Enjoy the World of Music

ISBN (Library of Congress) 0-87799-370-X

❏ Ministry   ❏ Communication
❏ Understanding Ourselves   ■ Choral Technique/Teaching
❏ Understanding Teenagers   ❏ Leadership

Summitt, Pat
RAISE THE ROOF
The Inspiring Inside Story of the Tennessee Vols

Broadway Books
New York, 1998

ISBN (Library of Congress) 1-889411-01-9

❏ Ministry
❏ Understanding Ourselves
❏ Understanding Teenagers

❏ Communication
❏ Choral Technique/Teaching
■ Leadership

Swanson, Frederich J.
MUSIC TEACHING IN JUNIOR HIGH
AND MIDDLE SCHOOL

Meredith Press
New York, 1973

ISBN (Library of Congress) 72-94283

❏ Ministry
❏ Understanding Ourselves
❏ Understanding Teenagers

❏ Communication
■ Choral Technique/Teaching
❏ Leadership

Tannen, Ph.D., Deborah
THAT'S NOT WHAT I MEANT
How Conversational Style Makes or Breaks Relationships

Ballentine Books
New York, 1986

ISBN (Library of Congress) 0-345-37972-1

❏ Ministry
■ Understanding Ourselves
■ Understanding Teenagers

■ Communication
❏ Choral Technique/Teaching
❏ Leadership

Vardey, Lucinda
MOTHER TERESA
A Simple Path

Ballentine Books
New York, 1995

ISBN (Library of Congress) 0-345-37945-2

❏ Ministry
❏ Understanding Ourselves
❏ Understanding Teenagers

❏ Communication
❏ Choral Technique/Teaching
■ Leadership

Viorst, Judith   Fawcett Gold Medal
NECESSARY LOSSES   New York, 1986
The Loves, Illusions, Dependencies and Impossible . . .

ISBN (Library of Congress) 0-449-13206-4

❏ Ministry   ❏ Communication
   Understanding Ourselves   ❏ Choral Technique/Teaching
   Understanding Teenagers   ❏ Leadership

Von Oech, Roger   Harper Perennial
A KICK IN THE SEAT OF THE PANTS   New York, 1986
Using Your Explorer, Artist, Judge and Warrior to be More. . .

ISBN (Library of Congress) 0-06-015528-0

   Ministry   ❏ Communication
   Understanding Ourselves   ❏ Choral Technique/Teaching
   Understanding Teenagers   ❏ Leadership

Von Oech, Roger   Warner
A WHACK ON THE SIDE OF THE HEAD   New York, 1983
How You Can Be More Creative

ISBN (Library of Congress) 0-446-39-158-1

   Ministry   ❏ Communication
   Understanding Ourselves   ❏ Choral Technique/Teaching
   Understanding Teenagers   ❏ Leadership

Yancey, Philip   Zondervan
DISAPPOINTMENT WITH GOD   Grand Rapids, 1988
Three Questions No One Asks Aloud

ISBN (Library of Congress) 0-310-51781-8

   Ministry   ❏ Communication
   Understanding Ourselves   ❏ Choral Technique/Teaching
❏ Understanding Teenagers   ❏ Leadership

Yancey, Philip   Zondervan
WHAT'S SO AMAZING ABOUT GRACE?   Grand Rapids, 1997

ISBN (Library of Congress) 0-310-21327-4

■ Ministry   ❏ Communication
■ Understanding Ourselves   ❏ Choral Technique/Teaching
■ Understanding Teenagers   ❏ Leadership

Yarrington, John   Augsburg Fortress
BUILDING THE YOUTH CHOIR   Minneapolis, 1990
Training and Motivating Teenage Singers

ISBN (Library of Congress) 0-8066-2454-X

❏ Ministry   ❏ Communication
❏ Understanding Ourselves   ❏ Choral Technique/Teaching
■ Understanding Teenagers   ❏ Leadership

CHAPTER 48

Movies

The movies listed below are both for your enjoyment as well as to gain more insight into the current youth culture. Each movie portrays a strong depiction of individual teenagers, adults who deal with them, the struggles of kids within a modern youth culture, or all of the above. Watch and listen carefully with your teenagers in mind. You will come away with better insight and increased wisdom in dealing with the daily challenges of being a youth choir director.

1980	ORDINARY PEOPLE
Robert Redford	*Donald Sutherland, Mary Tyler Moore, Timothy*
Cue Values	*Hutton, Judd Hirsch*

Family disfunction cripples teenagers as well as adults. Living with and protecting the family secret destroys all who hold it. Caring adults, with a divine combination of tough love and compassion can make an enormous difference in helping troubled kids survive and move toward emotional and spiritual health.

1981	ON GOLDEN POND
Mark Rydell	*Katherin Hepburn, Henry Fonda, Jane Fonda, Doug*
Cue Values	*McKeon, Dabney Coleman*

Superb exposé on intergenerational family relationships and how they affect the teenager in the house.

1983	THE OUTSIDERS
Francis Coppola	*All-star cast: C. Thomas Howell, Matt Dillon, Ralph*
Cue Values	*Machio, Patrick Swayze, Rob Lowe, Emilio Estevez,*
	Tom Cruise

The all-star cast is barely recognizable, because they are all just young kids, before they hit it big in show business. Amazing that each one of the newcomers in 1983 later became big-time stars in the '90s. We never know what our kids will become. The gang was not looking for a fight, only for love. Rich imagery, timeless applications.

1985	THE BREAKFAST CLUB
John Hughes	*Emilio Estevez, Paul Gleason, Anthony Michael*
Cue Values	*Hall, Judd Nelson, Molly Ringwald*

Kids are looking for intimacy, many times in all the wrong places. When home and school fail them, many have no place to go. Youth choir could help fill in that gap. How differently this group of kids would have looked if they each had a loving, Christian community around them.

1986	NOTHING IN COMMON
Garry Marshall	*Tom Hanks, Jackie Gleason, Eva Marie Saint,*
Cue Values	*Hector Elizondo*

Children, even successful adult children, suffer greatly from the dysfunction families experience during their adolescence. It takes a lot of work to work through the process of pain.

1986	HOOSIERS
David Anspaugh	*Gene Hackman, Barbara Hershey, Dennis Hopper*
Cue Values	

Impossible odds can be solved and redemption of relationships experienced by communication, care, and compassion. Great flick to watch with your teenagers, perhaps using the bus VCR on choir tour.

1989   DEAD POET'S SOCIETY
Peter Weir   *Robin Williams, Robert Sean Leonard, Ethan Hawke*
Cue Values

The value of a caring, creative, passionate teacher in the lives of teenagers cannot be measured. Heavy with plenty of applications for youth choir directors. Inspires the teacher in all of us.

1990   AWAKENINGS
Penny Marshall   *Robert De Niro, Robin Williams, Ruth Nelson*
Cue Values

To every life, there is a window of opportunity in which to be productive, address key issues, and move into the future. Any time we work with people, there is always going to be mystery in the ministry.

1991   THE PRINCE OF TIDES
Barbra Streisand   *Barbra Streisand, Nick Nolte*
Cue Values

Children's and teenager's soundtracks are being created continuously. If not properly death with in adolescence, they are repressed and surface in dangerous ways throughout adulthood. Incredible pain surfaces in the movie, and we wonder how it has been suppressed all those years. Many teenagers are repressing incredibly painful memories today which will bite hard during adulthood.

1992   SISTER ACT
Emile Ardolino   *Whoopi Goldberg, Maggie Smith, Kathy Najimy*
Cue Values

Kids need someone to lead them who have not given up on them. Vision, dreams, and imagination can save kids' lives, as well as the whole community.

1992   WHERE THE RED FERN GROWS, PART 2
Jim McCullough, Sr.   *Doug McKeon, Wilford Brimley, Chad McQueen*
Cue Values

Soundtracks learned in adolescence continue to play throughout life. Coming to terms with disappointment must be confronted as a teenager or it will be much harder to work through later in life.

1993   THE SANDLOT
David M. Evans   *Tom Guiry, Mike Vitar, Patrick Renna, Marty York*
Cue Values

When a community of kids grows up together, conquers common enemies and experiences the fun of the sport, the emotional ties that bind are stronger than we might imagine. Fun flick to watch with your teenagers.

1993   SISTER ACT 2: BACK IN THE HABIT
Bill Duke   *Whoopi Goldberg, Kathy Najimy, Barnard Hughes*
Cue Values

Teamwork wins the day, even when it has seemed impossible.

1993   MRS. DOUBTFIRE
Chris Columbus   *Robin Williams, Sally Field, Pierce Bronson, Polly*
Cue Values   *Holiday, Lisa Jakub, Matthew Lawrence, Mara Wilson*

The parental tie between parents and children is strong indeed, even when incredible odds are against them. Kids will make all kinds of allowances for parents if true love is shown.

1994   THE ST. TAMMANY MIRACLE
Jim McCullough, Sr.   *Mark-Paul Gosselaar, Soleil Moon Frye, Jamie Luner*
Cue Values

Relationships are more important than winning, friendship more valuable than sport, and a community of teamwork crossed a number of barriers.

1995   MR. HOLLAND'S OPUS
Stephen Herek   *Richard Dreyfus, Glenne Headly, Jay Thomas,*
       Olympia Dukakis

To adults who grew up as teenagers under a caring, motivating teacher, that educator and the experience he provided are more valuable than the memories of a hundred pop stars.

1996   THE PREACHER'S WIFE
Penny Marshall   *Denzel Washington, Whitney Houston,*
Cue Values   *Courtney B. Vance*

Ministry can be very discouraging and seem fruitless at times. Sometimes, just when we are about to give up, a touch from God comes along to see us through, if we look for it.

1997   GOOD WILL HUNTING
Gus Van Sant   *Matt Damo, Robin Williams, Ben Affleck*
Cue Values

Many teenagers are undermotivated and underestimated. Pain covers and quells a multitude of talent and courage. A sensitive adult at the right place and the right time can help break those barriers.

1998   PATCH ADAMS
Tom Shadyac   *Robin Williams, Monica Potter, Daniel London*
Cue Values

Laughter and fun are therapy for those in emotional and physical pain. It must not be denied.

1999   OCTOBER SKY
Joe Johnston   *Jake Gyllenhaal, Chris Cooper, Laura Dern*
Cue Values

Adult mentors and teachers have powerful effects on teenagers who are not receiving proper time, attention and affirmation at home. In our choirs are tomorrow's future leaders, inventors, and innovators.

CHAPTER 49

Youth Choir Repertoire

I n the immediate pages which follow, I have sought to provide the youth choir director with twenty years' worth of quality repertoire. If your youth choir learns and memorizes twenty anthems per year, the four hundred titles listed can theoretically last you and your group for two decades.

Contributing composers: 161 over a six-hundred year period
Publishers represented: 76

Difficulty Rating

You will note the anthems are listed in categories of difficulty, 1 being the simplest and 9 the most difficult. Within these categories, the anthems are listed alphabetically by the first word of the title.

Information on Publisher and Catalogue Number

All ordering information is provided.

Text, Scriptural References

In order to provide further assistance, we have included information regarding the text. Many are scriptural texts. On these, the scripture sources are given.

Features and Teaching Values

Information is provided as to particular information of interest and suggested teaching values in the youth choir setting.

Out of Print Anthems

We know a few of these anthems are out of print. For re-printing information and permissions, please contact the publisher.

Plenty of Others

This is by no means considered a comprehensive list of quality youth choir anthems. We readily acknowledge that many more titles exist which will work wonderfully in the youth choir setting. We attempt to present only a representative listing. Thankfully, there are also numerous anthems in various stages of production, and for those who continue to write meaningful youth choir literature, we are very grateful.

A Canticle for Advent	Schaefer	SAB	Augsburg	11-10880	1998
Keyboard, minimal handbells, gong	Veni Emmanuel		Difficulty Rating: 1		

Likeable piece which has class and is easy to conquer. Beautiful streaming melodic lines. Unison singing, simple writing, although very beautiful.

A Lenten Prayer	Near	Two-part	Aureole	AE9	1999
Organ	Lent		Difficulty Rating: 1		

Easily attainable, beautiful melody and harmony mostly in thirds.
Prayer text. Good entree into part singing.

An Advent Prayer	Pote	Two-part	Hinshaw	HMC-765	1984
Keyboard	Advent		Difficulty Rating: 1		

Thoughtful, prayerful setting which practically sings itself. Very enjoyable. Gentle and fluid lines. Tuning, independence of voices. Vocal production in the treble upper registers.

Blest Are They	Haas	SATB	GIA Publications	G-2958	1986
Keyboard/Guitar	Matthew 5:3-12, The Beatitudes		Difficulty Rating: 1		

Simple, beautiful melodic lines, lovely synthesis of text and music. Can easily be used with congregation or in any number of creative ways. Solo cues provide excellent training ground for young soloists/worship leaders. Beatitudes text provides superb material for spiritual training and development through devotionals and discussion.

Cantate	Lightfoot	Two-part	Choristers Guild	CGA-794	1998
Keyboard	Psalm 96		Difficulty Rating: 1		

Easy and fun. Most groups will memorize in one session. Easy access and yet a substantial text of praise. Independence of voices. Mixed meter. Energy and articulation.

God, I Look Up   Hopson   Two-part   Choristers Guild CGA811   1998
Piano   Psalm 8   Difficulty Rating: 1
Much appeal for young teenage voices. Fun, bouncy, and catchy without being trite. Consonant articulation and vowel unity. Rhythm must be felt internally. Dynamic variation and energy.

I Will Greatly Rejoice Pote   Two-part   Church Street 0-7673-9305-8 1982
Piano   Isaiah 61   Difficulty Rating: 1
Happy, fun piece for any type of youth choir or ensemble. Good rhythmic and melodic appeal. In 6/8. Opportunities to teach energy without rushing. Nice section for working with head voice of girls in descant.

Keep Me As The Apple of Your Eye
                          Kosche   Two-part   Choristers Guild CGA-A800   1998
Piano or organ   Psalm 17:1-2 (adapted)   Difficulty Rating: 1
Delightful little piece which practically sings itself. Super piece for baby dedication service. Text is strong and opens the door for numerous avenues of theological discussion. Long, melodic lines, full yet sensitive singing. Marvelous prayer which can be used in a number of ways.

Night Song   Ailor   SAB   Beckenhorst   BP1523   1998
Piano   Advent   Difficulty Rating: 1
Simple and beautiful. Independence of voices. Perfect for young youth choirs.

Prayer for Guidance   Pote   Two-part   Hinshaw   HMC-244   1977
Keyboard   Psalm 25   Difficulty Rating: 1
Lovely, versatile prayer for variety of uses. Sustained line, efficient choral sound, and tuning. Independence of voices.

Rejoice, Rejoice! For Christ is Born
                          Larson   Two-part   Church Street 0-7673-9315-5 1998
Piano   Advent   Difficulty Rating: 1
Delicate melody provides good synthesis for text. Happy, peaceful sound. Easy for most any group to conquer and memorize. Congregation may join near end. Even experienced choirs benefit from singing simple melodies. Unify vowels, build phrase movement and strive for tuning and balance.

Shine, Advent Candle, Shine

| | Shafferman | Two-part | Alfred | 4268 | 1992 |

Piano or organ   Advent   Difficulty Rating: 1

Beautiful phrases, easy to conquer. Adaptable for any kind of youth ensemble, choir, or duet. Suggestion: Allow one of your teenage piano players to accompany this one.

Someday My Lord Will Come

| | Purifoy | SATB | Word | CS-2769 | 1975 |

Piano/keyboard   Original   Difficulty Rating: 1

Kids almost always gravitate to this fun piece. Energy in sound, consonants, attacks, releases, tuning, independence of voice parts.

Three Advent Prayers   R. Edwards SATB   MorningStar MSM-50-0028A 1999

Piano/keyboard and full   Advent or General   Difficulty Rating: 1
orchestration available
from publisher (MSM-50-0028B).

Sweet melodic lines, some harmony in places. Easy to use with congregation. Breath control, stagger breathing, legato singing.

Thy Holy Wings   Burkhardt Two-part MorningStar MSM-50-5552 1999

Piano, oboe, clarinet and cello.   Psalm 25   Difficulty Rating: 1

Very flexible. Performance and worship possibilities are great. Lovely text and beautiful connection between words and music. A feel for global music. Melodic lines are beautiful and intervals gracefully leap.

We Gather to Gather   Hopson   Two-part Agape   HH 3946   1994

Piano and C instrument (included)   Netherlands Folk Hymn Difficulty Rating: 1

Traditional melody with fresh running treatment of accompaniment. A usable anthem for virtually any choral situation. Good way to get the choir to memorize. This piece will flow easily and should be quickly conquered. Attention to dynamics and vocal production in higher sections.

All Things Work Together for Good

| | Carter | Two-part | Providence | PP117 | 1990 |

Keyboard   Romans 8:28   Difficulty Rating: 2

Catchy yet with substance, musically as well as textually. Accuracy and articulation of rhythms. Fine piece for beginning youth choir. Even though simple, teaching opportunities abound.

Angel Carol — Page — Two-part — Alfred — 7960 — 1996
Piano with handbells (included)   Polish Carol   Difficulty Rating: 2
Lovely little piece which is adaptable for choir, ensemble, or duet. Independence of lines, flowing melodic lines, simple counterpoint.

Ascribe to the Lord — Martin — SAB/SATB — Monarch — 10/1846M — 1998
Keyboard   Psalm 29   Difficulty Rating: 2
Fun, happy and joyful! Kids love this piece! Good synthesis of text and music. Rhythmic accuracy, dynamics.

Be Thou My Vision — Hopson — SATB — Brookfield — 08740491 — 1995
Piano and C instruments (included)   Traditional   Difficulty Rating: 2
Fresh setting of old hymn. Youth will find this piece interesting because it is familiar and in a fresh setting. Transparent, lightly accompanied lines. "Solo" lines for both girls and boys. Last stanza is canon-like passage with soprano descant. Balance and tuning

Bethlehem Town — Paige — Two-part — Flammer — EA5144 — 1999
Keyboard   Advent   Difficulty Rating: 2
Approachable beginning to part singing. Pleasing melody and overall effect of the piece is strong. Independence of lines. Developing choral sound. Lends itself to good text study.

Come Follow Me — Althouse — SAB — Alfred — 4255 — 1992
Keyboard   Various scriptures   Difficulty Rating: 2
Superb youth choir piece for any setting. Fine text, pleasing music. Also available in SATB #4254. Transparent voice writing, tuning, text articulation, particularly in lower passages.

Gonna Be a Great Day — Martin — Two-part — Alfred — 4937 — 1999
Keyboard. Instrumental parts for alto and tenor sax, trumpet 1 and 2, trombone 1 and 2, guitar, bass, and percussion #18913. Also available SATB #18911.
Incorporates "Great Day"   Difficulty Rating 2
Exciting program opener or closer. Easter or general text. Familiar, yet new. Lots of fun. Rhythms, independence of lines, communication of text, tuning.

He is Lord of All   Harlan   SATB   GlorySound A-6955   1995
Keyboard   Romans 11:33-36; Isaiah 40   Difficulty Rating: 2
Lovely melody, rich harmonies, a natural youth choir piece which will almost sing
itself. Legato, smooth lines with sustained energy. Tuning, consistent vocal color
through the various ranges. Superb text and music relationship.

Here I Am, Lord   Pote   3-pt. mixed Hope   GC 977   1996
Piano or Organ   Commitment   Difficulty Rating: 2
Arrangement from "Here I Am, Lord," from the children's musical, "Rescue in the
Night." Wonderful melody and extraordinary, though simple message Singing clean,
clear, in tune melodic lines. Very sweet piece which every youth choir could sing.
Very adaptable to many situations. Outstanding opportunities for text discussion.

If We Sing at All   Pethel   SATB   GlorySound A-6568   1990
Piano or Keyboard   Contemporary, contains   Difficulty Rating: 2
                             phrases of "Holy, Holy, Holy"
Beautifully simple lines and graceful phrases. Opportunities abound for teaching
rhythms, blend, tuning, and balance. Text is thoughtful and motivating.

In This Very Room   Harris   SATB   Alexandria House R-H0202   1979
Keyboard   Contemporary   Difficulty Rating: 2
Simple beauty. Will work with practically any group of teenagers. Emotional, sweet,
yet not overdone. Rhythmic integrity throughout. Tuning of transparent melodies
and harmonies. Accompaniment is sparse, and although supportive, leaves the voices
purposely exposed in places.

In Your House, O Lord   Tuner/Wingate   SAB StevenSong SSC-2126   1996
Piano or Keyboard   Contemporary   Difficulty Rating: 2
Lovely, flowing melodic lines. Harmony emerges naturally and easily. Memory comes
quickly. Dynamics. The presence of God in our lives and the importance of corporate
worship.

Long Time Ago   Martin   SAB   High Street JH 544   1996
Piano   Advent   Difficulty Rating: 2
Gorgeous, haunting melody which flows freely. Teens will sing it easily and enjoy the
variety. Beautiful for working lines and phrases. Elegant and gentle. Short *a cappella*
section is good exposure to this medium. A sure winner for any Advent.

Lord, I Stretch My Hands to You Althouse SATB Providence PP 131 1992
Piano (Also available in SAB). Based upon Charles Wesley Difficulty Rating: 2
A superb youth choir piece. Text, music, and pathos are wonderful for this age group.
Building a legato line. Harmonies are simple and beautiful. Ballad-like writing which
symbolizes peace.

Love One Another Hopson Two-part Choristers Guild CGA741 1996
Piano John 13; Matthew 25 Difficulty Rating: 2
Creative and fresh setting of timely text. Melody moves gently and securely. Second
voice takes melody and upper voice is counter-melody. Good vocal training, sustaining of breath.

Make Me a Servant Harlan/Williams SAB Brookfield 08741388 1998
Keyboard Original Difficulty Rating: 2
Simple, beautiful prayer. Memorable for gentle phrases and simple, transparent vocal
lines. Tuning and balance.

May the Peace of the Lord Wagner Two-part Hope A-606 1988
Keyboard. Handbell parts avail. #1314 Benediction Difficulty Rating: 2
Lovely, gentle piece. Flows like a clear stream. Easy success, and yet not trite.
Substance in text and classy music. Independence of lines. Very flexible for usage in
many settings. Rhythms totally together.

O *Magnify the Lord with Me* Pethel Two-part GlorySound EA-5063 1985
Keyboard Psalm 34:3 Difficulty Rating: 2
Calypso feel. Highly rhythmic and much fun. Very singable and magnetic quality.
Rhythms. Rhythms. Rhythms. Articulation of consonants. Terraced dynamics.

Palm Branches Nolan SA(T)B Harold Flammer D 5494 1998
Piano, handbell part Palm Sunday Difficulty Rating: 2
included on pages 11-12.
Gentle melody in 6/8. Very nice musical treatment of text and rhythm. Handbells
add festive feel. Sing smooth melodic lines in 6/8 time. Dynamic variations, crescendo, decrescendo. Very singable and playable, even for young choirs.

Psalm 139   Pote   SATB   Choristers Guild CGA-610   1992
Piano   Psalm 139   Difficulty Rating: 2
Wonderful piece for beginning youth choir or a seasoned group. Very singable, very
well-crafted. Fresh setting for magnificent text. Sure to be a favorite with most youth
choirs. Gentle melodic lines, independence of voices, tuning, dynamic variation.

Revive Us Again   Hayes   SATB   GlorySound A 7204   1998
Piano. Parts available from   Old Gospel   Difficulty Rating: 2
publisher for sax, trumpets,
trombones, bass, guitar, drums (LB 5456).
Fun and rhythmic. Rhythm and feeling choral music of an expanded style. Fun to
sing.

Risen Indeed   Martin   SATB   High Street JH533   1993
Keyboard   Easter   Difficulty Rating: 2
Fun, fun, fun! Simple to learn, quick to memorize. Rhythmic precision, dynamic variation, independence of voices. Excellent for younger choirs, but exciting for older, as
well.

Stand Fast in the Lord   Page   Two-part   Flammer   EA-5119   1992
Keyboard   Philippians 4: 1-7   Difficulty Rating: 2
Very kind piece of music. Lines flow like a river, and voice parts are beautiful and
well-fitted to both music and text. Good entree into part singing. Independence of
lines.

Teach Me, O Lord   Nolan   Two-part   GlorySound   EA5147   1999
Keyboard. Guitar, bass, and   Psalm-like Prayer   Difficulty Rating: 2
drum parts available #LB5514.
Magnetic music, excellent merging of interesting music elements: melody, rhythm,
harmony. Prayer text provides good devotional material. Very likable selection which
makes teaching it a privilege.

The Armor of God   Allen   Two-part   Lillenas   AN-8098   1992
Keyboard. Orchestration   Commitment   Difficulty Rating: 2
available #OR-2258.
Kids will find the rhythms enjoyable and easy. Much appeal to younger voices.
Rhythms and phrasing. Articulation of text and rhythmic integrity.

The Artist	Martin	SATB	Flammer	A7214	1998
Keyboard		Contemplative		Difficulty Rating: 2	

Gentle melody in ballad style. Usable in variety of ways with variety of groups.
Smooth phrasing, independence of voice parts, stagger breathing, dynamics, tuning.

The Last Supper	Pote	SATB	Choristers Guild	CGA-532	1989
Piano with optional piano and bass.		Mark 14		Difficulty Rating: 2	

Very usable and beautiful setting for youth in communion. Easy and transparent lines.
Easy divisi between tenor and bass and soprano and alto. Phrasing, dynamics, and
choral ambiance emphasized.

They Crucified My Lord	Carter	3-part	Hope	JC 316	1992
Keyboard/Piano/Organ	Traditional spiritual			Difficulty Rating: 2	

Haunting melodic lines and harmonies, yet easy to hear. Thoughtful text to powerful
for teenagers to ponder. Basic choral principles on many levels are implied in this
anthem.

They Shall Soar Like Eagles	Manzo	SA/TB	Fred Bock	BG2023	1986
Keyboard. Flute obligato included.		Isaiah 40:29-31		Difficulty Rating: 2	

Easy and free. Very versatile and usable in many settings. Use with variety of voice
parts. Sustained supported, and fluid melodic lines. Soars like an eagle. Lovely and
very singable.

Two Songs of Hope	Edwards	SATB	MorningStar	MSM-50-2507A	2000
Keyboard. Orchestration		Selected Scriptures		Difficulty Rating: 2	

available #MSM-50-2507B.
First selection, "Canticle of Comfort" was originally entitled "Comfort for Columbine"
in memory of the students injured and killed in Colorado. "Truly, God is Able" was
originally entitled "Canticle for Kenya." Chorus-like songs which incorporate limited
four-part sections. Smooth and gentle, usable on many levels, including with congregation.

We Are One	Hayes	SAB	GlorySound	D5481	1998
Piano. Parts available for guitar,		Original Unity		Difficulty Rating: 2	

bass, and drums from publisher (LB5463).
Also available in SATB (A 7209).
Much-needed message for today's church. Strong text and nice music. Independence
of voices. Flexibility allows use in many settings. Community of faith explored.

We Come Rejoicing   Pethel   SATB   Choristers Guild   CGA816   1998
Piano   Psalm 63 (adapted)   Difficulty Rating: 2
Wonderful energetic selection for call to worship or general use. Very singable and
fun. Accompaniment is very supportive of voice parts. Several teaching opportunities
here. See how quickly your kids can commit this one to memory. It can be done in
one rehearsal.

What Can I Bring   Pethel   SAB   Hope   GC900   1989
Keyboard   Advent   Difficulty Rating: 2
Gorgeous for choir or ensemble, trio, or solo. Smooth, seamless lines and flowing
melody. Harmonies very simple.

A Carol Trilogy   Fettke   SATB   Genevox   0-7673-9292-2   1997
Keyboard and/or Orchestra   Advent   Difficulty Rating: 3
(0-7673-9293-0)
Three Christmas settings for choir, orchestra and congregation. Very youth friendly
and usable separately or together. Includes "O Come, O Come Emmanuel," "How
Great Our Joy," and "Angels We Have Heard on High." Great entree into having kids
sing with orchestra. Works well for use with chamber orchestra (string quartet, winds,
piano).

A Jubilant Song   Lightfoot   Two-part   Sacred Music   10/1026   1993
Piano   Psalms and Ancient Latin   Difficulty Rating: 3
Superb anthem which sounds much more difficult than it is. Exciting and indeed
jubilant. Mixed meter between 6/8 and 9/8 from beginning to end. Shift of accents is
brilliant, great teaching tools. Piece is fun and yet has the same effect as singing a
good vocalise.

Angels Looked Down   Curry   SATB   GlorySound   A7027   1996
Piano and/or organ and orchestra.   Communion/Holy Week   Difficulty Rating: 3
Orchestration available from
publisher (LB 5368).
Strong, creative text. Incorporates hymn, "I Stand Amazed" by Charles Gabriel. Dark
and heavy, ambiance and effective choral communication and focus required.

Be Still   Beebe   Two-part   Hinshaw   HPC-7012   1979
Keyboard   Psalm 46   Difficulty Rating: 3
Classic youth choir anthem. Excellent for young group, still challenging for older
kids. Rhythms, articulation, observance of rests, accents, and dynamics.

Be Thou My Vision   Wagner   SAB   Flammer   D-5379   1985
Keyboard   Ancient Irish   Difficulty Rating: 3
Very fine, flexible and easy arrangement for kids. Usable in choir or ensemble. Long
sustained, supported lines. Vowel formation.

Behold, I Stand at the Door   Thornton/King   SA(T)B
                                       Broadman   4566-45   1983
Keyboard   Revelation 3:20   Difficulty Rating: 3
From the youth musical, "Choices." Rhythms, tuning, and dynamics. Still relevant
text and style.

Bought with a Price   Sleeth   Two-part   Hinshaw   HMC-542   1981
Piano, Optional SATB   1 Corinthians 6, Micah 6   Difficulty Rating: 3
Elegant and pleasant setting of needed text. Choir beginning to sing parts will bene-
fit. Truly lovely lines which must be kept smooth and silky.

Come Down, O Lord   Pethel   SATB   Hope   GC-860   1984
Keyboard   Prayer   Difficulty Rating: 3
Easy call to prayer or general worship anthem. Memorable melody. Basic choral train-
ing. Attacks, releases, proper breathing and phrasing. Dynamic variations.

Coming Home   Allen   SATB   Purifoy   479-03110   1985
Keyboard   Hymn   Difficulty Rating: 3
Features and includes drama (The Prodigal Son) which coordinates with the piece.
Hymn text is set to new fresh music. Simple but pretty music which is easy to con-
quer and sing well. Drama and song work well together for teaching opportunities.

Dance and Sing for the Lord ...   Hopson   Two-part
Piano and Tambourine   Choristers Guild   CGA 749   1998
(part included in choral score)   Isaiah 11:1-7   Difficulty Rating: 3
Popular ancient Hebrew folk melody. Fun and exciting. Independence of voices.
Establishing part singing could never be easier than on this piece. Delightful.

Delight Yourself in the Lord   Barrett   SAB   GlorySound   D 5475   1997
Piano. Guitar, drums and bass   Psalm 37   Difficulty Rating: 3
parts available from publisher (LB5419).
Good setting of much-needed text. Instruments add youth appeal and interest. Text
provides superb devotional material for youth choirs. Music is joyous, fun and enjoyable.

Didn't My Lord Deliver Daniel   Emerson   Three-part   Jenson   40326168   1992
Keyboard   Resurrection   Difficulty Rating: 3
Traditional spiritual set in new surroundings. Workable in virtually all youth choirs
or ensembles. Rhythms, spiritual style, good entree into part sing. Enjoyable.

Easter is Here   Williams/Paige SAB   Harold Flammer D 5490   1998
Keyboard   Resurrection   Difficulty Rating: 3
Lilting piece which dances from beginning to end. Fun, easy, and very approachable.
Holding firm the tempo in 6/8. Independence of voices. Optional bass line appears
near the end. Fun and easy to conquer.

Friends   Smith/Taylor   SAB   Word   3010311168   1982
Keyboard   Contemporary   Difficulty Rating: 3
Youth favorite through the years. Speaks to them on the relational level as few songs
will. Rhythms, rhythms, rhythms. Dynamics and articulation of text.

Gather the People   Pethel   SATB   Hope   CG861   1984
Keyboard   Joel 2: 15-32   Difficulty Rating: 3
Easy and exciting, usable in most any youth choir situation. Flexibility in usage.
Strong vocal lines, driving rhythms, and stout harmonies at the end.

Gaudete   Batastini   SATB   GIA Publications G-3056   1987
A cappella with handbells,   Renaissance Carol   Difficulty Rating: 3
finger cymbals, and tambourine.
Sung with energy and fire, very exciting and moving piece. Quite energetic, loud, and
strong. *A cappella* unison melody lines. Simplicity provides perfect setting for choral
training on numerous levels.

Glorious Is Thy Name, O Lord   M. Edwards   SATB
Piano. Orchestration available   Church Street   06630-3565-3   1999
from publisher (06330-0430-8).   Old Hymn Text   Difficulty Rating: 3
Delightful, dancing setting of the old hymn. Baroque-feel. Light and bouncy throughout. Good teaching opportunities in singing lightly at top range. Tuning, phrasing and
dynamics.

Go Out with Joy   Perry   Three-part Alfred   4949   1994
Keyboard   Isaiah 55: 12   Difficulty Rating: 3
Straight forward, sensitive, and appealing anthem. Independence of voice parts.
Accompaniment is very supportive. Syncopation enlivens the joyous message is easily
taught.

God is Our Refuge and Strength   Pote   SATB
                                      Hope   A-583   1986
Keyboard. Trumpet parts available   Psalm 46   Difficulty Rating: 3
#A-583-B.
Youth choir classic, every teenager should sing this piece. Easy assymetrical rhythms
and mixed meter. Exciting and easy to learn and memorize. Strong soprano descant.

God So Loved the World   Homan   Unison   Choristers Guild   CG-447   1988
Keyboard. Flute part included.   John 3:16   Difficulty Rating: 3
Easy and pleasant, melodic line is beautiful and flowing. Usable on many levels, with
many combinations of voices. Support and sustain of open sound on long lines.

Honor and Praise   Paris/Kirkland   SATB   Allegris   AG-1017   1996
Piano and/or Orchestration (OR-2314)   Praise   Difficulty Rating: 3
Contemporary Christian feel, easy-going anthem provides color and contemporary
feel for choir or ensemble. Simple three-part for girls provides nice introduction into
three-part singing. Independence of voices.

How Far Is It to Bethlehem?   Pethel   SATB   Somerset   AD 2048   1993
Piano with flute (included).   Traditional English Carol   Difficulty Rating: 3
Easy, thoughtful piece which provides variation and color for worship or Christmas
concert. Basic, good music which is pleasing and smooth. Nice accompaniment assists
voices. Good entree into four-part singing. Nice "solo" lines for both boys' and girls'
sections.

I Want to Walk as a Child of the Light	Lamberton	SATB	MorningStar
Organ or Keyboard	MSM-50-8813		1998
	Devotion	Difficulty Rating: 3	

Catchy, singable lines. Perfectly suited for young voices. Good introduction into part singing. Rubato lines. Unison passages spotlight need for balance. Easily teachable and approachable for kids.

I Will Serve You, Lord	Berry	SATB	GlorySound	A 7103	1997
Piano. Drums, guitar, and bass		Commitment	Difficulty Rating: 3		
parts available from publisher (LB5404).					

Contemporary feel. Very singable and strong. Strong statement of commitment and desire to minister. Crescendo from beginning to end.

I'll Lead You Home	Allen	SATB	Allegris	AG-1011	1995
Keyboard		Service	Difficulty Rating: 3		

Solo feel throughout. Good message for kids. Rhythms, independence of lines and devotional possibilities from text.

If I Have My Ticket	Moore	SATB	Belwin	SV9130	1991
Keyboard. Also available		Gospel Spiritual	Difficulty Rating: 3	
in TTB #SV9131.				

Fun and magnetic for teenagers. Enjoyable as well as challenging, particularly for younger voices. Rhythms, syncopation, style. Tuning of unison lines.

In His Presence	Lawrency	SATB	Brentwood	OT1085	1988
Keyboard. Orchestration		Praise and Devotion	Difficulty Rating: 3	
available #OR-1085.				

Beautiful, contemporary melody and well-written harmonies. Can be in a variety of ways for worship. Smooth, gentle lines. Articulation of text in lower registers. Creating a mood and a stillness in the presentation.

It Is a Good Thing to Give Thanks	Butler	Three-part	Agape	EB9213	1982
Keyboard		Psalm 92	Difficulty Rating: 3		

Catchy, running melodies and simple counterpoint. Pleasing and simple. Good introduction into part singing. Variation in articulation within the piece. Rhythmic accuracy. Dynamics.

Jesus, Precious Jesus   Blankenship   SATB   Broadman   4554-92   1975
Keyboard   Contemporary   Difficulty Rating: 3
Superb youth choir selection. Timeless, beautiful, and elegant. Independence of voic-
es. Dynamics, gentle articulation. Text makes for good devotional material.

Little One, Holy One   Lau   SATB   Lorenz   E221   1995
Keyboard   Advent   Difficulty Rating: 3
Kind, delicate choral selection to bring warmth and tenderness to any program or
worship service. Flowing lines, treatment of beginning and backside of each phrase.
Nuance, tone, and intonation.

Lord Most Holy   Hayes   SATB   Genevox   3100-33   1995
Piano. Orchestration available   Devotional Prayer   Difficulty Rating: 3
from publisher (3000-54).
Reverent musical lines appropriate for almost any worship setting. Call to worship or
general worship use. Prayer-like and meaningful as response.

Many Gifts, One Spirit   Pote   SAB   Coronet   392-41417   1986
Keyboard   Contemporary, Unity   Difficulty Rating: 3
Allen Pote's consummate youth choir anthem. Kids will want to sing it every time
they are together. Also available in SSA #392-41466 and SATB #392-41388. Fine
introduction into part-singing. Easy four-part. Tuning and transparent vocal lines. Can
be made stunning.

Messiah   Allen   SATB   Purifoy   479-13094   1987
Keyboard   Praise   Difficulty Rating: 3
Catchy and a favorite of many choirs. Quick and driving, yet also tender as well.
Rhythmic impulse, hemiola feel throughout. Superb praise piece.

O Be Joyful   Van   SATB   Walton   WDW-1007   1995
Guitar, harp, or piano   Advent   Difficulty Rating: 3
Unique, unusual piece with strong appeal for youth. Lovely, gentle melody which
incorporates a different sound from the ordinary. Interesting and enjoyable learning.

O Give Thanks   Martin   SAB   GlorySound   D5414   1991
Keyboard   Psalm 105:1-5   Difficulty Rating: 3
Rhythmic, joyful, and fun. Melody dances and harmonies are quite simple. Excellent
entree into part singing. Very approachable for most youth choirs.

O God, Creator   Marcello   Two-part MorningStar MSM-50-9420 1998
Piano or Organ   Psalm 8   Difficulty Rating: 3
Extremely flexible, the two voices can be virtually of any mixture. Delightful introduction into the Baroque. Light, delicate feel. Tuning and terraced dynamics are of
the essence.

Serenity   Jones   SAB   Jackman Universe 392-00883   1996
Piano, flute. String parts also   St. Francis of Assisi   Difficulty Rating: 3
available #392-00883.
Lovely setting for kids, calming, soothing text and music which enhances it. Legato
singing. Good introduction into 3-part singing. Excellent for young voices as well as
more mature groups.

Shout for Joy   Greer   SATB   Church Street   0-7673-9309-0   1998
Piano   Psalm 100   Difficulty Rating: 3
Exciting, singable, and fun! Intensive, concentrated singing, rhythmic impulse is
strong. Dynamic variation paramount.

Sing a Joyful Song   Pethel   SATB   Hope   C5008   1999
Keyboard. Brass parts Isaiah 23:16 & Ephesians 5:19   Difficulty Rating: 3
available #C5008B.
Jubilant and energetic anthem of praise. Useful in many worship settings. Rhythms.
Independence of line, good for beginning part-singing. Flows and almost sings itself.

Sing Joyful Song   Hopson   SATB   Hope   C 5008   1999
Piano with brass. Brass parts   Isaiah 23, Ephesians 5   Difficulty Rating: 3
available from publisher (#C5008B).
Joyous, easy piece which will come together quickly, sounding more difficult than it
is. Driving rhythms and fun melodies. Good introduction to *a cappella* with a few
easy isolated measures. Crescendo and descrendo.

Sing of the Glory   Paige   SATB   Harold Flammer A 6805   1993
Piano   Praise   Difficulty Rating: 3
Fun, easy melody with some harmony that is basically two-part doubled. Good selection for young or inexperienced choir. Independence of voice parts. Articulation of consonants. Dynamic variations.

The Joyful Sound   Allen   Two-part Lillenas   AN-8081   1989
Keyboard. Orchestration   Spiritual   Difficulty Rating: 3
available #OR-2188.
Jazzy spiritual with lots of rhythmic movement and shuffle beat. Rhythms and style.

The Lord is My Shepherd   Pote   SATB   Choristers Guild CGA-551 1993
Keyboard   Psalm 23   Difficulty Rating: 3
Wonderful melody and harmonies provide superb fresh setting of the text.
Dynamics, phrasing, stagger breathing, tuning of unison lines. Good piece for training younger voices. Good music for any youth choir.

The Morning Trumpet   Burroughs SATB   Candella   JRS-4033   1997
Keyboard or orchestra (orchestration   Sacred Harp   Difficulty Rating: 3
available from publisher JRO4033) with
two trumpets (included in choral score).
Fun, simple, and exciting. Great entree into Sacred Harp tunes and texts. Exciting use of trumpets. Voice parts very approachable for teen voices.

They Carried My Lord Away Martin   SATB   Alfred   4242   1997
Piano   Lent or Holy Week Difficulty Rating: 3
Powerful pathos and text. Dark and moving. Independence of lines. Phrases sustained and energized throughout.

They Crucified My Lord   Owens   SAB   MorningStar MSM-50-3409 1998
Organ and Keyboard   African-American Spiritual   Difficulty Rating: 3
Great piece with much pathos and nuance. Superb devotional material. Transparent voice parts make tuning and balance key issues.

Waiting for a King   Martin   SATB   Triune   10/1632T   1997
Piano with optional C instrument (included).   Advent   Difficulty Rating: 3
Tranquil and peaceful, yet expectant. Child-like feel and simple beauty. In 3/4, teach
the dotted rhythms to be perfectly on time. Excellent use of dynamic variation which
needs to be maximized. Smooth, flowing lines and long, four-measure phrases.

We Bring Our Thanks   Schram   SAB   Flammer   D5483   1998
Keyboard   Thanksgiving   Difficulty Rating: 3
Excellent text for offertory, Thanksgiving or general use. Music is serene and
thoughtful. Pretty melodic lines. Legato singing. Independence of voices, dynamics
and style.

Westminster Carol   Nygard   SAB   Hinshaw   HMC-860   1986
Keyboard   "Angels We Have Heard on High"   Difficulty Rating: 3
Delightful, fun and easy to learn, colorful piece which will bring quick success for
most groups. Articulation variations throughout, from staccato to legato. Appealing
setting which provides confidence to the choir.

What Wondrous Love Is This   Burkhardt   Two-part MorningStar
Organ or keyboard, with optional   MSM-60-3002   1998
treble instrument and handbells.   American Folk Hymn   Difficulty Rating: 3
Simple and elegant. Beautiful lines and transparent harmonies. Hymnody.
Independence of voices, line, phrases, and dynamics.

Worthy and Faithful and Righteous   Sterling   SATB Genevox   4172-67   1986
Keyboard   Praise   Difficulty Rating: 3
Very contemporary sound. . . almost new age sonorities. Rhythm and flowing har-
monies. Text articulation is a challenge with this anthem.

I Will Keep My Eyes on You   Berry   SATB   Daybreak   08740970   1997
Piano   Prayer   Difficulty Rating: 4
Pensive piece which concentrates upon the presence of God in everyday life.
Teenagers will relate immediately to text. Gentle unison lines. Harmony makes good
sense and is easy to hear. Good choir theme song. Discipleship and sensitivity to the
Spirit of God.

A Thanksgiving Prayer   Larson   SATB   Lorenz   10/1702L   1998
Piano   Thanksgiving   Difficulty Rating: 4
Lovely setting of Thanksgiving and unity text. Calm, reassuring, and gentle. Musically perfect for kids voices. Melodic lines are well-crafted and easy to sing well. Harmonies are simple though rich. Warm, friendly presentation needed.

All I Have   Pethel   SATB   Coronet Press 392-41937   1995
Piano/keyboard   Commitment   Difficulty Rating: 4
Long melodic lines, quite singable and satisfying, four-part sections are easily attainable, moderate range. Creating musical lines, breath control, stagger breathing, legato singing, text teaches strong personal commitment.

All That Lasts   Angerman SATB   Harold Flammer A 7260   1998
Piano   Devotional
Running piano accompaniment, very supportive of voices. Good text for throw-away society. Simple and tasteful lines. Two-part most of the time, but four-part is easy to negotiate. Good starter kit for four-part singing. Dynamics, legato articulation.

Alleluia! Gloria! Magnificat! Noel!   Music   SATB   Concordia 98-2897 1990
Keyboard. Percussion instrument cues included.   Difficulty Rating: 4
Delightful tune and text put together cues included. Rhythms, combining of many elements to form an exciting effect.

Alleluia! Hear the Sound   Paslay   SAB   Hinshaw   HMC 1300   1993
Keyboard   "Brethren We Have Met to Worship"   Difficulty Rating: 4
Fresh and vibrant setting of old hymn. Language more inclusive than the original. Rhythms, style, dynamics, phrasing. Good introduction into mixed meter.

Almighty Father   Harlan   SATB   GlorySound #A6898   1999
Keyboard   Psalm-like   Difficulty Rating: 4
Great text of promise and hope. Music is simple and yet classy, gentle and yet triumphant. Also available in TTBB #C 5075. Excellent introduction into TTBB for boys. Not difficult but challenging and interesting. Beautiful sounds, harmonies are colorful and parts are well-written.

Amazing Grace/Kum ba ya   Beery/Musser   SATB   Flammer   A-6668   1991
Keyboard   Traditional   Difficulty Rating: 4
Fresh setting of combination of tunes. Enjoyable and fun for kids. Transparent
melodies and flowing harmonies. Tuning of unison lines and balance of voice parts.

Be of Good Cheer   Purifoy   SATB   Purifoy   479-02014   1983
Keyboard   John 16: 33   Difficulty Rating: 4
Fun and filled with life, choral parts are easy once the basic rhythm is mastered.
Good theme song for youth choir. Teenagers warm to this piece immediately.
Rhythmic themes and variations provide colorful learning for any age of youth choir.
Keep it light and joyful, never heavy.

Behold! Rise Up! Go Tell! Shine!   Hayes   SATB   Alfred   18046   1998
Piano with optional brass, available   Four Carols   Difficulty Rating: 4
from publisher (#18300). Also available in SATB (#18045).
Delightful medley combination of "Behold that Star," "Rise Up, Shepherd and
Follow," "Go, Tell It on the Mountain," "This Little Light of Mine." Voice parts are
easy and very singable with all familiar melodies. Separation and independence of
lines. Good introduction into part singing.

Bethlehem Wind   Martin   SATB   Alfred   16440   1997
Piano   Advent   Difficulty Rating: 4
Flowing, gentle piece for color and mood in any Christmas program or worship ser-
vice. Legato, tuning, attacks and releases, good introduction into 4-part singing.

Bound for Greater Things   Medema/Scott   SATB   GlorySound   A-6849   1993
Piano and/or guitar, electric   Spiritual   Difficulty Rating: 4
bass, percussion (LB-5314).
Approachable Medema piece. Very enjoyable for kids as well as for the listener.
Communication of text. Energy and enthusiasm.

Carols Around (And a Round)   Nygard   SAB   Hinshaw   HMC-703   1984
Piano   "Dona nobis pacem," "The First Noel,"
                    "It Came Upon the Midnight Clear."   Difficulty Rating: 4
Fun and interesting setting. Artistic connection of carols. Legato singing, melodic
lines, phrasing, tuning.

Come to the Water   Foley   SATB   OCP Publications   9489   1993
Piano, guitar and solo   Isaiah 55, Matthew 28   Difficulty Rating: 4
C instrument.
Swing tempo and lots of youth appeal. Performance notes and suggestions included.
Excellent for getting singers moving with the rhythms they are singing. Bring many
musical elements together.

Come, Spirit of Our Father's Heart   Martin   SATB   CPP   Belwin   BSC00273   1993
Keyboard   Contemporary Prayer   Difficulty Rating: 4
Beautiful melody and gentle ambiance. Long, legato lines, breath control, stagger
breathing, and tuning. Prayer text invites discussion and inclusion in personal devotional life.

Crucified with Christ   Dengler   SATB   GlorySound   A7167   1997
Piano   Galatians 2:15-21 (adapted)   Difficulty Rating: 4
Strong text for young Christians. Thoughtful setting provides a fresh context for
foundational text. Excellent devotional text for kids. Music is clean, forthright, and
strong. Very strong, emotional ending which pronounces the power of Christ to save.

For Future Generations   Allen   SATB   Benson   25986-0671-7   1994
Keyboard. Orchestration   Commitment   Difficulty Rating: 4
#25986-0671-R.
Provides excellent musical connection with Cue theme of mentoring. Powerful and
convicting. Text provides many opportunities to teach Christian truth. Rhythms and
harmonies are strong, driving and focused.

For the Beauty of the Earth   Courtney   SATB   Beckenhorst   BP 1533   1998
Piano and flute. Flute part   Traditional 19th Century   Difficulty Rating: 4
available from publisher (BP1533A).
Lovely setting incorporating DIX tune. Gorgeous, crystal-like melodic lines. Gentle
music with lovely sonorities.

From All that Dwell Below the Skies   Young   SATB   Galaxy   1.2186.1   1960
Organ or piano   Isaac Watts   Difficulty Rating: 2
Sugar stick anthem for many adult choirs. Most youth can handle without difficulty.
Strong and powerful. Long, strong, exposed melodic lines. Unison singing. Divisi parts
at the end provide superb opportunity for energetic, efficient choral tone.

Goin' to the Holy City   Williams/Martin SATB   GlorySound A 7243   1998
Piano (optional) with guitar, bass,   Contemporary Spiritual   Difficulty Rating: 4
and drums (LB5473). Bass soloist.
Fun and celebrative. Hope and promise for future. Rhythms, balance between bass
soloist, instruments, and choir. A team effort.

Hear Your People Singing   Choplin   Three-part   Alfred   17933   1998
Keyboard and/or guitar, bass   Communion, Advent, Pentecost
and drums. Instrumental parts   Difficulty Rating: 4
available from publisher (17935).
Excellent setting for worship use. Flexible and appealing. Gentle and easy. Sharp
rhythms. Excellent training grounds for young soloists. Congregation may also participate.

Here Is Water, Lord   Martin   SATB   Glory Sound A-6963   1995
Keyboard   Original, incorporating "Shall We Gather at the River"
                                              Difficulty Rating: 4
Wonderful, flowing water accompaniment. Very supportive of voices. Clever juxtapo-
sition of texts and themes. Beautiful, long, melodic lines. Choral sustaining power
and phrase direction. The very creative use of the water imagery makes for fine teaching opportunities.

Hodie   Althouse Two-part   Alfred   5854   1993
Keyboard   Advent in Latin and English   Difficulty Rating: 4
Dancing piece, festive and fun. Also available in SAB #5853 and SATB #5852.
Internal rhythmic impulse. Diction, balance, and tuning, particularly in unison sec-
tions.

Holy Is the Lord   Schubert/Bock SATB   Gentry   JG473   1982
Organ or Piano   Traditional   Difficulty Rating: 4
Classical setting with easy vocal lines. Very well arranged and usable in many settings.
Long, legato lines. Tuning, balance, breath control, vowel formation.

I Have Loved You   Larson   SATB   Beckenhorst BP1514   1997
Keyboard   John 15: 9-12 (adapted)   Difficulty Rating: 4
Features Southern Harmony tune WONDROUS LOVE. Running melodic lines and
very supportive accompaniment. Ambiance and intensive communication of the textual message. Gorgeous lines and rich texture.

I Will Bless the Lord   Williams/Nolan   SAB or SATB   GlorySound   D 5476   1997
Piano with orchestration   Psalms (adapted)   Difficulty Rating: 4
available from publisher (LB5423).
Strong, moving melody with totally supportive accompaniment underneath. Very
adaptable from various choral situations. Rhythms, independence of voice parts,
dynamic variations, phrasing.

I Will Rejoice   Martin   SAB   GlorySound   D5411   1990
Keyboard   Habakkuk 3: 18   Difficulty Rating: 4
Dancing melody and easy harmonies. Changing meters, dynamics, rhythmic articula-
tion.

Let The Children Come   Williams/Martin   SATB   Alfred   4299   1993
Keyboard with children's   Mark 10:13-16 (adapted) Difficulty Rating: 4
choir, soloist, or ensemble.
Tender piece, perfect for intergenerational worship leadership. The piece almost
sings itself. Beautiful lines, inspiring harmonies, creative combination of children's
and youth/adult voices.

Let the Praise Go Round   Boyce   SAB   H.W. Gray   GCMR 3375   1977
Organ and/or Piano   Praise   Difficulty Rating: 4
Strong praise composition which instills strong singing skills. Good introduction into
melisma. Independence of voices is easy to hear. Many choirs will be raised to their
next musical level by singing this piece.

Lift Up Your Heads, O Mighty Gates   Hopson   SATB   Brookfield Press   08741788
Piano and handbells (included).   Psalm 24 (adapted)   Difficulty Rating: 4   1998
Delightful setting which will work easily in the youth choir or adult choir setting.
Strong substantial anthem which appeals to the best choral sounds a choir can pro-
duce. Simple handbell part adds brilliance and festive feel.

Look to the Rose   Martin   SATB   Flammer   A6923   1994
Keyboard   Contemporary   Difficulty Rating: 4
Fascinating text and well-suited music. Teenagers will warm to this immediately.
Long sustained lines, relationship of vowels to consonants in legato phrasing.
Beautiful lines and lovely effect.

Lord, Make Me An Instrument of Thy Peace   Lindh   SATB
                                    Choristers Guild   CGA612   1992
Piano/Keyboard   St. Francis   Difficulty Rating: 4
Gently moving anthem written to the memory of a teenager, Abe Graham who died
of cancer at age 16. Flows like a mighty, yet calm river. Repetition brings about more
commitment each time it appears. Legato singing with long lines and delicate color.
Ambiance rekindles long tonal memory. Balance and blend. Dynamic contrast.
Communication of text. Powerful, purposeful prayer for teenagers.

Now Sing We All Noel   Young   SATB   Sacred Music   S-120   1972
A cappella   Advent   Difficulty Rating: 4
Double choir, yet quite easy and approachable. Sings well and provides variety of
potential uses. Independence of voices. Larger choirs will find dividing their forces for
this piece will enhance the strength of both. Simple to teach.

Peace I Leave With You   Landes   SATB   MorningStar MSM-50-5000 1998
Organ   John 14: 27   Difficulty Rating: 4
Lovely melodic lines, superb setting for benediction. Short and sweet. Choral rich-
ness in melody and harmony.

People Need the Lord   Colvard   SATB   Sparrow 5746/1762-76011-5 1983
Keyboard   Contemporary   Difficulty Rating: 4
Hot in the '80s, this is still a very powerful piece, particularly for groups who have
not experienced it. Smooth lines and gentle articulation. Tuning and fine-tuning of
harmonies. Challenge is to produce smooth, gentle treatment.

Pray for Me   Smith   SATB   Word   301049016X   1988
Keyboard   Intercession   Difficulty Rating: 4
Somewhat trendy, but still a favorite of many kids. Good contrasting piece for con-
certs. Superb in worship when theme is prayer. Choir must think as a small group.
Tight rhythms and melodic turns. A unifying piece on several fronts.

Remember Me   Berry   SATB   Daybreak Music   08741269   1996
Piano/Keyboard   Holy Week, Communion   Difficulty Rating: 4
Very likable, singable lines. Gentle, appealing melody and harmonies. Sustained lines,
balance, tuning. Opportunities for theological discussions.

Savior, Like a Shepherd Lead Us   arr. Armstrong SATB
            Concordia   98-3326   1997
Keyboard   Hymn   Difficulty Rating: 4
Fresh setting for old hymn. Harmonies are rich and full. Tuning and balance between voices. Good for working on male sound.

Seekers of Your Heart Tunney/Hart SATB Word 3010425163 1985
Keyboard   Devotional   Difficulty Rating: 4
Much youth appeal, and a favorite of many. Text is easily relatable to teenagers. Flowing, gentle lines, isolated *a cappella* section. Possibilities for soloist and duet sections.

Shout for Joy   Pethel SATB Hope   GC 888   1988
Piano/Keyboard   Psalms (adapted)   Difficulty Rating: 4
Exciting, contagious piece which brings forth the best energy out of teenagers. Quite adaptable to fit many situations. Memory comes easy. Teaching opportunities abound in the areas of rhythm, balance, and independence of voices.

Sing for Joy   Purcell/Hopson SAB Jenson 43319010   1980
Keyboard   Psalm 100: 1-3   Difficulty Rating: 4
From "Come, Ye Sons of Art." Fine teaching opportunities on every level. Fine music.

Sing Out a Song   Besig   SATB GlorySound A-6552   1989
Keyboard. Brass and percussion Psalm-like   Difficulty Rating: 4
parts available #LB-5236.
Energetic and catchy. Excellent call to worship or for use at beginning of concert. Rhythms, in-tune unison singing, good entree into part-singing and divisi.

Sing Out, Children of God Barrett   SATB GlorySound A7183   1997
Keyboard. Parts of guitar,   Praise   Difficulty Rating: 4
bass and drums #LB5430.
Easy, yet substantial for teenagers, both musically and textually. Good training on all levels. Rhythms, independence of lines. Dynamics, phrasing, articulation of syncopation.

Sing to Him a Song of Praise   Berry   SATB   Word   301 0877 161   1996
Piano and/or orchestra   Psalmic   Difficulty Rating: 4
(301 0594 259).
Fun, delightful, and joyful. Easy parts provide good entree into four-part singing.
Rhythmic precision and choral range at the end. Vocal/choral instruction.

Sing We Noel   Young   SATB   Laurel Press 10/1920LA   1998
A cappella   Advent   Difficulty Rating: 4
Fun, joyful Christmas piece for worship or caroling. Dynamic variations. Clean articu-
lation. Vowel formation.

Surely, the Lord Is In This Place   Colvin   SATB   Word   3010101163   1977
Keyboard   Genesis 28: 16-17   Difficulty Rating: 4
Fine setting for quiet, contemplative service. Prayerful and moving. Long legato lines
on top of flowing eighth-note accompaniment. Harmonies rich and beautiful. Text -
musical relationship superb. Teaching opportunities abound.

Take My Yoke Upon You   Williams/Nolan   SATB   Harold Flammer   A7158 1997
Piano   Matthew 11 (adapted)   Difficulty Rating: 4
Fine text for Holy Week, Lent or general worship use. Isolated *a cappella* sections.
Gentle lines and flowing melodies.

The Solid Rock   Peterson   SATB   GlorySound A-5921   1980
Keyboard   Old Hymn   Difficulty Rating: 4
Delightful, fun, and exciting, this piece virtually always works with kids. 3/8 - 4/8 time
seems difficult but is easy to feel. Keep eighth note constant throughout. To be taken
as quickly as it can be done cleanly. Lots of fun.

The Son of God in Tears   Williams/Martin   SATB   Harold Flammer   A7278 1998
Piano or Organ   Holy Week   Difficulty Rating: 4
Powerful text dealing with the last week in the life of Christ. Music and text are filled
with pathos and emotion. Smooth expressing of melodic lines and harmonies.
Communication of text through the simple beauty of the music.

The Stars Look Down   Larson   SATB   Flammer   A7231   1998
Keyboard   Advent   Difficulty Rating: 4
Beautiful lines and good synthesis of music and text. Melody incorporates phrases of "O Little Town of Bethlehem." Smooth, legato singing, intonation, and seamless lines.

What Do the Stars Do?   Porterfield   SSA   Alfred   11602   1995
Piano   19th Century (Rosetti)   Difficulty Rating: 4
Appealing and attainable piece for young girls' ensemble. Independence of voices, gentle melodic lines, beautiful harmonies. Accompaniment provides excellent support for voice parts.

Whisper! Whisper!   Althouse   SAB   Alfred   5839   1998
A cappella   Advent   Difficulty Rating: 4
Easy yet exciting neo-spiritual. Kids are sure to enjoy. Good introduction into *a cappella* singing. Dynamics and unity of rhythm. Two short solos, one female and one male.

You Are My Song   Berry   SATB   Genevox 0-7673-3048-X   1996
Piano and/or orchestra (0-7673-3053-6).   Praise   Difficulty Rating: 4
Pretty melodic line, begins gently, builds, and ends softly. Simple three-part harmony for girls. Melodic lines allow fluidity of choral tone.

You Are There   Medema   SATB   Brier Patch Music   #BP204   1993
Keyboard   Comfort   Difficulty Rating: 4
Beautiful and flowing. Powerful, relevant text. Part-singing made simple. Beautiful lines and perfect wedding of text and music.

Advent Celebration   Paige   SATB   Harold Flammer   A 7213   1998
Piano   Advent   Difficulty Rating: 5
Jubilant, joyous piece which dances off the page. Rhythms in changing meters. Simple back and forth between 6/8, 3/8 and 9/8. Running 16th note accompaniment provides energy and flowing line. Nice, easy four-part.

Arise! Shine!   Williams/Martin   SATB   GlorySound A7063 1996
Keyboard, Orchestration   Isaiah 60: 1-6 (adapted) Difficulty Rating: 5
(LB 5360), Track (MC 5189).
Exciting, rhythmic, and moving, brings energy to worship service or concert.
Rhythmic integrity, dynamic variation, stylistic shifts. The spiritual lesson of coming
into God's presence with joy.

As Long As I Have Breath   Farrar   SATB   Beckenhorst   BP 1298   1987
Keyboard   Psalm-like   Difficulty Rating: 5
Beautiful lines and full rich harmonies, although not difficult. Good introduction
into divisi within sections. Meaningful text for kids, fine entree into choir devotional.

At the Break of Day   Cox   SATB   Hinshaw   HMC-1311   1993
Piano or organ and violin   Origins from Brazil, translated by Ralph Manuel
or C instrument.   Difficulty Rating: 5
Lovely prayer setting. Melody is unique and rich. Motion in melody and harmony.
Balance between voices and instruments. Text lends itself to devotional for choir.

Beneath the Cross of Jesus Wood   SATB Sacred Celebrations   10/1014   1994
Keyboard   Traditional Hymn   Difficulty Rating: 5
Fresh setting of St. Christopher tune. Very melodic and flowing. Superb for either
youth ensemble or choir. Flexible and usable in many settings. Parts are written creatively and very well. Blending of vowels and choral nuances. Excellent devotional
text for kids.

Break Forth Mountains   Ford   SATB   Hinshaw   HMC-1598   1998
Piano, flute, tambourine, claves.   Isaiah 55, Psalm 98   Difficulty Rating: 5
Fun, exciting piece full of rhythm and movement. Balance between voices and instru-
ments. Rhythm lends itself to movement. Tempo changes throughout.

Call on Him   Leavitt   SATB   Hal Leonard 08596405   1992
Piano and C instrument;   Psalm 116 (adapted)   Difficulty Rating: 5
also full orchestration available from publisher.
Excellent selection for youth choir. Text is powerful and assuring. Clean rhythms,
tuning within harmonies, and balance. Good, easy introduction into three-part boys
and girls in very isolated sections.

Carols and Candlelight   M. Edwards   SATB   Church Street 0-7673-9689-9   1999
Piano. Orchestration available   Traditional Carols   Difficulty Rating: 5
from publisher (0-6330-0297-6).
Gentle, mellow collection of four carols. Superb for youth at Christmas. Congregation may join in places if desired. Smooth, sensitive lines. Gentle sustained singing
which helps teenagers internalize the texts. Rich, deep and festive.

Celebrate! Christ the Lord is Risen   Williams/Shackley   SATB   Harold Flammer
                                              A 7262   1998
Keyboard   Easter or general   Difficulty Rating: 5
Strong, powerful and driving accompaniment. Choral lines are fun and joyful.
Excellent piece to encourage energetic singing. Rhythm, formation of consonants,
mood change to and from the B-section.

Changed   Fettke   SATB   Word   301-0108168   1979
Keyboard   I Corinthians 15:51-52 (adapted)   Difficulty Rating: 5
Exciting selection regarding the Second Coming of Christ. Long, flowing, smooth
lines. Range toward the end makes vocal coaching necessary.

Come to the Table   Pote   SATB   Coronet Press 392-41678   1992
Piano   Communion   Difficulty Rating: 5
Combination of melody, text and rhythms make for fine youth choir anthem.
Flowing 6/8, allows the working of energized phrases and clear, crisp rhythm. Steady
tempo between accompanist and choir.

Enter the Joy   Medema   SATB   Brier Patch BP 101   1993
Keyboard   Original, Joy and Praise   Difficulty Rating: 5
Intriguing text and interesting musical setting. Easter-like feeling. Good opportunity
to develop soloists on stanzas. Lovely imagery and very singable choral lines. Perfectly
suited for teenage voices.

Even His Name Is Holy   Allen   SATB   Genevox   0-7673-3324-1   1997
Keyboard. Orchestration   Praise   Difficulty Rating: 5
available #0-7673-3326-8.
Worshipful and beautiful setting which provides meditative quality at the beginning
or centerpiece for worship. Flowing melodic lines. Begins soft, ends soft, strong in "B"
section. Some girl's three-part divisi.

Give Us a Vision   Choplin   SATB   Purifoy   10/1149   1994
Keyboard   Prayer   Difficulty Rating: 5
Strong text for teenagers. Parts are simple but sound is full and rich. Rhythmic preci-
sion, singing with long legato lines, tuning in the upper registers.

Gloria In Excelsis Deo   Crandal   SAB   OCP Pub.   10511   1996
Keyboard   Advent   Difficulty Rating: 5
Terrific setting of traditional Latin text. Fine interest and energy. Superb teaching
piece, yet will be easy because it's fun learning. Mixed meter. *A cappella* section adds
to energy. Fine teaching on every level.

Great Is Thy Faithfulness   Courtney   SATB   Beckenhorst BP1522   1998
Keyboard and flute or other   Fresh Setting of Traditional
C instrument. Available from   Difficulty Rating: 5
publisher (BP1522-A).
Text which every Christian would benefit from knowing and committing to memory.
Tastefully done. Unison melodic lines are rich and smooth. Harmonies are easily
attainable for most kids. Descant toward the end.

Hark the Glad Sound   Curry   SATB   Monarch   10/1896 M   1998
Piano with optional brass and   "Gloria in Excelsis" Difficulty Rating: 5
percussion. Parts available from the publisher (30/1328M).
Delightful, rhythmic piece which is attainable for most youth choirs. Rhythmic accuracy. Good opportunity for the girls and boys to enjoy a little healthy competition in
rehearsal. Exciting and fun.

Have Thine Own Way   Burroughs SATB   Alfred   17974   1998
Keyboard   Gospel Song; Isaiah 64:8   Difficulty Rating: 5
Fresh setting of lyric gospel song for kids. In 6/8. Underpinning of running sixteenth
notes against dotted quarter note melody. Soaring dynamics and freedom of tempo.

He Came Here for Me   Nelson   SATB   Boosey & Hawkes   5370   1960
Piano, harp, or organ   Devotional   Difficulty Rating: 5
Ethereal, beautiful, haunting melody which matches the mystery of the text.
Seamless singing and tuning of parallel octaves. Excellent discussion piece for theolog-
ical truths of the incarnation of Christ.

He Chose to Die   Drennan   SATB   GlorySound   A7168   1997
Piano with cello.   Communion or Holy Week   Difficulty Rating: 5
(Part included in choral score).
Very imaginative and innovative. A new textual slant on Christ's purpose and pas-
sion. Wonderful color and expression in melodic lines. Superb devotional material
and beautiful music to bring it all together.

Hosanna   Pote   SATB   Choristers Guild CGA-596   1989
Keyboard. Optional guitar and bass.   Matthew 21:9   Difficulty Rating: 5
Fun, happy, and easy to feel, the joy flows freely. Precise, uncompromising rhythms.
Nice contrast of mood to be maximized within piece.

I Have Felt the Hand of God   Courtney   SATB   Beckenhorst   BP1518   1997
Piano   Devotional   Difficulty Rating: 5
Gorgeous little piece which is a youth choir favorite. Excellent down-to-earth theology. Music is winsome and flowing. Fine wedding between vocal lines and accompaniment.

I Will Yet Praise Him   Shepperd SATB   Gladsong   11-10853   1997
Piano   Psalm 42 and 43   Difficulty Rating: 5
Solo-like lines in all voices. Appealing for its accompaniment and melodic unique-
ness. Unison lines. Flowing melodies and rich harmonies. Quiet strength and power.

I'll Sing the Praise of Jesus   Courtney   SATB   Beckenhorst   BP1383   1991
Keyboard   Old Hymn   Difficulty Rating: 5
Bright nuances provides a favorite feel for sensitive kids. Text is strong and devotional
in nature. Long, sustained lines. Tuning and balance of lovely harmonies.

Infant Holy, Infant Lowly   Wood   SATB   Sacred Music   10/1700 S   1998
Piano, organ and flute.   Polish Carol   Difficulty Rating: 5
(Flute part included in choral score).
Beautiful color piece for Christmas program. Usable for ensemble or the whole choir.
Gentle voice leading and lovely melodies. Harmonies are rich and full. Isolated *a cap-
pella* sections.

Jesus is Born   Smith   SATB   Logia   98-3370   1997
Keyboard and Triangle   Advent   Difficulty Rating: 5
Joyous and celebrative, an exciting new sound with much energy and interest for
kids. Mixed meter, independence of voices, dynamics, articulation.

Joyful, Joyful   Allen   SATB   Allegris   AG-1025   1997
Keyboard. Orchestration available   Advent and General Use   Difficulty Rating: 5
#R-2326.
Very recognizable but different, quite singable and enjoyable. Rhythms, easy voice
parts provide entree into part singing. Large, demanding ending.

Jubilate Deo   Anderson SATB   Concordia 98-2470   1980
Keyboard   Psalms 98 and 100   Difficulty Rating: 5
Exceedingly flexible piece which can be sung in practically any combination of voices. Quick, joyful, and fun. Independence of lines, Latin or English text, excellent
vocal/choral training.

Keep Your Lamps   Thomas   SATB   Hinshaw   HMC-577   1982
A cappella with   Spiritual, loosely taken from Gospels   Difficulty Rating: 5
conga drums.
Fine spiritual setting for all youth Rhythm, singing a cappella, tuning, dynamic contrast. The spiritual lesson of being prepared and alert.

Kyrie   Schubert/Ehret   SAB Hal Leonard HL 00007711 1970
Piano or Organ   Kyrie eleison   Difficulty Rating: 5
Transcription of Kyrie from the Schubert Mass in G. Simple text in Latin Excellent
introduction into the classics. Dynamic contrasts, variation in articulation. Rich,
smooth lines.

Lord of the Dance   arr. Ferguson   SATB   Galaxy   1.5260   1990
Organ or Piano   Shaker Hymn   Difficulty Rating: 5
Fun introduction into Early American choral music. Freedom in singing, stressing of
prominent consonants and words. Independence of lines.

Lord, For Thy Tender Mercies Sake   Farrant   SATB   E. C. Schirmer   374
A cappella   Renaissance   Prayer of Confession and Commitment
                                                        Difficulty Rating: 5
Rich, choral texture and very singable lines. Not difficult to conquer, and once
accomplished, very usable in any youth choir setting. Rich in resources for teaching.
Smooth, choral lines, and rich harmonies. Spiritual formation through prayer, confes-
sion, commitment.

Lord, Work a Miracle   Choplin   SATB   GlorySound A7111   1997
Keyboard. Parts for string bass,   Contemporary   Difficulty Rating: 5
drums, and guitar available #LB5399.
Exciting rhythmic piece. Text regarding the miracles of the early ministry Jesus.
Rhythms sharp and totally accurate. All the style is written into the rhythms and
music. Good text for devotional study.

O Holy Night   Hayes   SAB   Alfred   17786   1998
Piano, optional parts for brass, saxes,   Traditional (Wright)   Difficulty Rating: 5
and percussion available from the publisher (#17788).
Interesting setting for kids. Much appeal for youth, in gospel shuffle feel. Piano part
is fun to hear and will inspire enthusiastic singing. Good training in gospel style.
Divisi harmonies for girls throughout, adaptable, but fun to learn. Range toward the
end for upper voices.

O Night of Nights   Lau   SATB   Hinshaw   HMC1586   1997
Keyboard and Organ   Contemporary Advent Difficulty Rating: 5
Based upon O WALY WALY. Lovely choral treatment of wonderful new text. Easy
parts and beautiful unison lines. Dynamics and some freedom of tempo throughout.

On This Day Angels Sing Gilpin   SAB   Alfred   17986   1998
Piano   "Piae Cantiones"   Difficulty Rating: 5
Flowing choral sounds of Advent celebration. Excellent training for independence of
three parts. Easy to isolate and work section by section. Dynamic contrast. Sign language suggested to highlight the singing of the refrain, which features angel-like
sequencing harmonies.

Once Upon a Night   Choplin   SATB   Harold Flammer   A7132   1997
Keyboard, Flute and guitar.   Advent   Difficulty Rating: 5
Flute part is included. Guitar
part available from publisher. (LC5089)
Beautiful melody and sweet setting. Easy for teenagers to grasp and master. Adaptable
for soloist, ensemble, or entire choir. Close harmonies and long, flowing melodies.
Gentle interpretation of legato singing.

Only Jesus Knew   Dengler   SATB   Harold Flammer   A7273   1998
Piano with oboe or other   Holy Week or Communion
C instrument. (Part included on pages 13-14).   Difficulty Rating 5
Haunting line which captures the pathos of the upper room scene with Jesus and the
disciples. Focuses upon tenor and bass parts. Teaches independence of tenor and bass
voices. Toward the end, good teaching possibilities for choral treatment of thick texture. Teaching possibilities on every front: musical, spiritual, theological.

Out of the Depths   Schalk   SAB   MorningStar   MSM-50-3410   1999
Organ   Psalm 130   Difficulty Rating: 5
Great color piece for concert or communion service. A different kind of piece for
your youth choir, and yet one which will be appreciated greatly when mastered.
Haunting melody which stays in the head long after the rehearsal. Long, flowing
lines. In 4/2 time, this piece allows theory education on time signatures. Excellent
training ground for young voices.

Praise the Lord Our God Forever   Mozart/Ehret   SATB   Fred Bock
                                                              B-G0176   1980
Keyboard   Psalm-Like   Difficulty Rating: 5
Fine setting for teenagers. Challenging and fun for any youth choir. As in all classical
music, teaching opportunities abound. Counterpoint, independence of line. Balance.

Psalm 23   Bass   SATB   Broadman   4561-08   1959
Keyboard   Psalm 23   Difficulty Rating: 5
Colorful and very approachable setting of text. Interesting and attainable for kids.
Balance, independence of lines, color and nuance in choral sound.

Seek First the Kingdom of God   Allen   SATB   Lillenas   AN-2646   1994
Keyboard. Orchestration available   Matthew 6:25-34 & Proverbs 3: 5-6
#OR-2257.   Difficulty Rating: 5
Written for Florida Baptist All State Choir. Perfect for youth choirs. Can be successfully sung with small group. Spiritual teaching abounds. Easy voice parts and simple
rhythms throughout. Independence of voice lines.

Servants of Almighty God   Patterson   SATB   GlorySound A7254   1998
Keyboard. Parts for guitar, bass, and   Praise   Difficulty Rating: 5
drums available #LB5482.
Strong choral sound with equal voice parts. Exciting piece which grows all the way to
the end. Teaching of part-singing. Dynamics, *a cappella* section at beginning, strong
impulse to the end.

The Gift   Courtney SATB   Beckenhorst BP 1558   1999
Piano   Advent   Difficulty Rating: 5
Great text for teenagers in a consumer-oriented society. Creative and thoughtful.
Good opportunities for blended singing, unison and in harmony. Triple meter pro-
vides a strong pulse forward and a soul-searching quality throughout. A couple of
short, nice *a cappella* passages.

The Lord is My Keeper   Page   SATB   MorningStar MSM-2506A   2000
Keyboard with handbells and flute.   Difficulty Rating: 5
Orchestration available #MSM-2506B.
Beautiful melody and heavenly harmonies. Rich, simple, of the same quality as Page's
"Creation Will Be at Peace." Long, legato lines. Vocal training in upper registers.
Tuning in unison. Part sections are sensible and easy to hear. Wonderful teaching
opportunities on all levels.

This Holy Place   Hayes   SATB   Genevox   4173-23   1987
Keyboard   Devotional   Difficulty Rating: 5
Gentle melody and treatment of text. Very flexible and usable in many worship settings. Opportunities for soloists or small groups to sing various sections. Long lines
and beautiful message.

Walk Worthy   Martin   SATB   Purifoy   10/1079-2   1994
Keyboard   1 Corinthians 1: 9-14   Difficulty Rating: 5
Excellent natural youth choir anthem. Text and music fit well together and combine
for a powerful effect. Usable on many levels, in many sizes of groups. Accuracy of
rhythms. Tuning in unison sections, balance where parts emerge. Good training
grounds for upper registers of all voices.

What Shall I Render to My God   Lovelace   SATB   E.C. Kirby   90578   1955
Organ or Piano   Charles Wesley   Difficulty Rating: 5
Sugarstick possibility for any strong youth choir. Excellent text and strong, powerful
music. Independence of line. Developing efficient vocal sound. Phrasing, dynamics,
articulation and style.

Wings Like Eagles   Pote   SATB   Hope   C 5049   1999
Organ or Piano   Isaiah 40:28-31   Difficulty Rating: 5
Enjoyable throughout and challenging in places. Range provides fine teaching opportunities. Independence of voices, good mixture of easy melody and more difficult
harmonic passages.

Wings of the Dawn   Spencer   SATB   GlorySound A-6183   1985
Keyboard   Psalm 139   Difficulty Rating: 5
Superb, wonderful youth choir selection for any time. Excellent for teaching part-
singing. Each line is a melody of it's own and yet is quite interesting as a whole.
Beautiful and moving. Text is perfect for devotional material.

With Wings as Eagles   Williams/Harlan SATB   Lillenas AN-2609   1989
PIano/keyboard and   Isaiah 40:28-32 and Habakkuk 3:17-18
orchestration available   Difficulty Rating: 5
from publisher (MU-2170D).
Lovely melodic lines and counterpart. Close harmonies and legato throughout.
Ending strong and powerful. Breath control, vowel formations, rhythmic accuracy,
dynamics.

You Are My All in All   Jernigan/Greer   SATB   Word   301-0937-164   1996
Keyboard, orchestration available   Praise   Difficulty Rating: 5
from publisher (301-0651-252).
Baroque feel, light and energetic throughout. Very happy, joyful anthem of celebration. Baroque-like rhythms and articulation throughout. Light and easy to commit to
memory. Bright rhythms and sustained lines.

A Blessing of Peace   Schwoebel SATB   Hinshaw   HMC-906   1987
Keyboard   Book of Common Prayer   Difficulty Rating: 6
Lovely benediction. A little demanding but short, a good entree into demanding literature because it is so brief (30 measures). Vocal production in isolated high-range
measures. Excellent and interesting alto line. Beautiful in every way.

A Manger Carol   Harlan   SATB   Hinshaw   HMC-919   1987
Keyboard   Traditional   Difficulty Rating: 6
Tune taken from American Folk Song. Fresh setting with colorful harmonies. Good
introduction of two against three, though not difficult. Development of bass sound
in the lower registers. Training in harmony abounds.

Be Not Afraid   Courtney SATB   Beckenhorst BP1388   1992
Piano or Keyboard   Isaiah 43:1-4   Difficulty Rating: 6
Crystal melody, biblical text with a promise, movie-score-like accompaniment,
although not overdone, and gorgeous harmonies. Soprano descant optional on last
"stanza." Beautiful, free melodic lines. Singing legato against a triple subdivision.
Harmonic balance. Dynamic variation. Individuation of parts. Two against three.
Communication of text. A consummate youth choir anthem.

Canticle of Hope   Williams/Martin SATB Harold Flammer   A6983 1995
Keyboard   Isaiah 25 (adapted)   Difficulty Rating: 6
A cappella beginning. Written for the people of Oklahoma City following the bombing of the Federal Building. Gentle, peaceful, yet powerful piece. Text and context
offer rich teaching opportunities. Good simple introduction to 3-part singing for
both boys and girls (limited and easy). Excellent possibilities for spiritual formation.

Christ is the Rock   Larson   SATB   Lorenz   10/2163M   1999
Keyboard. Brass and percussion   Incorporates the "The Solid Rock"
parts available #30/1398M.   Difficulty Rating: 6
Joyous, rhythmic and quick. Fun to sing and excellent youth appeal. Parts are easy
and make perfect sense. Articulation of text. Energy and focus required to sing effectively.

Clap Your Hands   Roberts   SATB   Broadman   451-622   1967
Piano/keyboard with   Psalm 47   Difficulty Rating: 6
some *a cappella*.
Fine, exciting writing, very creative treatment of text. Lends itself to numerous creative usages: liturgical dance, hand claps, added instruments, shortened version for call to worship or introit. Rhythm, independence of voices, *a cappella* singing in limited section, choral energy, praise in worship.

Come Before His Presence with Singing   Purifoy   SATB   Purifoy
                                                 479-03024   1984
Keyboard, organ   Psalm 85,96 and 100   Difficulty Rating: 6
Exciting, driving, and inspiring. Excellent introduction into part singing and laying foundation for stronger sections in the youth choir. Dramatic and magnetic.

Creation Will Be at Peace   Page   SATB   Alfred   4248   1992
Piano. Handbell parts available   Isaiah 11: 6-9   Difficulty Rating: 6
from publisher (No. 12392).
Octavo also available in SAB arrangement (No. 5898).
Beautiful, kid-friendly setting. Lovely melodic lines and gentle harmonies. Teaching possibilities about: silky singing, breath support and control, stagger breathing, phrasing. Excellent material for choir devotional.

Do You Hear What I Hear? Simeone   SATB   Shawnee   A708   1962
Keyboard. Instrumental parts for   Traditional   Difficulty Rating: 6
brass also available. Choral parts available in SSA, SAB, or TTBB.
Fun and popular arrangement for kids' Christmas program. Independence of voices, good training in both unison and part work. Divisi in places toward the end.

Fairest Lord Jesus   Cox   SATB   Brookfield Press 08741812   1999
Piano   Anonymous German Hymn   Difficulty Rating: 6
New tune for traditional text. Very fresh and singable. Lovely melody provides many lessons in phrasing and articulation. Tuning, balance and unified vowels are essential.

Gloria   Spevacek Three-part Jenson   437-07050   1987
A cappella   Praise   Difficulty Rating: 6
Bright, cheerful praise anthem for use in a variety of settings. Also available in SSA #437-07023 and SATB 437-07034. *A cappella* singing. Rhythmic impulse throughout must be felt internally.

God and God Alone Fettke SATB Word 3010369166 1984
Keyboard Praise Difficulty Rating: 6
Many have used this with adults. Works well with teens also. Strong statement of faith and praise. Powerful singing from beginning to end. Hymn-like stability through-out, providing power and some good vocal demand as well. Good challenge . . . not too much . . . for kids.

God Shall Wipe Away All Tears Kirk SATB Tempo 5-3038 1976
Keyboard Revelation 21:1-4 Difficulty Rating: 6
Outstanding text for today's youth. Hope, promise, and future. Singing with artistry and sensitivity. Dynamic variations maximized. Flowing lines and rich harmonies.

God's Love Made Visible Brubeck SATB Shawnee A-1469 1998
Keyboard, instrumental parts (string Mexican Advent Difficulty Rating: 6
bass, guitars, trumpets, and Latin American percussion) #LB-171.
Great introduction into global music. In English but undeniable Latin beat and melody. In 5/4 time, an excellent and exciting entree into assymetrical rhythms. Challenging but very usable.

Hark, the Voice of Jesus Calling Manuel SATB MorningStar
MSM-50-6011 1999
Keyboard Hymn Difficulty Rating: 6
Strong meaningful setting which provides textual reality check for kids. Gentle with strong youth appeal. Fine choral selection for teenagers. Moving parts require training in sustaining, stagger breathing, and phrasing. Lovely lines and beautiful melodies and harmony. Superb devotional material.

Hold My Hand Medema SATB Brier Patch BP102 1993
Keyboard Comfort Difficulty Rating: 6
Classic Medema, but this is one of the easier selections. Fun to sing. Exacting rhythms, good interval training, lends itself to solos on stanzas.

Hurry, Shepherds, Run! Wagner SATB Somerset AD2034 1989
Fun, driving piece which brings out group's energy and focus. Rhythms. Independence of voices. Articulation of text. Tuning.

I am the Way, the Truth, and the Light   Young   SATB   Sacred Music   E40   1965
Keyboard   John 14:5-6   Difficulty Rating: 6
Stout, classic anthem for any choir. Call to worship or general usage. Intensive unison
singing, emerging parts are strong and triumphant."B" section is soft and reflective.
Great contrast in styles within the piece.

I Will Glorify Your Name   Berry   SATB   Church Street   0-7673-9304-X   1998
Piano and/or organ and orchestra.   Praise   Difficulty Rating: 6
Orchestration available from publisher (0-7673-9331-7).
Easy, joyous and pleasant music. Singing powerfully even through various dynamic
levels. Range toward the end provides good vocal training ground.

I Will Sing   Crouch   SATB   MorningStar MSM-50-2502A   1999
Piano/keyboard will full   Psalm 104:5, 33-35 (adapted)
orchestration available from publisher (MSM-50-2502B).   Difficulty Rating: 6
Delightful melody and counterpart. Harmonically very approachable and attainable.
Lighthearted and dancing. Independence of voice parts, marvelous wedding of text
and music, vocal training opportunities in every measure. Great new music.

I Will Sing Praise   Martin   SATB   Purifoy   10/1144   1994
Piano   Praise   Difficulty Rating: 6
Exuberant and joyful. Fun and energetic piece which will draw the interests of
teenagers. Isolated mixed meter for text emphasis. Lots of unison and easy voice parts.
The musical work on this will be fun enough that it will not seem like work.
Rhythmic articulation.

If You Search with All Your Heart   Courtney   SATB   Beckenhorst BP1434   1994
Piano and or/Organ   Jeremiah 29:11-14   Difficulty Rating: 6
Superb youth choir piece for its text and musical beauty. Long, extended phrases will
need much stagger breathing and control. Tessitura is low at points. Excellent training
in keeping phrases alive and vital. Beautiful piece.

In the Bleak Midwinter   Harlan   SATB   Hinshaw   HMC 1590   1997
Keyboard   Traditional   Difficulty Rating: 6
Gorgeous setting with haunting and lovely tune. Choral parts are rich and colorful.
Unison lines, interval training, tuning, balance of choral sound. Superb teaching oppor-
tunities.

In Thee Is Gladness   Kallman   SATB   MorningStar   MSM-50-9058   1992
Organ or piano with optional   Praise   Difficulty Rating: 6
C instrument (included).
Intriguing piece which incorporates melodic line, children's voices or ensemble, and
whistling of tune. Good training in separation of boy's parts. Whistling of counter-
melody creates a good opportunity in teaching. Two-part section followed by chorale-
like section. Range toward the end is approachable and lands upon open vowels.

Jesus Calls Us   Manuel   SATB   MorningStar MSM-50-8822 1998
Keyboard   Hymn   Difficulty Rating: 6
Beautiful setting of old hymn. Simple melodic line and lovely harmonies.
Independence of voices, simple part singing. Phrasing and beautiful flowing lines.
Text is superb devotional material.

Know My Heart   Harlan   SATB   GlorySound A-6836   1993
Keyboard   Psalm 139   Difficulty Rating: 6
Marvelous text and musical setting for kids. As close to a sure winner as you will
find. Brilliant and timely. Beautiful, flowing soaring melodic lines. Triplet rhythms in
"B" section, which is also basically *a cappella*.

Make Me a Channel of Your Peace   Templ/Hayes SAB   Alfred   18317   1967
Piano or orchestra. Parts through   Prayer of St. Francis   Difficulty Rating: 6
publisher (18320). Anthem also available in SATB (18316) and SA (18318).
In memory of Princess Diana of Wales. Lovely voicing and beautifully set and
arranged. Seamless lines and beautiful "pulseless" forward movement. Fine craftsmanship.

My Jesus, I Love Thee   Sjolund   SATB   Hinshaw   HMC-935   1987
Keyboard. Flute or violin   Traditional Hymn   Difficulty Rating: 6
obligato included.
Wonderful arrangement of old hymn and tune. Beautifully put together and provides
strong appeal for younger singers. Obligato and accompaniment strongly support
voices. Seamless lines and phrases. Tuning and balance of rich harmonies, balance
with obligato. Good introduction into divisi within four parts.

None Other Lamb   Courtney SATB   Beckenhorst BP1301   1987
Keyboard   Holy Week, Communion   Difficulty Rating: 6
Clean, clear melodic lines. Tuning when parts emerge. Transparent piece which needs
full attention to details.

O Come, Emmanuel Burroughs   SATB MorningStar   MSM-50-0026 1999
Piano and handbells (included)   Traditional   Difficulty Rating: 6
O WALY WALY tune. Beautiful and seamless melody. Exceptionally well-suited for
young voices. Gentle and flowing phrases. Dynamics and calm energy throughout.
Accompaniment very supportive.

O Little Town of Bethlehem Helvey   SATB   Bookfield   08741566   1998
Piano and handbells (included)   Traditional   Difficulty Rating: 6
FOREST GREEN tune. Fresh and transparent setting which will bring new meaning
to the text. Good training on all levels.

Old Time Religion Medley Hayes   SATB   Alfred   16138   1997
Piano and or trumpets, trombones,   Old-time   Difficulty Rating: 6
guitar, bass. Parts available from the publisher (12241).
Great appeal for jazzy old-time music. Jazz feel. Musical accuracy amidst old-time
style. Dynamic variation. Lends itself to movement.

On Eagle's Wings   Joncas/Hayes SATB Alfred   16104   1991
Piano   Psalm 91 (adapted)   Difficulty Rating: 6
Excellent setting of the well-known text and tune. Flowing lines and beautiful harmonies. Independence and separation of voice parts. Great opportunities for teaching, musically and spiritually.

On the Third Day   Pote   SATB   Hope   F1000   1992
Keyboard, handbell parts included.   Apostles Creed   Difficulty Rating: 6
Separate brass and timpani parts available #F1000B.
A consummate Easter or festival selection. Works well on many levels and in many
venues. Very fun and exciting. Gradual crescendo from beginning to end. Rhythmic
articulation and energy sustained throughout.

Open Thou Mine Eyes   Harlan   SATB   GlorySound A-6722   1992
Keyboard   16th Century Text   Difficulty Rating: 6
The most kid-friendly setting of this fine text. Melody is gorgeous, harmonies rich,
and accompaniment quite supportive and imaginative. Crystal clear melodic lines,
rubato singing, balancing of rich, low harmonies.

Poor Man Lazarus   Hairston   SATB   Bourne Co. S-1001   1950
A cappella   Spiritual   Difficulty Rating: 6
Classic spiritual in style and content. Very youth choir friendly. Rhythmic precision,
harmonic balance, tuning. Training abundant, and this will only increase the joy and
fun of it.

Restore My Joy   Berry   SATB   Word   3010558163   1991
Keyboard. Orchestration available   Psalm 51   Difficulty Rating: 6
#3010271255.
Good fresh setting of well-used text. Moving, gentle, and yearning. Tuning in numerous unison sections. Balancing of harmonies within the low, rich harmonies. Range in
upper voices provides superb vocal training grounds.

Silver Star   Pote   SATB   Hope   C 5048   1999
Piano   Advent   Difficulty Rating: 6
Fresh, clean selection to bring color to any Christmas program or worship service. In
12/8, moving gently and freely as if through the air. Wonderful changes in key feeling
throughout gives it an unearthly feel. Keep energy in phrases.

Sing A New Song, Our Savior Is Born   Harris   SATB   Church Street 0-7673-9301-1
Piano and handbells (included}.   Advent   Difficulty Rating: 6   1977
Fun, exciting piece which has been around for years. Very usable in youth choir and
combination choral settings. In 6/4, lilts in 2 and is made interesting by recurring 3/2
feel. Contrasting *a cappella* B section is legato and sustained. Bells and piano return
and keep up the energy to the end.

Sing to God, Sing and Rejoice   Patterson   SATB   Triune   10/1807T   1998
Piano   Psalmic   Difficulty Rating: 6
Exciting and contagious melody. In 6/8, the text moves steadily and strongly through-
out. A light, gentle dance of praise. Bright.

Sing Unto God   Young   SATB   Carl Fischer N3861   1962
Keyboard and Organ   Psalm 68: 32   Difficulty Rating: 6
Stout and powerful expression of praise. Interesting moving accompaniment provides
a feel of dancing. Intensive unison singing and aggressive four-part *a cappella* section.
Not difficult, but keeps moving. Usage of limited mixed meter. Strong!

Sing Unto the Lord a New Song   Haydn/Hopson   SATB   MorningStar
                                                   MSM-50-2503A   1999
Piano/keyboard with full   From Mass No. 3 in D minor.
orchestration available from   Praise, Festive Celebration   Difficulty Rating: 6
publisher (MSM-50-2503B).
Great entree into classical style. Parts are easy to sing well and are relatively easy to
put together. Dynamic variations, terraced dynamics, vocal agility and singing free of
tension.

Stand Up and Bless the Lord   Allen   SATB   Lillenas   AN-8090   1993
Keyboard. Orchestration available #OR-2229.   Praise   Difficulty Rating: 6
Wonderful piece for teens which provides courage and inspiration. *A cappella* section
at beginning is simple yet challenging. Voice parts are almost of marching quality.
Much youth appeal, particularly in today's society.

Still, Still, Still   Luboff   SATB   Walton   W3003   1958
Keyboard   Austrian Carol   Difficulty Rating: 6
Absolutely gorgeous gentle piece which feels like snow. Lovely lines and artistically
crafted harmonies. Legato, soft, singing. Sustained, rich musical line and powerful
ambiance.

Tandi Tanga Jesus   Ellingboe   SATB   Augsburg   11-10602   1986
A cappella with percussion.   Traditional Namibian and Tanzanian
                                                   Difficulty Rating: 6
Excellent example of global music. Joyful, almost playful, and much fun. Short sentences of African text. Features a strong boy's section. Rhythms, African performance
practice. Joy in singing, joy in Christian walk.

The Cross   Martin/Courtney   SATB   Beckenhorst BP1526   1998
Piano or Keyboard   General, Original and Powerful   Difficulty Rating: 6
Exquisite accompaniment, gorgeous melody, and powerful synthesis of text and

music. Moderate range. Independence of voices, listening for balance and blend, communication of text. Colorful prayerful text spawns a dozen devotionals.

The Third Day Pote SATB Hope F 1000 1992
Piano, handbells. Separate parts Apostles' Creed (adapted)
for brass and percussion available from publisher (F 1000B). Difficulty Rating: 6
Extraordinary Easter anthem for any choir, youth or adult. Exciting. The thrill of powerful music washes over the piece. Independence of voices, great for vocal development, strong, full-throttle singing most of the way through.

We Will Need No Candle Martin SATB Flammer A-6947 1995
Keyboard Revelation 22:5 Difficulty Rating: 6
Beautiful, warm melody. Text is very descriptive and full of promise and hope. Legato singing. Phrasing and lines. Very transparent and worthy of as much precision and understanding as possible.

Welcome, Holy Child Haan SATB MorningStar MSM-50-1070 1998
Organ or piano, violin, cello, Advent Difficulty Rating: 6
and soprano soloist.
Lovely melody in combination with gentle Advent text. Soprano soloist soars in places, and yet range is moderate. String parts add much to ambiance. Good teaching opportunities for listening and balancing against soloist, obligato instruments and organ. Tuning and phrasing throughout.

With a Voice of Singing Shaw SAB G. Schimer 10226 1953
Keyboard Psalm-like Difficulty Rating: 6
Classic youth choir anthem. Also available in SATB #8103. Teaching possibilities abound. Excellent music for building choral foundation and strength. Nothing about this piece is less than great.

A Chosen People Berry SATB GlorySound A-7049 1996
Piano and/or orchestra. I Peter 2:4-10 Difficulty Rating: 7
Available from publisher (LB5383)
Strong message and powerful music. Choral confidence-builder. Melody is beautiful and seems to move forward toward the end. Easy three-part girls near end. Easy, yet strong.

A Christmas Caroll   Melton   SATB   Heritage   H459   1981
A cappella   16th Century   Difficulty Rating: 7
Rich, gentle setting with fine choral color and nuance. Soft singing, phrasing, close
yet simple harmonies. Medium high range in all voice parts.

A Mighty Fortress Is Our God Allen   SATB   Allegris   AG-1020   1996
Keyboard. Orchestration available   Luther   Difficulty Rating: 7
#OR2321
Exciting, driving arrangement of traditional hymn and tune. Much appeal for kids.
Rhythms, changing meter, dynamics, energetic singing.

A Never-ending Alleluia   Williams/Martin   SATB   GlorySound   A7250   1998
Keyboard with optional   Easter   Difficulty Rating:7
orchestration (LB5480).
Exciting, rhythmic and moving. Contagious. Includes a short excerpt of "Amazing
Grace." Musical mood swings, from sorrowful to glorious. Rhythmic integrity, energy.
Three part-girls near the end. Opportunities to teach vocal control (range).

American Hymn Sampler   Purifoy   SATB   Brookfield   08741842   1999
Piano and optional brass   Traditional Hymns   Difficulty Rating: 7
available from publisher (HL08741850).
Fun and cheerful. Good introduction into early American Hymns for kids who may
not know them. Rhythms and early American feel. B-section is slow and thoughtful
(My Shepherd Will Supply My Need). Strong choral ending. Good choice for broad-
ening repertoire.

Antiphonal Praise   Peterson   SATB   Triune   TUM 427   1992
A cappella. Optional brass parts included   Psalm-like   Difficulty Rating: 7
to cover the antiphonal choir parts, if desired.
Exciting call to worship or general praise anthem. If group can be divided physically,
it will increase effectiveness. Excellent selection for combining youth and adults,
allowing the youth to sing one choir and the adults the other. Good for teaching
intervals and musical confidence.

Be the One   Coates   SATB   Benson   OCT00235   1990
Keyboard   Contemporary Christian   Difficulty Rating: 7
Trendy in the early '90s, this is still a moving selection for kids. Focused challenge to
stand up for their faith. Energy throughout. Nice use of soloists. This piece works
best if sung on its own merit, not trying to duplicate the stylistic sounds of the studio recordings.

Blessed Are You   Courtney   SATB   Beckenhorst   BP 1538   1998
Piano   Matthew 5   Difficulty Rating: 7
Excellent setting of extended scripture passage. Four strong parts needed. Beautiful
suspensions and rich harmonies. Expressive musical qualities, phrasing, line, and
ambiance must be stressed.

Come, Holy Spirit   Cox   SATB   MorningStar   MSM-50-5409   1999
Piano or Organ   Prayer   Difficulty Rating: 7
Great text, beautiful wedding of words and music. Rich harmonies and beautiful
melody. Accompaniment is rich and supportive. Tuning, sustained lines, phrasing of
text and music. Range, soft high singing for girls' voices.

Create In Me   James   SATB   MorningStar   MSM-50-3043   1999
Piano or Harp   Psalm 51:10:-13   Difficulty Rating: 7
Soprano soloist, four-part choir and harp. Beautiful lines, melodies, and harmonies.
Accompaniment very supportive of vocal lines. Excellent training for choir in back-
ground. Choral parts are supportive and beautifully crafted. Stagger breathing,
smooth lines.

Esta Noche   Cunningham   SATB   Hinshaw   HMC 1274   1993
Keyboard with Latin American   Spanish   Difficulty Rating: 7
percussion. Pronunciation guide included.
Delightful, fun, and colorful to add spice to any Christmas program. Mariachi feel.
Superb lessons in diction, rhythm, and accuracy of parts. The lessons will be
painless—very fun to sing.

Every Valley   Beck   SATB   Beckenhorst   BP1040   1974
Piano or Organ   Isaiah   Difficulty Rating: 7
Strong and powerful choral setting. Great for good boys section. Training and developing basic choral sound. Vowels are rich and open, voice-leading and text assignment
for higher sections are perfect.

Family of Faith   Choplin   SATB   Monarch   10/1657M   1997
Piano   Unity   Difficulty Rating: 7
Warm, friendly piece which draws singers into it. Crisp rhythms, in-tune unison
singing, and easy harmony voice parts.

Father, Hear Thy Children Calling   Ellers   SATB   Jenson   402-06014   1982
A cappella   Prayer   Difficulty Rating: 7
Superb prayer anthem for a group to adopt as their own. Fanning out harmonies pro-
vide excellent interval training grounds and teaching of tuning and listening.
Beautiful and worth the extra work.

Follow Me   Wilson   Wilson   Lorenz   E14   1961
Piano   Henry Wadsworth Longfellow   Difficulty Rating: 7
Strong, "thinker" text which paints word pictures at every turn. Fine for devotional
material as well as for musical advancement. Short selection. Strong unison singing,
independence of voice parts. Powerful choral drama. In many ways easy, because it is
so short. Excellent entree into more substantial literature.

Footprints in the Sand   Martin/Angerman   SATB   GlorySound   A-6998   1995
Piano, Orchestration (LB5351),   Contemporary   Difficulty Rating: 7
Track (MC5180)
Singable, catchy melody, fun. Rhythmic integrity, independence of parts, the constant
presence of Christ.

God Be in My Head   Hopson   SATB   MorningStar   MSM-50-6018   1999
Piano   Traditional Celtic Prayer   Difficulty Rating: 7
Beautiful flowing melody and sensible counterpoint. Lovely piece. Extraordinary text
for teenagers. Legato, singable lines will provide training on numerous levels: vowels,
phrasing, breathing, dynamics.

Greet the Dawning   Leech/Sanborn   SATB   Fred Bock   BG2022   1987
Piano and/or organ with optional   Call to Worship or General
handbells and timpani (included in choral score).   Difficulty Rating: 7
Very bright, fun, and catchy. Much rhythmic interest and congregational appeal.
Happy yet substantial. B-section is a complete surprise and delightful. Rhythms,
rhythms, rhythms! Range allows for good vocal teaching opportunities.

He Never Failed Me Yet   Ray   SATB   Jenson   44708014   1982
Piano, with optional parts for guitar,   Gospel   Difficulty Rating: 7
brass and rhythm available from the publisher.
Exciting piece to add variety to any repertoire. Lots of fun. Rhythms, sustained phrases, training in gospel feel.

Here I Am, Lord   Courtney   SATB   Beckenhorst BP1403   1981
Keyboard. Flute part available   Isaiah   Difficulty Rating: 7
#BP 1403A
Marvelous text, contemporary setting of scripture passage. Appealing music which stays with kids. Balance of background harmonies against dominant melody. High range and divisi for soprano in places. Works beautifully.

How Beautiful Are They   Berry   SATB   Hal Leonard   08740971   1997
Piano   Various Scripture Passages   Difficulty Rating: 7
Easy four-part singing. Range is extended upward toward the end to produce the exciting climactic section. Piece ends thoughtfully. Vowel formations, flowing melodic lines, rich and full harmonies.

I Have Longed for Thy Saving Health   Byrd/Whitehead   SATB
A cappella   H.W. Gray   CMR 1679   arr.1940/1968
                                             Psalm 119: 174-175   Difficulty Rating: 7
Gorgeous and simple motet with strong Psalm text. Fine color piece for any youth choir concert. Excellently crafted and arranged. Sustained lines and tuning are challenges throughout, but not at all unattainable for kids. Super training ground on many levels.

I'm Not Ashamed to Own My Lord   Kosche   SATB   MorningStar
A cappella   MSM-50-9111   1999
                                     Isaac Watts   Difficulty Rating: 7
Very singable harmonies and well-written voice leading. Tune based on ARLINGTON. Training galore on this one. Opportunities for fine-tuning boys' sound; it begins with two-part men *a cappella*. Very singable, very workable in any choir which has four strong parts.

If You Search With All Your Hearts   Courtney   SATB   Beckenhorst BP   1434
Piano and/or Organ   1994   Jeremiah 29:11-14   Difficulty Rating: 7
Superb connection between text and music. Scripture containing strong promise for
teenagers. Outstanding music. Long, flowing lines. Tuning, listening, and balance.
Excellent opportunities for teaching vowel formations.

Laudate Dominum   Mozart   SATB   EC Schirmer   2280   1948
Organ or piano and/or orchestra   Psalm 117 and Gloria Patri
scores available from publisher.   Difficulty Rating: 7
Soprano soloist.
Gorgeous entree into classical. Excellent place for an outstanding soprano soloist to
shine. Whether sung in Latin or English, this work provides superb foundational
background for musically serious youth choirs.

Leaning on the Everlasting Arms   Hayes   SATB   Alfred   16061   1996
Piano and/or trumpets, trombones,   Gospel   Difficulty Rating: 7
sax, bass, drums and electric guitar. Available from publisher (12252)
Fun and entertaining! Rhythm, rhythm. rhythm! Dynamic variations and crescendo
of energy toward the end.

Let Jesus Christ Be Praised   Patterson   SATB   Flammer   A7293   1999
Keyboard. Parts for brass and   Praise   Difficulty Rating: 7
percussion available #LB5525.
Strong anthem of praise with teenager appeal and new sounds, but with a definite
traditional feel. Psalm-like text provides good opportunities for text study and devotional. Independence of line. Vocal/choral training is valuable for several sections, particularly the ending. Excellent teaching piece, yet fun as well.

Let Us, With a Gladsome Mind   Hopson   SATB   MorningStar   MSM-50-7031
Organ with optional electric bass   Difficulty Rating: 7   1998
or synthesizer.
Super-exciting and joyful. Optional text provided for "Christ the Lord is Risen
Today." Rhythms and strong unison singing. Teenagers will love the rhythmic feel, and
yet the sturdiness of this piece.

Lightshine   Martin   SATB   GlorySound A7199   1998
Keyboard. Part for guitar, bass, and   Spiritual-like   Difficulty Rating: 7
drums #LB5453.
Fun and energetic setting for concert or informal worship. Rhythms, dynamics, and
choral drama. Limited mixed meter. Vocal training in higher ranges.

Mary, Mary   Martin   SATB   GlorySound A7178   1997
Piano. Parts for guitar, bass   Holy Week   Difficulty Rating: 7
and drums (LB5427).
Very innovative treatment of imaginative text. Jazz feel following plaintive beginning.
Fun and joyous. Range for upper voices near the end.

May the Lord Go With You   Page   SATB   Alfred   5893   1993
Keyboard or *a cappella*   Benediction   Difficulty Rating: 7
Beautiful text, lines, and synthesis of text and music. Very flexible usage. Flowing
choral lines, tuning and moving parts kept gentle and smooth.

O Come, Let Us Sing   Berry   SATB   Purifoy   26026   1990
Piano/Keyboard   Psalm 95:1-2   Difficulty Rating: 7
Immediately likeable and fun. Energized enthusiasm leaping from every bar. Dynamic
variation. B section provides a superb introduction to mixed meter in that it is quite
easy to feel. Mixed into the rhythmic figures are some short sustained sections for
variety. Worship is celebrative and joyful.

O Sons and Daughters   Larkin   SA(T)B   MorningStar MSM-50-4034 1998
Keyboard   Praise   Difficulty Rating: 7
Fun, joyful, exuberant. Changing meters and shifting accents make for fun singing.
High registers present opportunities for good vocal training.

Open the Gates   Dengler   SATB   H.W. Gray   GCMR9904   1999
Keyboard   Isaiah 26: 2-10   Difficulty Rating: 7
Anthem-like tradition and yet contemporary appeal. Balance, diction, tuning, and
rhythmic accuracy.

Praise the Lord Who Reigns Above   Cobb   SATB   Hinshaw   HMC-1502   1996
Keyboard   Charles Wesley   Difficulty Rating: 7
Outstanding, exciting piece. Will ignite the musical interest of teenagers. Exciting and exceedingly well-crafted. Mixed meter. Articulation, tuning of unison lines. Choral drama.

Prayer of St. Francis   Pote   SATB   Hinshaw   HMC-888   1986
Piano/Keyboard   Prayer of St. Francis   Difficulty Rating: 7
Commissioned for Montreat Youth Choir. Beautiful, fresh treatment of traditional text. Melodic line is elegant and warm. Singing well in unison. Tight harmonies in a couple of measures. Flowing tones and gentle phrasing. Dynamic contrasts. Text is a treasure-trove of teaching.

Procession and Hymn for Palm Sunday   Courtney   SATB   Beckenhorst   BP1536
Keyboard and handbells.   Luke 19   Difficulty Rating; 7   1998
Instrumental parts available #BP1536A.
Exciting piece which builds from quiet beginning to very strong ending. Incorporates the hymn "Hosanna, Loud Hosanna." Great festive piece for Palm Sunday. Beautiful beginning, exciting ending. Incorporates congregation if desired.

Psalm 47   Ellingboe   SATB   KJOS   Ed. 8890   1998
A cappella with percussion effects   Psalm 47   Difficulty Rating: 7
Fine, interesting piece which will work well in a variety of youth choir settings. Every youth choir should sing this one. Rhythms. Great interval training, good development of *a cappella* sound.

Recollection of Joy   Butler   SATB   Beckenhorst BP13467   1990
Keyboard   Philippians 1   Difficulty Rating: 7
Gorgeous piece which will surely become a favorite with most youth choirs. Teaching of the value of faith passed down, thinking of mentors who have gone before. Very emotional piece, and yet artistically beautiful and well-crafted.

Rejoice!   Courtney   SATB   Beckenhorst BP1466   1995
Keyboard. Parts for two C or   Philippians 4   Difficulty Rating: 7
Bb instruments available #BP1466A
Delightful setting, incorporates "Rejoice Ye Pure in Heart" with sounds of Handel's "Rejoice Greatly, O Daughter of Zion." Excellent repertoire for kids. Light, joyful

singing at beginning and end. "B" section is contrasting, very legato with some range and choral demands.

Run, Run, Shepherds   Page   SATB   Alfred   16000   1996
Keyboard   Advent   Difficulty Rating: 7
Rhythmic, moving, and fun. Rhythmic impulse, energy through dynamic shifts.

Savior, Like a Shepherd Lead Us   Bock   SATB   Word   CS-2394   1969
Piano   Traditional Hymn   Difficulty Rating: 7
Lovely setting of old tune. Basic traditional Bradbury melody, but arranged skillfully for choral group. Tight *a cappella* section at the beginning, middle and ending. Gentle, flowing lines. Close harmonies. Tuning and fine-tuning. Rubato singing throughout. Great opportunity for teaching independence of boy's voice parts.

Scenes from Gethsemane   Martin   SATB   Harold Flammer   A 7156   1997
Piano   Holy Week   Difficulty Rating: 7
Beautiful melodic line. Harmonies are rich and colorful. Devotional material abounds. Musically smooth and gentle. Ending is strong and robust.

Shout to the King Hosanna!   Patterson   SATB   Harold Flammer   A 7275   1998
Piano   Palm Sunday or Easter   Difficulty Rating; 7
Good, solid youth choir piece for about any occasion. Good for building boys and girls sounds separately. Rhythmic accuracy and dynamic variation needed, particularly near the end. Range is excellent. . . not too high, not too low.

Shut de Do   Hayes   SATB   Chancel   3010262167   1984
A cappella with rhythm instruments.   Contemporary   Difficulty Rating; 7
Well used in the '80s and early '90s, still a fun piece for those who have not yet experienced it. Highly rhythmic. Rhythms, rhythms, rhythms.

Sing Praise and Celebrate   Fischer   SATB   Flammer   A6951   1995
Keyboard   Psalm 118,95,96   Difficulty Rating: 7
Jubilant, up-tempo, rhythmic, and exciting. Sustaining melodic lines in 6/8. Easy voice parts make for strong introduction into 4-part singing. Very flexible piece.

Soon-All Will Be Done   Dawson   SATB   KJOS   T-102-A   1962
A cappella   Spiritual   Difficulty Rating: 7
Demanding singing, but much fun. Superb teaching in phrasing, consonants, and
dynamic variation.

The Lord Desires These Things   Larson   SATB   Beckenhorst   BP1530   1998
Piano   Excerpted from various scriptures   Difficulty Rating: 7
Superb treatment of text and music. Clean flowing lines, transparent harmonies and
excellent opportunities for devotional discussion.

The Wondrous Cross   Bass   SATB   Broadman Press   4563-39   1981
Piano or organ with orchestra parts   "When I Survey the Wondrous Cross"
available from publisher (4576-39).   Difficulty Rating: 7
Fresh and beautiful setting of tradition text. New melody. Anthem is masterfully
crafted. Fine teaching for independence of voices, theory, voice-leading. Dynamics
and phrasing.

There Is a Time   Courtney   SATB   Beckenhort   BP1463   1995
Piano or Keyboard   Ecclesiastes 3: 1-8   Difficulty Rating: 7
Fine selection for teenagers for textual as well as choral reasons. Fine melody, rich
harmonies. Ballad-type allows personal expression and conducting freedom. Rubato.

This Is My Father's World   Turner   SATB   Broadman   4565-64   1976
Keyboard   Traditional Hymn   Difficulty Rating: 7
Very fresh setting of old hymn, utilizing the Terra Patris tune. Rhythms, shifts in key
feelings, various articulation styles within piece. Strong ending. Accompaniment is
aggressive and supportive.

To God Be Joyful   Mozart/Hopson   SATB   Harold Flammer   A-6142   1984
Piano or Organ   Psalm 100 (adapted)   Difficulty Rating: 7
Also available SAB (D-5371).
Setting from "Regina Coeli" K108. Excellent introduction into classical style. Training
possibilities in dynamics, style, and flowing phrases. Excellent vocal a training poten-
tial.

To Love Our God   Hayes   SATB   Hinshaw   HMC-1576   1997
Piano   Ecclesiastes 1 & 12   Difficulty Rating: 7
Great youth choir piece. Provides excellent sound tracking and provides powerful imagery. Strong, sustained singing. Builds from beginning to end. Dynamic variation, tuning, sustained lines.

Treasures in Heaven   Clokey   SATB   Summy-Birchard   B-2010   1941
Organ or piano   Matthew 6 and 7   Difficulty Rating: 7
Elegant and gorgeous selection which teenagers will come to love. An acquired taste you never lose. Seamless lines, tonal support, vowels, and line. No time signature. Lovely for teaching God's truth as well as fine musicianship.

Two National Anthems   Crouch   SATB   MorningStar   MSM-50-2500   1999
A cappella   "The Star-Spangled Banner"   Difficulty Rating: 7
                              "O Canada"
Perfect youth-friendly settings of national anthems for use at sporting events. Phrasing, breath control, building dynamics.

Weave Me, Lord   Spencer   SATB   GlorySound A6322   1987
Keyboard   Contemporary   Difficulty Rating: 7
Marvelous imagery throughout for teenagers. Sure to stay with teenagers in future. Very likable piece. Independence of voices, smooth, running lines within the sections, excellent and approachable alto and tenor parts.

Write Your Blessed Name   Scott   SATB   Hope   A-632   1989
Piano   14th Century   Difficulty Rating: 7
Text to which teenagers will easily relate. Meaningful devotional content. Smooth singing , rich harmonies, flowing lines. Dynamic variations abound.

Your Love Lifted Me   Greer   SATB   Genevox   3120-12   1995
Piano and/or orchestra. Parts   Praise   Difficulty Rating: 8
available from publisher (3000-84).
Contemporary feel, full of energy and excitement. Strong, driving rhythm. Rhythm and energy a must. Three-part girls in places. Good training for obtaining a good energized choral sound.

A Clean Heart   Burroughs/Hayes SATB   Chrismon   CHC5014 ·
1999
Keyboard   Psalm 51: 10-13   Difficulty Rating: 8
Fine choral lines with creative harmonic tension. Accompaniment both imaginative
and supportive. Tuning of the tight harmonies. Upper register soft singing for basses.
Smooth articulation of text. Dynamic variation.

A Vision of You   Berry   SATB   GlorySound   A7116   1997
Piano   Devotional   Difficulty Rating: 8
Text of compassion and Christian response. Dynamics, balance in four-part sections,
negotiating range at the end of piece. Devotional material abounds.

An Acclamation of Praise   Pote   SATB   Hope   F1021   1998
Piano with brass and timpani parts   Psalm 89   Difficulty Rating: 8
available from publisher (F1021B).
Contagious and energetic setting of a bright psalm text. Asymmetrical rhythms. Very
catchy and bright. Range is high in places but can be handled by advanced youth
choirs. Fun!

And the Father Will Dance   Hayes   SATB   Hinshaw   HMC-637   1983
Piano   Zephania 3, Psalm 34   Difficulty Rating: 8
Unusual text combined with wonderful writing has made this a church music neo-
classic. Driving dancing rhythm in 6/8. Very fine B section in 4/4 which is slow and
legato. The dance returns and ends with full energy. Choir communication: joy.

Benediction   Lutkin   SATB   H.W. Gray   GCMR2479   Traditional
A cappella with the   Traditional Aaronic Benediction from Numbers
seven-fold Amen.   Difficulty Rating: 8
Every youth and adult choir member should know this piece. It is not difficult, but
will take some time to conquer. Luscious lines and beautiful classical feel. The synthesis of text and tune is flawless.

Christ Is In This Place   Pote   SATB   Hope   AP 448   1996
Piano, oboe, and cello (included).   Communion   Difficulty Rating: 8
Lovely fresh composition which brings together a contemporary feel with a substantial text and setting. Unison lines appear throughout, breaking into parts and coming
back together again. Easy to teach, simple to memorize, and quickly connects with
the heart.

Come Unto Me Blankenship SATB Broadman 45445-99 1975
A cappella Matthew 11:28-30 Difficulty Rating: 8
Modern classic for youth or adult choirs. Perfect for combination youth/adult. Gorgeous, thick, and rich, training in *a cappella* singing in all its beauty is necessary here. Harmonies are, at times, close and treacherous, but well worth any amount of work.

Dry Bones Hayes SATB Alfred 17792 1998
Piano. Instrumental parts for saxes, Traditional Spiritual
trumpets, trombones, rhythm and Difficulty Rating: 8
percussion available from publisher (17794).
Fun modern spiritual setting. Rhythms, varying tempo and "feels," syncopation.

Festive Praise Pote SATB Hope F 998 B 1991
Keyboard. Separate brass parts Psalm 92 Difficulty Rating: 8
available #F 998 B.
Exciting, challenging, and fun. Superb concert beginning or even concert theme. In 6/8, the piece dances off the score. Challenging from the standpoint of sustained energy from beginning to end of three-minute selection. Nice, yet easy shifts in key feelings and rhythmic impulses.

Go Forth Into the World in Peace Rutter SATB Hinshaw HMC-984 1988
Organ or Piano Book of Prayer Difficulty Rating: 8
Vintage Rutter, but on the easy side of his writings. Melodies and harmonies easily achieved. Range is approachable and not difficult. Singing with pulse-less line. Glassy smooth movement of harmonies and melody. Only 38 measures, a good introduction into Rutter for kids.

Go Out With Joy Harlan SATB Church Street 0-7673-9302 1988
Piano Isaiah 55:12 Difficulty Rating: 8
Exciting and very contagious. Superb call to worship or general anthem. Has a festive feel. Ranges are a little extreme, but still a great piece of music. Fun, rhythmic and energetic from top to bottom. Harmonies will need work, particularly in girls' divisi. High tenor tessitura.

Go Where I Send Thee   Caldwell/Ivory   SAT Earthsongs   W21
1995   Piano   Gospel Spiritual
Difficulty Rating: 8
Part of the Anton Armstrong Choral Series. Fine African music and superb choral arrangement. Rhythms. Style. Presentation.

Grant Us Your Peace Mendelssohn/Young   SATB   MorningStar   MSM-50-9095
Organ or keyboard. String   Martin Luther   Difficulty Rating: 8   1999
parts available #50-9095B.
Beautiful flowing setting. English and German text provided. Lovely and rich. Words provide good text study material. Lines are full of expressive qualities and the choral parts are tantamount to excellent vocalises.

Hail the Day Which Sees Him Rise   Williams/Pethel   SATB   Coronet   392-42134
Keyboard   Charles Wesley   Difficulty Rating: 8   1997
Includes "Christ the Lord is Risen Today." Superb and exciting Easter or general anthem. Rhythms. Excellent reinforcement and appreciation of hymnology.

Heaven's Gonna Be My Home   Barrett   SATB GlorySound A7315 1999
Keyboard. Brass, guitar, string bass,   Incorporating "The Unclouded Day"
and drum parts available #MD5017.   Difficulty Rating: 8
Fun, rhythmic and full of life. Great piece to add dimension and variety to a youth choir folder. Nice, easy entree into three-part girls. Syncopation and energetic choral sound.

Heavy   Nagy   SATB   High Street   JH552   1998
A cappella   Holy Week   Difficulty Rating: 8
Haunting and powerful piece for kids. Rich harmonies, powerful images and pathos. Good musical teaching possibilities on every level. Text is perfect devotional material.

I Will Rejoice   Harlan   SATB   GlorySound   A-6934   1995
Keyboard. Brass and percussion   Psalm-like   Difficulty Rating: 8
parts available #LB-5341.
Delightful, upbeat, with Contemporary Christian feel. Singing energetically and smoothly with rolling accompaniment underneath the choral lines. Attacks, releases, consonants.

I Will Sing Praises to the Lord   Lutz   Two-part, SATB   National Music   CH 34
Organ or Piano   .   Psalm-like   Difficulty Rating: 8   1987
Exciting, fun, and rhythmic. Once learned, dances will be well-retained. Assymetrical rhythms, though not difficult. Phrasing and dynamics. Choral drama.

I Will Sing with the Spirit   Rutter   SATB   Hinshaw   HMC-1386   1994
Keyboard   I Corinthians 14:15   Difficulty Rating: 8
Gorgeous setting of the scripture text. Very flexible and can be done with many combinations of voices. Musical craftsmanship of the first order. Floating soprano lines and gentle lower three voices. Fine interval training and dynamic variations.

I'll Follow My Lord and Santo, Santo   Pote   SSATTBB   Hope   AP452   1998
Piano and optional guitar (chord symbols).   Argentine   Difficulty Rating: 8
Great global music piece to add color and uniqueness to choir's repertoire. Divisi is not difficult. Spanish text in one short section. Delightful. Needs bodily movement in performance.

Jesus Paid It All   Sterling   SATB   GlorySound   A-6223   1985
Piano   Traditional (Hall)   Difficulty Rating: 8
Has become a classic for some choirs. Interesting and moving. Creative treatment of melody. Close harmonies toward the end. Falsetto ending for boys.

Jesus, Thou Joy of Loving Hearts   Bass   SATB   Church Street   07-673-1493-X   1997
Keyboard. Orchestration available   Prayer Hymn   Difficulty Rating: 8
from publisher.
Mendelssohn-like quality, impeccably crafted, beautiful setting in every way. This is a classic that every teen should sing. Choral teaching abounds. Lovely melodic line sung separately by girls, then boys, breaking into four parts. Independence of voice parts, close and rich harmonies. Devotional opportunities abound.

Jubilate Deo   Crocker   SATB   Jenson   47110014   1985
Keyboard. Full orchestration   Psalm 100   Difficulty Rating: 8
available #47110015.
Delightful, joyful, and not nearly as complicated as it sounds. Fine choral craftsmanship. Festive. Good introduction into mixed meter. Range is somewhat demanding, but excellent workout for young singers. Energy stays high.

Let There Be Praise   Greer   SATB   Word   301-0328168
1986   Keyboard. Orchestration available
#301-0066252.   Contemporary Psalm-like   Difficulty Rating: 8
Driving and flowing, the energy never ends. Accompaniment is strong and supportive.   Rhythms. Limited mixed meter. Range in upper voices.

Look at the World   Rutter   Unison/SATB   Hinshaw   HMC-1527   1996
Piano or Organ   Creation   Difficulty Rating: 8
Includes optional unison choir along with SATB chorus. The SATB sections are
repeating refrains. Typical Rutter beauty. Singing with seamless line and articulation.
Tuning and close harmonies. Phrasing and dynamics weave their ways through this
delightful creation.

Lord, Make Us Instruments of Thy Peace Gerig   SATB   Schmitt   07046   1975
A cappella   St. Francis   Difficulty Rating; 8
Beautiful and rich setting of traditional text. Rich harmonies provide a superb training ground for kids' developing voices, particularly the development of bass and
soprano sections.

Make a Joyful Noise   Harlan   SATB   GlorySound   A-6258   1986
Keyboard   Psalm 100   Difficulty Rating: 8
Magnetic, fun, and driving, a great way to begin a concert or worship service. Terrific
youth choir piece for advanced choirs or for those who want to advance. Good intro-
duction to girls' divisi. The piece launches and doesn't stop until the end.
Demanding but not harmful to young voices. Training on all levels.

My Shepherd Will Supply My Need   Wilberg   SATB   Hinshaw   HMC1424   1995
Harp (keyboard), flute, and oboe.   Isaac Watts from Psalm 23   Difficulty Rating: 8
American folk hymn melody slightly modified with exquisite accompaniment.
Gentle, seamless setting with ethereal quality from beginning to end. Simple, beauti-
ful singing with floating choral sound. Ensemble blend is paramount. Must maintain
concentration through piece, even when not singing. Strong spiritual promises.

My Song Is Love Unknown Childs SATB MorningStar MSM-50-3044 1999
Keyboard with optional congregation. 17th Century Difficulty Rating: 8
Congregational parts included with permission granted to photocopy. Fine and glorious choral selection. Beauty discovered around every musical corner. A challenge for even advanced youth choirs, anthem will stretch choir's musicianship, sustaining power, and sensitivities.

Now Sing We Joyfully Unto God Young SATB Shawnee A-651 1952
Keyboard. Orchestration available Psalm-like Difficulty Rating: 8
from publisher.
War horse of an anthem which contains both strength and dance-like quality. Teaching opportunities abound: rhythmic integrity, choral/vocal development.

Of The Father's Love Begotten Wohlgemuth SATB Hope A454 1973
A cappella 5th Century Traditional Difficulty Rating: 8
Superb work of art. Music history written small, from plainsong to organum to hymnody. A true classic. Unity of vowels, long sustained lines. Chant with harmonies. Fine training piece for young voices.

Our God Is With Us Allen SATB Genevox 0-7673-9676-6 1988
Keyboard. Orchestration available Advent Difficulty Rating: 8
#0-7673-9615-4.
Written by Michael W. Smith and performed by Stephen Curtis Chapman on his recent Christmas album. Rhythms, melody and blend of voices. Strong ending will require vocal training on upper registers of all voices.

Praise His Holy Name Hampton SATB Earthsongs 1998
Piano Gospel Spiritual Difficulty Rating: 8
Superb global music with African feel. Rhythms, range, articulation, and style.

Praise the Lord Handel/Hopson SATB Flammer A-5714 1974
Organ or Piano Psalmic Difficulty Rating: 8
From Judas Maccabeus, Nos. 33 and 34. Great entree into classical style. Rhythmic, fun, and basically easy for this style. Melismatic passages, independence of voices, terraced dynamics, crisp articulation of consonants.

Praise We Sing to Thee   Haydn/Luvaas SATB   KJOS   ED.2015
1945   *A cappella* Praise or General
Difficulty Rating: 8
Classical sound and style. Four-part throughout. Dynamics, independence of voices, crescendo and decrescendo.

Psalm IX   Butler   SATB   Beckenhorst BP 1232   1984
Piano   Psalm 9   Difficulty Rating: 8
Excellent interest and color, brilliant text setting. Extraordinary youth choir piece on several fronts. Teaching opportunities abound in intervals, dissonance, intonation, and rhythmic precision. Many youth choirs will be taken to the next music level by this piece.

Remember Me   Governor SATB   Beckenhorst BP1340   1989
Keyboard   Holy Week, Communion   Difficulty Rating: 8
Rich setting depicts the Last Supper. Lovely combination of voices. Supportive, flowing accompaniment throughout. Legato singing. Independence of voices. Harmonic balance throughout.

Salmo 150   Aguiar   SATB   Earthsongs Psalm 150   1993
A cappella   Psalm 150   Difficulty Rating: 8
Dynamite Brazilian piece which will be challenging and exciting for many advanced youth choirs. Rhythm, rhythm, rhythm. Accents and changing meters. Some Portuguese language, but very limited. Great fun!

Sing Unto the Lord   Yannarella SATB   Beckenhorst BP1173   1983
Keyboard   Scripture Adaptation   Difficulty Rating: 8
Fun and rhythmic, it seems to dance off the score. Tempo constant throughout, although styles significantly change back and forth. Excellent for independence of voices, staying in tempo, and articulation of consonants. Voice-parts interesting throughout.

Sunshine in My Soul   Coates   SATB   Shawnee   A-1066   1970
Piano   Gospel Song   Difficulty Rating: 8
Gospel rock style. A good beat and feeling throughout that does not drive but moves surely ahead. A pleaser. Harmonies and divisi at times make for a challenge, but a fun

one. Teenagers gravitate to the mood and rhythm. They will need to be encouraged to keep rhythms and harmonies clean.

Talitha Kum!   Williams/Martin SATB GlorySound   A7186   1997
Piano and many percussion   Mark 5:39-43 (adapted)   Difficulty Rating: 8
instruments
A musical account of Jesus raising a little girl from the dead. Exciting, moving, rhythmic and joyful. Excellent for teaching clean rhythms. Great teamwork piece which pulls together many elements. Assymetrical rhythms in places. Great, fun piece.

The Lord Bless You and Keep You   Rutter   SATB   Hinshaw HMC-570 1981
Organ. Orchestral parts available   Numbers 6:24   Difficulty Rating: 8
from publisher.
Superb craftsmanship and crystal clear harmonies. Melody is beautiful and soars triumphantly on "Amen." Excellent teaching potential on every musical level.

The Lord Reigns   Greer   SATB   Word   3010460163   1989
Keyboard/Organ   Psalms   Difficulty Rating: 8
Powerful and exciting praise anthem. Easy to feel and simple to sing. Range in places is high for all voices, but not unhealthy for kids. Good studies in rhythm and changing meters. Fun and worth the work.

Three Vacancies   Cox   SATB   MorningStar MSM-50-4038   1999
Piano   Original, Creative   Difficulty Rating: 8
Text is thoughtful treatment of the fact that the cradle, cross and grave are vacant. The music is rich and colorful. Teaching possibilities abound. Choir music must be highly energized to communicate text. Strong, flowing unison lines seem to burst into four-part passages. Mood, ambiance, dynamics, pathos.

Thy Will Be Done   Courtney SATB   Beckenhorst BP1263   1985
Keyboard   Matthew 26:36-42 (adapted)   Difficulty Rating: 8
Incredible synthesis of music and text. Colorful and powerful imagery and pathos. Intensity in choral singing. Savoring and sustaining every sound. The humanity of Christ and the reality of his sacrifice for us.

Trust in the Lord   Allen   SATB   Church Street 0-7673-9690-1
1999   Keyboard Devotional
Difficulty Rating: 8
Demanding musically and textually (spiritually). Lovely and quite singable for advanced youth choirs. Begins softly, strong in middle section, ends gently. Three-part divisi for girls. Four solid parts needed in SATB. Dynamics, phrasing, breathing.

Wade in the Water   Hayes   SATB   Alfred   5810   1993
Piano and/or instrumental ensemble.   Gospel   Difficulty Rating: 8
Parts available from publisher (7264).
Exciting, challenging and fun. Rhythmic energy and various "feels" about this anthem. Good imagery and opportunities for relating biblical stories.

When Morning Dawns   Medema   SATB   Brier Patch BP 104   1994
Keyboard   Isaiah Adapted   Difficulty Rating: 8
Dramatic and engaging, good for use as call to worship or general use in worship or concert. Includes portions of "O For a Thousand Tongues to Sing." Piece contains great variety. Teaching opportunities abound musically as well as spiritually.

A Gaelic Blessing   Rutter   SATB   Hinshaw   RSCM-501   1978
Keyboard. Organ and/or guitar.   Ancient Gaelic   Difficulty Rating: 9
Flowing melodies and harmonies. Gorgeous choral setting and perfectly suited for text. Challenging harmonically. Good candidate for section rehearsals prior to large group rehearsal. Serious choral selection suitable for youth choir.

African Noel   Thomas   SATB   Alfred   52747   1994
A cappella   Noel   Difficulty Rating: 9
Wildly exciting and contagious. Fun and full of energy. Tuning and rhythmic accuracy must be right on. Three-parts for both girls and boys. Fun and imaginative!

Alleluia   Manuel   SATB   Hinshaw   HMC-927   1987
A cappella   Alleluia   Difficulty Rating: 9
Gorgeous, rich *a cappella*. Contemplative. Good introduction into 8-part singing. Key center shifts provide excellent ear training.

At Bethlehem   Bass   SATB   Augsburg   11-10878   1998
Keyboard   Advent   Difficulty Rating: 9
Lovely, flowing anthem sensitively crafted with beautiful color and nuance. Long,
flowing lines, training in upper registers near the end.

Be Thou My Vision   Rutter   SATB   Hinshaw   HMC-1035   1989
Organ, piano, or orchestration   8th Century Irish   Difficulty Rating: 9
(available from publisher).
Flawless lovely melody with seamless connection between text and music.
Harmonies and transparent, rich, and full. Chant-like B section employs mixed meter.
Impeccably crafted. Flowing melody and melt-in-your-mouth harmonies provide
excellent teaching models for development of inner tactus. The text is powerful for
all, especially for teenagers and will encourage discussion and meditation.

Chill of the Nightfall   Scott   SATB   Hinshaw   HMC-1573   1997
Keyboard and orchestration   Advent   Difficulty Rating: 9
available from publisher.
Exquisite melodic line, harmonies are rich and full. Tender and imaginative text.
Unison singing on beautiful melody (both girls and boys). Four-part section is chal-
lenging and *a cappella*. High range for both girls and boys at the top of the melody.
Teaching opportunities abound.

Christmas Lullaby   Rutter   SATB   Hinshaw   HMC-1136   1990
Organ or Piano   Advent   Difficulty Rating: 9
Elegant and silky setting. A sure gem for the advanced youth choir. Rich harmonies as
only Rutter can write them. Independence of voices, divisi in middle section. Lovely.

Come Away to the Skies Mennicke SSATB   MorningStar MSN-50-9098 1999
A cappella   Charles Wesley   Difficulty Rating: 9
Early American tune, gorgeously and happily placed into this lovely setting. Light,
perfect for teenage voices. Training possibilities are considerable. Rhythmic integrity,
listening, unison singing, close, quick-moving harmonies, high range at the end.
Superb choral development is a given when serious work is done on this fine piece.

| *Come, Let's Rejoice* | Amner | SATB | Oxford | TCM 114 | 1988 |
| *A cappella* | | Psalmic | | Difficulty Rating: 9 | |

Dancing, lilting anthem perfect for call to worship, introit, or general use. Counterpoint, independence of lines, melismatic passages.

| *Deep River* | Burroughs | SATB | Hinshaw | HMC-1332 | 1993 |
| Piano/Keyboard | | Spiritual | | Difficulty Rating: 9 | |

Fresh treatment of old text. "A river runs through it" in the lovely, smooth accompaniment. Rich-textured and tight harmonies throughout. Smooth singing lines and harmonic balance. Difference between duples and triples within the beat. Choral color, sonority, and mood. The reality of heaven.

E'en So, Lord Jesus, Quickly Come	Manz	SATB	MorningStar	MSM-50-0001	1987
A cappella, also available for SSA		Revelation 22		Difficulty Rating: 9	
(MSM-50-0450) and					
TTBB (MSM-50-0900).					

Extraordinary piece which is worth every ounce of work you and the kids will put into it. Once learned, it is an eternal gift to all who sing it. Seamless lines, tuning, intervals, meter changes. Ranges in the middle of the piece provide superb vocal training possibilities.

| *Gloria (Heiligmesse)* | Haydn | SATB | Plymouth | FS-104 | Classical |
| Piano or Organ | | Advent or General | | Difficulty Rating: 9 | |

Latin and English texts provided. Delightful, painless way to introduce Classical period. This edition is in G major, a whole step lower than the original. Extraordinarily versatile and usable. Music appreciation. Rhythmic figures. Girls' head voice. As beneficial as a vocalise for tonal development. Text is celebrative and fun in either language, although Latin works best.

| *Go Down Moses* | Hayes | SATB | Hinshaw | HMC-704 | 1984 |
| Piano | | Spiritual | | Difficulty Rating: 9 | |

Superb, interesting and captivating choral setting for advanced youth choirs. Rhythms, introduction into choral jazz style. Very memorable biblical story of Moses' call to service by God.

God Be in My Head   Burroughs SATB   Alliance   AMPR011   1997
A cappella   Traditional 16th Century   Difficulty Rating: 9
One of the few settings of this text which is approachable to teens. Close harmonies, listening and balance needed. Range is extended upward for tenors and sopranos. Superb training ground for advanced youth choirs.

God Did   Allen   SATB   Lillenas   AN-1869   1999
Keyboard. Orchestration   Praise, Spiritual-Like   Difficulty Rating: 9
available #OR-2424.
Features solo with back-up ensemble. Good change of pace for concert or worship feature number. Rhythms, rhythms, rhythms, close harmonies, and style.

Great Day   Burroughs SATB   MorningStar   MSM-50-2504   1999
A cappella   Spiritual   Difficulty Rating: 9
Wonderful setting of old spiritual. Fresh and exciting. Isolation of the divisi parts in boys' and girls' sections. Excellent high range vocal training for sopranos and tenors. Lines are fun and fulfilling to sing.

He Was Wounded   Courtney SATB   Beckenhorst BP 1272   1986
Keyboard   Isaiah 53:3-6   Difficulty Rating: 9
Dark, heavy color piece for communion or general use. Short, but powerful. Leaps must be trained and tuned. Demanding in terms of range and sustaining of rhythms. On several levels, worth the extra work it requires to sing it well.

I Hear a Voice A-Prayin'   Bright   SATB   Shawnee   A-335   1955
A cappella   Spiritual   Difficulty Rating: 9
Exciting spiritual would be enjoyed by many youth choirs with four strong parts. Independence of voices, dynamics, ambiance, and passionate singing.

If Any Man Be in Christ   Bryce/Harlan SATB   Hinshaw   HMC-1282   1993
Piano, Organ or Keyboard   2 Corinthians 5:17, John 10:10
Difficulty Rating: 9
Asymmetrical rhythms throughout (though easily assimilated), A-B-A form, gorgeous B section. Ending is difficult, yet adaptable and attainable. Rhythmic integrity, smooth long lines in B section, strong biblical truth, even though text is masculine.

If God Is For Us   Pote   SATB   Triune   10/1438T   1996
Piano and two trumpets (included)   Romans 8   Difficulty Rating: 9
Good strong choral youth choir piece. Text is one which should be sung by all youth choirs. Rhythmic impulse marches forward throughout. Some range near the end, but very approachable. Good for independence of voices and acquiring a strong, focused sound from singers.

Jesus Born on This Day   Allen   SATB   Praise Song   08742056   1994
Keyboard. Orchestration   Advent   Difficulty Rating: 9
available #08742057.
Recorded by Mariah Carey and Walter Afanasieff. Great appeal for youth. Rhythms, divisi in girls voices. Range. Exciting setting.

Joseph Dearest, Joseph Mine   Helvey   SATB   Beckenhorst   BP 1529   1998
Two pianos, four hands   Traditional German Carol
                                          Difficulty Rating: 9
Beautiful and moving. Use of two pianos gives it depth and texture. Traditional German melody and text provide interest and contrast with the average youth choir piece. Singing sustained melodies and harmonies in 6/8 without bouncing the line. Very nice range for the bass section to affirm their lower voices. Rich and colorful for all parts.

O Clap Your Hands   Vaughan Williams   SATB   Galaxy   1.5000.1   1920
Organ or piano. Brass and   Psalm 47   Difficulty Rating: 9
timpani parts available.
War horse of an anthem. Challenging and festive. This year-long project will bring the choir to a new level of musicianship. Truly exciting. Independence of voice parts. Choral confidence. Vocal production in higher registers. Rhythm at quick tempo.

Open Thou Mine Eyes   Rutter   SATB   Hinshaw   HMC-467   1980
A cappella   Classic 16th Century   Difficulty Rating: 9
Incredibly beautiful plainsong with delicate harmonies. Tuning, vocal production, line, balance, and breathing.

Our Great and Glorious King   Sewell   SATB   Triune   10/1441T   1996
Organ   Hymn text "O Worship the King"   Difficulty Rating: 9
Based upon the organ piece, "Prelude in Classic Style" by Gordon Young. Chorale
singing, sustained lines. Powerful piece which teaches and trains in durability. Great
opportunities for vocal training.

Sing to the Lord a New Song   Bass   SATB   Alliance   AMP 0320   1998
Organ or Piano   Psalm 96   Difficulty Rating: 9
Exciting, challenging, and fun anthem which makes good use of a fine organ. The piece
seems almost an antiphonal setting where the organ and choir speak back and forth to
one another. Rhythms, close, high harmonies. Suggested for the most advanced high
school choirs only. Perfect for use with youth/adult combined choirs.

Sing Unto God (Judas Maccabeus)   Handel   SATB   Carl Fisher   CM7414   Baroque
Piano, Organ, or Orchestra   Classical   Difficulty Rating: 9
Melismatic passages, rhythmic and harmonic interest throughout, highly enjoyable
when conquered. Independence of voices, terraced dynamics, vocal development,
music history.

The Very Rocks Will Cry Out   Hayes   SATB   Ariose   S40060C   1984
Piano   Adapted from Various Biblical Sources
                    Difficulty Rating: 9
Exciting, fun, and holds much interest for teenagers, particularly rhythmically.
Excellent training for precise rhythms and articulation of consonants. Dynamics.

The Word Was God   Powell   SATB/divisi Gentry   JG2196   1996
A cappella   John 1:1-3   Difficulty Rating: 9
Superb *a cappella* selection to challenge a strong youth choir. Pleasant to sing and
beautiful to hear. Good introduction into eight-part singing. Strong rhythmic impulse
throughout, even during soft sections. Dynamics and accents.

What Child Is This?   Hopson   SATB   Hope   A-679   1994
Keyboard. String quartet parts   Advent   Difficulty Rating: 9
available #A 679 S.
Beautiful, fresh color, and maintaining a traditional feel. Very singable and rich.
Sustaining of melodic lines in 6/8. Tuning throughout. Close harmonies in places.
Some *a cappella*, but relatively easy to sing the parts.

Who Knows Where the Wind Blows   Martin   SATB   Triune   10/1313T
1995   Piano   John 3:7-8
Difficulty Rating: 9
Great contrast for most youth choir repertories. Interesting tempo changes. Good
strong choral beginning with numerous training opportunities. Good for solidifying
four parts. Should be a long-range project for most youth choirs.

Who'll Be a Witness for My Lord   Hairston   SATB   Bourne B214650-357   1957
A cappella   Spiritual   Difficulty Rating: 9
Rockin' spiritual with plenty of energy and appeal. Challenging and fun. Section
rehearsals indicated for the beginning of learning process. Ranges are high at end
with divisi. To be tackled only by motivated and advanced choir.

Zion's Walls   Copland   SATB   Boosey & Hawkes   OCTB6070   1954
Piano   Revivalist   Difficulty Rating: 9
Mixed meter, shifting accents, and fun rhythms. Very colorful anthem featuring brilliant accompaniment. Musical teaching possibilities are plenty. Imagery in text is simple, yet fascinating.

CHAPTER 50

You Will Have to Write the Rest . . .

W riting this book has been one of the greatest challenges of my life. The work has been very exciting because the whole subject holds such fascination and interest for me. I have tried to be as comprehensive as possible, although I realize even as I write these words that there are still hundreds, probably thousands, of pages left to write.

We will never be able to cover it all, because the subject of music is so big. The community of Christian believers is so expansive. The psychology of teaching is so complex. The current culture of teenagers is so diverse and changing by the minute. The psychology of leadership is so involved!

Comprehensive? No way. But provocative? I hope! Perhaps something you read was new to you, but more than likely it was an affirmation of what we all know about music, ministry, teenagers, and ourselves. Whether we have informed or affirmed, motivated or activated, stimulated or assimilated, we are grateful to have the opportunity to make a modest difference in the wonderful world of youth music ministry.

The real book is yet to be written. The blank pages which appear before us are in the forms of young teenagers who walk insecurely into our choir rooms looking for hope, purpose, and a future. With everything we do for them, with them, and beside them, we are helping to author the books of their lives. It is a huge responsibility, and there is no greater honor.

Keep singing. Keep teaching. Keep writing the book.

The eternal rewards are worth every ounce of energy you invest!

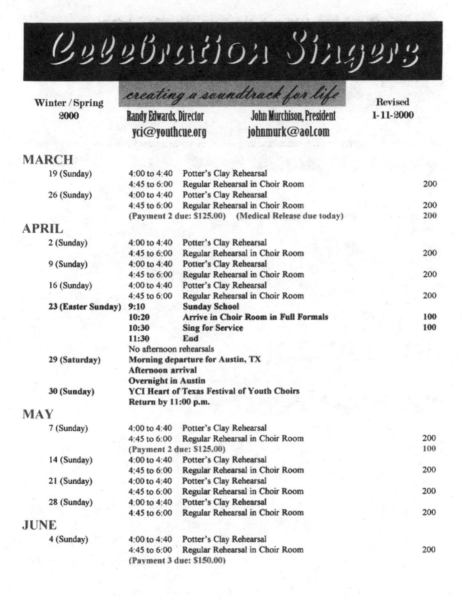

Celebration Singers

creating a soundtrack for life

Winter / Spring
2000

Randy Edwards, Director
yci@youthcue.org

John Murchison, President
johnmurk@aol.com

Revised
1-11-2000

MARCH

19 (Sunday)	4:00 to 4:40 Potter's Clay Rehearsal	
	4:45 to 6:00 Regular Rehearsal in Choir Room	200
26 (Sunday)	4:00 to 4:40 Potter's Clay Rehearsal	
	4:45 to 6:00 Regular Rehearsal in Choir Room	200
	(Payment 2 due: $125.00) (Medical Release due today)	200

APRIL

2 (Sunday)	4:00 to 4:40 Potter's Clay Rehearsal	
	4:45 to 6:00 Regular Rehearsal in Choir Room	200
9 (Sunday)	4:00 to 4:40 Potter's Clay Rehearsal	
	4:45 to 6:00 Regular Rehearsal in Choir Room	200
16 (Sunday)	4:00 to 4:40 Potter's Clay Rehearsal	
	4:45 to 6:00 Regular Rehearsal in Choir Room	200
23 (Easter Sunday)	9:10 Sunday School	
	10:20 Arrive in Choir Room in Full Formals	100
	10:30 Sing for Service	100
	11:30 End	
	No afternoon rehearsals	
29 (Saturday)	Morning departure for Austin, TX	
	Afternoon arrival	
	Overnight in Austin	
30 (Sunday)	YCI Heart of Texas Festival of Youth Choirs	
	Return by 11:00 p.m.	

MAY

7 (Sunday)	4:00 to 4:40 Potter's Clay Rehearsal	
	4:45 to 6:00 Regular Rehearsal in Choir Room	200
	(Payment 2 due: $125.00)	100
14 (Sunday)	4:00 to 4:40 Potter's Clay Rehearsal	
	4:45 to 6:00 Regular Rehearsal in Choir Room	200
21 (Sunday)	4:00 to 4:40 Potter's Clay Rehearsal	
	4:45 to 6:00 Regular Rehearsal in Choir Room	200
28 (Sunday)	4:00 to 4:40 Potter's Clay Rehearsal	
	4:45 to 6:00 Regular Rehearsal in Choir Room	200

JUNE

4 (Sunday)	4:00 to 4:40 Potter's Clay Rehearsal	
	4:45 to 6:00 Regular Rehearsal in Choir Room	200
	(Payment 3 due: $150.00)	

Celebration Singers

creating a soundtrack for life

Ark-La-Tex
February 25 - 27

Randy Edwards, Director
editor@youthcue.org

John Murchison, President
johnmurk@aol.com

Week Number
23

ORDER OF REHEARSAL

I Will Sing
Sing to the Lord a New Song
Hope, Peace, Joy and Love (Three Advent
Prayers #1)
Glorious Is Thy Name
Psalm 139
Greet the Dawning
The Cross
Tandi, Tanga Jesus
Truly, God is Able (Two Songs of Hope #2)
Footprints in the Sand
My Shepherd Will Supply My Neeed
Sing Unto God (Judas Macabbeus)

FESTIVAL SCHEDULE

	25 (Friday)	**5:30**	**Singers arrive in Sanctuary**	**300**
			Remember to eat dinner before you arrive.	
F			*Wear something comfortable to go with your*	
e			*Festival Ts, which will given to you when you*	
s		**10:30**	*arrive on Friday.*	
t			End	
i	**26 (Saturday)**	**8:30**	Festival activities all day	**300**
v		**4:00**	End	
a	**27 (Sunday)**		**Wear Festival *Blacks and T-shirts***	
l		**9:00**	**Sunday School / Worship**	
		2:00	**Grand Concert**	**300**

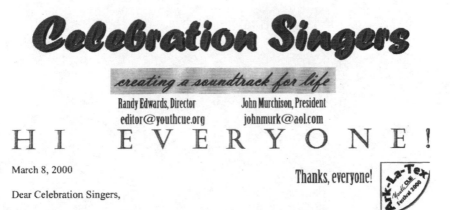

Celebration Singers

creating a soundtrack for life

Randy Edwards, Director   John Murchison, President
editor@youthcue.org   johnmurk@aol.com

H I   E V E R Y O N E !

March 8, 2000

Thanks, everyone!

Dear Celebration Singers,

Thank you for a great rehearsal last Sunday! A couple of reminders:

    1) **Keep remembering Joyce English and her daughter Ellen Pickett** in your prayers. They're doing fine but will appreciate all the prayers and cards you might send.

    2) **NO REHEARSAL THIS WEEKEND,** March 12! Have a great Venture Weekend.

    3) **Keep Randy in your prayers as he travels this week making preparations for tour.**

    4) **April 29 & 30 is the Heart of Texas Festival in Austin.** The weekend will cost $50 each and will include all your meals with the exception of dinner on Sunday evening. Sign-up begins soon. Stay tuned. We depart on Saturday April 29 @ 6:00 a.m. and will be back in Shreveport Sunday, April 30 @ 11:30 p.m.

Take care and we'll see you before long. Keep up with that classwork so the end of school doesn't come down on you like a ton of bricks (books?)

Love you all!
Randy

Coming at ya!

Sunday, March 19		No rehearsals due to Venture Weekend. Have fun!
Sunday, March 26	4:45 to 5:30	Short, check-in rehearsal (begin Austin sign-up)
Sunday, April 2	4:45 to 5:30	Short, check-in rehearsal (continue Austin sign-up)
Sunday, April 9	4:45 to 6:00	Full Rehearsal (Austin sign-up ends) (Begin Tour sign-up)
Sunday, April 16	4:45 to 6:00	Full Rehearsal (Continue Tour sign-up)
Sunday, April 23		No rehearsals due to Easter
Saturday, April 29	6:00 a.m.	(Depart for Austin)
Sunday, April 30	11:30 p.m.	(Arrive home from Austin)